PLANNING
PROGRAMMING
BUDGETING

PLANNING
PROGRAMMING
BUDGETING:

a systems approach to management

Edited by
FREMONT J. LYDEN
and
ERNEST G. MILLER
Graduate School of Public Affairs
University of Washington

MARKHAM PUBLISHING COMPANY
CHICAGO

MARKHAM POLITICAL SCIENCE SERIES
Aaron Wildavsky, Editor

First Published April 1968
Second Printing January 1969
Printed in U.S.A.
Library of Congress Catalog Card Number 67-29429

Preface

On August 25, 1965, President Johnson announced to his Cabinet members and other heads of agencies that he was introducing a new Planning-Programming-Budgeting System (PPBS) for all departments and agencies in the federal government. In his statement he indicated his conviction that the "system will improve our ability to control our programs and our budgets rather than having them control us. . . ."

The United States Bureau of the Budget subsequently issued Bulletin No. 66–3 (October 12, 1965) and a Supplement (February 21, 1966) to heads of executive departments and establishments. Bulletin 66–3 constituted the initial official explanation, instruction, and timetable for the inauguration of PPB by the various agencies, and the Supplement provided details on the reporting format of the two central documents to be used in the PPB system—the Program and Financial Plans (PFP) and Program Memoranda (PM). (Bulletin 66–3, the Supplement, and Bulletin 68–2, replacing 66–3, are included in the Appendix of this reader).

In two recent messages to Congress the President has given further emphasis to the importance of the PPB system. In his January message on the fiscal 1968 budget the President referred to the PPB system as "primarily a means of encouraging a careful and explicit analysis of Federal programs." In the March 17 message on the quality of American government he again highlighted the managerial implications of PPB, stating that the system has proved its worth many times over in the Defense Department and would now bring to each department and agency the most advanced techniques of modern business management. Under the PPB system each department, he said, must now:

Develop its objectives and goals, precisely and carefully;

Evaluate each of its programs to meet these objectives, weighing the benefits against the costs;

Examine, in every case, alternative means of achieving these objectives;

Shape its budget request on the basis of this analysis, and justify that request in the context of a long-range program and financial plan.

Regardless of whether PPB really constitutes something radically new under the administrative sun—and many argue that it does not—it does place a greater emphasis upon *program results* and *analytical techniques* which, if fully developed, promise to bring about marked changes in public management. These changes are gradually becoming apparent in the federal government, and they are beginning to have an impact at other governmental levels. Several states have already evidenced interest in utilizing the PPB approach, and a number of cities and counties are making initial efforts to explore its applicability.

The evolution and eventual outcome of PPB will be a matter for interpretation and judgment by future historical analysts, but in the meantime the contemporary public manager or student of public administration needs to know what the PPB approach to budgeting is, how it has developed up to this early point in time, how it relates to other kinds of budgeting approaches, how it is related to and underpinned by systems analysis generally, how it may be applied, and what its limitations and deficiencies may be. The readings in this book have been carefully assembled to serve these purposes. While several of the articles predate the PPB movement they present perspectives essential to an understanding of its implications. Other articles—particularly the two examples of systems analysis by Nicol and Maruyama—do not allude specifically to PPB but provide graphic illustrations of the type of program analysis necessary for applying PPB. Altogether this collection of readings constitutes a starting basis for an educated understanding of PPB and its implications in managerial as well as policy contexts.

For encouragement in preparing this volume we especially wish to thank Professors George Shipman, Dwight Waldo, and Aaron Wildavsky. We also wish to acknowledge our appreciation to Thomas Spring for overseeing the details involved in the preparation of the manuscript and to W. Richard Miller and Gary Marshall who assisted him.

Table of Contents

I.
PPB IN PERSPECTIVE

1.
PPBS
Comes to Washington*
VIRGINIA HELD

In May, 1966, all departments and most agencies of the United States government, in submitting to the Budget Bureau their rough spending plans for the fiscal year starting fourteen months later, began using for the first time the Planning-Programing-Budgeting System, or PPBS. The change has its source in the summer of 1965, when Lyndon B. Johnson ordered them to institute what he called a "revolutionary" new system, one which demands that departments and agencies define clearly the major objectives (or "programs") which they choose to pursue, that they apply systematic analyses to the alternative ways in which these objectives are being—or may be—sought, and that they plan their spending in long-range as well as one-year-ahead terms. This does not sound very revolutionary; indeed, it sounds merely sensible. Oddly enough, it may actually be both.

RAND AND THE D. O. D.

In initiating this new approach, the President is applying throughout the government an approach toward more rational decision-making which has already swept through the Defense Department. "Program budgeting" was introduced into the Department of Defense in 1961. Previously, defense expenditures had been considered in traditional line-item form, focusing on categories such as maintenance, supplies, personnel, and equipment; and the budget presented by the Secretary of Defense was really a combination of Army, Navy, and Air Force budgets. The deficiencies, as explained by Alain C. Enthoven, Deputy Assistant

*Reprinted from Virginia Held, "PPBS Comes to Washington," *The Public Interest*, No. 4 (Summer, 1966), pp. 102–115, by permission of the author and publisher. Virginia Held teaches philosophy at the City University of New York—Hunter College.

Secretary of Defense for Systems Analysis, were that the whole question of how much a weapon system *cost* was not brought in systematically, either to determine the feasibility of the program or to evaluate its efficiency. By 1960 it was apparent that the troublesome decisions of the Defense Department centered around the choice of vast weapon systems, each enormously expensive, designed for various military missions (such as strategic retaliation and continental defense). In order to be able to consider the "worth" of a weapon system as a whole, and to relate longer-range planning to annual budgets, the Defense Department's comptroller, Charles J. Hitch, at Secretary of Defense Robert McNamara's direction, instituted a new system of program budgeting. The United States defense effort has, as a result, been broken down into nine basic "programs": Strategic Retaliatory Forces, Continental Air and Missile Defense Forces, General Purpose Forces, Airlift and Sealift Forces, Reserve and National Guard Forces, Research and Development, General Support, Military Assistance, and Civil Defense. Each is composed of certain "program elements" (such as Polaris submarines and Minutemen missiles) which are intended to accomplish a common military mission.

The groundwork for the reorganization of the Defense Department budget had been laid by several studies. The Hoover Commission on Organization of the Executive Branch of the Government had made a general recommendation in its 1949 report that the government adopt a budget based upon functions, activities, and projects, which it designated a "performance budget." David Novick of the RAND Corporation presented in 1954 a systematic exposition of how the new technique could be applied effectively to military spending. In his RAND study, called *Efficiency and Economy in Government Through New Budgeting Procedures,* and on subsequent occasions, Novick proposed a method of "program budgeting" and recommended its adoption by the Defense Department. The Committee for Economic Development issued a policy statement in 1955 called *Control of Federal Government Expenditures;* it also advocated a refashioning of the entire federal budget along "program" lines. The term "program," as then used by the Bureau of the Budget, designated combinations of activities, such as procurement of equipment, training of personnel, and so forth, rather than their objectives. With the 1954 RAND study for the Defense Department, however, the term "program" came to mean the ultimate goal of many interdependent activities.

When Charles Hitch first took office as Defense Department Comptroller in 1961, he expected to introduce program budgeting over a period of several years. But McNamara speeded up the process and decided that the budget for fiscal 1963 should be formulated in terms of major programs and weapon systems. The results of this reorganization, and of the evaluations it has made possible, led to recommendations that the approach be extended to civilian affairs. David Novick suggested that RAND conduct research on the government-wide applicability of program budgeting; this led to a collection of papers edited by Novick, and recently published by Harvard University Press under the title, *Program Budgeting—Program Analysis and the Federal Budget,* and the advice "to introduce into the nondefense areas of the federal government the kind of program analysis that has been installed in the Department of Defense as an integral part of the planning, programming, and budgeting process." In line with this and other recommendations, the government is now in the process of doing just this.

THE ROLE OF THE BUDGET

Since every governmental program is only as extensive as the money put into it, the place where decisions—whether rational or not—concerning the division of the national effort are most apparent, is in the federal budget. The budget is the central expression of how the government's finite resources will be allocated, the terms of the annual cease-fire, as it were, within the executive branch, between the competing claims of different advocates for more money for defense, or agriculture, or new welfare programs.

Once the amounts have been fixed in the budget, which the President will then present to Congress, the major decisions have for the most part been made. Congress can, of course, upset the settlement temporarily by decreasing or increasing some aspects of some programs, and dissatisfied agencies can breach the cease-fire and help one congressional faction or another. But as George A. Steiner puts it in his chapter of the recent RAND study, . . . "despite the wide publicity frequently given to changes made by the Congress in the budget presented by the President, important alterations are usually relatively few and minor." Hence it is in the executive process of putting together a budget that the impact of the new approach will be most apparent.

The greater part of a federal budget is what it is because of what it was. All those programs already made mandatory—such as farm price supports or veterans' pensions—have to be paid for. Defense expenditures, which have used up over half of the total of federal expenditures for the past fifteen years, have not changed drastically from year to year. The region of discretion, then, is distinctly limited. But as in other human affairs, it is those few decisions that are open to conscious choice which cause anguish. And it is to the resolution of such anguish that the new intellectual techniques are directed.

WHAT IS A PROGRAM?

Establishing just what a program may or may not be involves the conceptual distinguishing and grouping of various objectives and activities; alternative conceptualizations are always possible, and are often floating about. Charles Hitch and Roland McKean, whose book *The Economics of Defense in the Nuclear Age* (published as a paperback last year by Atheneum) has become a classic in its field, discussed the problem of discerning a defense program: "Let us illustrate the distinction between a program and an object [of expenditure]. . . . Certain activities of the Air Force, the Army, and the Navy produce retaliatory striking power or deterrence, and these activities might be grouped together and called a program. In providing deterrence, the Services use missiles, manpower, food, paper clips, and transportation—intermediate items which might be called 'objects of expenditure.' . . .

"Just what one means by an 'end-product' or a 'program' is not unambiguous. The line of demarcation between programs and objects is not clear-cut. Is the Military Air Transport Service a program or simply an activity supporting, say, the Tactical Air Program? Or is even the latter merely something to be purchased for a program that might be called 'deterrence and fighting of limited wars'? Even such tasks as providing nuclear striking power and providing forces for limited war have interrelationships. Neither is solely a supporting activity of the other, yet each can influence the credibility and effectiveness of the other. It may seem that one is driven to regard every military item and activity as an object purchased for and contributing to one program—national security.

"Despite these complexities, officials do find it helpful to think in terms of several programs, and there is hope of developing categories that will be even more meaningful. After all, our only chance of pondering the gains as well as the costs of defense budgets is to think in terms of rather broad aggregations of activities."

The Defense Department budget has thus been divided into the nine major programs already mentioned and over 800 "program elements," which are the forces, weapons, or support systems, and other types of integrated activities by means of which the programs are to be achieved. But the possibilities for regrouping are almost endless.

Officials trying to decide what to include or exclude from various civilian programs face analogous difficulties. Education, for instance, is one of the most dispersed activities of the government. In the fiscal 1965 budget, funds for education were dispersed through more than forty agencies. The United States Office of Education's expenditures constituted only about one-fifth of the total federal education budget, and efforts are only now under way to distinguish what could be conceived of as *the* education program of the federal government.

A member of the executive involved with the new system has said that the President's directive on program budgeting is forcing some agencies to consider, virtually for the first time, just what their objectives are. Officials of the Justice Department, for example, being lawyers, traditionally think it is their clients, not they themselves, who have objectives. But formulations of the Department of Justice's objectives are now being considered in terms of such categories as reduction and prevention of crime, protection of internal security, assurance of civil rights under law, maintenance of competition in the business community, and so on.

Melvin Anshen, in the opening chapter of RAND's *Program Budgeting* sums up the scope of the undertaking:

"The central issue is, of course, nothing less than the definition of the ultimate objectives of the federal government as they are realized through operational decisions. Set in this framework, the designation of a schedule of programs may be described as building a bridge between a matter of political philosophy (what is government for?) and the administrative function of assigning scarce resources among alternative governmental objectives. The unique function of a program budget is to implement the conclusions of a political philosophy through the assignment of resources to their accomplishment. . . . In a number of areas no clear objectives have ever been laid down. This undesirable condition has prevailed in the field of international aid and investment, but it can also be found in many domestic areas including, among others, agriculture, transportation, education, and unemployment."

One problem which may become troublesome is that of frankness. How honest can an agency be in declaring its intentions without getting into difficulties, how open about its criteria of evaluation? If the Department of Agriculture, for instance, is trying to shift a lot of people out of farming, will it be wise to advertise this objective? If the State Department values a program that induces in the leaders of foreign countries a healthy respect for United States power, should it say so in a public analysis? How much program budgeting may aggravate "the honesty problem" remains to be seen.

THE END OF ABSOLUTES

The importance of thinking in program terms is that, in addition to clarifying objectives, it helps move discussion away from the fairly useless absolutes of (a) what fixed amounts of money to spend no matter what the goals, or (b) what fixed objectives to achieve no matter what the costs.

Starting out with an immovable sum, and deciding how to spend it makes little sense for an entity such as the United States Government. (It appeared to be the favored approach of President Eisenhower's Budget Director, Maurice Stans, who liked to tell department secretaries to be sure not to exceed certain fixed amounts of money in their requests.) Critics of this approach point out that since revenues are subject to increase, it should be acknowledged that, if the nation's security requires stronger defenses, or a program to combat unemployment, no fixed amount of spending should be imposed as a precondition to which all subsequent decisions must conform.

But the opposite approach, that of viewing needs or objectives as thoroughly immovable, is no more satisfactory. Congressman often ask military officials to tell them, honestly, what they "really need." Senator Chavez, for instance, said to General Maxwell Taylor, in Congressional hearings on appropriations for Eisenhower's defense program, "We would like to know what you need and not what the Budget Bureau thinks you should have." The question, however, is unanswerable. If money is no problem at all, some people need Cadillacs and caviar; generals and department heads are no exception. Governments, like individuals, traditionally find ways to spend what is available.

Alan Peacock and Jack Wiseman, in their book *The Growth of Public Expenditure in the United Kingdom,* published in 1961, tried to assess the validity of the "law" of ever-increasing state expenditures formulated by the German economist Adolph Wagner in 1883. Wagner had said, on the basis of observations of Western European countries, that pressures for social progress inevitably lead to increasing state activity and hence to a growth of governmental expenditures, and that "in the long run the desire for development of a progressive people will always overcome . . . financial difficulties." Peacock and Wiseman found upon analyzing British figures that it seemed to be the other way around: expenditures increase because revenues increase. With a given tax system and constant tax rates, government revenues grow as the economy grows, and governments arrange to use up their incomes. But discovering which is cause and which effect may be less important than acknowledging the futility of regarding the levels of either revenues or expenditures as absolute in trying to make federal budget decisions.

Explaining the point with regard to defense plans, Hitch and McKean say:

"There is no budget size or cost that is correct regardless of the payoff, and there is no need that should be met regardless of cost.

"On the one hand, there is no presumption that the defense budget is now, or should be, near any immovable upper limit. As far as physical and economic feasibility is concerned, national security expenditures could be raised (within a two- or three-year transition period) by, say, $30 billion per year. With appropriate changes in tax rates and monetary policy, this could be done without causing severe inflation.

"From existing levels, in other words, outlays for defense activities can be raised if we really want to raise them—if we feel that we need extra defense programs more than other things."

"On the other hand," Hitch and McKean continue, "there is no particular national security program that we need in an absolute sense. . . . A list of the 'desirable' items that could strengthen our defense would be almost endless. Where does one draw the line (without reference to cost) between what is needed and what is not? There are no clear-cut 'minimal' needs, either for defense as a whole or for particular programs. . . . Outlays for various programs *can* be cut if we feel that we need other things even more. It is up to us to choose."

THE METHODS OF CHOICE

Along with facilitating an awareness of the objectives to be sought, PPBS provides for the application of a battery of new techniques, such as systems analysis and cost-benefit analysis in an effort to increase the possibilities of making rational choices between alternative means. The terms used to designate these techniques are not yet at a stage of precise definition. As Gene H. Fisher states in his chapter on "cost-utility analysis," the term he favors, in the RAND study on program budgeting, the terms "cost-benefit analysis," "cost-effectiveness analysis," "systems analysis," "operations research," and "operations analysis" all "convey the same general meaning but have important different meanings to different people."

David Novick explains one important distinction: "Cost-effectiveness analysis of alternative forces and weapon systems . . . stems basically from operations research in World War II. But operations research is concerned with the analysis of alternative tactics with basically given weapon systems (e.g. in bombing a bridge, whether to go across it or down the middle), while the emphasis in cost-effectiveness analysis is on forward planning. Freedom to allocate one's resources is usually severely limited in typical problems of operations research, whereas the purpose of cost-effectiveness analysis is to examine the effects of such alternative resource allocations. . . ."

While these techniques remain in their present healthy state of disorderly and inventive and sometimes exuberant development, precise definitions may be of less interest than a few glimpses at how they may be shaped and used in specific decision-making situations.

One of the most useful books for this purpose, partly because of its conceptual openness, is a collection of papers edited by Robert Dorfman under the title *Measuring Benefits of Government Investments* (Washington, D.C., The Brookings Institution, 1965). The authors attempt to expand and apply cost-benefit concepts to various areas of federal and local governmental activity, such as providing outdoor recreation, preventing high-school drop-outs, investing in highways, and undertaking urban renewal, where questions of how to quantify social 'costs' and 'benefits' become crucial. "It is no accident," the editor explains, "that benefit-cost analysis had its origin and highest development in the field of water resources. That is the field in which . . . the highest proportion of outputs —water and power—are saleable commodities bearing relevant market prices." This volume steers clear of the relatively easy cases of dams and levees, where costs and benefits are more quantifiable in terms of money, and enters foggier territory. Dorfman notes that the book's "preoccupation with conceptual problems and comparative neglect of technical expedients is probably a symptom of the youngness of the field. . . . The work of extending the methods of benefit-cost analysis and of criticizing and appraising these extensions has only just begun."

For the purpose of grasping a few basic concepts of cost-benefit analysis, however, it may be useful to revert to reservoirs for a moment and to look at one simple case offered by Otto Eckstein, who has written two books on cost-benefit analysis in connection with water resource development. In his little book *Public Finance* (Prentice-Hall, 1964), he gives the following table showing, for a Brink Valley, estimated flood damage without protection in a typical year and the lowered damage figures when progressively more ambitious flood protection plans were initiated:

Plan	Annual Cost of Project	Average Annual Damage	Benefit (Reduction of Damage)
Without protection	0	$38,000	0
Plan A—levees	$ 3,000	32,000	$ 6,000
Plan B—small reservoir	10,000	22,000	16,000
Plan C—medium reservoir	18,000	13,000	25,000
Plan D—large reservoir	30,000	6,000	32,000

Benefits exceed costs in all plans, but Plan C is the best because the marginal benefit of going from the lesser plan to it continues to exceed the marginal cost of spending the extra money. Although it costs $8,000 more than Plan B, it will avert $9,000 more in damages. But a further increment, going to Plan D, would cost an extra $12,000, yet yield only $7,000 in additional benefits. Hence it would fail the test of having marginal benefits exceed marginal costs.

In the Dorfman volume, a paper by Ruth P. Mack and Sumner Myers, of the Institute of Public Administration and the National Planning Association, respectively, attempts to provide an analysis in cost-benefit terms that could be used to evaluate governmental expenditures on outdoor recreation. Benefits are calculated on the basis of what the authors call "merit-weighted user-days," which take into account various sorts of recreation for various sorts of people under varying conditions. The simple measure of "user-days"—a function of the numbers of people expected to use a park and of the lengths of time of their stays—is weighted to take into account that some user-days are better than others. The weighted figures include such social judgments as: that a day spent by a child in the wilderness has more lasting value than an adult's picnicking in a crowded, noisy park; that the marginal utility of additional recreation declines as larger amounts are made available; that equity requires government to provide relatively more recreational opportunities to those who most need them and can least afford private alternatives, plus many others. In ways too complex to examine here, alternative parks under consideration for a given expected number of users are then evaluated in terms of the "merit-weighted user-days" which they could be expected to provide.

Hitch and McKean in their book present conceptual frameworks, together with a mathematical appendix which becomes impossible for the non-specialist, for choices between alternative military forces. As a simplified hypothetical example, they take a situation with one input, say a fixed budget of B billion dollars and two possible outputs. A planner is assumed to be deliberating about what proportion of the B billion dollars to spend on a strategic bombing force and what proportion on an air defense force. Using enemy targets that could be destroyed and the number of attacking enemy bombers that could be shot down as the two outputs to which he would attach values, the planner could construct a curve showing maximum combinations which could be bought with the B billion dollars. Each point on the curve then represents an "efficient" use of resources, because at any point on it, it is possible to increase one valuable output only by decreasing the other. To select a point on the curve representing the "optimal" use of his budget amount, a planner needs what the economists call "indifference curves" to intersect it. Indifference curves reflect preferences for some combinations of target destruction and kill potential over others. The optimal point is a point of intersection of the original curve with as high an indifference curve as possible.

In many actual situations, an analysis can only yield calculations on efficient systems; trying to choose optimal ones may largely require reliance on intuitive judgment. But the range within which such judgment must be made can often be narrowed.

One of the central problems of any analysis is the choice of a criterion, or test of preferences, which would suggest the best combination of desirable factors. Simultaneously maximizing gain while minimizing cost seems appealing but is no criterion because, as Hitch and McKean point out, "there is no such policy possible." "Maximum gain is infinitely large, and minimum cost is zero. Seek the policy that has that outcome, and you will not find it." One common preference is to choose that policy which has the highest ratio of "effectiveness," or achievement of desirable objectives, to cost. The maximizing of this ratio is then the criterion, but choices should be bounded by common sense from assuming extreme forms, as for instance in overkill situations. It often happens that the ratio reduces itself to maximum effectiveness for a given budget.

What are usually required are analyses that straddle a problem, that calculate what, given a certain scale of objectives, can minimize costs, or what, given assumed amounts of money to spend, can maximize achievements. The best formulation here as in other deliberations, tends to depend on which one is intuitively assessed as offering 'reasonable' levels.

An example of an analysis that is to be made when the data is in, as the use of analytic techniques expands from the Defense Department, where most actual analyses are classified, to other areas of government, is an evaluation of the Office of Economic Opportunity's Job Corps and Neighborhood Youth Corps. The two corps are alternative ways of pursuing certain of the poverty program's objectives. The Job Corps takes youngsters and puts them in residential camps, keeping them there twenty-four hours a day, seven days a week. It teaches them to read and write, and it trains them for a job. The Neighborhood Youth Corps takes youngsters of the same age group, and gives them work for thirty-five hours a week, paying them the minimum wage. They live at their own homes. Although very different, and designed for different kinds of enrollees, the objective of both organizations is to make youngsters employable, and attempts can be made to measure their relative effectiveness.

It is known already that the Job Corps costs about four times as much per youth as the Neighborhood Youth Corps. "The large differential in costs," an OEO working memorandum states, "makes assessment of payoff critical. It is, for example, estimated that $100 increase in annual income, discounted at 5 per cent, justifies the expenditure of $1,500 in training." Although economic considerations need not constitute the basis on which a decision to expand or decrease either program is made, they are at least worth looking into in planning future efforts to combat poverty.

Kermit Gordon, a former member of the Council of Economic Advisers, and Budget Director under Presidents Kennedy and Johnson, has recently suggested a series of possible applications of economic analysis to existing governmental programs. One suggestion is an evaluation of the program the United States has for sugar. "The U.S. sugar program," Gordon says, "incorporates import quotas, domestic production quotas, import duties, an excise tax on sugar refining, and graduated subsidies to U. S. cane and beet sugar producers. Over the years, the program has been used to promote increased domestic production at the expense of imports. On the average, over the past decade or so, domestic prices have been roughly double the world price of sugar. The present combined costs to the U. S. Government and to the U. S. sugar consumer of our sugar program have been estimated at about $500 million a year; that is, we spend on sugar about $500 million more than we would spend if there were no U. S. sugar program. (This does not include the federal subsidy for irrigation water to sugar beet growers.) Estimated net income of all U. S. cane and beet growers is about $140 million per annum. Thus, the total cost of the program is more than three times the net income of producers.

"Presumably," Gordon continues, "the purpose of the program is to support the incomes of U. S. sugar growers and to assure to U. S. consumers a reliable supply of sugar at relatively stable prices. It should not exceed the talents of economists to devise alternative programs which would achieve these objectives at substantially lesser costs than the present program."

One of the most imaginative attempts to evaluate the effectiveness of programs with hard-to-assess objectives is a method devised by David Osborn, Deputy Assistant Secretary of State for Educational and Cultural Affairs. Built into this system, which is being programmed by the Franklin Institute Research Laboratory in Philadelphia, is the view that the agency's various activities have multiple and overlapping objectives, and that a conceptual structure delineating end programs through alternative means does not adequately reflect such overlapping. Osborn recommends a scheme of cross-multiplying the costs of the activities with a number representing the rank of its objectives on a scale. For instance, the exchange of Fulbright professors may contribute to "cultural prestige and mutual respect," "educational development," and gaining "entrée," which might be given scale numbers such as 8, 6, and 5, respectively. These numbers are then multiplied with the cost of the program, and the resulting figure is in turn multiplied with an ingenious figure called a "country number." The latter is an attempt to get a rough measure of the importance to the United States of the countries with which we have cultural relations. It is arrived at by putting together in complicated ways certain key data, weighted to reflect cultural and educational matters, such as the country's population, gross national product, number of college students, rate of illiteracy, and so forth. The resulting numbers are then revised in the light of working experience, as when, because of its high per capita income, a certain tiny middle-eastern country turns out to be more important to the United States than a large eastern European one. At this point, country numbers are revised on the basis of judgment and experience, as are other numbers at other points. But those who make such revisions have a basic framework to start with, a set of numbers arranged on the basis of many factors, rather than single arbitrary guesses. As Osborn explains it: "We debate the numerical results we come up with but it becomes a revision process. The analysis gives us approximations to work with. If you break up your judgment into various parts you have something to talk about."

Because of the imaginative, and sometimes conceptually playful nature of these techniques, which nearly all agree still constitute an art rather than a science, critics sometimes contend that the attempt to assign numerical values to such amorphous objectives as what an educational exchange program is aiming at, or what urban renewal is trying to accomplish, are of little use, and may be misleading. Misused, the techniques may lead to a focus on less important but measurable factors, such as dollar costs and miles of highway constructed, let us say, and to the neglect of less quantifiable factors such as the social and aesthetic costs and benefits of programs.

One point of such analyses may be, however, that when many guesses go into a calculation, the deficiency of any one of them is less crucial than if the only thing guessed at, intuitively, is the outcome, such as that exchanging professors is more valuable than exchanging dance troupes, or that programs for pre-schoolers will do more to ease poverty than money spent on housing.

William Gorham, an Assistant Secretary in the Department of Health, Education and Welfare and an economist who recently moved up from the Defense Department to introduce into HEW the kind of analyses that have been helpful in resolving defense decision problems, finds non-quantifiable considerations already so profuse in an agency such as HEW that there is hardly any danger for some time of introducing too much calculation.

In efforts such as those to prevent high-school drop-outs, for instance, about all that is known now is how much is being spent. To evaluate them one has to specify objectives—which may not lead to eradicating drop-outs altogether—and then to compare the merits of achieving different levels of high-school education. One of the principal benefits of finishing high school is the higher expected earning capacity of graduates. The more that is spent to reduce the drop-out rate, the greater the expected income of the population. Looked at in this way, the economic benefits and costs of achieving different levels of high school completion can be compared and can at least help determine the efficacy of such programs.

Gorham says of his experience in dealing with military problems that the dominant characteristics in a decision are often not those that can be measured, but if one does what is possible with numbers, it leads those involved in a decision to be clear about the non-or less-quantifiable factors on which the decision may be based, and such an influence is often useful.

THE LOCUS OF DECISION

The problems of defining what is rational and what is not and of deciding whether rational choices—if possible at all—are better than those made on the basis of intuitive feelings, involve high-level philosophical thinking. But to assert that it is advisable to know what one is doing may be a modest claim susceptible of general approval. What the new intellectual techniques, such as those used in PPBS, attempt to provide are methods by which those who make the decisions about how the government should direct its efforts can increase their awareness of the conditions and consequences of their choices and can clarify the elements that, explicitly or implicitly, enter into their judgments.

Various unforseeable and irrational factors will continue, sometimes rightly, to influence final decisions. And debates about which sorts of considerations *are* the rational ones are bound to remain lively. Congress, for instance, may cut an unpopular engineering project which the Department of the Interior declares rewarding, or, because of the pressures upon it, vote more money for a given defense component than Administration calculations deem effective. A department head may override his professional advisers for political reasons, good or bad. But the knowledge which the new techniques can provide may be used to raise the contests over such issues to a more responsible level. And those who object to the language of game-playing and payoff may simply not yet have understood the extent to which these techniques can embody a distinctively moral concern for alternative values.

Several of those RAND and Defense Department alumni now preparing to apply quantitative analyses to broader domains have made the point that the factors to be considered are probably more measurable in the case of domestic programs than in the case of defense. It is at least easier to measure jobs created, or numbers of people moved across an income figure representing a "poverty line," than it is to measure "deterrence."

Joseph Kershaw, now analyzing poverty programs, recently compared the problem for the two fields. He finds it easier to make such analyses for poverty programs because there is already so much information available—population and income and other statistics—even though the information is often not quite what one wants. He thinks objectives are somewhat easier to define, and to quantify for the poverty program than for the defense program, and furthermore, he observes, "we're playing the game against nature, whereas the Defense Department is playing, of course, against a very active player, or coalition of players," who can design their policies to confound those of the United States, and this "makes it possible for us to do things with more confidence than the Defense Department can."

To the extent that various forces lead those with political power to look to those with expert knowledge for advice on ways to increase the effectiveness with which government pursues its objectives, and thus to rationalize its efforts, the role of new intellectual techniques such as PPBS is likely to grow. And as the influence of government in shaping the national society continues to expand, any possible improvement in its capacity to make "better" choices becomes more significant.

There appears to have been in recent years a significant shift in the kind of advice the politicians call upon most. The supervisory outlook of New Deal government, shaped by lawyers apt to think in terms of governmental regulation and control of the nation's enterprises, has become less popular. Those that seem to have come to the fore are the economists, who think in terms of the effective management and development not only of the American economy but of the enterprise of government itself.

Participants in governmental decisions concede that foolish and wasteful choices are often made simply because those who make them do not know many of the things intelligent analyses can tell them. Yet even if those holding a political power of decision which continues to be primary develop no greater good-will nor desire to be rational, increased reliance upon the new techniques remains probable because, as Kermit Gordon expresses it, "analyses become powerful weapons in the arsenal of persuasion," as political wills confront one another and struggle toward resolution.

2.
The Road to PPB:
*The Stages of Budget Reform**
ALLEN SCHICK

Among the new men in the nascent PPB staffs and the fellow travellers who have joined the bandwagon, the mood is of "a revolutionary development in the history of government management." There is excited talk about the differences between what has been and what will be; of the benefits that will accrue from an explicit and "hard" appraisal of objectives and alternatives; of the merits of multi-year budget forecasts and plans; of the great divergence between the skills and role of the analyst and the job of the examiner; of the realignments in government structure that might result from changes in the budget process.

This is not the only version, however. The closer one gets to the nerve centers of budget life—the Divisions in the Bureau of the Budget and the budget offices in the departments and agencies—the more one is likely to hear that "there's nothing very new in PPB; it's hardly different from what we've been doing until now." Some old-timers interpret PPB as a revival of the performance budgeting venture of the early 1950's. Others belittle the claim that before PPB decisions on how much to spend for personnel or supplies were made without real consideration of the purposes for which these inputs were to be invested. They point to previous changes that have been in line with PPB, albeit without PPB's distinctive package of techniques and nomenclature. Such things as the waning role of the "green sheets" in the central budget process, the redesign of the appropriation structure and the development of activity classifications, refinements in work measurement, productivity analysis,

*Reprinted from Allen Schick, "The Road to PPB: The Stages of Budget Reform," *Public Administration Review,* 26:4 (December, 1966), pp. 243–258, by permission of the author and publisher. Allen Schick is associate professor of political science at Tufts University.

and other types of output measurement, and the utilization of the Spring Preview for a broad look at programs and major issues.

Between the uncertain protests of the traditional budgeteer and the uncertain expectations of the *avant garde,* there is a third version. The PPB system that is being developed portends a radical change in the central function of budgeting, but it is anchored to half a century of tradition and evolution. The budget system of the future will be a product of past and emerging developments; that is, it will embrace both the budgetary functions introduced during earlier stages of reform as well as the planning function which is highlighted by PPB. PPB is the first budget system *designed* to accommodate the multiple functions of budgeting.

THE FUNCTIONS OF BUDGETING

Budgeting always has been conceived as a process for systematically relating the expenditure of funds to the accomplishment of planned objectives. In this important sense, there is a bit of PPB in every budget system. Even in the initial stirrings of budget reform more than fifty years ago, there were cogent statements on the need for a budget system to plan the objectives and activities of government and to furnish reliable data on what was to be accomplished with public funds. In 1907, for example, the New York Bureau of Municipal Research published a sample "program memorandum" that contained some 125 pages of functional accounts and data for the New York City Health Department.[1]

However, this orientation was not *explicitly* reflected in the budget systems—national, state, or local—that were introduced during the first decades of this century, nor is it *explicitly* reflected in the budget systems that exist today. The plain fact is that planning is not the only function that must be served by a budget system. The *management* of ongoing activities and the *control* of spending are two functions which, in the past, have been given priority over the planning function. Robert Anthony identifies three distinct administrative processes, strategic planning, management control, and operational control.

Strategic planning is the process of deciding on objectives of the organization, on changes in these objectives, on the resources used to attain these objectives, and on the policies that are to govern the acquisition, use, and disposition of these resources.

Management control is the process by which managers assure that resources are obtained and used effectively and efficiently in the accomplishment of the organization's objectives.

Operational control is the process of assuring that specific tasks are carried out effectively and efficiently.[2]

Every budget system, even rudimentary ones, comprises planning, management, and control processes. Operationally, these processes often are indivisible, but for analytic purposes they are distinguished here. In the context of budgeting, *planning* involves the determination of objectives, the evaluation of alternative courses of action, and the authorization of select programs. Planning is linked most closely to budget preparation, but it would be a mistake to disregard the management and control elements in budget preparation or the possibilities for planning during other phases of the budget year. Clearly, one of the major aims of PPB is to convert the annual routine of preparing a budget into a conscious appraisal and formulation of future goals and policies. Management involves the programming of approved goals into specific projects and activities, the design of organizational units to carry out approved programs, and the staffing of these units and the procurement of necessary resources. The management process is spread over the entire budget cycle; ideally, it is the link between goals made and activities undertaken. *Control* refers to the process of binding operating officials to the policies and plans set by their superiors. Control is predominant during the execution and audit stages, although the form of budget estimates and appropriations often is determined by control considerations. The assorted controls and reporting procedures that are associated with budget execution—position controls, restrictions on transfers, requisition procedures, and travel regulations, to mention the more prominent ones —have the purpose of securing compliance with policies made by central authorities.

Very rarely are planning, management, and control given equal attention in the operation of budget systems. As a practical matter, planning, management, and control have tended to be competing processes in budgeting with no neat division of functions among the various participants. Because time is scarce, central authorities must be selective in the things they do. Although this scarcity counsels the devolution of control responsibilities to operating levels, the lack of reliable and relied-on internal control systems has loaded central authorities with control functions at the expense of the planning function. Moreover, these processes often require different skills and generate different ways of handling the budget mission, so that one type of perspective tends to predominate over the others. Thus, in the staffing of the budget offices, there has been a shift from accountants to administrators as budgeting has moved from a control to a management posture. The initial experience with PPB suggests that the next transition might be from administrators to economists as budgeting takes on more of the planning function.

Most important, perhaps, are the differential informational requirements of planning, control, and management processes. Informational needs differ in terms of time spans, levels of aggregation, linkages with organizational and operating units, and input-output foci. The apparent solution is to design a system that serves the multiple needs of budgeting. Historically, however, there has been a strong tendency to homogenize informational structures and to rely on a single classification scheme to serve all budgetary purposes. For the most part, the informational system has been structured to meet the purposes of control. As a result, the type of multiple-purpose budget system envisioned by PPB has been avoided.

An examination of budget systems should reveal whether greater emphasis is placed *at the central levels* on planning, management, or control. A *planning orientation* focuses on the broadest range of issues: What are the long-range goals and policies of the government and how are these related to particular expenditure choices? What criteria should be used in appraising the requests of the agencies? Which programs should be initiated or terminated, and which expanded or curtailed? A *management orientation* deals with less fundamental issues: What is the best way to organize for the accomplishment of a prescribed task? Which of several staffing alternatives achieves the most effective relationship between the central and field offices? Of the various grants and projects proposed, which should be approved? A *control orientation* deals with a relatively narrow range of concerns: How can agencies be held to the expenditure ceilings established by the legislature and chief executive? What reporting procedures should be used to enforce propriety in expenditures? What limits should be placed on agency spending for personnel and equipment?

It should be clear that every budget system contains planning, management, and control features. A control orientation means the subordination, not the absence, of planning and management functions. In the matter of orientations, we are dealing with relative emphases, not with pure dichotomies. The germane issue is the balance among these vital functions at the central level. Viewed centrally, what weight does each have in the design and operation of the budget system?

THE STAGES OF BUDGET REFORM

The framework outlined above suggests a useful approach to the study of budget reform. Every reform alters the planning-management-control balance, sometimes inadvertently, usually deliberately. Accordingly, it is possible to identify three successive stages of reform. In the first stage, dating roughly from 1920 to 1935, the dominant emphasis was on developing an adequate system of expenditure control. Although planning and management considerations were not altogether absent (and indeed occupied a prominent role in the debates leading to the Budget and Accounting Act of 1921), they were pushed to the side by what was regarded as the first priority, a reliable system of expenditure accounts. The second stage came into the open during the New Deal and reached its zenith more than a decade later in the movement for performance budgeting. The management orientation, paramount during this period, made its mark in the reform of the appropriation structure, development of management improvement and work measurement programs, and the focusing of budget preparation on the work and activities of the agencies. The third stage, the full emergence of which must await the institutionalization of PPB, can be traced to earlier efforts to link planning and budgeting as well as to the analytic criteria of welfare economics, but its recent development is a product of modern informational and decisional technologies such as those pioneered in the Department of Defense.

PPB is predicated on the primacy of the planning function; yet it strives for a multi-purpose budget system that gives adequate and necessary attention to the control and management areas. Even in embryonic stage, PPB envisions the development of crosswalk grids for the conversion of data from a planning to a management and control framework, and back again. PPB treats the three basic functions as compatible and complementary elements of a budget system, though not as co-equal aspects of central budgeting. In ideal form, PPB would centralize the planning function and delegate *primary* managerial and control responsibilities to the supervisory and operating levels respectively.

In the modern genesis of budgeting, efforts to improve planning, management, and control made common cause under the popular banner of the executive-budget concept. In the goals and lexicon of the first reformers, budgeting meant executive budgeting. The two were inseparable. There was virtually no dissent from Cleveland's dictum that "to be a budget it must be prepared and submitted by a responsible executive. . . ."[3] Whether from the standpoint of planning, management or control, the executive was deemed in the best position to prepare and execute the budget. As Cleveland argued in 1915, only the executive "could think in terms of the institution as a whole," and, therefore, he "is the only one who can be made responsible for leadership."[4]

The executive budget idea also took root in the administrative integration movement, and here was allied with such reforms as functional consolidation of agencies, elimination of independent boards and commissions, the short ballot, and strengthening the chief executive's appointive and removal powers. The chief executive often was likened to the general manager of a corporation, the Budget Bureau serving as his general staff.

Finally, the executive budget was intended to strengthen honesty and efficiency by restricting the discretion of administrators in this role. It was associated with such innovations as centralized purchasing and competitive bidding, civil service reform, uniform accounting procedures, and expenditure audits.

THE CONTROL ORIENTATION

In the drive for executive budgeting, the various goals converged. There was a radical parting of the ways, however, in the conversion of the budget idea into an operational reality. Hard choices had to be made in the design of expenditure accounts and in the orientation of the budget office. On both counts, the control orientation was predominant.

In varying degrees of itemization, the expenditure classifications established during the first wave of reform were based on objects-of-expenditure, with detailed tabulations of the myriad items required to operate an administrative unit—personnel, fuel, rent, office supplies, and other inputs. On these "line-itemizations" were built technical routines for the compilation and review of estimates and the disbursement of funds. The leaders in the movement for executive budgeting, however, envisioned a system of functional classifications focusing on the work to be accomplished. They regarded objects-of-expenditure as subsidiary data to be included for informational purposes. Their preference for functional accounts derived from their conception of the budget as a planning instrument, their disdain for objects from the contemporary division between politics and administration.[5] The Taft Commission vigorously opposed object-of-expenditure appropriations and recommended that expenditures be classified by class of work, organizational unit, character of expense, and method of financing. In its model budget, the commission included several functional classifications.[6]

In the establishment of a budget system for New York City by the Bureau of Municipal Research, there was an historic confrontation between diverse conceptions of budgeting.

In evolving suitable techniques, the bureau soon faced a conflict between functional and object budgeting. Unlike almost all other budget systems which began on a control footing with object classifications, the bureau turned to control (and the itemization of objects) only after trial-and-error experimentation with program methods.

When confronted with an urgent need for effective control over administration, the bureau was compelled to conclude that this need was more critical than the need for a planning-functional emphasis. "Budget reform," Charles Beard once wrote, "bears the imprint of the age in which it originated."[7] In an age when personnel and purchasing controls were unreliable, the first consideration was how to prevent administrative improprieties.

In the opinion of those who were in charge of the development of a budget procedure, the most important service to be rendered was the establishing of central controls so that responsibility could be located and enforced through elected executives. . . . The view was, therefore, accepted, that questions of administration and niceties of adjustment must be left in abeyance until central control has been effectively established and the basis has been laid for careful scrutiny of departmental contracts and purchases as well as departmental work.[8]

Functional accounts had been designed to facilitate rational program decisions, not to deter officials from misfeasance. "The classification by 'functions' affords no protection; it only operates as a restriction on the use which may be made of the services."[9] The detailed itemization of objects was regarded as desirable not only "because it provides for the utilization of all the machinery of control which has been provided, but it also admits to a much higher degree of perfection than it has at present attained."[10]

With the introduction of object accounts, New York City had a threefold classification of expenditures: (1) by organizational units; (2) by functions; and (3) by objects. In a sense, the Bureau of Municipal Research was striving to develop a budget system that would serve the multiple purposes of budgeting simultaneously. To the bureau, the inclusion of more varied and detailed data in the budget was a salutory trend; all purposes would be served and the public would have a more complete picture of government spending. Thus the bureau "urged from the beginning a classification of costs in as many different ways as there are stories to be told."[11] But the bureau did not anticipate the practical difficulties which would ensue from the multiple classification scheme. In the 1913 appropriations act

there were 3992 distinct items of appropriation. . . . Each constituted a distinct appropriation, besides which there was a further itemization of positions and salaries of personnel that multiplied this number several times, each of which operated as limitations on administrative discretion.[12]

This predicament confronted the bureau with a direct choice between the itemization of objects and a functional classification. As a solution, the bureau recommended retention of object accounts and the total "defunctionalization" of the budget; in other words, it gave priority to the objects and the control orientation they manifested. Once installed, object controls rapidly gained stature as an indispensable deterrent to administrative misbehavior. Amelioration of the adverse effects of multiple classifications was to be accomplished in a different manner, one which would strengthen the planning and management processes. The bureau postulated a fundamental distinction between the purposes of budgets and appropriations, and between the types of classification suitable for each.

. . . an act of appropriation has a single purpose—that of putting a limitation on the amount of obligations which may be incurred and the amount of vouchers which may be drawn to pay for personal services, supplies, etc. The only significant classification of appropriation items, therefore, is according to persons to whom drawing accounts are given and the classes of things to be bought.[13]

Appropriations, in sum, were to be used as statutory controls on spending. In its "Next Steps" proposals, the bureau recommended that appropriations retain "exactly the same itemization so far as specifications of positions and compensations are concerned and, therefore, the same protection."[14]

Budgets, on the other hand, were regarded as instruments of planning and publicity. They should include "all the details of the work plans and specifications of cost of work"[15] In addition to the regular object and organization classifications, the budget would report the "total cost incurred, classified by *functions*—for determining questions of policy having to do with service rendered as well as to be rendered, and laying a foundation for appraisal of results."[16] The bureau also recommended a new instrument, a *work program*, which would furnish "a detailed schedule or analysis of each function, activity, or process within each organization unit. This analysis would give the total cost and the unit cost wherever standards were established."[17]

Truly a far-sighted conception of budgeting! There would be three documents for the three basic functions of budgeting. Although the bureau did not use the analytic framework suggested above, it seems that the appropriations were intended for control purposes, the budget for planning purposes, and the work program for management purposes. Each of the three documents would have its specialized information scheme, but jointly they would comprise a multi-purpose budget system not very different from PPB, even though the language of crosswalking or systems analysis was not used.

Yet the plan failed, for in the end the bureau was left with object accounts pegged to a control orientation. The bureau's distinction between budgets and appropriations was not well understood, and the work-program idea was rejected by New York City on the ground that adequate accounting backup was lacking. The bureau had failed to recognize that the conceptual distinction between budgets and appropriations tends to break down under the stress of informational demands. If the legislature appropriates by objects, the budget very likely will be classified by objects. Conversely, if there are no functional accounts, the prospects for including such data in the budget are diminished substantially. As has almost always been the case, the budget came to mirror the appropriations act; in each, objects were paramount. It remains to be seen whether PPB will be able to break this interlocking informational pattern.

By the early 1920's the basic functions of planning and management were overlooked by those who carried the gospel of budget reform across the nation. First generation budget workers concentrated on perfecting and spreading the widely approved object-of-expenditure approach, and budget writers settled into a nearly complete preoccupation with forms and with factual descriptions of actual and recommended procedures. Although ideas about the use of the budget for planning and management purposes were retained in Buck's catalogs of "approved" practices,[18] they did not have sufficient priority to challenge tradition.

From the start, federal budgeting was placed on a control, object-of-expenditure footing, the full flavor of which can be perceived in reading

Charles G. Dawes' documentary on *The First Year of the Budget of The United States.* According to Dawes,

. . . the Bureau of the Budget is concerned only with the humbler and routine business of Government. Unlike cabinet officers, it is concerned with no question of policy, save that of economy and efficiency.[19]

This distinction fitted neatly with object classifications that provided a firm accounting base for the routine conduct of government business, but no information on policy implications of public expenditures. Furthermore, in its first decade, the bureau's tiny staff (forty or fewer) had to coordinate a multitude of well-advertised economy drives which shaped the job of the examiner as being that of reviewing itemized estimates to pare them down. Although Section 209 of the Budget and Accounting Act had authorized the bureau to study and recommend improvements in the organization and administrative practices of federal agencies, the bureau was overwhelmingly preoccupied with the business of control.

THE MANAGEMENT ORIENTATION

Although no single action represents the shift from a control to a management orientation, the turning point in this evolution probably came with the New Deal's broadening perspective of government responsibilities.

During the 1920's and 1930's, occasional voices urged a return to the conceptions of budgeting advocated by the early reformers. In a notable 1924 article, Lent D. Upson argued vigorously that "budget procedure had stopped halfway in its development," and he proposed six modifications in the form of the budget, the net effect being a shift in emphasis from accounting control to functional accounting.[20] A similar position was taken a decade later by Wylie Kilpatrick who insisted that "the one fundamental basis of expenditure is functional, an accounting of payments for the services performed by government."[21]

Meanwhile, gradual changes were preparing the way for a reorientation of budgeting to a management mission. Many of the administrative abuses that had given rise to object controls were curbed by statutes and regulations and by a general upgrading of the public service. Reliable accounting systems were installed and personnel and purchasing reforms introduced, thereby freeing budgeting from some of its watchdog chores. The rapid growth of government activities and expenditures made it more difficult and costly for central officials to keep track of the myriad objects in the budget. With expansion, the bits and pieces into which the objects were itemized became less and less significant, while the aggregate of activities performed became more significant. With expansion, there was heightened need for central management of the incohesive sprawl of administrative agencies.

The climb in activities and expenditures also signaled radical changes in the role of the budget system. As long as government was considered a "necessary evil," and there was little recognition of the social value of public expenditures, the main function of budgeting was to keep spending in check. Because the outputs were deemed to be of limited and fixed value, it made sense to use the budget for central control over inputs. However, as the work and accomplishments of public agencies came to be regarded as benefits, the task of budgeting was redefined as the effective marshalling of fiscal and organizational resources for the attainment of benefits. This new posture focused attention on the problems of managing large programs and organizations, and on the opportunities for using the budget to extend executive hegemony over the dispersed administrative structure.

All these factors converged in the New Deal years. Federal expenditures rose rapidly from $4.2 billion in 1932 to $10 billion in 1940. Keynesian economics (the full budgetary implications of which are emerging only now in PPB) stressed the relationship between public spending and the condition of the economy. The President's Committee on Administrative Management (1937) castigated the routinized, control-minded approach of the Bureau of the Budget and urged that budgeting be used to coordinate federal activities under presidential leadership. With its transfer in 1939 from the Treasury to the newly-created Executive Office of the President, the bureau was on its way to becoming the leading management arm of the federal government. The bureau's own staff was increased tenfold; it developed the administrative management and statistical coordination functions that it still possesses; and it installed apportionment procedures for budget execution. More and more, the bureau was staffed from the ranks of public administration rather than from accounting, and it was during the directorship of Harold D. Smith (1939–46) that the bureau substantially embraced the management orientation.[22] Executive Order 8248 placed the President's imprimatur on the management philosophy. It directed the bureau

to keep the President informed of the progress of activities by agencies of the Gov-

ernment with respect to work proposed, work actually initiated, and work com-
pleted, together with the relative timing of work between the several agencies of
the Government; all to the end that the work programs of the several agencies of
the executive branch of the Government may be coordinated and that the monies
appropriated by the Congress may be expended in the most economical manner pos-
sible to prevent overlapping and duplication of effort.

Accompanying the growing management use of the budget process for the appraisal and improvement of administrative performance, and the scientific management movement with its historical linkage to public administration, were far more relevant applications of managerial cost accounting to governmental operations. Government agencies sought to devise performance standards and the rudimentary techniques of work measurement were introduced in several agencies including the Forest Service, the Census Bureau, and the Bureau of Reclamation.[23] Various professional associations developed grading systems to assess administrative performance as well as the need for public services. These crude and unscientific methods were the forerunners of more sophisticated and objective techniques. At the apogee of these efforts, Clarence Ridley and Herbert Simon published *Measuring Municipal Activities: A Survey of Suggested Criteria for Appraising Administration,* in which they identified five kinds of measurement—(1) needs, (2) results, (3) costs, (4) effort, and (5) performance—and surveyed the obstacles to the measurement of needs and results. The latter three categories they combined into a measure of administrative efficiency. This study provides an excellent inventory of the state of the technology prior to the breakthrough made by cost-benefit and systems analysis.

At the close of World War II, the management orientation was entrenched in all but one aspect of federal budgeting—the classification of expenditures. Except for isolated cases (such as TVA's activity accounts and the project structure in the Department of Agriculture), the traditional object accounts were retained though the control function had receded in importance. In 1949 the Hoover Commission called for alterations in budget classifications consonant with the management orientation. It recommended "that the whole budgetary concept of the Federal Government should be refashioned by the adoption of a budget based upon functions, activities, and projects."[24] To create a sense of novelty, the commission gave a new label—performance budgeting—to what had long been known as functional or activity budgeting. Because its task force had used still another term—program budgeting—there were two new terms to denote the budget innovations of that period. Among writers there was no uniformity in usage, some preferring the "program budgeting" label, others "performance budgeting," to describe the same things. The level of confusion has been increased recently by the association of the term "program budgeting" (also the title of the Rand publication edited by David Novick) with the PPB movement.

Although a variety of factors and expectations influenced the Hoover Commission, and the commission's proposals have been interpreted in many ways, including some that closely approximate the PPB concept, for purposes of clarity, and in accord with the control-management-planning framework, performance budgeting *as it was generally understood and applied* must be distinguished from the emergent PPB idea. The term "performance budgeting" is hereafter used in reference to reforms set in motion by the Hoover Commission and the term "program budgeting" is used in conjunction with PPB.

Performance budgeting is management-oriented; its principal thrust is to help administrators to assess the work-efficiency of operating units by (1) casting budget categories in functional terms, and (2) providing work-cost measurements to facilitate the efficient performance of prescribed activities. Generally, its method is particularistic, the reduction of work-cost data unto discreet, measurable units. Program budgeting (PPB) is planning-oriented; its main goal is to rationalize policy-making by providing (1) data on the costs and benefits of alternative ways of attaining proposed public objectives, and (2) output measurements to facilitate the effective attainment of chosen objectives. As a policy device, program budgeting departs from simple engineering models of efficiency in which the objective is fixed and the quantity of inputs and outputs is adjusted to an optimal relationship. In PPB, the objective itself is variable; analysis may lead to a new statement of objectives. In order to enable budget-makers to evaluate the costs and benefits of alternative expenditure options, program budgeting focuses on expenditure aggregates; the details come into play only as they contribute to an analysis of the total (the system) or of marginal trade-offs among competing proposals. Thus, in this macroanalytic approach, the accent is on comprehensiveness and on grouping data into categories that allow comparisons among alternative expenditure mixes.

Performance budgeting derived its ethos and much of its technique from cost accounting and scientific management; program budgeting has drawn its core ideas from economics and systems analysis. In the performance budgeting literature, budgeting is described as a "tool of management" and the budget as a "work program." In PPB, budgeting is an allocative process among competing claims, and the budget is a statement of policy. Chronologically, there was a gap of several years between the bloom of performance budgeting and the first articulated conceptions of program budgeting. In the aftermath of the first Hoover report, and especially during the early 1950's, there was a plethora of writings on the administrative advantages of the performance budget. Substantial interest in program budgeting did not emerge until the mid-1950's when a number of economists (including Smithies, Novick, and McKean) began to urge reform of the federal budget system. What the economists had in mind was not the same thing as the Hoover Commission.

In line with its management perspective, the commission averred that "the all-important thing in budgeting is the work or service to be accomplished, and what that work or service will cost."[25] Mosher followed this view closely in writing that "the central idea of the performance budget . . . is that the budget process be focused upon programs and functions—that is, accomplishments to be achieved, work to be done."[26] But from the planning perspective, the all-important thing surely is not the work or service to be accomplished but the objectives or purposes to be fulfilled by the investment of public funds. Whereas in performance budgeting, work and activities are treated virtually as ends in themselves, in program budgeting work and services are regarded as intermediate aspects, the process of converting resources into outputs. Thus, in a 1954 Rand paper, Novick defined a program as "the sum of the steps or interdependent activities which enter into the attainment of a specified objective. The program, therefore, is the end objective and is developed or budgeted in terms of all the elements necessary to its execution."[27] Novick goes on to add, "this is not the sense in which the government budget now uses the term."

Because the evaluation of performance and the evaluation of program are distinct budget functions, they call for different methods of classification which serve as an intermediate layer between objects and organizations. The activities relate to the functions and work of a distinct operating unit; hence their classification ordinarily conforms to organizational lines. This is the type of classification most useful for an administrator who has to schedule the procurement and utilization of resources for the production of goods and services. Activity classifications gather under a single rubric all the expenditure data needed by a manager to run his unit. The evaluation of programs, however, requires an end-product classification that is oriented to the mission and purposes of government. This type of classification may not be very useful for the manager, but it is of great value to the budget-maker who has to decide how to allocate scarce funds among competing claims. Some of the difference between end-product and activity classifications can be gleaned by comparing the Coast Guard's existing activity schedule with the proposed program structure on the last page of Bulletin 66-3. The activity structure which was developed under the aegis of performance budgeting is geared to the operating responsibilities of the Coast Guard: Vessel Operations, Aviation Operations, Repair and Supply Facilities, and others. The proposed program structure is hinged to the large purposes sought through Coast Guard operations: Search and Rescue, Aids to Navigation, Law Enforcement, and so on.

It would be a mistake to assume that performance techniques presuppose program budgeting or that it is not possible to collect performance data without program classifications. Nevertheless, the view has gained hold that a program budget is "a transitional type of budget between the orthodox (traditional) character and object budget on the one hand and performance budget on the other."[28] Kammerer and Shadoan stress a similar connection. The former writes that "a *performance* budget carries the program budget one step further: into *unit costs.*"[29] Shadoan "envisions 'performance budgeting' as an extension of . . . the program budget concept to which the element of unit work measurement has been added."[30] These writers ignore the divergent functions served by performance and program budgets. It is possible to devise and apply performance techniques without relating them to, or having the use of, larger program aggregates. A cost accountant or work measurement specialist can measure the cost or effort required to perform a repetitive task without probing into the purpose of the work or its relationship to the mission of the organization. Work measurement—"a method of establishing an equitable relationship between the volume of work performed and manpower utilized"—[31] is only distantly and indirectly related to the process of determining governmental policy at the higher levels. Program classifications are vitally linked to the making and implementation of policy through the allocation of public resources. As a general rule, performance budgeting is concerned with the *process of work* (what methods should be used) while program budgeting is concerned with the *purpose of work* (what activities should be authorized).

Perhaps the most reliable way to describe this difference is to show what was tried and accomplished under performance budgeting. First of all, performance budgeting led to the introduction of activity classifications, the management-orientation of which has already been discussed. Second, narrative descriptions of program and performance were added to the budget document. These statements give the budget-reader a general picture of the work that will be done by the organizational unit requesting funds. But unlike the analytic documents currently being developed under PPB, the narratives have a descriptive and justificatory function; they do not provide an objective basis for evaluating the cost-utility of an expenditure. Indeed, there hardly is any evidence that the narratives have been used for decision-making; rather they seem best suited for giving the uninformed outsider some glimpses of what is going on inside.

Third, performance budgeting spawned a multitude of work-cost measurement explorations. Most used, but least useful, were the detailed workload statistics assembled by administrators to justify their requests for additional funds. On a higher level of sophistication were attempts to apply the techniques of scientific management and cost accounting to the development of work and productivity standards. In these efforts, the Bureau of the Budget had a long involvement, beginning with the issuance of the trilogy of work measurement handbooks in 1950 and reaching its highest development in the productivity-measurement studies that were published in 1964. All these applications were at a level of detail useful for managers with operating or supervisory responsibilities, but of scant usefulness for top-level officials who have to determine organizational objectives and goals. Does it really help top officials if they know that it cost $0.07 to wash a pound of laundry or that the average postal employee processes 289 items of mail per hour? These are the main fruits of performance measurements, and they have an importance place in the management of an organization. They are of great value to the operating official who has the limited function of getting a job done, but they would put a crushing burden on the policy-maker whose function is to map the future course of action.

Finally, the management viewpoint led to significant departures from PPB's principle that the expenditure accounts should show total systems cost. The 1949 National Security Act (possibly the first concrete result of the Hoover report) directed the segregation of capital and operating costs in the defense budget. New York State's performance-budgeting experiment for TB hospitals separated expenditures into cost centers (a concept derived from managerial cost accounting) and within each center into fixed and variable costs. In most manpower and work measurements, labor has been isolated from other inputs. Most important, in many states and localities (and implicitly in federal budgeting) the cost of continuing existing programs has been separated from the cost of new or expanded programs. This separation is useful for managers who build up a budget in terms of increments and decrements from the base, but it is a violation of program budgeting's working assumption that all claims must be pitted against one another in the competition for funds. Likewise, the forms of separation previously mentioned make sense from the standpoint of the manager, but impair the planner's capability to compare expenditure alternatives.

THE PLANNING ORIENTATION

The foregoing has revealed some of the factors leading to the emergence of the planning orientation. Three important developments influenced the evolution from a management to a planning orientation.

(1) Economic analysis—macro and micro—has had an increasing part in the shaping of fiscal and budgetary policy.

(2) The development of new informational and decisional technologies has enlarged the applicability of objective analysis to policy making. And,

(3) There has been a gradual convergence of planning and budgetary processes.

Keynesian economics with its macroanalytic focus on the impact of governmental action on the private sector had its genesis in the underemployment economy of the Great Depression. In calling attention to the opportunities for attaining full employment by means of fiscal policy, the Keynesians set into motion a major restatement of the central budget function. From the utilization of fiscal policy to achieve economic objectives, it was but a few steps to the utilization of the budget process to achieve fiscal objectives. Nevertheless, between the emergence and the victory of the new economics, there was a lapse of a full generation, a delay due primarily to the entrenched balanced-budget ideology. But the full realization of the budget's economic potential was stymied on the revenue side by static tax policies and on the expenditure side by status-spending policies.

If the recent tax policy of the federal government is evidence that the new economics has come of age, it also offers evidence of the long-standing failure of public officials to use the taxing power as a variable constraint on the economy. Previously, during normal times, the tax structure was accepted as given, and the task of fiscal analysis was to forecast future tax yields so as to ascertain how much would be available for expenditure. The new approach treats taxes as variable, to be altered periodically in accord with national policy and economic conditions. Changes in tax rates are not to be determined (as they still are in virtually all states and localities) by how much is needed to cover expenditures but by the projected impact of alternative tax structures on the economy.

It is more than coincidental that the advent of PPB has followed on the heels of the explicit utilization of tax policy to guide the economy. In macroeconomics, taxes and expenditures are mirror images of one another; a tax cut and an expenditure increase have comparable impacts. Hence, the hinging of tax policy to economic considerations inevitably led to the similar treatment of expenditures. But there was (and remain) a number of obstacles to the utilization of the budget as a fiscal tool. For one thing, the conversion of the budget process to an economic orientation probably was slowed by the Full Employment Act of 1946 which established the Council of Economic Advisers and transferred the Budget Bureau's fiscal analysis function to the council. The institutional separation between the CEA and the BOB and between fiscal policy and budget-making was not compensated by cooperative work relationships. Economic analysis had only a slight impact on expenditure policy. It offered a few guidelines (for example, that spending should be increased during recessions) and a few ideas (such as a shelf of public works projects), but it did not feed into the regular channels of budgeting. The business of preparing the budget was foremost a matter of responding to agency spending pressures, not of responding to economic conditions.

Moreover, expenditures (like taxes) have been treated virtually as given, to be determined by the unconstrained claims of the spending units. In the absence of central policy instructions, the agencies have been allowed to vent their demands without prior restraints by central authorities and without an operational set of planning guidelines. By the time the bureau gets into the act, it is faced with the overriding task of bringing estimates into line with projected resources. In other words, the bureau has had a budget-cutting function, to reduce claims to an acceptable level. The President's role has been similarly restricted. He is the *gatekeeper* of federal budgeting. He directs the pace of spending increases by deciding which of the various expansions proposed by the agencies shall be included in the budget. But, as the gatekeeper, the President rarely has been able to look back at the items that have previously passed through the gate; his attention is riveted to those programs that are departures from the established base. In their limited roles, neither the bureau nor the President has been able to inject fiscal and policy objectives into the forefront of budget preparation.

It will not be easy to wean budgeting from its utilization as an administrative procedure for financing ongoing programs to a decisional process for determining the range and direction of public objectives and the government's involvement in the economy. In the transition to a planning emphasis, an important step was the 1963 hearings of the Joint Economic Committee on *The Federal Budget as an Economic Document.* These hearings and the pursuant report of the JEC explored the latent policy opportunities in budget making. Another development was the expanded time horizons manifested by the multi-year expenditure projections introduced in the early 1960's. Something of a breakthrough was achieved via the revelation that the existing tax structure would yield cumulatively larger increments of uncommitted funds—estimated as much as $50 billion by 1970—which could be applied to a number of alternative uses. How much of the funds should be "returned" to the private sector through tax reductions and how much through expenditure increases? How much should go to the states and localities under a broadened system of federal grants? How much should be allocated to the rebuilding of cities, to the improvement of education, or to the eradication of racial injustices? The traditional budget system lacked the analytic tools to cope with these questions, though decisions ultimately would be made one way or another. The expansion of the time horizon from the single year to a multi-year frame enhances the opportunity for planning and analysis to have an impact on future expenditure decisions. With a one-year perspective, almost all options have been foreclosed by previous commitments; analysis is effective only for the increments provided by self-generating revenue increases or to the extent that it is feasible to convert funds from one use to another. With a longer time span, however, many more options are open, and economic analysis can have a prominent part in determining which course of action to pursue.

So much for the macroeconomic trends in budget reform. On the microeconomic side, PPB traces its lineage to the attempts of welfare economists to construct a science of finance predicted on the principle of marginal utility. Such a science, it was hoped, would furnish objective criteria for determining the optimal allocation of public funds among competing uses. By appraising the marginal costs and benefits of alternatives (poor relief versus battleships in Pigou's classic example), it would be possible to determine which combination of expenditures afforded maximum utility. The quest for a welfare function provided the conceptual underpinning for a 1940 article on "The Lack of a Budgetary Theory" in which V. O. Key noted the absence of a theory which would determine whether "to allocate x dollars to activity A instead of activity B."[32] In terms of its direct contribution to budgetary practice, welfare economics has been a failure. It has not been possible to distill the conflicts and complexities of political life into a welfare criterion or homogeneous distribution formula. But stripped of its normative and formal overtones, its principles have been applied to budgeting by economists such as Arthur Smithies. Smithies has formulated a budget rule that "expenditure proposals should be considered in the light of the objectives they are intended to further, and in general final expenditure decisions should not be made until all claims on the budget can be considered."[33] PPB is the application of this rule to budget practice. By structuring expenditures so as to juxtapose substitutive elements within program categories, and by analyzing the costs and benefits of the various substitutes, PPB has opened the door to the use of marginal analysis in budgeting.

Actually, the door was opened somewhat by the development of new decisional and informational technologies, the second item on the list of influences in the evolution of the planning orientation. Without the availability of the decisional-informational capability provided by cost-benefit and systems analysis, it is doubtful that PPB would be part of the budgetary apparatus today. The new technologies make it possible to cope with the enormous informational and analytic burdens imposed by PPB. As aids to calculation, they furnish a methodology for the analysis of alternatives, thereby expanding the range of decision-making in budgeting.

Operations research, the oldest of these technologies, grew out of complex World War II conditions that required the optimal coordination of manpower, material, and equipment to achieve defense objectives. Operations research is most applicable to those repetitive operations where the opportunity for qualification is highest. Another technology, cost-benefit analysis, was intensively adapted during the 1950's to large-scale water resource investments, and subsequently to many other governmental functions. Systems analysis is the most global of these technologies. It involves the skillful analysis of the major factors that go into the attainment of an interconnected set of objectives. Systems analysis has been applied in DOD to the choice of weapons systems, the location of military bases, and the determination of sealift-airlift requirements. Although the extension of these technologies across-the-board to government was urged repeatedly by members of the Rand Corporation during the 1950's, it was DOD's experience that set the stage for the current ferment. It cannot be doubted that the coming of PPB has been pushed ahead several years or more by the "success story" in DOD.

The third stream of influence in the transformation of the budget function has been a closing of the gap between planning and budgeting. Institutionally and operationally, planning and budgeting have run along separate tracks. The national government has been reluctant to embrace central planning of any sort because of identification with socialist management of the economy. The closest thing we have had to a central planning agency was the National Resources Planning Board in the 1939–1943 period. Currently, the National Security Council and the Council of Economic Advisors have planning responsibilities in the defense and fiscal areas. As far as the Bureau of the Budget is concerned, it has eschewed the planning function in favor of control and management. In many states and localities, planning and budgeting are handled by separate organizational units: in the states, because limitations on debt financing have encouraged the separation of the capital and operating budgets; in the cities, because the professional autonomy and land-use preoccupations of the planners have set them apart from the budgeteers.

In all governments, the appropriations cycle, rather than the anticipation of future objectives, tends to dictate the pace and posture of budgeting. Into the repetitive, one-year span of the budget is wedged all financial decisions, including those that have multi-year implications. As a result, planning, if it is done at all, "occurs independently of budgeting and with little relation to it."[34] Budgeting and planning, moreover, invite disparate perspectives: the one is conservative and negativistic; the other, innovative and expansionist. As Mosher has noted, "budgeting and planning are apposite, if not opposite. In extreme form, the one means saving; the other, spending."[35]

Nevertheless, there has been some *rapprochement* of planning and budgeting. One factor is the long lead-time in the development and procurement of hardware and capital investments. The multi-year projections inaugurated several years ago were a partial response to this problem. Another factor has been the diversity of government agencies involved in related functions. This has given rise to various *ad hoc* coordinating devices, but it also has pointed to the need for permanent machinery to integrate dispersed activities. Still another factor has been the sheer growth of federal activities and expenditures and the need for a rational system of allocation. The operational code of planners contains three tenets relevant to these budgetary needs: (1) planning is future-oriented; it connects present decisions to the attainment of a desired future state of affairs; (2) planning, ideally, encompasses all resources involved in the attainment of future objectives. It strives for comprehensiveness. The *master plan* is the one that brings within its scope all relevant factors; (3) planning is means-ends oriented. The allocation of resources is strictly dictated by the ends that are to be accomplished. All this is to say that planning is an economizing process, though planners are more oriented to the future than economists. It is not surprising that planners have found the traditional budget system deficient,[36] nor is it surprising that the major reforms entailed by PPB emphasize the planning function.

Having outlined the several trends in the emerging transition to a planning orientation, it remains to mention several qualifications. First, the planning emphasis is not predominant in federal budgeting at this time. Although PPB asserts the paramountcy of planning, PPB itself is not yet a truly operational part of the budget machinery. We are now at the dawn of a new era in budgeting; high noon is still a long way off. Second, this transition has not been preceded by a reorientation of the Bureau of the Budget. Unlike the earlier change-over from control to management in which the alteration of budgetary techniques *followed* the revision of the bureau's role, the conversion from management to planning is taking a different course—first, the installation of new techniques; afterwards, a reformulation of the bureau's mission. Whether this sequence will hinder reform efforts is a matter that cannot be predicted, but it should be noted that in the present instance the bureau cannot convert to a new mission by bringing in a wholly new staff, as was the case in the late 1930's and early 1940's.

WHAT DIFFERENCE DOES IT MAKE?

The starting point for the author was distinguishing the old from the new in budgeting. The interpretation has been framed in analytic terms, and budgeting has been viewed historically in three stages corresponding to the three basic functions of budgeting. In this analysis, an attempt has been made to identify the difference between the existing and the emerging as a difference between management and planning orientations.

In an operational sense, however, what difference does it make whether the central budget process is oriented toward planning rather than management? Does the change merely mean a new way of making decisions, or does it mean different decisions as well? These are not easy questions to answer, particularly since the budget system of the future will be a compound of all three functions. The case for PPB rests on the assumption that the form in which information is classified and used governs the actions of budget-makers, and, conversely, that alterations in form will produce desired changes in behavior. Take away the assumption that behavior follows form, and the movement for PPB is reduced to a trivial manipulation of techniques—form for form's sake without any significant bearing on the conduct of budgetary affairs.

Yet this assumed connection between roles and information is a relatively uncharted facet of the PPB literature. The behavioral side of the equation has been neglected. PPB implies that each participant will behave as a sort of "Budgetary Man," a counterpart of the classical "Economic Man" and Simon's "Administrative Man."[37] "Budgetary Man," whatever his station or role in the budget process, is assumed to be guided by an unwavering commitment to the rule of efficiency; in every instance he chooses that alternative that optimizes the allocation of public resources.

PPB probably takes an overly mechanistic view of the impact of form on behavior and underestimates the strategic and volitional aspects of budget-making. In the political arena, data are used to influence the "who gets what" in budgets and appropriations. If information influences behavior, the reverse also is true. Indeed, data are more tractable than roles; participants are more likely to seek and use data which suit their preferences than to alter their behavior automatically in response to formal changes.

All this constrains, rather than negates, the impact of budget form. The advocates of PPB, probably in awareness of the above limitations, have imported into budgeting men with professional commitments to the types of analysis and norms required by the new techniques, men with a background in economics and systems analysis, rather than with general administrative training.

PPB aspires to create a different environment for choice. Traditionally, budgeting has defined its mission in terms of identifying the existing base and proposed departures from it—"This is where we are; where do we go from here?" PPB defines its mission in terms of budgetary objectives and purposes—"Where do we want to go? What do we do to get there?" The environment of choice under traditional circumstances is *incremental;* in PPB it is *teletic.* Presumably, these different processes will lead to different budgetary outcomes.

A budgeting process which accepts the base and examines only the increments will produce decisions to transfer the present into the future with a few small variations. The curve of government activities will be continuous, with few zigzags or breaks. A budget-making process which begins with objectives will require the base to compete on an equal footing with new proposals. The decisions will be more radical than those made under incremental conditions. This does not mean that each year's budget will lack continuity with the past. There are sunk costs that have to be reckoned, and the benefits of radical changes will have to outweigh the costs of terminating prior commitments. Furthermore, the extended time span of PPB will mean that big investment decisions will be made for a number of years, with each year being a partial installment of the plan. Most important, the political manifestations of sunk costs—vested interests—will bias decisions away from radical departures. The conservatism of the political system, therefore, will tend to minimize the decisional differences between traditional and PPB approaches. However, the very availability of analytic data will cause a shift in the balance of economic and political forces that go into the making of a budget.

Teletic and incremental conditions of choice lead to still another distinction. In budgeting, which is committed to the established base, the flow of budgetary decisions is upward and aggregative. Traditionally, the first step in budgeting, in anticipation of the call for estimates, is for each department to issue its own call to prepare and to submit a set of estimates. This call reaches to the lowest level capable of assembling its own estimates. Lowest level estimates form the building blocks for the next level where they are aggregated and reviewed and transmitted upward until the highest level is reached and the totality constitutes a department-wide budget. Since budgeting is tied to a base, the building-up-from-below approach is sensible; each building block estimates the cost of what it is already doing plus the cost of the increments it wants. (The building blocks, then, are decisional elements, not simply informational elements as is often assumed.)

PPB reverses the informational and decisional flow. Before the call for estimates is issued, top policy has to be made, and this policy constrains the estimates prepared below. For each lower level, the relevant policy instructions are issued by the superior level prior to the preparation of estimates. Accordingly, the critical decisional process—that of deciding on purposes and plans—has a downward and disaggregative flow.

If the making of policy is to be antecedent to the costing of estimates, there will have to be a shift in the distribution of budget responsibilities. The main energies of the Bureau of the Budget are now devoted to budget preparation; under PPB these energies will be centered on what we may term *prepreparation*—the stage of budget-making that deals with policy and is prior to the preparation of the budget. One of the steps marking the advent of the planning orientation was the inauguration of the Spring Preview several years ago for the purpose of affording an advance look at departmental programs.

If budget-making is to be oriented to the planning function, there probably will be a centralization of policy-making, both within and among departments. The DOD experience offers some precedent for predicting that greater budgetary authority will be vested in department heads than heretofore, but there is no firm basis for predicting the degree of centralization that may derive from the relatedness of objectives pursued by many departments. It is possible that the mantle of central budgetary policy will be assumed by the bureau; indeed, this is the expectation in many agencies. On the other hand, the bureau gives little indication at this time that it is willing or prepared to take this comprehensive role.

SOME BASIC DIFFERENCES BETWEEN BUDGET ORIENTATIONS

Characteristic	Control	Management	Planning
Personnel Skill	Accounting	Administration	Economics
Information Focus	Objects	Activities	Purposes
Key Budget Stage (central)	Execution	Preparation	Pre-preparation
Breadth of Measurement	Discrete	Discrete/ activities	Comprehensive
Role of Budget Agency	Fiduciary	Efficiency	Policy
Decisional-Flow	Upward-aggregative	Upward-aggregative	Downward-disaggregative
Type of Choice	Incremental	Incremental	Teletic
Control Responsibility	Central	Operating	Operating
Management Responsibility	Dispersed	Central	Supervisory
Planning Responsibility	Dispersed	Dispersed	Central
Budget-Appropriations Classifications	Same	Same	Different
Appropriations-Organizational Link	Direct	Direct	Crosswalk

CONCLUSION

The various differences between the budgetary orientations are charted in the table presented here. All the differences may be summed up in the statement that the ethos of budgeting will shift from justification to analysis. To far greater extent than heretofore, budget decisions will be influenced by explicit statements of objectives and by a formal weighing of the costs and benefits of alternatives.

NOTES:

The author is indebted to Henry S. Rowen and Paul Feldman of the Bureau of the Budget and to the many federal officials who guided him during a summer's sojourn along the road to PPB.

[1]New York Bureau of Municipal Research, *Making a Municipal Budget* (New York: 1907), pp. 9–10.
[2]Robert N. Anthony, *Planning and Control Systems: A Framework for Analysis* (Boston: 1965), pp. 16–18.
[3]Frederick A. Cleveland, "Evolution of the Budget Idea in the United States," *Annals of the American Academy of Political and Social Science,* LXII (1915), 16.
[4]*Ibid.,* p. 17.
[5]See Frank J. Goodnow, "The Limit of Budgetary Control," *Proceedings of the American Political Science Association* (Baltimore: 1913), p. 72; also William F. Willoughby, "Allotment of Funds by Executive Officials, An Essential Feature of Any Correct Budgetary System," *ibid.,* pp. 78–87.
[6]U. S., President's Commission on Economy and Efficiency, *The Need for a National Budget* (Washington: 1912), pp. 210–213.
[7]Charles A. Beard, "Prefatory Note," *ibid.,* p. vii.
[8]New York Bureau of Municipal Research, "Some Results and Limitations of Central Financial Control in New York City," *Municipal Research,* LXXXI (1917), 10.
[9]"Next Steps . . .," *op. cit.,* p. 39.
[10]"Next Steps . . .," *op. cit.,* p. 67.
[11]"Some Results and Limitations . . .," *op. cit.,* p. 9.
[12]"Next Steps . . .," *op. cit.,* p. 35.
[13]*Ibid,* p. 7.
[14]"Next Steps . . .," p. 39.
[15]"Some Results and Limitations . . .," *op. cit.,* p. 7.

[16]*Ibid.,* p. 9.

[17]"Next Steps . . .," *op. cit.,* p. 30.

[18]See A. E. Buck, *Public Budgeting* (New York: 1929), pp. 181–88.

[19]Charles G. Dawes, *The First Year of the Budget of the United States* (New York: 1923), preface, p. ii.

[20]Lent D. Upson, "Half-time Budget Methods," *The Annals of the American Academy of Political and Social Science,* CXIII (1924), 72.

[21]Wylie Kilpatrick, "Classification and Measurement of Public Expenditure," *The Annals of the American Academy of Political and Social Science,* Vol. 183 (1936), 20.

[22]See Harold D. Smith, *The Management of Your Government* (New York: 1945).

[23]Public Administration Service, *The Work Unit in Federal Administration* (Chicago: 1937).

[24]U. S. Commission on Organization of the Executive Branch of the Government, *Budgeting and Accounting* (Washington: 1949), 8.

[25]*Ibid.*

[26]Frederick C. Mosher, *Program Budgeting: Theory and Practice* (Chicago: 1954), p. 79.

[27]David Novick, *Which Program Do We Mean in "Program Budgeting?"* (Santa Monica: 1954), p. 17.

[28]Lennex L. Meak and Kathryn W. Killian, *A Manual of Techniques for the Preparation, Consideration, Adoption, and Administration of Operating Budgets* (Chicago: 1963), p. 11.

[29]Gladys M. Kammerer, *Program Budgeting: An Aid to Understanding* (Gainesville: 1959), p. 6.

[30]Arlene Theuer Shadoan, *Preparation, Review, and Execution of the State Operating Budget* (Lexington: 1963), p. 13.

[31]U. S. Bureau of the Budget, *A Work Measurement System* (Washington: 1950), p. 2.

[32]V. O. Key, "The Lack of a Budgetary Theory," *The American Political Science Review,* XXXIV (1940), 1138.

[33]Arthur Smithies, *The Budgetary Process in the United States* (New York: 1955), p. 16.

[34]Mosher, *op. cit.,* p. 47–48.

[35]*Ibid.,* p. 48.

[36]See Edward C. Banfield, "Congress and the Budget: A Planner's Criticism," *The American Political Science Review,* XLII (1949), 1217–1227.

[37]Herbert A. Simon, *Administrative Behavior* (New York: 1957).

II.
BUDGETING
AND THE POLITICAL PROCESS

3.
Budgeting in a Political Framework*
JESSE BURKHEAD

The factors which determine the allocation of public expenditures are shaped by the machinery of government and by the private pressures which are brought to bear on the decision-makers. As V. O. Key stated, in commenting on the absence of criteria for determining whether X dollars should be allocated to activity A rather than to activity B,

Perhaps the approach toward the practical working out of the issues lies in the canalizing of decisions through the governmental machinery so as to place alternatives in juxtaposition and compel consideration of relative values.[1]

The development of an adequate approach to decision-making in the allocation of public resources must recognize the interrelation of (1) the governmental machinery, and the administrator and legislator therein, in providing a mechanism for arriving at decisions; and (2) the influence of groups that are affected by public expenditures in shaping and molding the decision. Beyond these two, there is the influence of the facts—the measurement of specific benefits which have come and can come from specific expenditures.

The organizational structures which are established for decision-making and the procedures which are involved enter into all aspects of public budgeting and will be treated in other places in this volume.[2] At this point only two aspects of this complex will be examined—the political character of decision-making in government with specific reference to the position of the administrator, and the influence of interest groups.

A. ROLE OF THE ADMINISTRATOR

In the first important writings on public administration at the turn of

*Reprinted from Jesse Burkhead, *Government Budgeting,* New York: Wiley, 1956, pp. 44–50, by permission of the author and publisher. Jesse Burkhead is professor of economics at the Maxwell School, Syracuse University.

the century, decision-making in government was analyzed in terms of a separation between "politics" and "administration." Writing primarily about American government, influenced by the formal separation of legislative and administrative authority, and motivated by a desire to support civil service systems, the early theorists stressed that policy was formulated primarily by the legislature and that it was the responsibility of the administrator to carry out this policy in accordance with certain principles which were intended to guide him.[3] Such policy determinations as were made within administrative agencies were the responsibility of appointed officials, subject to removal and control of elected officials. The formulation of policy rested exclusively with those who could be directly controlled by the electoral process.

In recent years a quite different approach has come to dominate the analysis of decision-making in government. It has been pointed out by such observers as Appleby that a distinction between policy and administration is not descriptive of the operating reality of government; that the legislature makes policy, of course, but so do administrators; that the administrator is subject to many of the same kinds of political pressures in making his decisions as are the legislators; that policy is made where decisions are made; and that this is not confined to the upper reaches of the hierarchy of a government agency, nor to the corridors of the legislature.[4]

This approach to decision-making illuminates a good number of problems which, up to this time, had not been well understood. It emphasizes that power and authority in government do not reside in elected representatives alone, and it centers attention on the importance of securing responsibility in administration. The administrator is not responsible solely to elected representatives, to the chief executive, or to the Congress. The administrator operates—makes decisions—in an extremely complex pattern of responsibility. The materials for his decisions come from many and diverse sources, as Appleby says:

The process of democratic public administration is one of group judgment at each hierarchal level, judgment of groups of levels, group judgment subject to review, modification, revocation, and punitive action in any one of the many higher levels as consequences of the judgment's having come to bear upon citizens and having become subject to the reaction of citizens. It is a process in which facilities of appeal and levels of review are more numerous, various, and open than in any other action-laden process yet devised. It is a process carried on in an environment more critical and more politically active and potent than the environment of any other administrative

*process. It is a process in which the pattern of responsibility runs to public
representativeness of many kinds and roles, to subordinates, to associates in the same
unit, to contiguous and related units with somewhat different responsibilities, to
higher executive levels where repose broader responsibilities; it runs outward to
special publics, outward from higher levels to other and larger publics, outward and
upward from executive agencies to the Chief Executive, to the Congress, and to the
general public.*[5]

Further, there can be no separation of economics from politics in governmental decision-making. "The intermingling of economics and politics within the executive branch is just one aspect of the general inter-
twining of politics and administration."[6] Economic considerations are not
of a higher order than political considerations. Both must be merged in
the materials which are the basis of policy decisions. "If economists are
to be of greater service in advising on public policy, they must recognize
frankly the inseparability of economic and political analysis and gird
themselves to do a better job."[7] The same point has been made by Congressman Cannon in commenting on United States government programs:

*. . . no economic program rightly called the federal government's will ever show
much resemblance to an economist's dream—or even to the composite picture of the
dreams of a thousand economists. The reason is obvious. Legislation is political
business. It is the business of compounding distinct and divergent interests into
progressively broader understandings and agreements.*[8]

The pattern of responsibility which is inherent in any governmental
program may be illustrated by a relatively simple example—an example
which will also incidentally illustrate some of the difficulties in determining the efficiency of governmental operations.

Suppose that a city council, after reviewing the demands for various
municipal services for the forthcoming year, authorizes a lump sum of
$250,000 for the public library for operating purposes. Suppose that the
librarian has freedom to determine his program within the limits of this
appropriation and decides to curtail the purchase of new books, spending the funds which are saved on the encouragement of the use of the
library. Lighting facilities are improved; the reading room is brightened
up with curtains; some new chairs are purchased for the children's
room; the periodicals are placed on open shelves. In addition, the librarian devotes his energies to publicizing the facilities of the library. He
makes speeches in the public schools and before clubs and organizations.
He arranges for book review luncheons. He sponsors a Great Books scs-

sion every week in the library. Let it be assumed that his efforts are successful, and at the end of the year the use of the library is greatly increased. Whereupon, the community's demand for library facilities is enlarged, and in the next annual budget the city council sees fit to increase the appropriation to $300,000. The librarian can now purchase the new books that he did not buy the year before.

Has the librarian acted in an "efficient" fashion? As a result of his decisions the city ends up by spending more, not less, on the library. Citizens find that they devote more of their spare time to reading and less to other leisure-time activities. If they formerly patronized night clubs, thereby absorbing a quantity of police protection services, it may be that the number of police prowl cars can now be reduced.

This hypothetical case illustrates a number of the characteristics of the operations of the public sector and the role of the administrator therein.

First, it is evident that the administrator, as in this not extraordinary situation, may have great leeway in the determination of policy, that is, in the determination of what constitutes a "good" library.

Second, the resources which are available to the administrator are by no means rigidly limited. He can create the demand that additional resources be devoted to the program which is under his supervision. It may be noted that these additional resources might be diverted from other governmental programs, or they might represent a net addition to governmental resources, that is, the city council may authorize higher taxes in order to provide an increase in funds for the library.

Third, the community does not have a set of values that determine the amount of resources which will be used for the operation of libraries or any other governmental function. These values are operationally determined and are always in the process of being determined. The community decides that it wants a library. The librarian then shapes the community's demand for libraries by the way in which he administers. The kind and size of the library will be determined by the librarian's program and by the response of the community to that program.[9]

Fourth, the form in which the budget is presented and approved will determine the distribution of decision-making power between the administrator and the legislature. In the case here it was assumed that the librarian had considerable freedom to allocate the funds available to him. But if the city council were to specify in advance each detail of expenditure in the librarian's budget, his decision-making authority would be drastically limited.

Fifth, budget-making provides the occasion for periodic review and reassessment of community needs and resources. The community does and should change its mind about libraries from time to time. The periodicity inherent in budgeting provides the occasion for translating these policy changes into operating programs.

B. INTEREST GROUPS AND THE BUDGET

Decisions concerning the size of the budget, the distribution of revenues, and the distribution of expenditures are political decisions, which both reflect and affect the possession of power by economic groups and classes. The decisions that emerge and are called public policy are greatly influenced by the interplay and the resolution of forces which may be generally described as interest groups.[10] There are, of course, other influences at work. The analysis of interest groups does not constitute an inclusive approach to political behavior. The dynamics of personal leadership, the role of organized political parties, the influence of cultural values, creeds, and dogmas, the structure of an economic system—all of these and many more will shape that which is called public policy. Interest groups are singled out here because of their particular impact on budgetary decisions.

It was noted that the public sector is characterized by the absence of readily measurable criteria to guide the allocation of resources. It is not possible to determine, beyond the possibility of controversy, that X dollars spent on A will produce more "good" for society than X dollars spent on B. However, one of the ways by which it can be determined whether it is wise to spend X dollars on A rather than on B is to ask persons interested in A and B what they think.

This is one aspect of interest group activity which is of greatest importance for public budgeting, and which influences decisions made by administrators in the formulation of the budget and decisions made by legislators who modify and adopt the budget. Organizations and associations, whether they be representative of employees, manufacturers, or farmers, or representative of the vitreous china manufacturers of Syracuse, New York, or the growers of corn in Emmet County, Iowa, or representative of predominantly non-economic groups such as veterans and religious organizations, must and should make their views known on matters which affect them. In this way policy-making officials will become informed of the probable consequences of their decisions. This is a part of the adequate knowledge and consideration which officials must possess before their decisions can be made responsibly.

The fact that the interest groups have a legitimate role to play in relation to the formulation of governmental policy need not mean that the decision-maker is a helpless pawn in the hands of the dominant groups. In some cases the decision-making administrator may act solely to affirm the compromises that are reached by the interaction of forces beyond his control. But in other cases there is opportunity for the organization of compromise, for the sublimation of issues, for the invention of solutions, and for the assertion of what is deemed to be a larger and wider interest as a counter to what is deemed a narrower and special interest. When these possibilities exist, the administrator, as Redford has said,

. . . should have competence in measuring possibilities and in discovering techniques for manipulating organism in terms of directive. It is the function of the political superstructure to see that he does not forget that his manipulative powers are subordinate powers, to be exercised in terms of the community purpose embodied in directives. It must also be the function of the political superstructure to provide some guiding concept of public purpose.[11]

In making decisions the administrator can play a partially independent role in the formulation of policy.[12] To him the public delegates some discretion. In some circumstances the administrator can assume active leadership in shaping and molding community support for or against specific proposals. The possibilities of this sort will vary in accordance with the program and in accordance with influences which are at work in the interest groups and in organized political parties. The relationship of the administrator to the community is not a static one.

NOTES:

[1]V. O. Key, Jr., "The Lack of a Budgetary Theory," *American Political Science Review,* December 1940, p. 1142.

[2]For example, Chapter 10 deals with budgetary decisions at the agency level, Chapter 11 with the central budget office, and Chapter 12 with the legislature. [Ed. note: This text reference and footnote refer to the Burkhead book.]

[3]See, for example, Frank J. Goodnow, *Politics and Administration* (New York: Macmillan Co., 1900), esp. pp. 1–22. For an excellent summary of the development of this doctrine of "separation of powers" as applied to public administration see Dwight Waldo, *The Administrative State* (New York: Ronald Press Company, 1948), pp. 104–129.

[4]See, in particular, Paul H. Appleby, *Policy and Administration* (University,

Ala.: University of Alabama Press, 1949), pp. 1–25; *Morality and Administration* (Baton Rouge: Louisiana State University Press, 1952), pp. 121–140.

[5]*Morality and Administration,* p. 251.

[6]Paul H. Appleby, "The Influence of the Political Order," *American Political Science Review,* April 1948, p. 274.

[7]Bertram M. Gross, in a review of *The Nineteen Fifties Come First* by Edwin G. Nourse, *American Political Science Review,* September 1951, p. 872. Nourse's views are somewhat different from those expressed here. See his *Economics in the Public Service* (New York: Harcourt, Brace & Company, 1953), esp. pp. 5–28.

[8]Clarence Cannon, "Congressional Responsibilities," *American Political Science Review,* April 1948, p. 308.

[9]See Norton E. Long, "Public Policy and Administration: The Goals of Rationality and Responsibility," *Public Administration Review,* Winter 1954, pp. 22–31. For a very different view of the determination of community values, and the role of the administrator therein, see Simon, *Administrative Behavior,* pp. 186–188; also, Clarence E. Ridley and Herbert A. Simon, *Measuring Municipal Activities* (Chicago: International City Managers' Association, 1938), pp. 1–9.

[10]Political scientists have written at length on this subject, and from various points of view. See, for example, the early work of E. Pendleton Herring, *Group Representation Before Congress* (Baltimore: John Hopkins Press, 1929); and *Public Administration and the Public Interest* (New York: McGraw-Hill Book Co., 1936). Also, Avery Leiserson, *Administrative Regulation* (Chicago: University of Chicago Press, 1942); David B. Truman, *The Governmental Process* (New York: Alfred A. Knopf, 1953); V. O. Key, Jr., *Politics, Parties and Pressure Groups* (New York: Thomas Y. Crowell Co., 1948). Apart from the earlier work of the institutionalists, such as Veblen and Commons, few economists in recent years have devoted very much attention to group and organizational problems. Important contributions, however, are Robert A. Brady, *Business as a System of Power,* (New York: Columbia University Press, 1943); Kenneth E. Boulding, *The Organizational Revolution* (New York: Harper & Bros., 1953); John Kenneth Galbraith, *American Capitalism* (Boston: Houghton Mifflin Co., 1952); Chamberlain, *A General Theory of Economic Process,* esp. pp. 259–281.

[11]Emmette S. Redford, *Administration of National Economic Control* (New York: Macmillan Co., 1952), p. 231.

[12]There are important dissents to this view, particularly from those who

emphasize that governmental decision-making is bound by the interest groups and their influence. See Earl Latham, *The Group Basis of Politics* (Ithaca: Cornell University Press, 1952), pp. 1–53, where it is contended that the characteristic which distinguishes government from other groups is that it is endowed with "officiality," an endowment which occurs only after interest group influences have been resolved and compromised. Also, Herbert Agar, *The Price of Union,* (Boston: Houghton Mifflin Co., 1950), where this approach is applied to the analysis of political parties and their lack of principles.

4.

Public Attitudes Toward Fiscal Programs*

EVA MUELLER

Insights into people's attitudes toward fiscal programs are needed both by policy-makers and fiscal theorists. Although popular preferences cannot be regarded as a mandate to policy-makers, information on how people feel and what they want should be available and should have some bearing on policy decisions.

Personal interview surveys can throw light on the citizen's attitudes toward various government spending programs, the level of taxation, and budget deficits. More important, surveys can give us some understanding of the nature of people's fiscal preferences—their origin, congruence, and stability.

Theoretical work on the problem of budget determination by economists quite properly has emphasized such criteria as fiscal soundness, economic stability, economic growth, and income redistribution. At the same time it is agreed that, in addition to promoting these ends, fiscal policy should be governed by a welfare criterion. The maximum-welfare principle of budget determination requires that marginal outlays be allocated between private and public goods and between alternative government programs in accordance with consumer preferences.[1] If this principle is to advance the discussion of budget determination, it is necessary (1) to search for methods which can reveal people's preferences for public services, and (2) to gain some understanding of the nature of these preferences. This paper is directed toward both of these problems.

Section I will discuss the potentialities and limitations of sample surveys in measuring attitudes toward fiscal programs, based on data col-

*Reprinted by permission of the author and publisher from Eva Mueller, "Public Attitudes Toward Fiscal Programs," *Quarterly Journal of Economics,* Vol. 77, No. 2 (May, 1963), 210–235, copyright by the President and Fellows of Harvard College. Eva Mueller is professor of economics at the University of Michigan.

lected by the Survey Research Center of The University of Michigan on an experimental basis. Some comparisons will be made with voting systems. In Section II a brief account of major empirical findings to date will be presented. Section III will be concerned with the congruence and stability of fiscal preferences. It will be demonstrated that certain aspects of the preference system for public goods and services are not clearly crystallized in the consumer's mind; hence these attitudes have elements of inconsistency and may change easily under the impact of new information or new circumstances. In Section IV some of the determinants of attitudes toward fiscal programs will be explored. Particular interest centers around the role of considerations of direct personal benefit in shaping attitudes.

I. SAMPLE SURVEYS AS A TOOL FOR MEASURING ATTITUDES TOWARD FISCAL POLICIES

Attitudes toward government spending programs, taxes and deficits are a complex matter. Moreover, answers to survey questions may be influenced by the wording of the questions. Therefore, the answer to a single question (such as is sometimes posed in public opinion polls) is likely to be misleading. For example, people might be asked: "Do you think the federal government is spending about the right amount on improving our roads, or should it spend more, or less?" By itself the distribution of answers to this inquiry is difficult to interpret. However, if corresponding questions were asked also about school construction and slum clearance, one would be in a position to draw conclusions such as this: more people see a need for additional spending on school construction than see a need for more spending on highways. In other words, one can make valid comparisons between answers to parallel questions relating to different expenditures or taxes. Second, one can compare the answers by different subgroups of the population to the same question. By this procedure it might be learned that people in one section of the country feel a greater need for road improvement than people in another section, or that people with college training are more likely to favor outlays for schools than people with less education. Third, one can make comparisons over time of answers to identical questions. If more people favor an increase in defense spending now than some time ago, we are entitled to infer that concern about national security has intensified. Fourth, one may measure an attitude by asking not one but a series of questions on the same topic; the results would show to what extent and how answers are influenced by the context in which the attitude is explored.

Personal interview surveys can be conducted so as to allow people to explain their opinions fully in their own words. For instance, some people may explain that they are opposed to greater outlays on roads because they generally favor economy in government; others may be against greater outlays on roads because they own no car; still others may feel that the existing roads are good and not too overcrowded; still others may oppose spending on roads because they believe that additional defense spending is more urgent. The frequency of various reasons for holding an opinion is a crucial piece of information for the policymaker who wants to obtain a full understanding of popular preferences.

Finally, surveys can yield information on functional relationships between variables. For example, they can show whether people who favor higher government spending also favor higher taxes; or they can tell us how strongly preferences for various fiscal policy alternatives are related to political party identification.

Voting systems designed to reveal public preferences toward fiscal programs have been discussed extensively in the public finance literature.[2] It would appear that a well-designed personal interview survey with a representative sample of the population could provide a more adequate picture of people's attitudes and preferences than a popular referendum in which the total electorate could register their opinions in the voting booth. The drawback of any voting system is that it is impossible in the context of an election to ask people to respond to a lengthy series of carefully interrelated questions; nor is it possible to call for anything but "yes" or "no" answers (at most, one might get people to assign varying numbers of points to a series of alternatives). Of course, sample surveys are subject to sampling errors; but it takes a probability sample of only 2,000 cases to keep the sampling error below 4 percentage points. Inadequate questions may bring about reporting errors of much more serious magnitude.

Yet there is one danger in public opinion surveys which may be present to a lesser extent in a popular referendum. People may be asked in a survey to judge various policies, when they have little knowledge or conviction about the issues involved. An *ad hoc* answer may then be given which does not reflect any clearly formulated attitudes or preferences. Prior to an election, the issues involved usually are discussed by public figures, in the mass media, and by the candidates, so that the level of information and preparation may be higher than in the case of an unexpected interview. However, it is clear that many people have little knowledge and no opinion even about proposals, for instance regarding bond issues, that appear on the ballot.[3] This raises the question of the existence of preferences and their stability, which will be dealt with in Section III. We turn first to an examination of the nature of current attitudes.

II. SOME SURVEY FINDINGS

The data on consumer attitudes toward government expenditures, the level of taxation, and deficits were collected as part of three surveys conducted in 1960 and 1961. The three surveys were concerned primarily with other economic problems, and the questions on attitudes toward federal fiscal policies were added for exploratory purposes. In each sur-

TABLE I

NUMBER OF PROGRAMS FOR WHICH PEOPLE FAVOR SPENDING
MORE OR LESS THAN NOW

Number of Programs	(1) More spending favored in general [1]	(2) Less spending favored [1]	(3) More spending favored even if taxes had to be raised [2]
	%	%	%
None	6	39	14
One	7	22	36
Two	9	16	19
Three	12	10	11
Four	15	6	8
Five	14	3	4
Six	12	1	3
Seven	8	1	2
Eight or more	15	1	2
Not ascertained	1	1	1
Total	100	100	100
Number of cases	2256	2256	956

1. Question asked in June and November 1961.
2. Question asked only in November 1961.
The questions were:
   "The government spends money on many things. On this card is a list of some of the things on which the government spends money. How about . . . (specific program) . . . do you think the government should be spending more money, less money, or about the same amount?"   (The question was repeated for each program.)
   "You said the government should spend more money on . . . (name items) . . . ; if the government had to raise taxes to finance the additional expenditures, *then* for which of these things would you favor spending more money?"

vey a nationwide cross-section of households was selected for interview. In complete families the husband was designated as respondent in half the cases, the wife in the other half (the choice was made by a random procedure); in families where the head was not married, the head was automatically the respondent.

The finding which emerges most clearly from the survey data is that a large majority of the American people have favorable attitudes toward a number of major government expenditure programs. These attitudes are closely connected with the widely held belief that the federal government has great capabilities for influencing the level of economic activity and for bringing about the proper functioning of the economy.[4] The inquiry began by handing respondents a card showing a list of eleven "things on which the government spends money."[5] For each category of expenditure respondents were asked to indicate whether in their opinion the government should spend more money than now, less money than now, or about the same amount. The first column of Table I shows that only 6 per cent of the people interviewed did not think that any of the government programs enumerated should be enlarged. Sixteen per cent checked the answer "more" only once or twice, about half checked it three to six times, and a fourth checked it seven times or more. The table also shows (column 2) that 39 per cent did not advocate the reduction of any government program, and about the same proportion would like to see one or two programs cut back. Very few people checked the answer "less should be spent" for more than three of the eleven items listed on the card. These distributions of answers clearly point to widespread support for many government programs.

At the same time attitudes toward individual programs differ sharply. In Table II programs are listed in order of the frequency with which the answer "spend more" was checked. Over half of the people interviewed expressed the opinion that more money than now should be spent for (1) help to older people, (2) help for needy people, (3) education, (4) slum clearance and city improvement, and (5) hospitals and medical care. Only a small percentage feel that less money should be spent on any of these programs. There were four others programs: public works, defense, support for small business, and highway construction, to which between one-third and one-half of those interviewed would like to see more funds allocated. Finally there were a number of programs which received support in the sense that the proportion who said that the government should spend more money than now was greater than the proportion who said that the government should spend less. There were

TABLE II

ATTITUDES TOWARD GOVERNMENT PROGRAMS

Program	Government should spend . . .					More even if taxes had to be raised[2]
	More	Less	Same	No opinion	Total	
	%	%	%	%	%	%
Help for older people	70	3	23	4	100	34
Help for needy people	60	7	28	5	100	26
Education	60	7	25	8	100	41
Slum clearance, city improvement[1]	55	9	24	12	100	3
Hospital and medical care	54	9	28	9	100	25
Public works[1]	48	11	31	10	100	3
Defense, rearmament[2]	47	6	34	13	100	30
Support for small business[1]	37	11	31	21	100	3
Highway construction	36	10	45	9	100	13
Unemployment benefits	29	14	45	12	100	10
Parks, recreational facilities	27	15	48	10	100	7
Space exploration[2]	26	32	28	14	100	14
Support for agriculture	20	26	34	20	100	6
Help to other countries[2]	7	53	28	12	100	2

1. Question asked only in June 1961.
2. Question asked only in November 1961.
3. Not available.
For questions: see Table I.

only three programs for which the answer "spend less" was more frequent than the answer "spend more."

It appears from Table II that a rank ordering of public preferences can be achieved by survey methods. We are justified in concluding, for example, that additional aid to older people or to education would meet with more widespread public approval than additional outlays on parks and recreational facilities or aid to the unemployed. However, some caution in interpretation is necessary. Many people may respond to these survey questions on the basis of the values which they see in the programs and possibly on the basis of feelings about present adequacy. Few are in a position to judge whether better services might not be provided from present outlays or whether additional funds could indeed be utilized to good advantage (for example, in the case of space exploration).

The questions analyzed so far were posed without reference to methods of financing. In order to see whether people were prepared to pay for the many increases in spending for which they indicated their support, a further question was asked. After respondents had expressed their attitudes toward each government program, the interviewer summarized the programs checked "spend more" and asked: "You said the government should spend more money on . . .; if the government had to raise taxes to finance the additional expenditures, then for which of these things would you favor spending more money?" In other words, people were asked to reconsider their previously stated preferences. It was suggested to them that they may not have thought of the necessity of raising taxes to finance the additional expenditures; and they were asked whether in this case they would still adhere to their previous opinion. The third column of Table I shows that many people revised their opinions in response to the new question. They listed considerably fewer government programs on which they favored additional spending, but they still expressed a desire for the expansion of a number of government services. Half of the people said they would be willing to pay more taxes for two or more expanded programs, while only 14 per cent were unwilling to pay higher taxes for any government programs.[6] Yet there is no single program so popular that a majority would be prepared to pay higher taxes for it.

The rank ordering of programs is not changed greatly if extent of support is judged by the proportion of the people who are willing to pay more taxes for each program. Education heads the list according to this second ranking, with 41 per cent favoring greater outlays for education, even if these additional outlays would require tax increases. Help for older people ranks second in this list, followed by defense, help for needy people, and expenditures for hospitals and medical care. The proportion who, when reminded of taxes, adhered to their original opinion that more should be spent is highest for education and defense; it is particularly low for support to agriculture, parks and recreation facilities, aid to the unemployed, and highway construction.

The choice posed by this line of questioning is, of course, not sufficient. There are two alternative means by which stepped-up government programs might be financed: deficit spending and reductions in less preferred government activities. People's attitudes toward budget deficits and taxes may be clarified by considering this broader range of alternatives.

There is no evidence that the *existing* federal debt causes great concern or uneasiness. In the fall of 1961 only about half of the people interviewed knew that deficits were being incurred, and a substantial proportion of those who were aware of federal deficits were unable to answer a question about possible effects of deficits on business conditions. The small group who did have an opinion consisted of 8 per cent who saw favorable effects (more money being spent, more income and employment), 10 per cent who argued that there is no effect, and 15 per cent who saw unfavorable effects. Unfavorable effects cited were, in addition to feelings of insecurity and fiscal unsoundness, the possibility that taxes would have to be raised or that inflation would ensue.

Predominantly negative attitudes toward deficits were expressed, however, when the advisability of *additional* deficits came under discussion. In the fall of 1961, in order to raise the problem of new sources of funds, people were asked: "If the cold war with Russia should cost us *more* money during the next few years, do you think the government should raise taxes, or spend less on other things, or go further into debt?" The alternative of going further into debt was almost unanimously rejected, as Table III indicates. Most people probably could not support their antipathy to growing deficits by acceptable economic arguments. The tradition that the government budget should be balanced may have some relation to the maxim that one's private budget should be balanced. It is a belief which appears to be so well established that it is not contingent on economic circumstances.

TABLE III

OPINIONS ABOUT THREE METHODS OF FINANCING ADDITIONAL COLD WAR COSTS
(November 1961)

Method of Financing	All Families	Family Income				
		Under $3000	$3000–4999	$5000–7499	$7500–9999	$10,000 and over
	%	%	%	%	%	%
Raise taxes	29	21	31	35	36	29
Spend less on other things	62	62	62	60	60	68
Go further into debt	4	3	3	4	9	6
Depends; uncertain; not ascertained	11	18	9	7	6	9
Total	1	1	1	1	1	1
Number of cases	956	246	197	256	106	106

1. Columns add to more than 100 per cent since some few respondents suggested a combination of methods.
The question was:
  "If the cold war with Russia should cost us more money during the next few years, do you think the government should raise taxes or spend less on other things, or go further into debt?"

Debt *reduction* is favored by many people, but it clearly has less priority in most people's minds than the expansion of a number of government programs. In connection with taxes we shall discuss "habituation," i.e., getting accustomed to a level of taxes which, when first reached, seemed "too high." There is no specific empirical evidence that habituation also occurs in connection with the national debt; but such an inference would probably be quite safe. In November 1960 and in June 1961 people were asked: "Some people say that there will be some disarmament and therefore our government will spend *less* on arms and defense. Suppose this is the case, what would you say should be done with the money saved?" Table IV shows that only 14 per cent of the people interviewed (and 22 per cent of those with incomes over $10,000) spontaneously suggested debt reduction; an even smaller proportion suggested tax cuts, while about half answered that the government should then spend more on other programs, particularly public welfare programs, public construction programs, and education.[7]

Spontaneous answers to a non-suggestive question usually bring forth

TABLE IV

ALTERNATIVE USES OF DEFENSE SAVINGS SPONTANEOUSLY MENTIONED
(November 1960 and May–June 1961)

Alternative Uses	All Families	Family Income				
		Under $3000	$3000–4999	$5000–7499	$7500–9999	$10,000 and over
	%	%	%	%	%	%
Reduce government debt	14	11	13	13	18	22
Reduce income taxes	10	6	9	12	14	20
Public welfare programs	20	27	23	17	15	14
Education (other than school building)	13	10	12	15	17	17
Build schools, highways, etc.	10	7	12	11	11	11
Increase financial help to other countries	3	1	2	3	3	3
Other	15	10	18	16	18	21
Uncertain	15	24	13	13	8	6
Not ascertained	13	14	12	14	12	9
Total	1	1	1	1	1	1
Number of cases	2690	677	569	684	306	343

1. Adds to more than 100 per cent because respondents were allowed more than one mention.
The question was:
   "Some people say that there will be some disarmament and our government will spend less on arms and defense. Suppose this is the case, what would you say should be done with the money saved?"

those matters which are salient to the respondent. Nevertheless some alternatives, such as debt reduction, may have been overlooked. Therefore the inquiry about possible uses of defense savings was carried further by suggesting five specific possibilities and asking people to rank these in order of preference. The five choices were: (1) increase financial help to other countries; (2) reduce government debt; (3) reduce income taxes; (4) build schools; highways, and the like; (5) step up public welfare programs to help needy people in the United States. Table V shows for each alternative the proportion of people who ranked it first, second, third, etc. It appears that over half of the people interviewed ranked the two domestic expenditure programs—public welfare spending and public construction—first and second. Reduction in taxes and in the public debt were typically ranked third and fourth, while foreign aid tended to be the least preferred use of the money. A substantial minority—about one in four—put debt reduction ahead of expenditure programs *and* tax reduction, but many more assigned a relatively low priority to debt reduction.

One may conclude from the admittedly limited data regarding attitudes toward the public debt that the status quo is accepted by the majority of people without serious misgivings. A desire to see the debt reduced is present but is not very meaningful, since the desire for additional government programs seems to be stronger. On the other hand, any departure from the status quo in the direction of a significant increase in public debt is disliked and evokes fears of financial irresponsibility.

Attitudes toward taxes also seem to be characterized by a widespread acceptance of the status quo, that is, acceptance of prevailing levels of taxation. But, while in the case of the debt any dissatisfaction takes the form of a feeling that it should be reduced, in the case of taxes there is diversity of opinion: a sizable minority believes that it might be advisable to step up taxes; and another sizable minority is eager to have taxes reduced.

Table I above clearly points to some willingness to accept *tax increases.* It shows that half of the people interviewed said that they were prepared to pay additional taxes in order to make possible larger outlays on two or more government programs. Later in the interview, it may be recalled, people were asked to choose between three alternative methods of financing additional cold war expenditures—raising taxes, spending less on other things, or going further into debt. Given these alternatives, about 30 per cent clearly expressed themselves in favor of higher taxes

(Table III). This then is a group which seems to be willing to pay additional taxes, at least for a program which they view as being important.

Regarding *tax reductions,* people first were asked a non-suggestive question which they had to answer in their own words: In case a reduction in defense spending should become feasible, what should be done with the money saved? Only 10 per cent replied spontaneously "reduce taxes," as Table IV indicates. Many more people mentioned alternative spending programs. Table V shows that when people were asked specifically to rank five alternative uses of defense savings, some who had not thought of tax reduction previously ranked it as their first or second choice. In all, 37 per cent ranked tax reduction first or second, and only a slightly smaller proportion ranked it fourth or fifth.

The finding that most Americans feel no pronounced dissatisfaction with the prevailing level of taxation may be explained in part by "habituation."[8] Survey Research Center studies have shown repeatedly that visible advances in the cost of living are strongly resented, when they first occur. Many people know about them, and this knowledge adversely affects their willingness to buy. Later consumers become accustomed to the new price level, and after a year or two the original resentment diminishes.[9] Data on attitudes toward taxes collected in June 1951 suggest that tax increases also are resented at first, but then are gradually accepted. It may be recalled that Congress enacted a tax increase in September 1950. Although this increase was occasioned by war, 40 per cent of the people were of the opinion in June 1951 that taxes should be reduced, and another 40 per cent argued that *no* further increases should be made. Most significantly, about 60 per cent explained spontaneously in 1951 that "taxes already are high." This figure stands in sharp contrast to the 20 per cent who gave a similar response in 1961. Habituation to prevailing tax rates was undoubtedly facilitated by rising real incomes.

Acceptance of current tax levels may also be explained by the fact that most people are not social innovators, nor do they feel that they understand fiscal problems. Hence the majority of Americans do not formulate ideas as to how the level of taxation, much less the system of taxation, might be altered. Of course, strong dissatisfaction would lead people to visualize alternative levels of taxation and to express a preference for something other than the status quo. Because of habituation, dissatisfaction is unlikely to persist, however, except under extreme circumstances.

One important implication of the findings presented is lack of con-

TABLE V
ATTITUDES TOWARD ALTERNATIVE USES OF DEFENSE SAVINGS
(November 1960 and May–June 1961)

Ranking	Public welfare programs	Build schools, highways and the like	Reduce government debt	Reduce income taxes	Increase financial help to other countries
All Families (Number of cases = 2700)					
	%	%	%	%	%
Ranked as first choice	30	23	24	16	3
Ranked as second choice	22	31	15	21	5
Ranked as third choice	19	24	16	24	9
Ranked as fourth choice	17	13	29	22	11
Ranked as fifth choice	5	2	8	11	60
Not ascertained	7	7	8	6	12
Total	100	100	100	100	100
Income under $3000 (Number of cases = 677)					
	%	%	%	%	%
Ranked as first or second choice	64	52	29	32	5
Ranked as third choice	14	23	15	27	7
Ranked as fourth or fifth choice	12	13	41	27	70
Not ascertained	10	12	15	14	18
Total	100	100	100	100	100
Income $3000–7499 (Number of cases = 1253)					
	%	%	%	%	%
Ranked as first or second choice	54	56	38	38	8
Ranked as third choice	20	23	18	24	9
Ranked as fourth or fifth choice	20	15	37	32	74
Not ascertained	6	6	7	6	9
Total	100	100	100	100	100
Income over $7500 (Number of cases = 649)					
	%	%	%	%	%
Ranked as first or second choice	41	53	51	39	9
Ranked as third choice	23	25	14	20	11
Ranked as fourth or fifth choice	29	16	30	35	71
Not ascertained	7	6	5	6	9
Total	100	100	100	100	100

The questions were:
"Some people say that there will be some disarmament and therefore our government will spend less on arms and defense. Suppose this is the case, what would you say should be done with the money saved?"

"Here are some suggestions that have been made. Please tell me which use of the money appears best to you, which is second best, third, etc." (A card listing the five alternatives was shown to the respondent.)

gruence in people's thinking about fiscal programs.[10] Although there is strong support for the extension of a number of government programs, only a minority of the people interviewed would like to see taxes raised, and hardly anyone would like to see these expenditures financed by deficits.[11] One explanation might be that each citizen would prefer to have some government programs reduced in order to allow greater scope for others which interest him. This explanation is contradicted by the finding (Table II) that for only three out of fourteen major government programs is there a sizable group of people who advocate a reduction in spending, while for the remaining eleven programs the group favoring increased spending is much larger than the group favoring cut-backs.

An alternative explanation is consistent with our findings and with recent psychological research. Although there is considerable evidence that people strive to avoid dissonance or incongruence (by problem-solving behavior or suppression), dissonance may be tolerable when the conflicting desires or beliefs are peripheral to the person's psychological field. In the case of fiscal policies, the average citizen does not have to make decisions in which his conflicting preferences are confronted. He may not even think about (or discuss) fiscal problems enough to be bothered by lack of congruence. Hence in that area he may remain unaware of contradictions, look the other way, or just hope that more knowledgeable people in government will make the right decision for him.

By contrast, if a consumer wants a new TV set *and* a new washing machine and he can afford only one of these without drawing on his savings (which he dislikes), he is in a cross-road situation. He must deliberate until he arrives at a decision as to which course of action he prefers. Thus, while we have reason to assume that preference functions for alternative uses of private funds (including the savings alternative) have some firmness and consistency, our findings raise doubt whether the corresponding concept of a preference function for alternative fiscal policies is fruitful. We shall pursue this problem further in the next two sections by examining the congruence and stability of fiscal preferences and their origin.

III. THE CONGRUENCE AND STABILITY
OF FISCAL PREFERENCES

Attitudes toward fiscal programs undoubtedly vary in stability. At the one extreme there are attitudes which are long-standing stereotypes, firmly rooted in people's thinking and seldom consciously re-examined.

The conviction that deficits are bad is probably of that kind. At the other extreme may be fleeting notions which also have not been carefully thought through, being of little salience at the moment. In between are many attitudes which are rational in the sense that they are based on some degree of deliberation. These attitudes are related to values, preceptions and group belonging, but can be modified by environmental changes and new information. Their stability and congruence depend in part on external conditions, in part on the extent to which they are integrated into the central attitude structures of the individual.[12]

Besides the contradiction between attitudes toward spending and attitudes toward means of financing already discussed, three other kinds of findings appear in the survey which suggest that some fiscal policy attitudes are not very certain or firm. First, the data presented above show that variations in the wording of questions have considerable influence on the answers received. This is most evident in connection with the tax questions. When people who expressed themselves in favor of increased spending on a variety of government programs were reminded of tax costs, a substantial proportion revised their opinions. Yet half of the people indicated that they would be willing to pay additional taxes for two or more government programs (Table I). When some time later in the same survey, it was suggested that cold war costs might rise, only about 30 per cent chose higher taxes as a means of financing these additional outlays, while over 60 per cent "voted" in favor of reducing other government programs. To be sure, the questions differed, and in strict logic one might favor additional taxes in one context but not in the other. Still it appears that people's reactions to any proposed tax change would be strongly influenced by the reasons for the tax change and the political and economic circumstances under which it occurred.

Second, in addition to the over-all contradictions in attitudes, there is evidence of vacillation at the individual level. Two examples may be presented to illustrate the point. The two examples were selected intentionally to display the problem of vacillation. A number of other questions which have been compared show more harmonious responses. In the November 1961 survey people were asked both of the following questions:

If the cold war with Russia should cost us more money during the next few years, do you think the government should raise taxes, or spend less on other things, or go further into debt? And (in the context of a discussion of the recession): There has been discussion about reducing taxes at the present time. Do you think this would be a good idea or a bad idea?

TABLE VI

COMPARISONS OF RESPONSES TO TWO TAX QUESTIONS BY
IDENTICAL RESPONDENTS (1961)

Attitude Toward Tax Reduction	If the cold war should cost more in the future, how should it be financed?		
	Raise taxes	Spend less on other things	Go further into debt
	%	%	%
Good idea	32	42	34
Pro-con	4	6	6
Bad idea	59	42	49
Depends, uncertain	5	10	11
Total	100	100	100
Number of cases	220	529	35

For questions: see text.

The answer to these two are related in Table VI. While people who favored raising taxes in case of additional cold war costs were more frequently opposed to cutting taxes in 1961 than others, the differences were relatively small.

In Table VII people are classified into three groups according to their interest in additional government expenditures. One might assume that the proportion who advocate financing the cold war by cutting down on other programs (rather than by raising taxes) would be greater for the

TABLE VII

COMPARISON OF ATTITUDES TOWARD TAXES AND TOWARD SPENDING
BY IDENTICAL RESPONDENTS (1961)

If the cold war should cost more in the future, how should it be financed? [1]	Number of programs on which more spending is favored [2]		
	Zero to two	Three to five	Six or more
	%	%	%
Raise taxes	22	27	40
Spend less on other things	65	65	54
Go further into debt	4	3	8
Depends; uncertain, not ascertained	15	10	7
Total	[3]	[3]	[3]
Number of cases	276	424	244

1. For question: see Table III.
2. For question: see Table I.
3. Columns add to more than 100 per cent, since some respondents suggested a combination of methods.

TABLE VIII

RESPONDENT'S REACTIONS TO VARIOUS POLICY ISSUES (1956 AND 1960)

Reaction	The government ought to help people get doctors and hospital care at low cost		The United States should give economic help to poorer countries even if those countries can't pay for it [1]		If cities and towns need help to build more schools, the government in Washington ought to give them the money they need	
	1956	1960	1956	1960	1956	1960
	%	%	%	%	%	%
Agree strongly	40	46	21	29	49	38
Agree, but not strongly	15	12	22	23	19	18
Not sure; depends	20	22	32	28	18	20
Disagree, but not strongly	8	6	10	6	5	8
Disagree strongly	17	14	15	13	9	15
Not ascertained	2	2	2[2]	1	2[2]	1
Total	100	100	100	100	100	100
Number of cases	1358	1358	1358	1358	1358	1358
Rank order correlation coefficient between 1956 and 1960 response	r = .45		r = .25		r = .34	

1. The substantial level of agreement with this statement is not inconsistent with the unfavorable showing of foreign aid in Table II. Here we see that many people agree that the United States should give *some* foreign assistance. Table II indicates that very few people favor *more* spending on foreign aid.
2. Less than half of 1 per cent.

group that favored expanding few or no programs than for the group favoring expansion of most or all projects under discussion. Such a relationship is evident, but again it is far from strong. In fact, over 50 per cent of those who advocated expansion of six or more government programs chose "spending less on other things" as the best means of paying for additional cold war costs.

A third evidence of inconsistency and instability was obtained from a set of re-interviews in the fall of 1960 with respondents first interviewed prior to the 1956 election.[13] Respondents were presented with a number of statements in 1956 and asked to express their agreement or disagreement. These same people were presented with the identical statements four years later and were asked to react to them once more. Thus it is possible to determine what proportion took the same position at both times and what proportion took a different position after four years. The statements related to a variety of topics: isolationism, the over-seas stationing of American troops in peace time, a full employment guarantee by the government, the proper sphere of government versus private business, racial equality in housing and employment, and school desegregation. Also included were three statements concerning government expenditure programs:

If cities and towns around the country need help to build more schools, the government in Washington ought to give them the money they need. The United States should give economic help to poorer countries of the world if those countries can't pay for it. The government ought to help people get doctors and hospital care at low cost.

Table VIII shows people's reactions to the three fiscal policy statements in 1956 and 1960. The over-all change in attitudes over the four year period was relatively small, with medical aid and foreign assistance showing some increase in popular support and school construction showing some decline in response to environmental changes over the four year period. Yet many more individuals shifted position than would have been necessary to bring about the over-all change. That is, some people shifted from approval to disapproval, others moved in the opposite direction.[14] At the bottom of Table VIII are shown the rank order correlation coefficients between the first and second response, using a five-point scale ranging from "strong approval" to "strong disapproval."[15] For all three fiscal issues the rank order correlation coefficients are quite low. However, reactions to the other political issues posed yielded rank order correlation coefficients within the same range. Attitudes toward school desegregation together with medical care were most stable (rank order correlation coefficients of .45), while attitudes toward foreign economic aid were the least stable (.25). The other issues are clustered in the interval from .25 to .37.

It may be inferred that many citizens find it difficult to appraise the wisdom of major foreign and domestic policies. Because of the complexities involved, people often do not seem to come to a clear conclusion as to what stand they should take. Instability and incongruence of expressed attitudes are the logical consequence of such uncertainty. Attitudes toward fiscal policies do not differ from attitudes toward other difficult political and social policy problems in this respect.

IV. GROUP DIFFERENCES IN ATTITUDES TOWARD FISCAL POLICIES

This section will examine group differences in attitudes toward fiscal policies with the aim of throwing some light on the problem of attitude

TABLE IX

NUMBER OF PROGRAMS FOR WHICH PEOPLE FAVOR SPENDING
MORE THAN NOW (1961)

Number of Programs	Family Income			
	Under $3000	$3000–7500	$7500–10,000	$10,000 and over
	More spending favored in general			
	%	%	%	%
None	8	5	4	7
One or two	17	14	18	16
Three or four	23	28	29	32
Five or six	28	26	27	25
Seven or more	23	26	21	19
Not ascertained	1	1	1	1
Total	100	100	100	100
	More spending favored even if taxes had to be raised[1]			
	%	%	%	%
None	18	13	9	15
One	33	35	40	37
Two	25	19	15	12
Three or four	12	20	20	24
Five or more	8	12	14	11
Not ascertained	4	1	2	1
Total	100	100	100	100

1. Question asked only in November 1961. For questions: see Table I.

formation. We shall first attempt to distinguish between those groups which are more or less likely to benefit by a given policy in order to see how far considerations of direct personal benefit govern attitudes. We shall also examine the relation of attitudes toward fiscal programs to income, education, age, and political party affiliation. Finally, we shall relate the need felt for more government services to the need felt for major consumer goods and services.

Beginning with income group comparisons, the data show that it is *not* true, as is sometimes supposed, that upper income groups are less favorably disposed toward the extension of government programs than lower income groups. The number of programs for which people would like to see the government spend more money is almost identical in all major income groups; the same is true of the number of programs for which people are willing to pay higher taxes (Table IX). The answer "spend less" does occur, however, slightly more frequently among upper than among lower income groups.

While the desire for extended government services is pronounced in all income groups, Table X shows that there are distinct differences in

TABLE X

INDEXES OF ATTITUDES TOWARD GOVERNMENT PROGRAMS (1961)

	Index Values of Attitudes toward Spending[1] Family Income		
Program	Under $3000	$3000–7500	$7500 and over
Education	43	59	53
Help for older people	68	67	64
Slum clearance[2]	42	52	37
Hospital and medical care	54	45	33
Unemployment benefits	26	17	-2
Help for needy people	63	51	39
Support for agriculture	8	-3	-27
Public works[2]	44	38	24
Help to other countries[3]	-38	-46	-51
Defense[3]	35	42	45
Space exploration[3]	-18	-2	5
Highway construction	18	28	27
Parks	1	17	11
Support for small business[2]	20	27	30

1. Index value represents per cent advocating increased spending minus per cent advocating decreased spending; "no change" answers are disregarded.
2. Question asked only in May–June 1961.
3. Question asked only in November 1961.
For question: see Table I.

the kinds of services which are desired. In Table X a summary measure is used which shows the proportion who want more spent on a particular program minus the proportion who want less spent. Positive index values indicate that the proportion favoring expansion of a particular program exceeds the proportion favoring reduction; negative figures indicate the opposite. For example, if 40 per cent want to see a particular program enlarged, 50 per cent want no change, and 10 per cent want a reduction, the index value is 30 (40 minus 10). All income groups strongly support more aid for older people and more aid for education. In addition, certain programs which are of direct benefit primarily to lower income groups are more widely advocated among those with smaller incomes than among the well-to-do. Aid to the needy, aid for the unemployed, hospital and medical care, and public works fall into that category. By contrast, aid to small business and highway construction receive widest support in the upper income groups. In all, considerations of direct personal benefit seem to have some influence on attitudes toward fiscal programs; yet it is clear that other considerations are at work also and may even be more decisive.

TABLE XI

ATTITUDES TOWARD SPENDING IN RELATION TO SELF-INTEREST

Type of Expenditure	Index Values of Attitudes toward Spending[1]			
		Repeatedly unemployed	Seldom unemployed	Never unemployed
Unemployment benefits		60	33	15
	Under 35 years old	35–54	55–64	65 years old and over
Help for older people	57	70	66	69
		Farmers	Other occupations	
Support for agriculture		9	−8	
		Under 45: no children	Children under 18 in family	Over 45: no children
Education		64	58	41
		Own *no* car	One car	Two or more cars
Highway construction		14	28	28
	Central Cities	Suburban areas	Adjacent areas	Rural areas
Slum clearance and city improvement	48	54	43	35

1. Index value represents per cent advocating increased spending minus per cent advocating decreased spending; "no change" answers are disregarded.

The role of immediate self-interest can be tested by a number of additional comparisons. The index values shown in Table XI are computed as in Table X. The self-interest principle would suggest, for example, that people who are repeatedly unemployed would favor larger unemployment insurance benefits, while those who are never unemployed would favor no increase or even a decrease, or that expenditures to help older people would be increasingly favored with advancing age.

Except in the case of unemployment compensation, these comparisons confirm the idea that direct personal benefit offers only a partial explanation of attitudes toward fiscal programs. In the case of unemployment compensation closer knowledge and a different understanding of the problem among the unemployed may account for some of the observed differences, not merely self-interest. Regarding the other programs, many people expressed themselves in favor of greater expenditures from which they were not likely to reap direct personal benefit. They seemed to realize that the benefit of most government programs should be assessed from the point of view of the national welfare as a whole.[16] National benefit, in contrast to personal benefit, is difficult to assess. Looking at this broader frame of reference, many people might feel incapable of judging which course of action the government should pursue. Such feelings of ignorance or inability to choose between alternative possibilities must result in uncertainty or vacillation, and hence may account for some instability and inconsistency in attitudes toward fiscal programs.[17]

If this interpretation of the data is correct, there should be greater congruence of attitudes among the upper income and better educated groups than among the lower income and less educated. The data confirm this inference in the sense that they show the upper income and better educated groups to be somewhat *more* willing to pay taxes (presumably to finance the government programs which they advocate) than other groups. The proportion of people who ranked tax reduction first or second, when asked to consider alternative uses of free public funds, was about the same in all income groups (Table V). But a direct inquiry whether taxes should be raised in 1951 and an inquiry whether they should be lowered in 1956 both indicated that lower income groups are more eager for tax reduction than are the well-to-do. Questions about the advisability of tax reductions asked in 1961 and 1962 show that in both years opposition to tax cuts was more frequent among upper than among lower income groups, although the differences between income groups were greater in 1961 than in 1962.[18] If the data on attitudes toward tax reductions are classified by education, it appears that willingness to pay taxes also rises with education. Indeed the income differences in attitudes toward taxes may to some extent reflect educational differences. The finding that upper income groups have somewhat more favorable attitudes toward taxes than lower income groups stands in sharp contrast to the frequently expressed opinion that the well-to-do, who pay much larger amounts of taxes, are more resentful of the tax burden than those in the lower income brackets.

Relatively favorable attitudes by upper income groups toward taxes may reflect in part greater opposition to budget deficits. In the fall of 1961 awareness that the federal government had been running deficits increased sharply with income; 82 per cent of those with incomes of $10,000 or more had this information, as compared with only 38 per cent of those with incomes under $3,000. When asked to rank in order of preference five alternative uses of possible defense savings, debt reduction was ranked first or second by 29 per cent of those in the lowest income group, 38 per cent of those in the middle group, and 51 per cent of those with incomes over $7,500. Very similar differences in attitudes toward debt appear when comparisons are made between people with grammar school, high school, and college education. Not only is the general public not aware of the problems which economists see in a program of debt reduction, but education does not help here.

It seems, then, that the greater willingness of the upper income and better educated groups to pay taxes grows out of the desire to secure adequate government services and at the same time to avoid deficits. Possibly a greater feeling of financial latitude also has some influence.[19] The analysis of attitudes by income and education suggests that there are differences in the frequency of what we have called incongruent attitudes between these groups, which may be attributed to differences in information and understanding.

Age differences in attitudes toward fiscal policies are small and take the form of somewhat greater fiscal conservatism among people who are fifty-five and over than among those in the younger and middle-age brackets. By fiscal conservatism is meant less eagerness to step up government spending programs, coupled with a greater desire to reduce debt and to lower taxes (or avoid tax increases), in other words a more limited scope of government activity.

To what extent are attitudes toward fiscal policies different for Republicans and Democrats? We cannot concern ourselves here with the question whether identification with a party and its dominant ideology shapes attitudes toward fiscal policies or whether these attitudes exist first and help to determine party identification. Even in the second case party identification might be important because it could reinforce, or fail to reinforce, prior attitudes. The relationship between partisan preference and attitudes toward fiscal policies was analyzed by Campbell, Converse, Miller, and Stokes as part of an intensive Survey Research Center study of the 1956 election.[20] The study shows that attitudes toward taxes are unrelated to party identification. The kind of political party ideology or attitude structure that can be shown to have a bearing on party identification does not include attitudes toward the level of taxation as one of its components. On the other hand, attitudes toward social welfare activity by the government show some association with party preference, being viewed more favorably by Democrats than by Republicans.

The data collected in November 1960 on five alternative uses of available public funds (Table V) can be broken down by party preference and confirm these findings. They show that 35 per cent of Democrats and 39 per cent of Republicans ranked tax reduction as their first or second choice, while 30 per cent in both parties ranked it fourth or fifth. On the other hand, public construction programs (schools, highways, and the like) were ranked first or second by 49 per cent of Republicans and 59 per cent of Democrats; public welfare programs were ranked first or second by 45 per cent of Republicans and 60 per cent of Democrats. Finally, debt reduction was ranked first or second by 45 per cent of Republicans and 29 per cent of Democrats. Despite these differences, the finding which must be emphasized is that party identification does not contribute greatly toward the explanation of attitudes toward fiscal policies.

One further idea, which seems to underlie *The Affluent Society* deserves brief discussion—the idea that a strong desire for private goods and services dulls the need felt for public services.[22] Our data show first that in our affluent society the desire for extensive government services is very widespread, despite our preoccupation with private consumption. Second, the 1961 survey contained a series of questions on expenditure plans of consumers, the items ranging from food, clothing, and housing to recreation, hobbies, and travel. There was a moderate positive correlation between the number of private expenditures that people intend to step up and the number of government programs they would like to see enlarged. This suggests that feelings of financial well-being generate favorable attitudes toward private *and* public spending. Feelings of financial stringency, on the other hand, make for caution regarding private spending and economy-mindedness regarding public spending.[23]

We have analyzed some of the reasons for the uncertainty of fiscal attitudes. If fiscal preferences were based primarily on notions of immediate self-interest or benefit, little uncertainty should arise in most cases; hence we should expect a considerable degree of stability. Similarly, if these attitudes were derived from party identification, they should be nearly as firm as party preferences. We find that party identification has only a weak relationship to fiscal policy attitudes. The relationship of fiscal preferences to personal benefit is more pronounced, yet personal benefit appears to be only a partial determinant. Many people favor expenditures (for example on education, city improvement, or help for needy people) from which they themselves will not derive any direct advantage. It appears that people attempt to judge fiscal programs from the point of view of both national and immediate personal benefit.

Judging fiscal policies in terms of national or long-term general benefit seems, however, to be a task beyond the grasp of many people. The difficulty of the problem, combined with the fact that no decisions or action are required which demand its solution, discourages deliberation and inhibits the crystallization of ideas and preferences. Consciously or unconsciously, people delegate responsibility for making such decisions to their elected representatives and to the experts. Yet, to the extent that fiscal preferences have been formulated by the public, they should be known to the elected representatives and leaders of the people. Such information could then become one important consideration bearing on fiscal decisions, but, of course, not the only one.

In turn the public is receptive to guidance and information. Given the uncertainty with which people view many fiscal issues, their preferences may be considerably affected by the reasons they see for a proposed policy change and by the personalities advocating it. Although people feel at a loss to judge many questions of fiscal policy, this does not mean that they are unwilling to learn. On the contrary, surveys indicate that most Americans attach considerable importance to governmental decisions and grope for explanations, however unsophisticated. In order to explain their decisions effectively, political leaders ought to have a clear picture of prevailing opinions, whether these are traditional beliefs or uncertain notions. What is needed then is an active two-way flow of information. Policy-makers need to learn where the preferences of large numbers of people are at variance with their own. Ideally, the two-way flow of information would stimulate discussion of the underlying issues and could reduce any large gaps between the views of the citizenry and the views of their elected representatives.

NOTES:

This study was made possible by a grant from the Rockefeller Foundation to the Survey Research Center of The University of Michigan for theoretical analysis of economic survey data. The author also wishes to express her gratitude to Dr. George Katona who contributed valuable suggestions at all stages of this study and to Wallace Wilson for his participation in the analysis.

[1]More precisely, the maximum-welfare principle of budget determination as formulated by Pigou and Dalton requires, first, that resources should be allocated among different public uses so as to equalize the marginal return of satisfaction for each type of outlay; second, it requires that public expenditures be pushed to the point where the utility of the marginal expenditure dollar equals the utility of the marginal tax dollar. For further discussion see Richard A. Musgrave, *The Theory of Public Finance* (New York: McGraw-Hill, 1959), pp. 110–15.

[2]This literature is reviewed in Musgrave, *op. cit.,* Chap. 6, pp. 116–35.

[3]In 1958–59 a heated controversy took place in the state of Michigan regarding the imposition of an income tax. The problem was extensively discussed in the mass media and by public figures from the governor to business and labor leaders. Nevertheless a survey conducted in Detroit in early 1959 showed that 18 per cent of all adults could not say whether a sales or an income tax would be better for Michigan, and a considerably larger proportion had no definite opinion on the relative fairness of income, sales and property taxes. See Elisabeth J. L. David, "Public Preferences and the Tax Structure: An Examination of Factors Related to State and Local Tax Preferences," unpublished Ph.D. thesis, The University of Michigan, 1961.

[4]This point is treated more fully and documented by George Katona, *The Powerful Consumer* (New York: McGraw-Hill, 1960), pp. 174–75 and 231–32.

[5]The specific items on the card are listed in Table II below. Three items were dropped from the list after the first round of data collection and three others added, as indicated in Table II.

[6]The question was asked in what appeared to be an unbiased and understandable form; yet alternative wordings were possible. One might have referred specifically to the respondent's tax bill ("your taxes"). The actual wording of the question was meant to imply increases for all tax-

payers. Again, one might have asked *first* what programs people would be willing to pay higher taxes for, and *second* what programs should be undertaken, if free funds were available. How such changes in the question would have affected the level of positive responses cannot be predicted without further experimentation; it is unlikely that they would have significantly altered the rank ordering of the various programs.

[7]It may be pointed out here that the majority of respondents paid little heed to the introductory sentence regarding disarmament. People answered in terms of their preferences between various fiscal alternatives, rather than in terms of a program particularly suited to replace spending on arms and defense. Nevertheless, one clear conclusion regarding the disarmament problem can be drawn from our data: If disarmament should become possible, there are a number of major government spending programs which many people would like to see stepped up in place of defense spending. The fear that the government, in order to maintain full employment, might have to undertake projects little valued by the public is without foundation. This problem has been discussed by Emile Benoit in *Economic Impacts of Disarmament*, U.S. Arms Control and Disarmament Agency Publication 2 (Washington: U.S. Government Printing Office, 1962), and in "The Propensity to Reduce the National Debt Out of Defense Savings," *American Economic Review*, LI (May 1961), 455–59, with some reference to Survey Research Center data.

[8]It does not follow from this finding that a tax reduction would have no favorable psychological effects. More recent Survey Research Center studies on attitudes toward tax reduction will appear in the forthcoming book, *The 1962 Survey of Consumer Finances*, Survey Research Center, Institute for Social Research, (Ann Arbor: University of Michigan, 1963).

[9]For further detail see George Katona and Eva Mueller, "Consumer Attitudes and Demand, 1950–52," Survey Research Center, Institute for Social Research, (Ann Arbor: University of Michigan, 1953), pp. 16–26; and Eva Mueller, "Consumer Reactions to Inflation," *Quarterly Journal of Economics*, LXXIII (May 1959).

[10]The term "congruence" is used in this paper to denote harmony among attitudes. It is looser than the term "consistency," which is used where the answer to one question strictly pre-determines the logical answer to another question.

[11]Favorable attitudes toward additional expenditures also have been found to coexist with dislike of additional taxes in Germany and Sweden. See Günter Schmölders, *Das Irrationale in der Öffentlichen*

Finanzwertschaft (Hamburg: Rowohlt, 1960).

[12]The distinction between habitual ways of thinking and genuine decisions is treated by George Katona, *Psychological Analysis of Economic Behavior* (New York: McGraw-Hill, 1951), Chap. 4.

[13]These data were collected as part of a continuing program of election studies directed by Angus Campbell, Philip E. Converse, Warren E. Miller, and Donald E. Stokes, *The American Voter* (New York: Wiley, 1960).

[14]For a more general analysis of the problem of response instability, see George Katona, "Changes in Consumer Expectations and Their Origin," *The Quality and Economic Significance of Anticipations Data,* a Conference of the Universities—National Bureau of Economic Research (Princeton: Princeton University Press, 1960), pp. 53–82.

[15]The coefficient is the tau-beta due to Maurice Kendall *(Rank Correlation Methods;* London: Charles Griffin, 1948), applicable to a table with unlimited numbers of ties, and hence useful for bivariate distributions with ordered categories. I am indebted for this analysis to Dr. Philip Converse.

[16]The distinction in the public finance literature between individual benefit and collective benefit has been criticized by Gerhard Colm, "The Theory of Public Expenditures," *Essays in Public Finance and Fiscal Policy* (New York: Oxford University Press, 1955), pp. 27–43. Our data suggest that even the individual citizen often does not make such a differentiation. Hence the notion that individual benefit can serve as a criterion for taxation appears artificial. See, however, Musgrave, *op. cit.,* pp. 87–88.

[17]Schmölders reports that in West Germany expenditures for social welfare, science and culture, aid to farmers, and road improvement are designated as being of "utmost importance" by people irrespective of personal benefit. He argues that these favorable attitudes represent national stereotypes rather than opinions based on deliberation.

[18]The term upper-income group refers here to people with incomes of $10,000 and over. The number of cases with incomes over $25,000 in the survey is too small to analyze this group separately; conceivably antipathy to taxes might be stronger in that group.

[19]There is, however, no evidence that a man with a $10,000 income who seeks an upper-middle class standard of living and a college education for his children feels more financial latitude than a man with a $5,000 income and more modest aspirations.

[20]*Op. cit.,* Chaps. VIII and IX.

[22]J. Kenneth Galbraith, *The Affluent Society* (Boston: Houghton Mifflin, 1958).

[23]For a further discussion of this problem, see George Katona, "Consumers—Wasters or Investors?" *Challenge,* Vol. 10 (Dec. 1961), 14–16.

III.
APPROACHES TO PLANNING
AND PROGRAM BUDGETING

5.

The Planning Process: A Facet Design*

YEHEZKEL DROR

Introduction[1]

A close perusal of the large and growing literature dealing with different kinds of planning, shows a transfer of the focus of attention from ideological discourses on the desirability of planning to examination of substantive problems associated with the planning process, such as its nature, the phases of planning, conditions for successful planning, planning techniques, etc.[2] This change of emphasis in discussions on planning went hand-in-hand with recognition of the basic nature of planning as a methodology of rational thought and action, rather than a specific blueprint for one or another definite course of action.[3]

Emancipation of the concept of planning from any ideological annotations or connotations other than a belief in the ability of *homo sapiens* to engage to some extent in the shaping of his future and a belief in the desirability of his doing so[4] is an essential prerequisite for scientific examination of planning as a basic social-administrative process; but in order to be able to approach the study of planning in a really scientific and systematic way, we need first of all a much closer and more refined examination of its components and elements than is generally found in the literature dealing with it. In fact, it is very interesting to note that, despite the growing number of articles and books dealing with planning on one level or another, only a few efforts have been made recently to

*Reprinted from Yehezkel Dror, "The Planning Process: A Facet Design," *International Review of Administrative Sciences,* Vol. 29, No. 1 (1963) 44–58, by permission of the author and publisher. Yehezkel Dror is associate professor of political science and public administration at Hebrew University, Jerusalem.

develop a systematic approach to the study of planning as an administrative process.[5] Even authors well known for their original contributions to the administrative sciences have often failed to deal adequately with the planning phase of institutional action.[6] A more systematic approach to the study of planning, utilizing more refined concepts and more advanced research designs and methods, is urgently needed, if we want our knowledge on this basic and often crucial phase of organizational action to be in line with the progress being made in other areas of administrative science—such as communication theory and formal organization—and if we want knowledge to contribute to the improvement of the rapidly spreading practice of planning.[7]

In this paper an effort is being made to deal with one of the first phases of a systematic study of planning, namely a preliminary concept analysis—or, to use a more technical term, facet design—trying to identify the main factors and variables composing the planning process and shaping it. We will first explain and justify the methodological rationale and objective of this paper and discuss briefly its significance for the study of planning as a part of administrative sciences; then we will define our subject-matter and proceed to the presentation of the various primary and secondary facets of planning; finally, we will point out some lines for empiric research, based on the facet-design and directed at various problems of planning identified with the help of the facet design.

METHODOLOGY[8]

The concept of facet design, as first developed by Louis Guttman[9] and as applied to the study of various phenomena[10] is based on R. A. Fisher's approach to the design of experiments[11] and tries to systematize the construction of a semantic structure which identifies the different elements and variables of which the phenomenon to be studied is composed and by which it is shaped.

A short citation from the paper by Louis Guttman in which the concept of facet was first proposed will serve to clarify the general methodological significance of this concept:

Perhaps the most practical way of defining the concept is in most general terms. Consider a set A of any elements a_1, a_2 . . ., and a set B of any elements b_1, b_2 . . . Let C be the direct product[12] *of A and B: $C = A \times B$. That is, a typical element of C, say c, is a pair of elements $c = (a_j, b_k)$, one coming from A and the other from B. If A has m elements and B has n elements, then C has mn elements. We shall say that C is a two-faceted set, and that A and B are facets of C. A* *facet, then, is a set of elements. In general, C may be the direct product of any number of facets, not just two.*

Facet theory is useful for designing the universes of content of research projects. This aspect of the theory is part of facet design. Facet design may also refer to the population, P, being studied. The facet formula for a project can always be written in the general form: $P \times C = R$, where R is the set of possible responses of results.[13]

Application of the methodology of facet design to the study of the planning process is not easy because of the very complexity of the planning process, which results in a complex and multi-faceted set, in which each facet in turn is the product of a large number of secondary facets, which in turn are the product of various trietary facets which can be analyzed in terms of different sub-sets, and so on. Nevertheless, if the study of planning is to progress beyond impressionistic images or generalizations based on limited experience, it is essential that an effort be made to identify the main elements of planning, i.e. that a preliminary facet design of planning should be made.

Construction of a facet design is but a first, though very important, step which should, if possible, be followed by construction of a statistical or quasi-statistical structure designed for empirical research. While some of the primary and secondary facets to be presented in this paper form a simplex[14]—the primary facets being ordered in a simple order pattern from more external to more internal ones and the secondary facets being partly ordered from more simple ones to more complex and comprehensive ones—it may be necessary at a later stage to try and construct more complex structures for empiric research of planning.

In its present, rather amorphous form, the facet design of planning to be presented in this paper is intended to serve more as stimuli for directing thought towards basic problems than as a ready-made apparatus which can be directly applied to empiric investigations.[15] Nevertheless, even in its present form, the facet design should be of help for comparative study of planning instances,[16] and should serve as a checklist of factors to be considered and dealt with in any investigation of planning and in any attempt to set up, improve or analyze planning processes.

An additional remark must be made here on the relation between our facet design of planning and various "models of planning" and other discussions of some of the issues involving the planning process found in modern literature on decision-making, statistical decisions, theory of games, etc. Nearly all these models and discussions, insofar as they are relevant to our subject, deal with the sequential phases of rational action, providing various schemes or sequences which are designed to lead to rational outputs. If for some purposes some of these models can be regarded as parts of blueprints of an ideal flow-chart for the planning process, or parts of a system-analysis of the planning-process, then our facet design should be viewed as dealing with the environment and structure, or, to use a technical term, "space" within which the planning process takes place. Thus, we are dealing here with the first part of a general theory of the planning process, to be completed at a later date by a second paper, on the phases of the planning process.

THE CONCEPT OF PLANNING

Any effort to deal in a methodologically sound way with so elusive a phenomenon as planning must be anteceded by a more or less exact delimitation of the area of investigation, i.e. a definition of planning. While the validity of the definition is by its very nature limited to our world of discourse and adjusted to the purposes we have in mind, the definition should be in line with the more commonly accepted uses and meanings of the verbal referent "planning," so as to avoid unnecessary communication difficulties. Simultaneously, our definition must be wide enough to include planning processes taking place in different contexts and sharp enough to distinguish between planning and other related processes.

A short examination of some commonly used definitions will facilitate preparation of our own definition. Even leaving out of consideration definitions explicitly dealing with a limited area of planning—such as physical planning, economic planning, regional planning, etc.—we are faced with a wealth of definitions,[17] only a few of which can be quoted here. We will select our quotations so as to illustrate the main different approaches to the definition of the concept "planning."

One school of thought emphasizes the nature of planning as decisions concerning future action, as illustrated by the following definitions:

Planung ist die geistige Vor-Formung eines Organismus Organs oder eines Funktionsablaufs.[18]

Speaking generally, planning is deciding in advance what is to be done; that is, a plan is a projected course of action.[19]

Planning . . . is the working out in broad outline the things that need to be done and the methods for doing them to accomplish the purpose set for the enterprise.[20]

Another school of thought regards rationality and the utilization of knowledge as characterizing planning:

Planning is an organized effort to utilize social intelligence in the determination of national policies. It is based upon fundamental facts regarding resources, carefully assembled and thoroughly analyzed; upon a look around at the various factors which must be brought together in order to avoid clashing of policies or lack of unity in general direction; upon a look forward and a look backward. Considering our resources and trends as carefully as possible, and considering the emerging problems, planners look forward to the determination of the long-time policies.[21]

Planning consists in the systematic, continuous, forward-looking application of the best intelligence available to programmes of common affairs in the public field. . . . Planning is a continuous process, and necessitates the constant re-examination of trends, tendencies, policies, in order to adapt and adjust governmental policies with the least possible friction and loss. . . . Planning is not an end, but a means, a means for better use for what we have, a means for emancipation of millions of personalities now fettered, for the enrichment of human life. . . .[22]

Planning is one of the functions of the manager and, as such, involves the selection, from among alternatives, of enterprise objectives, policies, procedures, and programmes. It is thus decision-making affecting the future course of an enterprise. . . . Planning is thus an intellectual process, the conscious determination of courses of action, the basing of decisions on purpose, facts, and considered estimates.[23]

. . . Planning is more and more regarded as equivalent to rational social action, that is, as a social process for reaching a rational decision.[24]

Of special interest in this connection may be a similar definition by a Soviet economist:

By "Planning" we mean the fullest and most rational utilization of all work and of all the material resources of the community, in the light of a scientific forecast of the trends of economic development and with strict observance of the laws of social development.[25]

Some of the quoted definitions already include the evaluative element of being directed at the "social good." This element becomes predominant in some other definitions of planning:

Planning is the means by which the discipline of Science applied to human affairs will enable man to incarnate his purposes. It is the inevitable link between means and ends. Moreover, it is in itself an inspiring ideal. For once it is realized that there is no natural harmony of nature, no Divine or other purpose hidden beneath the flux and chaos of present planlessness, it becomes immoral to let poverty, ignorance, pestilence, and war continue if they can be obliterated by a plan. Although there is some disagreement as to the nature and desirable limits of planning, students of administration are all "planners."[26]

Planning is an activity by which man in society endeavours to gain mastery over himself and to shape his collective future by power of his reason. . . . Planning is nothing more than a certain manner of arriving at decisions and action, the intention of which is to promote the social good of a society undergoing rapid changes.[27]

Some modern students of public administration have tried to present more elaborate definitions of planning, composed of various elements:

Planning . . . is that activity that concerns itself with proposals for the future, with the evaluation of alternative proposals, and with the methods by which these processes may be achieved. Planning is rational, adaptive thought applied to the future and to matters over which the planners or the administrative organizations with which they are associated, have some degree of control.[28]

Planning is essentially a means of improving decisions and is therefore a prerequisite to action. It seeks to answer two vital questions: What is the purpose of an agency or a program, and what are the best means of achieving that purpose? However, policy, organization, and the social environment are in constant state of flux. This means that planning must be continuous and dynamic; it must anticipate change. Very broadly, administrative planning must consider political ends and the appropriate ways of achieving them. It must design effective operating procedures and provide supervisory techniques which will ensure that what has been planned is in fact being achieved. In the process planning touches upon every aspect of management, including decision-making, budgeting, coordination, communications, and problems of structure. Planning, in a word, is management.[29]

Taking into account this variety of definitions, it is not surprising that some authors get weary of the whole business and despair of any attempt at formulating a generally valid definition of planning:

Planning is a word of many meanings. To some it means a blueprint for the future; to others it means only foresight, and action with the forward policies of the government for regulation of the economy as a whole. To some it means government responsibility to take whatever action is necessary to ensure that the economic system operates efficiently, to others it means only that the government should correlate whatever functions it undertakes toward desired overall objectives.[30]

We could go on and quote a large number of additional definitions of planning; or we could choose to subject the various definitions to critical examination, showing that most of them are of limited validity, include irrelevant elements or are unsatisfactory in some other respect. But it seems that there is a better way to achieve our objective of clarifying the concept of planning as used in our paper, namely presentation of our own definitions of planning. As will be easily discerned, our definition relies on some of the quoted ones, covers most of the elements included in them, but is constructed in a different way designed to meet the needs of the study of planning within the framework of administrative sciences.

It seems to me that for the purposes of administrative sciences,[31] planning can usefully be defined as follows:

Planning is the process of preparing a set of decisions for action in the future, directed at achieving goals by optimal means.

This definition includes seven different elements. A short discussion of each of these elements in turn will clarify the meanings and implications of the proposed definitions and will introduce some of the concepts out of which the facet design of planning is to be composed.

1. PLANNING IS THE PROCESS

Planning is a process, i.e. a continuous activity taking place within a unit and requiring some input of resources and energy in order to be sustained. Planning as a process must be distinguished from a "plan." A "plan" can be defined as "a set of decisions for action in the future" and can be arrived at either through planning, or through some other—rational or irrational—methods of decision-making.

2. OF PREPARING

Planning is substantially—and, in most cases, also formally and legally—a process of *preparing* a set of decisions to be approved and executed by some other organs. Even if the same unit combines planning functions with authority to approve and execute, these are distinct, though interdependent, processes which must be kept analytically separate.

3. A SET

It is very important to emphasize the difference between planning and decision-making in general. While planning is a kind of decision-making, its specific characteristic in this respect is its dealing with a set of decisions, i.e. a matrix of interdependent and sequential series of systematically related decisions.

4. OF DECISIONS FOR ACTION

Planning is primarily directed at action and not at other objectives, such as pure knowledge, development of the planners and so on. Planning does in fact have various secondary results, such as executive development, better decision-making, training in teamwork, etc., but as long as those results are only secondary objectives, the planning function is not impaired. In fact, it is true that often a planning activity is engaged in as a device to mobilize support, improve public relations, and so on. If this is the case, the process is not planning in its full sense and the actual process in such cases will deviate in most respects from the characteristics and phases of the "pure type" planning process, as defined by us, which is essentially "action" or "execution" oriented.

5. In the Future

Nearly all definitions recognize that planning is directed towards the future. This is perhaps the most important characteristic of planning, introducing the elements of prediction and uncertainty and conditioning all aspects, problems and features of planning.[32]

6. Directed at Achieving Goals

The planning process cannot operate unless it has more or less defined goals to the achievement of which its recommendations for action in the future are directed. This does not mean that the planning process begins to operate with clearly defined objectives. Rather, in most cases, the first phase of the planning process consists in the formulation of operational planning objectives on the basis of rather ambiguous and undefined goals set before the planning process by some other, in most cases "policy," processes.[33]

7. By Optimal Means

The very nature of planning, as a process for rational shaping of the future according to our desires, depends on the means-ends relationship, which is basic to the planning process. The planning process is directed at suggesting the optimal means for achieving our goals, i.e. at selecting on the basis of rational processes—including collection of information, utilization of knowledge, systematic and integrative data processing, etc. —the optimal strategy for achieving the desired goals. The basic problem of planning methods, procedures and techniques, is provision of ways for identification of these optimal means with a minimum of input of resources.

It is upon these elements of the definition, that our facet design of planning is based.

THE FACETS OF PLANNING

Following the concept of facet, as developed by Louis Guttman, we will now present the primary facets and secondary facets of planning:
The four primary facets of planning appear to be the following:
Primary facet A. The general environment of the planning process.
Primary facet B. The subject matter of the planning process.
Primary facet C. The planning unit.
Primary facet D. The form of the plan to be arrived at.
Each of these primary facets is the product of a number of secondary facets, which in turn are the product of a series of tertiary facets, and so on. We will now proceed to an examination of these various facets and secondary facets and some of their sub-sets. In order to concretize our presentation, a few observations on the relative significance of the various elements of the facet design and some of their characteristics will be introduced from time to time, to point out some examples of possible lines for empiric investigation utilizing the tools provided by the facet design.

PRIMARY FACET A: THE GENERAL ENVIRONMENT OF THE PLANNING PROCESS

One of the more interesting characteristics of planning is its bi-directional relation with its environment: On the one hand, the planning activity is shaped and conditioned by various environmental factors; on the other hand, planning is in many cases directed at that environment, trying to shape it to a greater or lesser extent. While, therefore, the environment is not a fully independent variable, it nevertheless is at any point in time relatively fixed and is one of the primary facets shaping the planning process.

The main secondary facets of the general environment are:

A_1. The basic environmental factors which constitute the physical, demographic, ecologic, social, cultural, geo-physical, geo-economic, etc. phenomena which are the general background against which the planning process takes place.

A_2. The resources in manpower knowledge, capital, etc., which are potentially available for the planning process and for eventual plan-execution.

A_3. Various values, power-groups and ideologies which limit the alternatives to be considered by the planning processes, in terms of methods that can be used for plan-execution (e.g., force), of conditions for recruiting the necessary support for the planning process, of the actual resources that will be put at the disposal of plan-execution, etc. Neglect by the planners of these limitations results in utopian, non-realistic planning.

A_4. The terms of reference within which the planning process is to take place, including general goals set for the planning process; contextual goals, i.e. values and institutions which should not be impaired;[34] basic directives concerning some aspects of the working methods to be used during the planning process, such as giving an opportunity to interested persons to have a hearing; and so on.

It is these environmental elements which constitute the basic framework within which the planning process takes place and which also determine, or at least influence, directly and indirectly, the form of most of the other facets.

PRIMARY FACET B: THE SUBJECT MATTER OF THE PLANNING PROCESS

The subject matter of the planning process is the product of at least nine different secondary facets.

B_1. The structural relation between the subject matter and the planning unit.

B_2. The degree to which the subject matter is predetermined or elastic.

B_3. The degree of penetration.

B_4. The significance.

B_5. The orientation of the subject matter towards the planning process.

B_6. The extent to which the subject matter has already been subjected to planning.

B_7. The scope of the activity subjected to planning.

B_8. The demographic-territorial area related with the subject matter of the planning process.

B_9. The time-span.

Let us examine these secondary facets more closely, one by one.[35]

B_1. THE STRUCTURAL RELATION BETWEEN THE SUBJECT MATTER AND THE PLANNING UNIT

The structural relation between the subject matter of the planning process and the planning unit can take either of three forms, which constitute the sub-set of this secondary facet:

(a) The subject matter is structurally identical with the planning unit or a part of it, e.g., planning the future staffing of the planning unit or planning the work program of the planning unit.

(b) The subject matter belongs to an organizational structure of which the planning unit is itself a part, e.g., the personnel department planning the executive development scheme for the enterprise.

(c) The subject matter does not belong to an organizational structure of which the planning is itself a part, e.g., a central planning agency preparing a master plan for a town or an economic development plan for a region or state.

While these distinctions are, at least partly, relative ones, depending on the strictness or looseness of the organizational structure which serves as frame of reference for the analysis (e.g., one can regard a whole society as a kind of loose organizational structure), it helps in pointing out the basic difference between so-called "organizational planning" which is more "inner-directed," and various kinds of "outer-directed" planning.

B₂. THE DEGREE TO WHICH THE SUBJECT MATTER IS PREDETERMINED OR ELASTIC

There is a big difference between various planning instances in the extent to which the subject matter of the planning process is clearly delimited and defined when submitted to the planning unit or is left for the planning unit to determine the change from time to time. In general, it seems that planning units—driven by their *bona fide* sense of mission, their belief in their own expert knowledge and their empire-building drives— have a tendency to try and overcome even rigorously predetermined definitions of their subject matter, and to enlarge the scope of activities subjected to their planning.

B₃. THE DEGREE OF PENETRATION

Planning can penetrate more or less into its subject matter, trying to deal with all the elements and aspects of the subject matter or aiming only at its main directions and central factors. This is an important dimension for comparative study of planning cases because even if identical activities are subjected to planning, entirely different degrees of penetration may be aimed at.

B₄. THE SIGNIFICANCE OF THE SUBJECT MATTER OF THE PLANNING PROCESS

Depending on the subject matter of the planning process, the (public or private) character of the planning unit and of the organization to which it belongs and on the socio-political-ideological environment, the significance of the subject matter of a certain planning process will be viewed mainly from the angle of the organization engaging in the planning activity, from the angle of various political-economic-social interests, from a "public interest" angle, or various combinations of these different points of view.

Viewed from these different points of view, the subject matter of a planning process can be of high or low significance, either objectively—in the sense of the impact of the subject matter of the planning process on other areas of activity—or subjectively, the importance of the subject matter of the planning process according to various cognitions, values or ideologies.

B₅. THE ORIENTATION OF THE SUBJECT MATTER TOWARD THE PLANNING PROCESS

Depending on various trietary facets, the persons and institutions related with different subject matters can have a more passive or active and more positive or negative orientation towards the planning process (and the planning unit—these two are closely related in the public image). It is a moot point, in urgent need of research, which orientation of the subject matter towards the planning process provides better results in terms of the quality of the planning process; it seems that in most cases the planning process, and even more so the plan-execution process, needs a lot of active, positive support to be successfully maintained.

B₆. THE EXTENT TO WHICH THE SUBJECT MATTER HAS ALREADY BEEN SUBJECTED TO PLANNING

Prior subjection of the subject matter to planning does not only influence its orientation towards the present planning process, but creates various expectations, traditions and factors which are of much importance in shaping the future planning processes. In this respect, there are significant differences between different planning instances dealing with subject matters (or even an identical subject matter) subjected to more or less prior planning.

B_7. THE SCOPE OF THE ACTIVITY SUBJECTED TO PLANNING

Planning always deals with a delimited subject matter, which is defined in terms of functions, territorial units or other characteristics. Total planning, i.e. planning including within its subject matter all extra-personal, inter-personal (and perhaps even intra-personal) activities, is unimaginable outside of fantastic science fiction. The limitations of the human mind, the limitations of resources and the many competing alternative uses for them, the limits on maximum integrating capacity of organization, and the existence of strong opposition to planning of certain subject matters—all these limit planning at any given time to a selected, relatively small, number of subject matters. On the other hand, recognition of the inter-dependence of various aspects of activity, especially under conditions of rapid change (e.g., rapidly developing societies, rapidly growing enterprises), is one of the more important reasons for enlarging the scope of activities subjected to planning, leading in the direction of a comprehensive planning approach.

B_8. THE DEMOGRAPHIC-TERRITORIAL AREA RELATED WITH THE SUBJECT MATTER OF THE PLANNING PROCESS

The relation between planning and demographic-territorial area is a rather complex one, which has at least three distinct, though closely interrelated, possible aspects: Since all human activity takes place in space-time, by its very nature planning must, and does, take into account this fact, and delimits its scope within these dimensions. Even in the few cases, where the subject matter of planning is not defined in demographic-territorial terms (e.g., "all economic activities"), the fact that all material phenomena are distributed in space, will make it convenient, and even inevitable, to use some demographic-territorial subdivision as units for delegated planning purposes.

To this general consideration on the inherent role of space in human thought and activity, a second aspect of the relation between area and planning must be added: the specific importance of demographic-territorial units in social affairs. Beginning with the nearly instinctive, emotional attachment of an individual to his place of birth, and going through all levels of social institutions, the special role of territory in social life is always apparent.

A third aspect of the relation between demographic-territorial area and planning has its roots in the fact that one of the most important functions of every society is adjustment to its territory. Such adjustment is brought about to some extent by changing the physical environment and making the territory fit the needs of the society. In the field of planning this aim is reflected in the many planning activities having as their subject matter certain aspects of what we call territory. Such "earthbound" fields include landscaping, resources conservation, flood control, urban redevelopment, and many more.

In all these cases, the relation between demographic-territorial area and planning poses two problems, the solutions of which have to be reconciled somehow. First, the *technical-optimum* area for dealing with the subject matter of the planning activity must be defined; and second, this technical optimum area must be reconciled with the existing demographic-territorial units of social action and the limited freedom of the planning unit.

The best possible compromise between the two sets of areas will yield the *social-optimal* demographic-territorial area for the designed planning activity.[36]

B_9. THE TIME-SPAN

Each planning process deals with a certain, though not necessarily exactly predetermined, time-span. The selection of the optimum time-span for each planning activity depends on various factors, including the natural cycle of the subject matter of planning, the acute need for interference to change an unbearable situation, limitations on our ability to predict the future, our evaluation of present as against future needs, the desire that planning should serve as a guide to present actions and more.

We shall now proceed to the two remaining primary facets of planning which are of a somewhat more limited nature but exert a tremendous influence on the planning process.

PRIMARY FACET C: THE PLANNING UNIT

The characteristics of the planning unit are the product of seven main secondary facets:

C_1. THE BASIC NATURE OF THE PLANNING UNIT

Planning, as defined by us, can take place on the level of individuals and on the level of various institutions, such as a family, a tribal coun-

cil, etc. A special case of institutional planning which is of highest contemporary importance and which includes most socially significant
planning processes, is planning in and by bureaucratic structures. It is
this kind of planning, which is part of the subject matter of administrative sciences, at which our facet design is mainly directed.

Because of the underdeveloped state of neurology and individual psychology, we know nearly nothing of the factors conditioning and shaping planning on the individual level. This is all the more regrettable because, after all, organizational planning is also done by individuals, and
more knowledge of planning on the individual level may well contribute
much to the understanding and improvement of the administrative
planning process.

C$_2$. PRIMARY OR DELEGATED PLANNING UNIT

Delegated planning is planning which constitutes plan-execution from
the point of view of another planning unit; primary planning is planning pursued not as part of any higher level plan. In general, delegated
planning will be more detailed, for a shorter time-span and dealing with
a smaller subject matter.

The importance of this distinction can be illustrated by applying it to
a concrete issue, e.g., the optimum subject matter of city planning.
Some authors[37] rely on the precedent of large-scope city planning in the
United States during the big depression, including economic and social
spheres of social activity, to justify a similar large subject matter for city
planning today. But it seems that much of the enlarged scope of city
planning at that period was delegated planning, part of a national plan
to relieve unemployment and rehabilitate the economy. Therefore, what
happened then is not directly relevant to the problem whether, in the
absence of national planning of some subject matters, cities should deal
with them through primary planning.

C$_3$. STATUS

The status of the planning unit (including the status of the institution
and of the planners as individual role-bearers) influences the resources
which can be mobilized for the planning process, the extent to which
limitations on alternatives and similar externally determined limits imposed on the planning process can be overcome, and so on. In other
words, the status of the planning unit is closely correlated, though not
identical, with its power, which is an important factor in the strategy of
planning.[38]

C₄. VALUES, INFORMATION AND CHARACTER OF THE PLANNING UNIT

The planning process in all its phases calls for constant judgments involving the value systems, the information and the character of the decision-makers—the planning unit as a collection of individuals and the planning unit as an institution.[39] This is a factor of tremendous importance, having significant implications for the selection of planners,[40] their education and their control.[41]

C₅. RESOURCES AND MEANS

The resources in manpower, knowledge, equipment, time, etc. at the disposal of the planning unit and the planners are further important factors which have a definite influence on the planning process and must therefore be carefully considered.

C₆. WORK SYSTEMS, PROCEDURES AND METHODS

The systems, methods and procedures of work in the planning unit determine the detailed form of the planning process. The more important systems, procedures and methods deal with information gathering, data processing and decision-making. The introduction of electronic data processing equipment, while greatly increasing the possibilities of planning, introduces serious complexities into work systems, work methods and procedures and makes even more essential careful attention to consciously and rationally established explicit systems, procedures and methods through which the planning process is channelized.

C₇. ORGANIZATIONAL STRUCTURE

Last, but not least, the organizational structure of the planning unit raises difficult problems, especially concerning the distribution of functions between specialized overhead planning function and the ordinary line units in charge of day-to-day operations in regard to specific subject matters. Both in small- and large-scale, inner- and outer-directed planning, the organizational issues are most complex and the solutions adopted determine to a considerable degree the form taken by the planning process and its success or failure in fulfilling its tasks.[42] As yet, the organizational problems of planning are among the most neglected subjects, both in the study of planning and in organization theory.

Primary Facet D:
The Form of the Plan To Be Arrived at

D$_1$. The Realism of the Plan

We already mentioned cases of planning directed at political advantages, public relations, training objectives, etc. In these cases, it is not always necessary to arrive at the final phase of the planning process, i.e., preparation of a plan; and even if a plan is prepared, it is often purposely utopian in nature. Leaving such cases of "quasi-planning" aside, there is a legitimate span of more or less realism aimed at in the preparation of the plan. Indeed, a certain utopian element may be essential for gaining the necessary support and may be fully compatible with a realistic approach to planning and with successful plan-realization. In any case, the degree of realism of the plan to be arrived at is an important sub-facet influencing the entire "tone" of the planning process.

D$_2$. The Form of the Plan

The sub-set of this secondary facet includes various forms of plans: fixed-time plans, such as five-year or seven-year plans; conditional plans, to be executed at a given occurrence which might or might not happen at an unknown point in the future, such as most military operation plans; master plans, showing a blueprint of a desired state of affairs without setting down a fixed time-table for its achievement, such as many town plans; budgetary plans, constructed in terms of monetary units; work plans, constructed in terms of technical specification, drawings, etc.; and more.

The modern tendency seems to be in the direction of composite plans, including long-range and short-range time-tables, financial and physical breakdowns, conditional and predetermined elements and so on. It seems that the more complex and large-scale the subject matter of the planning process is, the more multiform and complex the plan has to be.

D$_3$. Degree of Details

The plan to be arrived at can be more or less detailed. In general, the larger the time-span to be covered by the plan, the more the plan will include general frameworks and directions, leaving details for later or delegated planning.

A related element of the sub-set is in whether the plan will be single-alternative, providing for one strategy of action, or multi-alternative, providing different strategies, for later selection in the light of developments of the optimal one.

CONCLUSIONS

Returning to the concept of facet as used in this paper, we can regard planning (P) as the product (in the mathematical sense of "cartesian product"[43] of primary facets A, B, C, D.

In other words, generally speaking,

Planning   =   (general environment) × (subject matter) × (planning unit) × (form of plan),

or, $P = A \times B \times C \times D$

Each primary facet in turn is the product of a number of secondary facets, namely:

$$A = A_1 \times A_2 \times A_3 \times A_4$$
$$B = B_1 \times B_2 \times B_3 \times B_4 \times B_5 \times B_6 \times B_7 \times B_8 \times B_9$$
$$C = C_1 \times C_2 \times C_3 \times C_4 \times C_5 \times C_6 \times C_7$$
$$D = D_1 \times D_2 \times D_3 \times D_4$$

We have thus 24 secondary facets of planning, each one of which—even if not regarded as the product of a series of trietary facets—can take different forms. Thus, we have

$$A_{1a}, A_{1b}, A_{1c}, \ldots d_{4a}, d_{4b}, d_{4c}, \ldots d_{4n}.$$

The form of some of the secondary facets (e.g., time-span) can be expressed in transitive but not fully comparable units (e.g., the secondary facet "significance"); still others can only be expressed by rough qualitative terms (e.g., most of the secondary facets related to the form of the plan to be arrived at). Following further elaboration of various classifications of the former of the various secondary facets, the basic problems are reached, which combination of forms do in fact appear in real planning instances; and what combinations give, under various conditions, the best results, and why.

In other words, we would like to know for which values of

$$a_{1i}, a_{2j}, \ldots d_{4n},$$

planning ($p = a \times b \times c \times d$) can exist in reality, and—given the values of some of the secondary facets—which values for the non-pre-determined secondary facets will maximize the quality[44] of the planning process (qp).

Available experience and impressionistic data provide some guidelines to these problems: thus, we would not expect long-range planning of a large-scope subject matter to go with very detailed plans and a high degree of penetration; we do not expect planning to succeed if the planners lack certain qualifications, and so on. But available material, based as it is on limited experience and subjectivistic impressions, does not permit many conclusions beyond such rather obvious and partly semantic ones. Only systematic empiric study, utilizing the best available research designs and methodologies, can perhaps provide us with valid and reliable answers to these and other problems and provide a sound basis for a more systematic approach to the study of the planning process as part of administrative sciences.

NOTES

[1]This article is based on a series of lectures given by the author at the Comprehensive Planning Course, Institute of Social Studies, The Hague, in 1960, 1961 and 1962. For an earlier effort, cf. Dror, "Dimensions of Planning," *Public Policy,* Vol. VII (1956), 112–127. The present version has been prepared while the author was a Fellow at the Center for Advanced Study in the Behavioral Sciences.

[2]Cf. John Friedman, "Introduction," *International Social Science Journal* Vol. XI, No 3 (1959), 327–328.

[3]One of the first authors clearly to recognize this difference was Hayek, who explicitly limited his anti-planning arguments to "planning" in the sense of a directed economy. Cf. F. A. Hayek, *The Road to Serfdom* (1944), p. 26.

[4]Cf. Dror, *op. cit.,* p. 114–118.

[5]The most important recent contribution is Le Breton and Henning, *Planning Theory* (Englewood Cliffs, N.J.: Prentice-Hall, Inc., 1961). See also the files of the *Journal of the American Institute of Planners,* which includes a number of significant papers on the planning process. Cf., e.g., John W. Dyckman, "Planning and Decision Theory," (review article), *ibid.,* Vol. 27, No. 4 (November, 1961), 335–345; John R. Seeley, "What is Planning? Definition and Strategy, *ibid.,* Vol. 28, No. 2 (May, 1962), 91–97; Paul Davidoff and Thomas A. Reiner, "A Choice Theory of Planning," *ibid.,* 103–115, and more. Important contributions to a theo-

ry of planning as an administrative process may also come from Operations Research. Cf. the various papers presented at the 22nd National Meeting of the Operations Research Society of America (November 7–9, 1962, Philadelphia, Pa.), which was devoted to "planning."

[6]Especially noteworthy is the failure to distinguish between planning and decision-making in general. E.g., cf. James G. March and Herbert H. Simon, *Organizations* (1958), who regard planning as identical with decision-making (p. 200).

[7]The lack of any framework theory on planning is clearly seen in the non-systematic way with which planning is dealt with in the thirty-eight passages from the best available texts and papers included in David W. Ewing (ed.), *Long-Range Planning for Management* (1958). Similarly the many recent contributions by social scientists to the "planning" literature, while often very interesting and contributing important insights, suffer from an outdated interest in the semi-ideological issue of "planning" vs. "non-planning" and the lack of clear conceptual frameworks. E.g., cf. most of the papers on social planning in *Transactions of the Fourth World Congress of Sociology* (International Sociological Association, 1919), Vol. II. For some short, but sharp and pointed and relevant remarks, cf. Bertram M. Gross, "When Is a Plan NOT a Plan?," *Challenge* (December, 1961).

[8]I am indebted to Professor Louis Guttman for his important help and suggestions concerning the methodological aspects of this paper.

[9]Louis Guttman, "An Outline of Some New Methodology for Social Research," *Public Opinion Quarterly*, Vol. 18 (1954), 395–404. Louis Guttman "What Lies Ahead for Factor Analysis?" *Educational and Psychological Measurement*, Vol. 18 (1958), 497–515. Louis Guttman, "Introduction to Facet Design and Analysis," *Proceedings of the Fifteenth International Congress of Psychology*, Brussels, 1957 (1959), 130–132. Louis Guttman, "A Structural Theory for Intergroup Beliefs and Action," *American Sociological Review*, Vol. 25, No. 3 (June, 1959), 318–328.

[10]Uriel G. Foa, "The Foreman-Worker Interaction: A Research Design," *Sociometry*, Vol. 18, No. 3 (August, 1955), 226–244. Uriel G. Foa and Louis Guttman, *Facet Design and Analysis of Data on Personality and Attitudes Related to Human Organization*, Israel Institute of Applied Social Research (1960).

[11]R. A. Fisher, *The Design of Experiments* (1951).

[12]"Not to be confused with the 'logical' product or 'intersection' of two sets."

[13]Louis Guttman, 1954, *op. cit.*, p. 399.

[14]Louis Guttman, "A New Approach to Factor Analysis: The Radex," in Paul F. Lazarsfeld (ed.), *Mathematical Thinking in the Social Sciences* (1954).

[15]This paper can also be regarded as trying to apply the "facet" concept to an administrative process as an experiment designed to test the usefulness of this methodological tool for administrative sciences in general.

[16]Experience at international seminars and congresses devoted to planning problems clearly shows the need for a basic theory as a framework for collecting and evaluating data. E.g., cf. the papers on Government Organization for Economic Planning submitted to the IIAS Round Table (Lisbon, 1961) and the 12th International Congress of Administrative Sciences (Vienna, 1962), and the secretariat working paper on Administrative Machinery for Planning in the ECAFE Region prepared for the Conference of Asian Economic Planners, New Delhi, 1961 (U.N. Economic and Social Council, Document E/CN.11/CAEP.1/L.3 of 11 August 1961). See also Barbu Niculescu, *Colonial Planning: A Comparative Study* (1958).

[17]E.g., cf. the collection of definitions quoted in John D. Millet, *The Process and Organization of Government Planning* (1947), pp. 2 et seq.

[18]Karl Stefanie-Allmayer, *Allgemeine Organisations-lehre* (1950), p. 136.

[19]William H. Newman, *Administrative Action* (1958), p. 15.

[20]Luther Gulick, "Notes on the Theory of Organization," *Papers on the Science of Administration* (1937), p. 13.

[21]Charles E. Merriam, "The National Resources Planning Board," in G. B. Galloway, (ed.), *Planning for America* (1941), p. 486.

[22]National Resources Board, *A Report on National Planning and Public Works* (1934), pp. 83–84.

[23]Harold Koontz and Cyril O'Donnel, "The Nature and Purpose of Planning," in David W. Ewing, *op. cit.*, pp. 11, 12.

[24]Robert A. Dahl, "The Policies of Planning," *International Social Science Journal*, Vol. XI, No. 3, (1959), 340.

[25]C. H. Touretzki, "Regional Planning of the National Economy in the U.S.S.R. and Its Bearing on Regionalism," *ibid.*, 380.

[26]Dwight Waldo, *The Administrative State* (1948), p. 67.

[27]John Friedmann, "Introduction" (to series of articles on the study and practice of planning), *International Social Science Journal, op. cit.*, 327–329.

[28]Herbert A. Simon, Donald W. Smithburg and Victor A. Thompson, *Public Administration* (1950), pp. 423–424.

[29]John M. Pfiffner and R. Vance Presthus, *Public Administration* (1953), p. 83.

[30]Emmette S. Redford, *Administration of National Economic Control* (1952), p. 18.

[31]The dependence of the validity and utility of definition on the world of discourse within which the definition is to be used must be borne in mind.

[32]John Friedmann, *op. cit.*, p. 334, gives an interesting list of planning characteristics resulting from the futuristic orientation of planning:

"(a) It places a limit upon the time period over which projections into the future can be made without loss of practical significance for present decisions.

(b) It establishes the necessity for continuing planning analysis and assessment throughout the planning period and the constant re-evaluation and adjustment of means to ends.

(c) It suggests the use of expectational calculus in connection with statements about the future.

(d) It argues for the adoption of a system of framework or structural planning.

(e) It forces the careful consideration of flexibility in planning where the degree of flexibility explicitly introduced into a solution must be proportionate to the degree of uncertainty about future events. It is through an approach such as this that reason can come to terms with uncertainty."

[33]One of the most important, interesting and difficult problems in the study of planning is the actual and optimal relationships between "goal determination" and the planning process. I hope to deal with this issue in a later article on "Planning Phases"; the interested reader is referred to three papers which deal with this problem from different angles, namely: Edward C. Banfield, "Ends and Means in Planning," *International Social Science Journal, op. cit.,* 361–368; Charles E. Lindblom, "The Science of Muddling Through," *Public Administration Review,* Vol. 17 (1959), 79–88; and Philip E. Jacob and James J. Flink, "Values and Their Function in Decision-Making," *The American Behavioral Scientist,* Vol. 5, No. 9, Supplement (May, 1962).

[34]"Contextual ends are represented by social values and traditions that do not, in themselves, constitute the immediate objectives of planning but are sufficiently vital to make their preservation socially worth while." Friedmann, *op. cit.,* p. 330.

[35]Compare this list with the "dimensions of planning" as suggested by

Le Breton and Henning: complexity, significance, comprehensiveness, time, specificity, completeness, flexibility, frequency, confidential nature, formality, authorization, ease of implementation, ease of control. *Op. cit.,* pp. 22–56.

[36]It is incorrect to regard the technical-optimal area as the "desirable" area of action which is "distorted" by the "unfortunate" existence of nations, states, local units, etc. We have already mentioned the psychological importance for human happiness of emotional attachment to territories and the inevitability of territorial units of social action and their role in planning. Here it should be emphasized that these existing demographic-territorial units of social action have to play a most significant role in planning: The most important initiators are those who can mobilize loyalty, resources and support. The planner cannot and must not neglect these human and moral facts in favor of a quasi-mechanical "social engineering" approach.

[37]E.g., cf. Robert A. Walker, *The Planning Function in Urban Government* (1950).

[38]The politics of planning is a sadly neglected subject. With the exception of single-case studies on concrete planning instances and a few general studies dealing with some relationships between macro-planning and political regimes, only very little is known on this critically important subject. Cf. Meyerson and Banfield, *Politics, Planning and the Public Interest* (1955), Robert Dahl, "The Politics of Planning," *op. cit.;* this is another subject urgently in need of empirical study.

[39]On the importance of institutional values, cf. Simon, Smithburg and Thompson, *Public Administration* (1950), esp. chapters 3, 4, 5.

[40]"Where management cannot define in detail what is to be done (during the planning process), it must be unusually concerned about who is to do it and how they interact." Melvin Anshen, "Businessmen, Lawyers and Economists," in David W. Ewing, *op. cit.,* p. 99.

[41]For a discussion of some results of outdated values of planners and a suggestion to introduce feed-back data-processing mechanisms into the organizational structure of planning units in order to overcome some of the results of outdated values, cf. Ruth Glass, "The Evaluation of Planning," *International Social Science Journal, op. cit.,* 393–409.

[42]E.g., cf. H. Edward Wrapp, "Organization for Long-Range Planning," in David W. Ewing, *op. cit.,* pp. 59–79, and Royal Institute of Public Administration, *Administrative Organization for Economic Development* (Conference Report), esp. chapter III.

[43]Louis Guttman, 1954, *op. cit.,* p. 1.

[44]The measurement, or at least the comparative evaluation of which constitutes another basic and difficult problem in the study of the planning process.

6.

Toward a Theory of Budgeting*

VERNE B. LEWIS

The $64.00 question on the expenditure side of public budgeting is: On what basis shall it be decided to allocate X dollars to Activity A instead of allocating them to Activity B, or instead of allowing the taxpayer to use the money for his individual purposes? Over a decade ago V. O. Key called attention to the lack of a budgetary theory which would assist in arriving at an answer to this question.[1] Pointing out that budgeting is essentially a form of applied economics, since it requires the allocation of scarce resources among competing demands, Professor Key urged that this question be explored from the point of view of economic theory.

The purpose of this article is to analyze three propositions which are derived from economic theory[2] which appear to be applicable to public budgeting and to be appropriate building blocks for construction of an economic theory of budgeting. In brief, the three principles are:

1. Since resources are scarce in relation to demands, the basic economic test which must be applied is that the return from every expenditure must be worth its cost in terms of sacrificed alternatives. Budget analysis, therefore, is basically a comparison of the relative merits of alternative uses of funds.

2. Incremental analysis (that is, analysis of the additional values to be derived from an additional expenditure) is necessary because of the phenomenon of diminishing utility. Analysis of the increments is necessary and useful only at or near the margin; this is the point of balance at

*Reprinted from Verne B. Lewis, "Toward a Theory of Budgeting," *Public Administration Review*, 12:1 (Winter 1952), 42–54, by permission of the author and publisher. Verne B. Lewis is Deputy Representative of the United States Mission to the International Atomic Energy Agency.

which an additional expenditure for any purpose would yield the same return.

3. Comparison of relative merits can be made only in terms of relative effectiveness in achieving a common objective.

Part I of this article will be devoted to consideration of these principles. In Part II a proposal, which will be called the alternative budget procedure, will be outlined and analyzed in terms of the three principles. Primary emphasis throughout will be placed on the applicability of concepts developed by the economists to methods of analyzing budget estimates. The discussion is pointed specifically at problems of the federal government; the general ideas, however, should be equally applicable to state and local governmental units.

I

RELATIVE VALUE.

Budget decisions must be made on the basis of relative values. There is no absolute standard of value. It is not enough to say that an expenditure for a particular purpose is desirable or worth while. The results must be worth their cost. The results must be more valuable than they would be if the money were used for any other purpose.

Comparison of relative values to be obtained from alternative uses of funds is necessary because our resources are inadequate to do all the things we consider desirable and necessary. In fact, public budgeting is necessary only because our desires exceed our means. The desires of human beings are virtually unlimited. Although the supply of resources has been greatly expanded in recent decades, the supply is still short in relation to demands. It would be nice if we had enough to go around, but we do not. Some demands can be met only in part, some not at all.

Scarcity of resources in relation to demands confronts us at every level of public budgeting. Public services consume scarce materials and manpower which have alternative uses. If used for governmental activities, they cannot be used for private purposes. If used for Activity A of the government, they cannot be used for Activity B. Expressed in terms of money, the problem of scarcity arises in connection with appropriations. As individual taxpayers, we put pressures on Congress to hold down federal taxes so that a larger proportion of our already inadequate personal incomes will be available to satisfy our individual desires. In view of these pressures, Congress usually appropriates less than is requested by the President and interest groups. The President in turn usually requests the Congress to appropriate less than the total of the estimates submitted to him by agency heads. Rarely does an agency have sufficient funds to do all the things it would like to do or that it is requested to do by citizen groups.

Confronted with limited resources, congressmen and administrative officials must make choices. The available money will buy this *or* that, but not *both.* On what basis should the choice be made?

The economists, who specialize in problems of scarcity, have a general answer to this question. It is found in the doctrine of marginal utility. This doctrine, as applied to public budgeting, has been formulated by Professor Pigou as follows:

As regards the distribution, as distinct from the aggregate cost, of optional government expenditure, it is clear that, just as an individual will get more satisfaction out of his income by maintaining a certain balance between different sorts of expenditure, so also will a community through its government. The principle of balance in both cases is provided by the postulate that resources should be so distributed among different uses that the marginal return of satisfaction is the same for all of them. . . . Expenditure should be distributed between battleships and poor relief in such wise that the last shilling devoted to each of them yields the same real return. We have here, so far as theory goes, a test by means of which the distribution of expenditure along different lines can be settled.[3]

Other aspects of the marginal utility concept will be considered in later sections; here we want to note that this concept poses the problem in terms of relative values rather than absolutes. To determine the distribution of funds between battleships and poor relief we must weigh the relative value of the results to be obtained from these alternative uses. Is it worth while to spend an additional $1,000,000 for battleships? We can answer "yes" only if we think we would get more valuable results than would be obtained by using that $1,000,000 for poor relief.

When the economists approach the problem in terms of costs rather than results they arrive at the same conclusion. Fundamentally, as the economists indicate in their "opportunity" or "displacement" concept of costs, "the cost of a thing is simply the amount of other things which has to be given up for its sake."[4] If Robinson Crusoe finds he has time to build a house *or* catch some fish, but not *both,* the cost of the house is the fish he does not catch or vice versa. The cost of anything is therefore the result that would have been realized had the resources been used for an alternative purpose.

Of what significance from the point of view of budget analysis are these concepts of relative value and displacement cost? They indicate that the basic objective of budget analysis is the comparison of the relative value of results to be obtained from alternative uses of funds. If an analyst is convinced after reading the usual argument supporting a budget request that the activity in question is desirable and necessary, his task has just begun. To be justifiable in terms of making the most advantageous use of resources, the returns from an expenditure for any activity must be more desirable and more necessary than for any alternative use of the funds. On the other hand, a budget request for an activity cannot legitimately be turned down solely on the basis that the activity costs too much. Costs and results must be considered together. The costs must be judged in relation to the results and the results must be worth their costs in terms of alternative results that are foregone or displaced.

INCREMENTAL ANALYSIS.

If the basic guide for budget analysis is that results must be worth their costs, budget analysis must include a comparison of relative values. How can such a comparison of values be made?

The marginal utility concept suggests a way of approaching the problem. The method, briefly, is to divide available resources into increments and consider which of the alternative uses of each increment would yield the greatest return. Analysis of increments is necessary because of the phenomenon of diminishing utility. This means, roughly, that as we acquire more and more units of anything, the additional units have less and less use value. If enough units are acquired, an added unit may be of no value at all and may even be objectionable. To illustrate, four tires on a car are essential, a fifth tire is less essential but is handy to have, whereas a sixth tire just gets in the way. Although a sixth tire will cost as much as any of the first five, it has considerably less use value. In deciding how many tires to buy, we must therefore consider the use value to be derived from each *additional* tire.

Because of the phenomenon of diminishing utility, there is no point in trying to determine the *total* or *average* benefits to be obtained from total expenditures for a particular commodity or function. We must analyze the benefits by increments. If one million bazookas make a valuable contribution toward winning a war, we cannot assume that the contribution would be doubled if we had two million. Perhaps there are not enough soldiers to use that many. No matter how valuable bazookas might be in winning a war, a point would be reached sometime on the diminishing scale of utility where additional expenditures for bazookas would be completely wasted. Since we do not have enough resources to do all the things we would like to do, we certainly should not produce anything that will not or cannot be used.

But we cannot assume that we would make the best use of resources even if we produced no more bazookas than could be used. Perhaps the manpower and materials consumed in producing the last thousand bazookas would serve a more valuable purpose if they were used for producing additional hand grenades or some other item. This reasoning leads us back to the basic criterion for deciding how much should be spent for each activity. We should allocate enough money for bazookas so that the last dollar spent for bazookas will serve as valuable a purpose as the last dollar for hand grenades or any other purpose. If more than this amount is spent for bazookas, we sacrifice a more valuable alternative use. Thus, as is suggested by the marginal utility theory, maximum returns can be obtained only if expenditures are distributed among different purposes in such a way that the last dollar spent for each yields the same real return.

The marginal utility concept also indicates that a comparison of incremental values is meaningful and necessary only at or near the margins. When analyzing the value of the returns by increments of expenditure near the margins we would ask: How much will be sacrificed if proposed expenditures for Function A are reduced by $1,000? Can efficiency be increased so that output will not have to be reduced? What would be the consequences of lowering standards of quality? Of reducing quantities? Of postponing some portion of the work?

When these issues are explored, the pay-off question can be tackled. Would the sacrifices be greater or less if the $1,000 cut is applied to Function B rather than to Function A? This question brings up the most difficult and most critical problem. How can the values of unlike functions be compared? How can the value of an atom bomb and cancer research be compared? Or public roads and public schools? So far we have not indicated how this question can be answered. We have only narrowed the field by indicating that the value of functions must be compared by increments rather than in total and that the value of increments need only be compared near the marginal point of balance. Incremental analysis at the margins is just a tool, though a useful one, we believe. It does not supply the answers, but it helps to focus attention on the real points at issue.

RELATIVE EFFECTIVENESS.

The relative value of different things cannot be compared unless they have a common denominator. The common aspect of an atom bomb and cancer research, of public roads and public schools, is the broad purpose each is designed to serve. These items, as well as all other public and private activities, are undertaken to serve human needs and desires. We can only compare their values by evaluating their relative effectiveness in serving a common objective.

To revert to a previously used example, we do not make bazookas just for the sake of making bazookas. We make them because they help win wars. Although bazookas, hand grenades, and K-rations are unlike things, they serve a common military purpose. The relative values of these items can be weighed in terms of their relative effectiveness in fighting a war. We do not fight wars for their own sake either. They are fought for a larger purpose of national security. Economic aid to foreign countries also serves this purpose. Since they share a common objective, the relative value of military activities and economic aid can also be compared in terms of their effectiveness in achieving this objective.

Let us take a different type of case which is less general and more tangible than national security. Purchasing officers and engineers perform quite different functions. Yet, if they are working in an organization which does construction work, for example, they share the common objective of that organization. Operating within a ceiling on total expenditures, the head of the agency might be faced with this question: Would a part of the money allocated to the procurement section yield greater returns if transferred to the engineering section? This question involves value comparisons of unlike things, whether for a private firm or for a government agency. Moreover, the firm or the agency usually cannot express the contributions of procurement officers and engineers in terms of precise numbers. Nevertheless, reasonable men who are reasonably well informed arrive at substantially the same answer to such questions, provided the basic objective has been decided in advance. If the objective is to build a structure according to prescribed specifications in X months and at not to exceed Y dollars, this objective provides a common basis for evaluation. The answer will depend upon forecasts of facts and will also be influenced by relative need. For example, if design is on schedule but construction is being delayed because purchase orders are not being issued on schedule, additions to the procurement staff would probably yield greater returns than additions to the design staff. On the other hand, if design is behind schedule and, as a consequence, the procurement staff has no material requisitions to process, more design engineers would yield the greater return.

Evaluation in terms of relative effectiveness in achieving a common objective is, therefore, a second fundamental method of budget analysis.[5]

Evaluation in terms of common purposes is another way of saying that alternative means can be evaluated in terms of the end they are designed to achieve. That end can be considered, in turn, as a means of achieving a broader end. This process requires, of course, that the ultimate ends be somehow established. How can these fundamental decisions be made? In a democracy we are not so much concerned with how they are made as by whom they are made. The ideal of democracy is that the desires of the people, no matter how they are arrived at or how unwise they may be, should control the actions of the government. The representatives of the people in Congress make the fundamental decisions as to the ultimate aims of governmental services. These decisions, in the form of laws and appropriation acts, provide the basis for economic calculation by administrative agencies in the same way as consumer action in the market place provides the basis for decisions in the private economy.

We now have some basic elements of an economic theory of budgeting. The economic aim of budgeting is to achieve the best use of our resources. To meet this test, the benefits derived from any expenditure must be worth their cost in terms of sacrificed or displaced alternatives. As a first step in applying that test, we can use incremental analysis at the margins as a means of concentrating attention at the areas where comparison of values is necessary and meaningful. These values can be compared by determining their relative effectiveness in achieving a common purpose. Analysis in terms of common purposes requires a set of basic premises which are found in the ultimate ends or purposes established by Congress, acting for the people. This means that Congress is charged by the people with the basic responsibility for deciding what constitutes the "best use of resources," so far as the federal government is concerned.

PRACTICAL LIMITATIONS.

Although the propositions outlined above concerning relative value, incremental analysis, and relative effectiveness constitute, in a sense, a formula for budget analysis which appears to be theoretically sound, the formula is not always easy to apply. Precise numbers to use in the equations are frequently unavailable. Although the formula will work in a theoretically valid manner, even if one has to guess the numbers to put into the equation, the practical usefulness of the answers will depend upon the accuracy of the numbers.

One area where firm numbers are hard to get involves forecasts of future needs and conditions. As we have noted, value is a function of need and need changes from time to time. In comparing the relative value of guns and butter, for example, we will strike a balance between them at different points at different times depending upon whether we are engaged in a hot war, a cold war, or no war at all. The balance between public health and police will be struck at one point if communicable diseases are rampant at a time when the traffic accident rate is low. The balance will be struck at a different point if the state of public health is good but the accident rate is alarming.

Budgetary decisions have to be based not only on relative needs as they are today but also on forecasts of what the needs will be tomorrow, next year, or in the next decade. The point is illustrated most dramatically by the decision made by the federal government during World War II to try to develop an atomic bomb. At the time, no one knew whether a bomb could be made, or if it could be made in time to help win the war. Hence, the government in deciding to divert tremendous quantities of scarce resources to this purpose had to take a calculated risk. Its decision was based not on firm facts but on forecasts and hopes as to the values to be realized.

There are probably as many budget arguments over forecasts of needs as there are over the relative merits of the expenditures which are proposed to meet those needs.

Not only must budget decisions be based, in some cases, on sheer guesses as to future needs and future accomplishments, but often the nature of governmental activities is such that accomplishments in relation to costs cannot be precisely measured even after the fact. How can one tell, for example, how much fire damage was prevented for each $1,000 spent by the fire department for fire prevention?

Perhaps it was the frequent difficulty in obtaining precise numbers that led Professor Key to question the applicability of the marginal utility theory to public budgeting. He concluded:

. . . The doctrine of marginal utility, developed most finely in the analysis of the

market economy, has a ring of unreality when applied to public expenditures. The
most advantageous utilization of public funds resolves itself into a matter of value
preferences between ends lacking a common denominator. As such, the question is a
problem of political philosophy. . . .[6]

Whether firm numbers are available or not, judgments and decisions
have to be made. The lack of precise numbers does not invalidate the
basic principles or methods of calculation which we have outlined. The
methods have to be judged on the basis of whether or not they lead to
proper conclusions *if* it is assumed that the numbers used in the equations are the right ones. Obtaining the right numbers, though a fundamental and difficult problem, is separate and distinct from the problem
of developing methods of calculation.

On the other hand, Professor Key may have been questioning the
basic principle. It is perfectly true, as Key points out, that budgeting involves questions of value preferences which must be based on philosophy rather than science or logic. We agree that it is a problem for philosophers, but not exclusively, since the methods of the economists can
also be applied. The problem of value has long been one of the central
topics on the agenda of the economists. They do not approach the problem from the point of view of trying to develop an absolute standard of
value or from the point of view of trying to prescribe which ends, goals,
or objectives men should strive for. Rather they concentrate on methods
to be used to achieve the most valuable use of scarce resources as judged
by whatever standard of value men embrace. While the philosopher
helps us decide which goals we should strive for, the economist helps us
achieve those goals most efficiently. Thus, I believe, the economists' approach to the problem of value as expressed in the marginal utility
theory can be accepted as a useful approach for public budgeting.

The views outlined in this article concerning the applicability of the
methods of the economists to public budgeting run sharply counter to
the views of some economists. Ludwig von Mises, for example, contends,
in his book, *Bureaucracy,*[7] that there is no method of economic calculation
which can be applied to government. It can be shown, I think, that the
problem in government, so far as it exists, arises out of the lack of firm
numbers rather than out of the lack of a method.

Dr. Mises' central argument is that bureaucrats have no means of
calculating the relative usefulness of governmental activities because these
activities have no price in the market place. Therefore, he contends,
government agencies have no criterion of value to apply. In private busi-

ness, he points out (p. 26), "the ultimate basis of economic calculation is the valuation of all consumers' goods on the part of all the people" in the market place. Further, "economic calculation makes it possible for business to adjust production to the demands of the consumers" (p. 27). On the other hand, he argues, ". . . if a public enterprise is to be operated without regard to profits, the behavior of the public no longer provides a criterion of its usefulness" (p. 61). Therefore, he concludes, "the problem of bureaucratic management is precisely the absence of such a method of calculation" (p. 49).

We can agree with the part of his argument that says market prices provide a criterion of value which serves as a basis for economic calculation in private business; but we cannot agree that government agencies are completely lacking in such a criterion. As has been noted, appropriations, like market prices, indicate in quantitative terms how much the representatives of the people are willing to pay for goods and services rendered by the government. In appropriating funds, congressmen express their attitudes concerning the usefulness of governmental activities as definitely as individuals do when they buy bread at the corner bakery. Congressmen, in effect, are serving as purchasing agents for the American people.

What function does the market price criterion serve in determining whether an activity is worth its cost? One function is to provide the numbers necessary for determining how the cost of doing a particular job can be reduced to a minimum. Nothing, of course, is worth its cost if the same result can somehow be achieved at a lower cost. Market prices are as useful in government as they are in business in this regard. In constructing a road, a building, or a dam—even in running an office— the government has to pay market prices for the raw material and manpower it uses just as a private businessman does. If the guide to economic calculation is the market price, the government engineer has numbers to put into his equations just as his engineering brother in private industry has. Market prices provide the data he needs to calculate which combination of available materials, men, and machines will be least costly.

After all corners have been cut and the cost of doing a job has been reduced to the minimum, we face a broader question. Is the job worth doing? Dr. Mises undoubtedly would answer that a job is worth doing in private business if it yields a profit. In attempting to calculate whether a given activity will yield a profit, a businessman, however, faces some of the problems faced by government. He has to forecast market conditions. The numbers he forecasts may or may not be right. Likewise, a businessman cannot always determine even after the fact whether an individual activity has been profitable or not. No method has yet been found, for example, of measuring precisely how much of a company's profit or loss results from such activities as advertising, research, and employee welfare programs. Moreover, a businessman, if he wants to maximize profits, cannot engage in an activity just because it is profitable. It must be more profitable than alternative activities open to him. Thus, he is faced with the same problem of relative value as is the government official. Suppose it costs $1.00 a pound to recover scrap materials in a private factory and that the scrap can be sold on the market for $1.10 a pound, thereby yielding a profit of 10 per cent. Does it automatically follow that the scrap should be recovered? Not at all, since the firm might make a profit of 20 per cent if the men and materials were used instead for making new products.

The method of calculation by a government agency for a similar situation would be exactly the same. In fact, if government appropriations specified precisely the quantities, quality, standards, and maximum permissible unit prices for each government service, the problem of economic calculation would not only be exactly the same but the answers could be expressed in terms of a profit equivalent. If the agency could produce at a lower unit cost than specified by Congress, the funds saved would be comparable to profit and would be returned to the Treasury as a dividend to the taxpayers.

In many cases, however, government services are of such a nature that Congress cannot enact precise specifications. For example, the production of plutonium by the Atomic Energy Commission has not yet reached the stage where such specifications can be written. Congress, in effect, tells the commission to produce as much plutonium as it can, according to specifications deemed most suitable by the commission, with a total expenditure not to exceed X million dollars. The commission then has no basis for knowing exactly what dollar value is placed on a pound of plutonium by the Congress. Nevertheless, the commission is not without means of making economic decisions. The problem might be to decide whether it is worth spending Y dollars to recover scrap plutonium which accumulates during the manufacturing process. The decision can be made on the basis of comparison of alternative means of accomplishing a common objective. This objective is to produce the maximum amount of usable plutonium during a specified period within the limits of available funds and other resources. In the light of this objective the commission can afford to spend as much per pound for recovery as it has to spend to produce a pound of new plutonium. If it spent either more or less than this amount, the total usable quantity of plutonium produced during a period would be less than the potential maximum. Faced with this kind of problem, a private business would calculate in precisely the same way. The common objective of new production and recovery operations might be expressed in terms of dollars of profit rather than pounds of product, but the answer would be the same.

When the problem facing the government involves activities such as education, foreign relations, and public recreation where the goals are less tangible, where the results are less subject to measurement, and where the amount of results arising from an increment of expenditures is more difficult to determine, the numbers used in the equations will be less firm. Even so, we conclude, Dr. Mises' arguments notwithstanding, that the differences between business and government in economic calculation lie not so much in the methods of calculation as in the availability of precise numbers with which to calculate.

II

In the foregoing analysis of economic ideas in relation to public budgeting, we have stressed the importance of looking upon budgeting as a problem of relative values and have examined the applicability of two methods—incremental analysis and evaluation of relative effectiveness—in achieving a common objective to budget analysis.

On the administrative implications of these ideas, Professor Key has said, "Perhaps the approach toward the practical working out of the issue lies in canalizing of decisions through the governmental machinery so as to place alternatives in juxtaposition and compel consideration of relative values."[8]

The budget machinery of the federal government does accomplish this purpose. The federal budget forces a simultaneous, or nearly simultaneous, consideration of all the competing claims by the President and the Congress. Moreover, at each level in the administrative hierarchy, the budget forces consideration of the relative merits of competing claims within each jurisdiction.[9]

Budget estimates and justifications are rarely prepared in a manner, however, which makes it easy to compare relative merits. We shall, therefore, now outline a budget system designed to facilitate such comparisons and to apply other ideas derived from the preceding economic analysis. After outlining this system, we shall compare it with other budget methods now being used.

The system to be described will be called the alternative budget system. Under this procedure, each administrative official who prepares a budget estimate, either as a basis for an appropriation request or an allotment request after the appropriation is made, would be required to prepare a basic budget estimate supplemented by skeleton plans for alternative amounts. If the amount of the basic estimate equals 100, the alternatives might represent, respectively, 80, 90, 110, and 120 per cent of that amount. The number of alternatives might vary with the situation. Ordinarily, three alternatives would seem to secure a sufficient range of possibilities. In the interest of providing a safety valve, each subordinate might be permitted to prepare one or more additional alternative budgets totaling more than the top figure prescribed by his superior. In order to focus attention on problems near the margins, the amounts of the alternative budgets should range from a little less than the lowest amount that is likely to be approved to a little more than the recommended amount. Increments of 10 per cent might be appropriate in some cases; larger or smaller increments might be required in others.

The establishment of the alternative levels would have to start with the President. He would select alternative levels of over-all governmental expenditure, and he would establish corresponding alternative levels for each department or agency. The head of each department or agency would, in turn, establish alternative levels for each of his subordinates which would be consistent with the prescribed departmental levels.

In preparing the alternative budgets, the subordinate official would first indicate, as he does under present procedures, the nature, quantity, and quality of services his agency could render the taxpayers if the amount of the basic budget were approved. In addition, he would indicate the recommended revisions in the plan of service for each of the alternative amounts and the benefits or sacrifices which would result.

At each superior level the responsible official would review the alternative proposals submitted by his several subordinates and select from them the features that would be, in his opinion, the most advantageous to the taxpayers for each alternative amount set for him by the next highest organization level. Finally, the President would submit alternative budgets to the Congress. At this level the alternatives would reflect the major issues involved in determining the work program for the entire government.

The advantages of the alternative budget procedure will be brought out by comparing it with other budget methods and techniques now in use. For convenience, the other techniques will be labeled (a) open-end budgeting, (b) fixed-ceiling budgeting, (c) work measurement and unit costing, (d) increase-decrease analysis, (e) priority listings, and (f) item-by-item control. These methods are not mutually exclusive; some of them could very well be incorporated as features of the alternative budget plan. Some are used primarily in budget estimating, others in budget control.

OPEN-END BUDGETING.

Some agencies of the federal government (and in some years the Bureau of the Budget) permit subordinate officials to submit a single budget estimate for whatever amount the subordinate decides to recommend. This method has been used not only for preparing requests for appropriations but also for submission of allotment requests to agency heads after the appropriations have been made. This single estimate represents, by and large, the official's judgment as to optimum program for his agency for the ensuing year, tempered perhaps by his judgment as to what the traffic will bear in view of the general political and economic climate existing at the time. No restrictions are placed on him; the sky is the limit so far as the amount he can request is concerned. For this reason, we have selected the short title "open-end budgeting" as being descriptive of this method.

In justification for such a budget estimate, the official, in effect, says, "I think it is desirable (or important, or essential) that the taxpayers be given the services outlined in this budget. Such a program will cost X dollars. Any reductions in the amount requested will deprive the public of exceedingly valuable services." While such general statements are, of course, backed up by more or less specific facts and figures, the information provided leaves many gaps from the point of view of what the superior official needs in order to weigh the importance of each dollar requested by one subordinate against each dollar requested by other subordinates.

Statements which merely prove that a program is desirable do not fulfill the needs of a superior who is faced with the necessity of reducing the total amount requested by the subordinates, not because he thinks the requests are for undesirable or unnecessary purposes, but simply because the pattern is too big for the cloth. The subordinate's budget estimates and justifications, submitted to him under the open-end procedure, are deficient because they do not indicate specifically how plans would be changed if a smaller amount were available or specifically the subordinate's judgment as to the consequences of such a change in plans. Almost the entire burden, then, of ascertaining where the reductions can be made with the least harmful consequences is placed on the superior official, who naturally is less well informed on the details than are his subordinates.

In what way would the assistance rendered by the subordinate to his superior be enhanced if the alternative budget method were used? Under any circumstances the contribution of a subordinate official is limited by the fact that he is concerned with a segment rather than with the whole. His advice as to how much should be appropriated for his particular sphere of activities obviously cannot be accepted without careful scrutiny. He lacks information about other activities which would be necessary to make a comparison of relative importance. Even if he had complete information, he would be quite unique if he did not place a higher valuation on his own activities than others do. This generalization is borne out by the fact that the aggregate of requests from subordinate officials is invariably more than the public, acting through Congress, is willing to devote to public services.

The subordinate administrative official can be expected, however, to make a substantial contribution in advising the Congress and the President on the relative merits of competing demands within his own jurisdiction, even though he cannot be expected to weigh those demands against demands in other jurisdictions. The subordinate official can perform an indispensable service by comparing the relative effectiveness of each activity in achieving the goals of his agency and by indicating how he thinks any specified amount of money can best be distributed among the programs of his agency. His service in this respect is valuable not only because considerable technical knowledge and experience usually is required as a basis for arriving at such judgments, but also because the pressure of time may force the President and the Congress to rely greatly on his judgment.

This phase of the contribution of the subordinate official to budget-making is comparable to services I can get from an architect if I should decide to build a house. The architect's advice as to whether I should spend eight, twelve, or sixteen thousand dollars for a house is not very helpful. On the other hand, the architect can be very helpful in advising me as to how I can get the most of what I want in a house for any given sum I choose to spend.

Another way in which a subordinate can be of service is in advising his superiors on probable gains or losses from appropriating more or less for his portion of the government's work. This kind of contribution is comparable to the assistance an architect can render by analyzing the additional features in a house which can be obtained for each increment of cost, and by indicating the features that would have to be sacrificed if costs were reduced by specified amounts.

Alternative budgets prepared by subordinates would take advantage of both of these types of assistance. The subordinate would indicate his judgment as to the best way of using several alternative amounts and in addition he would analyze the benefits to be gained by each increment of funds.

FIXED-CEILING BUDGETING.

If the open-end procedure is one extreme, the fixed-ceiling method represents the opposite pole. Under this plan, a fixed ceiling is established in advance which the subordinate's budget estimate cannot exceed. Such a ceiling creates for the subordinate a situation similar to that facing the President if he should decide to recommend a balanced budget. Then the amount of anticipated revenues constitutes the ceiling on the amount of expenditures he can recommend.

Whatever the merits, or lack thereof, of allowing revenues to determine the total amount to be spent by the government, working to a set ceiling does have the advantage of forcing consideration, at the presidential level, of relative merits to a greater extent than is likely to prevail under open-end budgeting. In open-end budgeting, it is easy to keep adding items that appear to be desirable and thereby pass the buck to the next level of review in the event the total cost of the "desirable" items exceeds an acceptable figure. But prescribing a single fixed ceiling in advance for subordinate levels of the executive branch involves the danger of judging a case before the evidence is heard. The basic reason for requiring estimates from subordinate officials is that higher officials do not have enough detailed information, time, or specialized skill to prepare the plans themselves. How can these officials judge the merits of the experts' plans before they are submitted? In setting the ceiling figures in advance, how can one be sure that the ceiling for one function is not set too high and the ceiling for another too low?

The alternative budget plan, like the fixed-ceiling practice, forces consideration of relative merits within a given amount at each organization level, but the final decision as to amount does not have to be made by the superior until the evidence is in.

WORK LOAD MEASUREMENT AND UNIT COSTING.

Increasing emphasis has been placed in recent years on work load measurement and unit costing for budgetary purposes. The ultimate goal is to devise units of work and to determine unit costs wherever possible so that budget requests can be stated in this fashion: "It costs X dollars to perform each unit of this type of work. If you want us to perform 100 units, the cost will be 100 times X dollars. If you want only fifty units the cost will be fifty times X dollars."

This approach is useful for budgeting in many situations. It supplies some of the numbers needed for the economic calculation discussed in Part I. Precise, quantitative measures, if pertinent and feasible, are better than vague generalities. Some budget questions cannot be answered, however, in terms of work load and unit cost data. These data will show how many units are being done, but not how many should be done. They show what unit costs are, but not what they should be. They may or may not give an indication of the quality of the work, but they leave unanswered the question of the proper quality standards.

A further limitation on use of work load measurement is that the end product of many agencies is not measurable by any means yet devised. In other cases, the amount of work performed is not a measure of its significance or value. Some work is stand-by in character. Some facilities, for example, are maintained to meet emergencies if and when they arise. In such cases the less work there is to be done the better. Much of the work of military agencies and fire-fighters is of this type. In other cases, too, the amount of work performed is inadequate as an index of results. This is true with respect to many research projects and enforcement activities. In the case of research, it is the final result that counts, not the amount of work required to achieve the result. In enforcement work, the number of infractions dealt with is not an adequate measure since the ideal would be to have no infractions at all.

Lacking an adequate way of measuring or even identifying the end product in precise terms, it is still possible in many cases to develop significant measures of work load of subsidiary activities that contribute to the end product. Examples are number of letters typed, miles patrolled, or purchase orders processed. Detailed data of this type are useful in budgeting but their use is largely confined to the lower organization levels. The sheer mass of such data precludes their extensive use at higher levels.

The alternative budget proposal would permit use of work load and unit cost data to the extent feasible in each case. Under each alternative total figure, the number of units of work that could be performed, the quality standards, and unit costs could be shown. Thus the benefits to be derived from work load measurement would be fully utilized under the alternative budget procedure. In addition, the judgment of subordinates would be obtained on questions which cannot be answered by work load data alone. Such questions involve, for example, the gains or losses of performing alternative amounts of work, the achievement of alternative quality standards, and the effects of spending more or less per unit of work.

INCREASE-DECREASE ANALYSIS.

A common technique in the federal government is to require in budget estimates identification of the items representing increases and decreases as compared with the prior year's budget. Special explanations are required for the increases. Budget reviewers are frequently criticized for concentrating on the increases and giving too little attention to items in the base amount. This criticism is justified in part because the amount appropriated last year is not necessarily appropriate for this year and the activities carried on last year are not necessarily appropriate for this year. However, the sheer mass of work involved in reviewing budget estimates precludes examination of every detail every year. Even if it were possible, it would not be necessary, for conditions do not change so fast that every issue has to be rehashed every year.

The basic fault of the increase-decrease method is the fact that it does not require comparison of the relative values of the old and the new. While the proposed increase may be for an eminently desirable purpose, it does not necessarily follow that the appropriation of the agency should be increased. Perhaps other programs of the agency should be cut back enough, or more, to make room for the new. The alternative budget approach has all the advantages of the increase-decrease method without having this basic fault. It would require agencies to weigh the relative merits of all proposals, whether old or new, and thus would reflect the agency's evaluation of the importance of the proposed additions to the spending program in relation to the items composing the base.

PRIORITY LISTINGS.

Subordinates are required, in some cases, to indicate priorities of items included in their budget estimates or allotment requests to assist reviewers in determining where cutbacks should be made. Budgets for construction of physical facilities, for example, might contain a listing in priority order of the facilities proposed. The assumption underlying this method is that a budget reduction would be met by eliminating enough projects at the lower end of the list to bring the estimates down to the desired level. When that is the case priority listings are useful. Elimination of the lowest priority items, however, is only one of several means of reducing estimates. Some of the other types of adjustments are as follows: cheaper materials may be used in some or all of the facilities; the size, strength, or durability of the facilities may be decreased; or certain features may be eliminated or postponed until a later date. All of these types of adjustments can be reflected in alternative budgets since they all affect dollar requirements. The priority approach reflects only the one kind of adjustment.

ITEM-BY-ITEM CONTROL.

Approval of individual items of expenditure by higher authority is a common budgetary control technique. Equipment purchases, additions to staff, travel, expensive types of communications as well as entire projects, are frequently subjected to this type of control. An actual case will illustrate the problems involved. During World War II, the Secretary of the Navy was concerned about the expansion of the physical plant of the Navy in the continental United States. In an effort to assure that no facilities would be built unless vitally needed for war purposes and that costs and use of scarce materials would be minimized, the Secretary of the Navy required that all proposed construction projects should be subject to his approval. Prior to this approval they had to be screened at several different levels in the Navy Department. The projects were reviewed by officials in the sponsoring bureau, by the Bureau of Yards and Docks (to insure conformity to wartime engineering standards), by the Chief of Naval Operations (to determine their military necessity), and by a special committee in the Secretary's office composed mainly of civilian businessmen (to determine their over-all justification). Even with this series of reviews, the Secretary apparently was not convinced that outlays for facilities were being held down as much as they should be. The process was something less than satisfactory to subordinate officials, too, but for different reasons. They complained of the delays involved in getting a decision and of the amount of time and effort required to justify and re-justify each proposal at the several screening points.

The root of the difficulty, if the thesis of this article is sound, is that controls of individual items do not require or facilitate systematic consideration of relative desirability. Item-by-item control poses the problem at each level of review in these terms: Is the proposal desirable, or essential, or justified? A more pertinent question is: Is the proposal more essential than any alternative use of the funds?

The alternative budget procedure could be applied to this situation in the following manner: bureau chiefs, as well as officials at lower levels, if desired, would be asked to prepare alternative programs for construction of facilities for the period in question. The bureau chiefs in presenting these alternatives would, in effect, tell the Chief of Naval Operations and the Secretary, "If only X dollars are available, I recommend using the money this way . . .; if two X dollars are available, I think the money should be used this way. . . . The advantages and disadvantages of each plan are as follows: . . ." Having an opportunity to see the picture as a whole, having before him alternatives from which to choose, and having the judgment of his subordinates as to gains and losses resulting from each alternative, the Secretary, it would seem, would be able to make his decision fairly readily and with assurance. It is unlikely that he would have to spend as much time reviewing details as is necessary under the item-by-item approach. He would be in a better position to exercise his responsibilities while the subordinates would be freed from the delays, burdens, and irritations invariably involved in piece-by-piece screening processes.

In addition to the specific points discussed above, the alternative budget plan appears to have certain general advantages. It would, we believe, make budgeting a little more palatable to the technically minded operating official who must prepare and justify budgets. His role will be less that of a special pleader for *the* plan he thinks should be accepted and more that of an expert adviser. He will be less like an architect who tries to sell a client on a single plan costing a certain sum and more like an architect advising the client on the relative merits of several house plans and suggesting how the client can get the most for his money regardless of the amount he decides to spend.

Budget analysts under this plan would have a frame of reference which would enable them to operate more effectively. At present, much of their effort is directed toward determining desirability or necessity and not enough attention is given to issues of relative desirability. Under the plan suggested here, the primary job of the budget analyst would be to assist his superior in weighing the relative value of alternative uses of each increment of funds as a step in developing the alternatives to be submitted to the next higher level in the organization. Another aspect of his work would be to explore some of the many possible variations and combinations of features that could not be reflected in the limited number of alternatives formally submitted by the lower officials. Moreover, the analyst would have to check for accuracy, objectivity, and general adequacy the subordinate official's statements of the advantages and disadvantages of the alternatives submitted.

Another significant advantage of the alternative budget proposal is that it would make budgeting somewhat less authoritarian. It would make the budget recommendations of administrative officials less final without weakening in any way their usefulness.

At present, an item screened out of a budget by any administrative official even though it is of major importance is not considered at later stages unless it is brought to the attention of higher executive officials or the Congress by some method which is prohibited by the prevailing rules. To put it mildly, quite definite steps are taken to discourage later consideration. A bureau chief, for example, would be considered out of bounds if he appealed to the President for consideration of an item screened out of his budget by his departmental head. Any administrative officer is prohibited from recommending congressional consideration of any alternatives to the single proposal contained in the President's budget unless specifically requested to do so by a member of Congress. Publication of requests submitted by the departments to the President is also banned.

It is not at all unlikely that superior administrative officials or the Congress would want to adopt some of these screened-out items if they had an opportunity to consider them. Since Congress, in our form of government, is largely responsible for deciding what shall or shall not be done by the executive agencies, the wisdom of such strict censoring of proposals submitted for consideration by Congress seems questionable. Since the President's budget estimates are only recommendations, there would seem to be no disadvantage in his outlining the major alternatives from which he made his selection. In this way the views of subordinates who may have an honest difference of opinion with the President could be submitted to Congress for consideration openly and without subterfuge. After considering the evidence pertaining to each alternative, Congress could then take its choice. Since the making of such choices is involved in exercising congressional control over the purse strings—a control which historically and currently is a basic cornerstone of democratic government—the provision of information which will assist Congress in evaluating the major alternative courses is of vital importance.[10]

In general, the alternative budget plan is designed to emphasize throughout the budget process the economic ideas discussed in Part I of this article. Its purpose is to pose budget questions at every level in terms of relative value. It also is designed to make maximum use of the expert knowledge and judgment of officials at the lower organization levels by having them analyze, incrementally, the estimates of their agencies and evaluate the relative effectiveness of their several activities in achieving the goals of their organizations.

In proposing this system, I am not particularly concerned with detailed mechanics. There are undoubtedly other ways of accomplishing substantially the same results as this plan is designed to achieve. More important than the precise mechanics is the way of looking at budget problems, the approach to budget analysis and control which this plan reflects.

How practical is the alternative budget plan? How well will it work in practice? The answers to these questions depend in large measure on the relationships between superior and subordinate and between the administration and the Congress. Neither this system nor any other can work satisfactorily if the relations are strained, if the reviewer lacks confidence in the integrity or judgment of the official who is submitting the estimate, or if those who prepare the estimates are not sincerely interested in providing information which the reviewers need to form an intelligent judgment on the merits of the issues.

Perhaps undue faith in the rationality of man underlies the approach to budgeting outlined in this article. In real life, budget decisions are undoubtedly influenced to a greater or lesser extent by such non-economic and non-rational factors as pride and prejudice, provincialism and politics. These aspects deserve consideration, but they lie beyond the scope of this article. My primary purpose herein has been to stimulate further consideration of the economic aspects of budgeting.[11]

NOTES:

[1]V. O. Key, Jr., "The Lack of a Budgetary Theory," 34 *American Political Science Review,* 1137–44 (December, 1940).

[2]Ideas derived from Herbert A. Simon's works concerning the applicability of economic concepts to administration have been particularly useful for this purpose. See his *Administrative Behavior* (New York: Macmillan Co., 1947).

[3]As quoted by Key, *op. cit.,* p. 1139.

[4]L. M. Fraser, *Economic Thought and Language* (A. and C. Black Ltd., 1937), p. 103.

[5]This method, as it applies to public administration in general, has been extensively analyzed by Herbert A. Simon under the heading of the "criterion of efficiency," *op. cit.,* pp. 172–97.

[6]Key, *op. cit.,* p. 1143.

[7]Ludwig von Mises, *Bureaucracy* (New Haven: Yale University Press, 1944), p. 47.

[8]*Op. cit.,* p. 1112.

[9]See also, Simon, *op. cit.,* p. 214.

[10]Simon also has recommended submission of alternative budget plans to legislatures for substantially the same reason. *Op. cit.,* p. 195.

[11]Note on relation to a performance budget. A performance budget, as proposed by the Hoover Commission, would give primary emphasis to the result or end product to be obtained with the money spent by the government. The commission wisely criticized budget presentations that deal only with the ingredients that are required to produce the end product. Certainly first attention should be given to what is to be accomplished rather than to the people who have to be employed, or the materials which have to be bought, in order to accomplish the basic purpose.

Emphasizing performance or end results does not require us to ignore the ingredients or the means to the ends. It should not lead to that result. Important budget issues often involve only the means. While there may be agreement about purpose, the methods may be in dispute. For example, a conservation agency may be responsible for inducing producer-conservation of some natural resource. Should the objective be accomplished by an educational program, by regulatory action, or by subsidy?

The alternative budget plan is flexible enough to be adapted to the situation. Alternative purposes as well as alternative methods could and should be reflected in the alternative budget estimates. Whether greater emphasis would be placed on purposes than on methods would depend upon the nature of the problem.

7.

Comprehensive Versus Incremental Budgeting in the Department of Agriculture*

AARON WILDAVSKY and
ARTHUR HAMMANN

In the Spring of 1962, the Department of Agriculture shunted aside traditional methods of budgeting and attempted a comprehensive and simultaneous evaluation of all departmental programs. The purpose of this paper is to describe this experiment and to evaluate its results, especially as they bear upon the controversy surrounding incremental versus comprehensive approaches to decision-making. After a brief description of the rival positions in this controversy, the procedures used by officials in the Department of Agriculture in comprehensive budgeting are described. Then we attempt to determine the extent to which the intended objectives of comprehensive budgeting were achieved, and to describe a number of unanticipated consequences of using this approach. We conclude with a series of recommendations.[1]

THE CONTROVERSY

Whatever else they may be, budgets are manifestly political documents. They engage the intense concern of administrators, politicians, leaders of interest groups and citizens interested in the "who gets what and how much" of governmental allocations. Participants in budgeting use its political components as aids to calculation. They drastically sim-

*Reprinted from Aaron Wildavsky and Arthur Hammann, "Comprehensive Versus Incremental Budgeting in the Department of Agriculture," Administrative Science Quarterly, 10:3 (December 1965), 321–346, by permission of the author and publisher. Aaron Wildavsky is chairman of the department of political science at the University of California, Berkeley. Arthur Hammann is a teaching fellow in psychology at the University of Michigan. The name of the junior author was misspelled as Hammond in the original article.

plify their task by concentrating on the relatively small portion of the budget that is politically feasible to change. The previous year's budget, the largest part of which is composed of continuing programs and prior commitments, is usually taken as a base needing little justification beyond that offered in the past. Attention is normally focused on a small number of incremental changes, increases and decreases, calling for significant departures from the established historical base of the agency concerned. Parts of the total budget are given to various administrative agencies, appropriations subcommittees, budget bureau divisions, and other interested parties for special attention. This fragmentation is increased because all budgetary items are not evaluated together, but are dealt with in sequence by the various participants, so that only a small number of items need be considered by any participant at any one time. Heavy reliance is placed on receiving feedback from interested parties, if a decision turns out to have adverse consequences for others. The existing budgetary process, therefore, may be described as incremental, fragmented, and sequential.[2]

A large part of the literature on budgeting in the United States has been devoted to a critique of the present process.[3] Aids to calculation like the incremental method have been attacked as arbitrary and inefficient. The fragmented and sequential budgetary operations have been severely criticized for leading to a lack of coordination and a neglect of important values.

Failure to consider the budget as a whole, each item competing for funds with the others, has been characterized as irrational. Although many statements could be cited to show how long and how consistently these views have been held, only a few illustrations are presented here. Writing in 1924, E. Hilton Young asserted:

It must be a temptation to one drawing up an estimate to save himself trouble by taking last year's estimate for granted, adding something to any item for which an increased expenditure is foreseen. Nothing could be easier, or more wasteful and extravagant. It is in that way obsolete expenditure is enabled to make its appearance year after year long after reason for it has ceased to be.[4]

This often-repeated theme was echoed in 1941 by Benton Biser: "Appropriations generally are built upon the basis of the preceding year's expenditure, plus or minus any known items of increase or decrease, without considering whether or not the past year's experience is the result of efficient and economical administration."[5] Arthur Smithies was more positive: "In general final expenditure decisions should not be made until *all* claims on the budget can be considered"[6] (italics supplied).

These norms are still held by participants in budgeting. Maurice Stans, who was budget director under President Eisenhower, stated: *"Every item* in a budget ought to be on trial for its life *each year* and matched against *all* the other claimants to our resources"[7] (italics supplied). The critics would prefer a budgetary process in which coordination would be made the explicit concern of a central hierarchy, which would consider a wide range of alternative expenditures and investigate rather fully the consequences of each and the probability of their occurring. No item would be automatically included, and each would be considered anew every year in the light of its relative priority compared to other items. Instead of proceeding from a historical base, there would be no base at all; therefore, this comprehensive budget is called a "zero-base" budget.

While it is evidently possible to talk about comprehensive, zero-base budgeting, the question arises as to whether it is possible to put it into practice.[8] This question cannot be shunted aside as unimportant, when one considers the constraints imposed by limited time and comprehension, by the lack of theory to predict consequences or means to calculate them fully, by the widespread political consensus on many programs and the statutory necessity of proceeding with others, and by inability to resolve the perennial question of the comparability of different preferences held with varying degrees of intensity. A direct test of the comprehensive approach has not previously been possible because (to the best of our knowledge) no major attempt has been made to try a zero-base budget. The effort of the Department of Agriculture to work with a zero-base budget in 1962 provides, therefore, a unique and valuable opportunity to undertake a direct test of this approach. The analysis of a "deviant case" (when compared with the usual mode of budgeting) has special advantages in highlighting features of the budgetary process that might otherwise escape notice. Despite the disadvantage of working with one case, one can obtain insights from a close view of problems of budgetary calculation.[9]

The study is based on an extended series of interviews, during the summer of 1963, with budget officers, directors or assistant directors, and staff people in nearly every agency in the Department of Agriculture, as well as department level officials. We attempted to interview every person at a high level who was intimately involved in the zero-base budget experiment, and succeeded in interviewing at least one person in all but two small agencies. Our fifty-seven interviews constitute an overwhelmingly large sample of the important men available for discussion. All of the men interviewed were given an opportunity to comment upon a draft of this paper and to amplify their remarks to the senior author. Twelve re-interviews were undertaken in order to check on disputed points. Questions in the paper represent a transcription of notes taken during interviews or, when indicated, comments in letters written in response to the first draft.

PROCEDURES

The origin of the experiment in zero-base budgeting may be traced to three circumstances: (1) The general climate of opinion favored comprehensive budgeting. (2) A letter from Director of the Budget, David Bell, to the Secretary of Agriculture, Orville Freeman, suggested that a more comprehensive approach to budgeting was in order. Dated August 16, 1961, the crucial sentence reads: "I think we should in a real sense reconsider the basic funding for each program—'justify from zero' in the budgetary phase." (3) Freeman had a strong interest in budgetary problems, which he had developed as governor of Minnesota.[10] Comments like "The Secretary pushed this" or "The Secretary's interest was the motivating force" clearly indicate where department officials found the immediate impulse behind the proposal.

When the decision was made to do a zero-base budget, staff members in the department's Office of Budget and Finance made a quick survey of the literature and discovered that although much had been written criticizing the traditional methods of budgeting and advocating a comprehensive approach, there was little written about zero-base budgeting. After the staff members had consulted with leading department officials in order to get a clearer idea of the objectives, they began preparations.

In April, 1962, the Department Office of Budget and Finance sent out "Instructions for 1964 Agency Estimates," which called for radical changes.

A new concept has been adopted for the 1964 agency estimates; namely, that of zero-base budgeting. This means that all programs will be reviewed from the ground up and not merely in terms of changes proposed for the budget year. . . . The total work program of each agency must be subjected to an intensive review and evaluation. . . . Consideration must be given to the basic need for the work contemplated, the level at which the work should be carried out, the benefits to be received, and the costs to be incurred. . . .

The fact that certain activities have been carried out for a number of years will not, per se, adequately justify their continuation. Nor will the fact that programs are prescribed by statutory law necessarily be a controlling consideration. Program goals based on statutes enacted to meet problems or needs that are today of lesser priority must be re-evaluated in terms of present conditions.

It is implicit in the zero-based budget approach that the need for programs and their recommended magnitude in the fiscal year 1964 be clearly and specifically demonstrated. . . . The justifications should be prepared on the assumption that all *[italics supplied] information needed for making budget decisions should be included.*[11]

The instructions for preparing a zero-base budget required the agencies to make three major types of calculations: (1) justification of the need for agency activities and programs without reference to congressional mandate or past practice; (2) justification of the requested level of expenditure (fund obligations) based on the needs; (3) justification of the costs of the needed programs from the ground up. How did agency officials react to the demands placed upon them by the zero-base budget? How did they go about putting together the huge amount of information they were required to submit?

APPLICATION OF ZERO-BASE CONCEPT

All the agencies had serious difficulty in conceptualizing circumstances in which there were no legislative mandates, no past commitments, no consideration of items to be included because other participants in the budgetary process would demand it, no programs for which support could not conceivably be expected; in a word, no history or learning based on that history. The words of one official, "Justifying the whole program is silly; it just equals rehashing the original legislation" were echoed by many others. So the agencies either assumed or quickly decided that their programs were needed. Many programs were justified at least in part by references to the language of their enabling legislation, despite the statement in the instructions that this would not be an overriding consideration. Besides pointing to statutory requirements, the agencies gave priority to showing how their program met objectives of the Kennedy-Freeman program: increasing recreation facilities, aiding low-income groups, and generally advancing rural development. This is, of course, what the agencies would usually have done in justifying their budgets, except that more detail and greater documentation were provided. Furthermore, time was precious and in short supply. "We didn't have time to analyze much" was a typical comment, reflecting the tendency of efforts to be channeled into the large and pressing task of compiling supporting data.

One budget officer estimated that a "real examination" of the need for the programs carried out by his agency "would take at least a year." As a result, he explained, the continuation of major programs was not re-examined.

Agency people were far more concerned with the level of their programs than with whether there was a need for them at all. One stated, "We told our program people, 'These are the areas Congress has authorized us to participate in. Which need to be implemented in your state, and at what level?' "; and even here, "Mostly this was a justification of what we had." Program officials reported, apparently without realizing the implications for the theory behind the zero-base budget, that in preparing estimates, "We had to start from the previous year, then determine what increases we wanted for 1964." "Each staff officer reviewed his office. We all decided we needed what we had. Then we decided whether to ask for increases." The calculations involved in determining the precise figures were described by an agency head in terms generally applicable throughout the department: "In the matter of preparing budget estimates, the dollar emphases (priorities) are intended to represent a program which represents what the Secretary and Congress want to give emphasis to at that time. The dollar figures represent a compromise among the guidelines given by the need for the service (what the public has asked for), the wishes of the President and Secretary, and the indications given by Congress at 'Hill' hearings ('hold the line on this program next year!')." Other officials mentioned certain limiting factors—the availability of trained personnel or physical resources, which set upper limits to what they could do. It is apparent that agency people reduced their burden of calculation by actively seeking guidelines or constraints —what Congress would approve, what the statutes required, what could be done with available personnel and resources. The major calculating device was to take the budget of the past year or two and then consider increases or decreases.

Since the zero-base budget was designed to avoid this incremental procedure, we challenged the respondents to explain and defend their approach. Not all were aware at first that they were following an incremental procedure. At times the respondents became agitated: "You've got to start from where you are!" Two main grounds were advanced in support of this proposition. First, they knew most about their present status and could make some reasonable estimate of the effect of more or less money for particular programs. But they did not know what drastic changes, such as eliminating their programs, or cutting them in half, or doubling them, would mean: "Increases or decreases are about all we can swallow." Such comments were reinforced by observing that at department budget hearings, agency representatives were typically confronted with the same kinds of increase-decrease statements as in previous years: "How many people do you have now? What did you spend for that last year? What do you propose to do with the extra funds?"

The second argument was that the whole procedure was unreal. Why such a great effort for a procedure which nobody with experience could believe would lead to any significant results? Everybody knew that certain programs were mandatory, others could not be modified, still others had to be supported at approximately their current level, unless the President and the Secretary were prepared to make many more enemies than appeared to be the case: "We knock our heads against the wall and then we know it will all turn out the same." All this "waste of time and effort" when they might have been working on programs they could really do something about.

Considerations such as these were not entirely absent in the instructions for the zero-base budget, where one statement was: "One of the department's objectives will be to reduce over-all net expenditures for the Department of Agriculture in 1964 and subsequent years below presently estimated levels for 1962 and 1963." If the agencies were expected to make a fundamental analysis of the needs for their programs, regardless of budget changes, such an admonition would seem superfluous.[12]

"My first reaction was to jump out the window," an agency budget officer revealed. As the agencies began work to justify the cost elements in their estimates, however, the initial difficulties were forgotten in the attempt to meet the requirements set down for the zero-base budget. Those agencies whose activities or experience lent themselves easily to work-load analysis reacted differently from those whose activities made this procedure impossible or inappropriate for them. An agency with a well developed and widely accepted mode of work-load measures could meet the requirement that expenditures be justified from "the ground up" by attaching an explanation to tables of work-load statistics, supporting the expenditures. As one budget officer put it, "Work-load data is great for us. We're pioneers in this area. We'd been developing this data for years." A high-ranking official was explicit in stating that in his agency, "the zero-base approach made no difference, because to meet rapidly changing conditions, we're always preparing our budget zero-base style. Economic assumptions lead to size of expected program (required by statute), which leads to cost on basis of previous staffing and material needs. We don't know what the estimate will be until it pops out of the calculating machine."

For the agencies which did not or could not use work-load data, calculating the expected level of expenditures (budgetary obligations) in zero-base style was much more difficult, and the responsible officials tended to react much more negatively. "I don't know of any budget officer who liked zero-base budgeting," was a typical comment. "Work-load data is inappropriate for us," they explained. "It's not like building a bridge or something—you don't have 'units,' you have subject matter, and it is very difficult to know how many technical people are needed." Unable to talk in terms of so many applications processed, operations performed, or similar measures, the agencies with no work-load statistics had to find a substitute. In some cases an explanation of the problem was made, and the proposed levels of expenditure were justified by projecting the rate of growth of the previous few years into the future. A few agencies tried to develop new ways of dividing activities, although they did not think this realistic and expected no benefits from what they called "arbitrary categories." Developing supporting data meant breaking down costs differently and engaging in many hurried calculations without the feeling that something positive would result. As a result, these agencies were overburdened with work in which they had little confidence, although they did manage to submit estimates which were as much as ten or more times longer than previous ones. Six weeks after the instructions for the zero-base budget has been sent out, twenty-five sets of binders representing agency estimates, most taking up three feet of shelf space, appeared in the Office of Budget and Finance. "It nearly created a surplus storage problem," one official remarked in a pointed bit of humor.

COMPREHENSIVENESS OF ZERO-BASE APPROACH

"Theoretically," a department official said, "a zero-base budget is a way of evaluating needs and priorities more systematically and comprehensively than usual." How did the officials at the department level[13] analyze the voluminous material presented. Did they try to evaluate the relative merits of every item or program compared to every other? What procedures were actually used in making agency allowances?

The main problem was lack of time. "We knew we were getting into something horrendous," a respondent declared, "and it was obvious in advance that it would be impossible for all of us to analyze the material at all stages. The range of decision—the number of decisions to be made —increased almost infinitely. Although individual steps of the process at the department level were the same as always, this made such a quantitative difference as to amount to a qualitative one." Another official observed: "The stuff the agencies submitted was very complete, obviously too bulky for the Secretary himself to wade though." More direct confirmation came from an authoritative source, who said that the Secretary "didn't read a great deal of material; he only has time for summary material." But he did spend more time than before on the budget. Of the eight members of the Budget Committee of the Department—the undersecretary (chairman), six assistant secretaries, and the Director of Budget and Finance—it is doubtful that more than one or two actually had time to read all the material submitted. That the zero-base budget came up during the Billie Sol Estes episode and at a time when the appropriations bill was seriously behind schedule in Congress may have added to the time problem. The consensus, expressed by a high department official was: "There was too much material in the zero-base budget for us to digest and use. I haven't read it all." What, then, did they do with the material they could read and digest?

The crucial question centers around the degree to which comparisons were made as to the relative desirability of programs spanning several different agencies. Nothing approaching a comparison of every program with every other (or of most programs with each other) was made. On the contrary, the majority of comparisons made by department officials concerned programs and activities within individual agencies. An official explained: "Questions at department hearings were in the same categories as usual—Why this program? Why this level? What would alternatives cost?—but in more detail. In analysis, we didn't consider why sixty-five rather than sixty-four or sixty-six man-years for project X, but why three times as much for project X as project Y." Only in a few cases involving closely related programs in different agencies, where this had been the practice, were comparisons made across agency lines. In fact, most of the analysis, as in previous years, dealt with the justification of an individual program at a particular level of expenditure. "Unavoidably," a department official revealed, "we ended up talking about how much more, about increases. Budget people seem to talk about a budget request of $5 million when actually that's just the increase."

When we faced him with these findings a department official declared that:

The ideal of a zero-base budget is actually impossible: It would require investigating why each research lab is where it is (which is tough to trace), giving an objective measure of how much can be justified for research in a given area, etc. If you have the type of program where you can identify units of work, budgeting on zero-base is relatively simple. But in a case like the Department of Agriculture, that often doesn't work. Our activities are so varied as to make quantitative comparisons between programs impossible. I don't agree that just because we put emphasis on increases, no one pays attention to the rest of it. We are always evaluating some programs in a basic sense and always trying to make improvements in management. If we do [place emphasis on increases] it's because that's the way appropriations committees like to operate.

This official and others appear to be saying (1) that they do not know how to make the calculations required for a zero-base budget; and (2) that a comprehensive approach is not necessary, because they do, from time to time, investigate various programs intensively, within the limitations of their time and knowledge. It is clear that those who would like a zero-base budget will have to show how it can be done if they wish to see it put into practice.

THE STAFF

Those engaged in analyzing the budget at the department level did make a serious effort to avoid increase-decrease analysis. "Naturally," a staff man explained, "we were interested in the fact that a program would be a new investment; that fact might raise or lower [its] priority. But increases and decreases as such were for the Bureau of the Budget [and later for submission to Congress]; they weren't even included in the detailed justifications." This procedure raises a question of some interest. If, as we have seen, top officials manifested a preponderant interest in increases and decreases for the purpose of making recommendations on the budget, what purpose was served by providing them with different kinds of data and analysis?

When this question was posed to department people, they began to alter the rationale they had originally offered for the zero-base budget. Two major lines of thought developed. The first professed to see in the zero-base budget a combination of psychological reassurance and strategic utility: "There has been a great hue and cry about the size of the agriculture budget. The purpose of it [the zero-base budget] is to reassure, if we can, the Secretary, the Director of the Budget, the members of the appropriations committees, that money is not being wasted and that it is being used to carry out only the most important projects in work that furthers the national interest." Although related to the first in its emphasis upon the psychological aspect, the second *post-hoc* rationale leans on the benefits to be derived from any radical change in habits of work and thought. "We were interested," the proponents of this view asserted, "in the zero-base budget as a therapeutic device for agency and budget people. It's easy to get into the habit of doing things the same way. Starting out with the idea that nothing is sacred is therapeutic in itself. Any device which will encourage people to give a deeper and broader consideration to operations will lead to better understanding of what is going on and of areas where improvements might be made." Note that the focus has shifted from external phenomena like comprehensive calculation from the ground up, from analyzing programs comparatively, to internal psychological states like breaking up people's habitual patterns of thinking and reassuring leaders. To what extent did "better understanding" lead to improvements? Consider the consequences of the zero-base budget for budgetary decisions within the department. What difference did it make in the kinds of decisions made?

INTENDED OBJECTIVES

The major purpose of the zero-base budget was to examine all programs at the same time and from the ground up to discover programs continuing through inertia or design that did not warrant being continued at all or at their present level of expenditure. Money released by the discovery of these "obsolete" programs could lead either to a decrease in the over-all size of the funds requested by the Department of Agriculture or to a more rapid expansion of the highest priority programs than was possible under the traditional incremental approach to budgeting. In brief, detailed information about all programs would for the first time be available in one place at one time for departmental review. As a result, relative priorities of total amounts for all programs could be considered, not merely amounts of increase and decrease for some programs.

We therefore asked each respondent to tell us whether any decision made by him or by others could in any way be attributed to the zero-base budget. Did the agency or department officials recommend different programs, different amounts for programs, or distribute funds among programs differently as a result of the zero-base approach? For the most part, the answer was negative.

Most statements were variants of "I don't think it made a damn bit of difference," or, "I don't think anyone would honestly tell you that they changed their budget." Agency personnel continually reiterated their doubts that the department was adequately staffed to digest the vast amounts of material. Asked for evidence, the respondents usually replied that, "The figures we put in have never been referred to as far as I know" or, "It [the zero-base budget data] was sent across the street [where the department offices are located] and we never heard of it again." In a few cases the respondent hedged: "I don't know that I personally learned anything new or different, but . . . I suspect it did make some difference, but I'd hate to have to prove it." A couple of times an exceedingly small change was reported though not without qualification. Although there was "no difference in the over-all amounts requested or received from the department, analysis did lead to the transfer of $20,000 among programs. This analysis was, however, planned before the zero-base budget. . . ." An excess expenditure for files in one agency was also mentioned. In one instance a department official asserted, "I am confident that decisions were made which would not have been made or even considered in the absence of a zero-base budget." He could, however, give only one specific change—a reduction of $100,000 in an obsolete research program. The paucity of changes attributed to the zero-base budget is evident in the fact that this change was brought up repeatedly. (Many officials said they had heard of a change somewhere, but it always turned out to be this same change.) Another department official insisted that the zero-base budget procedure was not useful in "ferreting out all sorts of dark and sinister things that shouldn't be done, which would turn up quickly anyhow." Our general conclusion can be stated in the words of a person in a position to get a general view: "Some butterflies were caught, no elephants stopped."

There are a number of explanations for the paucity of changes. First, as an agency official put it, "Budgeting is continuous." Individual programs are constantly being evaluated. When authorizations run out, new studies are commonly undertaken and new justifications prepared. A change of party in the White House or the appearance of a new agency head often results in the re-evaluation of some programs. Interest in Congress or the Bureau of the Budget, demands by clientele groups, and changes in the economy or in technology may lead to intensive analysis of specific programs. These take place in addition to periodic reviews scheduled within the agency in order to adjust to changing circumstances. Second, some of the department's programs have always been budgeted more or less in zero-base fashion because their operations lend themselves to quantification. These include the price support programs of the Commodity Credit Corporation, which make up the largest single item in the budget. For such programs, justifying a $600,000 program and justifying a $100,000 increase in a $500,000 program amount to much the same thing. Therefore the requests coming from the agencies—certainly a major determinant of what departmental officials will approve—were quite similar to those of previous years. Third, it is the responsibility of administrators to see that resources are expended for the programs they believe have the highest priorities. The head of one of the larger agencies indicated that when he goes to Congress with a request for an increase in his agency's budget, he must always be ready to admit that the increase will finance work of lower priority than is already being done; otherwise he will be criticized because he has not already transferred funds to the higher priority activities. Nearly all agencies have many more programs than they can undertake or expand with the funds they have or are likely to get; they are not likely therefore, to allow an obsolete program to continue to drain resources from programs they deem more worth while.[14] Even those interested in expanding their organizations can seek expansion of those programs they believe most worth while.

The main reason that budgetary outcomes were not very different, however, is that the process by which budgets are calculated and justified is only one—and by no means the most important—determinant of program size, distribution, and content. Budget officials, particularly at the departmental level, continually qualified their remarks by saying that, after all, "The zero-base budget didn't affect the basic economic and political facts of life." There are mandatory programs like price supports for which expenditures must be made and which cannot be easily altered. The level of programs may depend a great deal on the state of the national economy (for service programs), on the existing state of knowledge and the availability of trained personnel (for research programs), and not on how programs are analyzed or written up. As many officials pointedly remarked, "Decisions are made on criteria other than the justification of the program itself. Frequently the figures are based on judgment factors of what the environment will permit taken in total." Whether political support exists for a program depends on party alignments in Congress and the executive branch, the preferences of the President, Director of the Budget, members of appropriations committees and other officials, and the activities of clientele groups. Budget people are well aware, for example, that the best possible justification may have little influence against a powerful budget-cutting drive. These factors find no place in the zero-base approach; therefore in a budgetary system in which there is necessarily much emphasis on "what will go,"[15] a zero-base approach will not necessarily make much difference.

Although there was widespread agreement that the zero-base budget did not significantly affect outcomes, nearly half of those interviewed commented quite favorably on the experience after it was over. Was this merely a show of bureaucratic loyalty or were there other reasons for the favorable attitude? This unexpected finding led us to ask further questions, which produced perhaps the most interesting findings in the study.

UNANTICIPATED CONSEQUENCES

Activities may have outcomes which are unanticipated, even unperceived, by the participants in the activity.[16] The preparation of a zero-base budget resulted in a number of unanticipated consequences, which were probably more important (and certainly more interesting) than its expected results.

One of the difficulties faced by reflective people engaged in budgeting is that they hold implicit beliefs about desirable methods of calculations —comprehensive and simultaneous evaluation of means and ends being considered as synonymous with rationality—while they practice quite different—incremental and sequential—methods. For the large minority who expressed positive feelings about zero-base budgeting, the experience appears to have satisfied a longing to believe that they were proceeding according to the canons of rational methods of calculation. When asked why they liked zero-base budgeting, they would answer by describing the method and pronouncing it good: "Considering everything from the ground up at the same time is, well, good, the right way to do it, and not just letting things grow like Topsy." "The major benefit may well have been the much more intensive, thoroughgoing review, from the bottom up." But if the zero-base budget did not lead to changes, did they perhaps learn more?

Here there was a sharp split in the responses of the large minority that approved of the zero-base budget. Some respondents claimed that they learned nothing new; they had known about all their operations before. How, then, was the zero-base budget helpful? Agency personnel answered that the department people must have benefited; department-level personnel answered that agency personnel had benefited. "The zero-base budget," said an agency man, was "enlightening to department officials who reviewed it. To us it was just an exercise." "We knew what was going on," department officials would say. "It was helpful in the agencies. I can't prove this, but I have no doubt that things turned up in the agencies that were never passed on." A variant of this argument was taken by an agency head: "I don't know that I personally learned anything new or different. But some of my staff who prepared material for me had clearer presentations than in other years." For these officials, the zero-base budget was good because it benefited other people.

The rest of the administrators who were favorably disposed toward zero-base budgeting did feel that they learned something new. Without exception these people had been in their positions less than three years and had not yet discovered how useful participation in budgeting and perusal of budgetary material could be in adding to their store of information. "I think everyone came out of this process with a great deal more information than they'd ever had before," a new appointee declared. "I went through all of the material, spent more time on budgeting than before [the previous two years], learned more about the scope of operations." Like others in his position, he knew what programs were being undertaken, but in some cases he had not realized the full extent of the operations until he read the budgetary data.

If this was the case, why did these officials not make use of the knowledge they had gained to alter their preferences or otherwise make somewhat different decisions? An important clue was furnished by one of these "learners" who remarked: "Some of these things I wouldn't have needed to know." Indeed, further questioning revealed that much of what was learned was simply not appropriate to the kinds of choices available to these men or, at least, was not perceived by them as being relevant in the context in which they operated.

Those who disliked the zero-base budget complained that they had done a lot of extra work, yet nothing had been changed as a result of their endeavors. Far from being unhappy at the absence of significant changes in their budgets, however, those who liked the zero-base budget seemed to find positive advantage in this circumstance. One official explained, the zero-base budget was good because "it tended to confirm what you had a notion of otherwise." It felt good "to satisfy yourself that you're doing a conscientious job," said another official, "instead of following the inevitable least resistance, less deep analysis, of the increases and decreases approach." The happy coincidence of making up a proper budget was a morale booster. Before they had come to the department they had heard complaints that many of its programs were wasteful and unnecessary. Now that it had been demonstrated in detail just what the Department of Agriculture was doing and why, they were more certain of the necessity of the programs for which they were responsible.[17] The strength of this feeling may go a long way toward explaining their favorable reaction to the zero-base budget and all its extra work— even—indeed, *especially* when few changes were made as a result of it.

The zero-base budget experiment had focused attention on the budgetary process. For the first time in many years, a Secretary of Agriculture had attended department budget hearings and had made it known that he considered budgeting of primary importance. As a 'result, many officials informed us that, "There was a higher interest in budgeting than ever before." Much more time was spent on budgeting: "I worked ninety hours a week and still didn't have nearly enough time." "A tremendous number of man-hours were involved. I spent at least twice as much time on budgeting this year, lots of Saturdays and evenings." Budget people discovered that their function was rated more highly as program people became more involved in budgeting and were "forced . . . to sit down and justify their programs." And, as program personnel worked on budget justifications, they liked the feeling of being more involved in their activities regardless of whether they wanted to change them. They might well have learned as much (or more) in other years if they had spent as much time and energy on budgeting. The zero-base approach had value here not so much because it was necessarily a better way of planning a budget, but because it was a *different* one which prompted them to focus their attention on budgeting.

A large part of the felt benefits of engaging in zero-base budgeting may stem, therefore, from the well-known Hawthorne effect[18] in which the content of the experiment is less important than the fact that the sense of importance of those engaged in the experiment is enhanced. Greater interest and attention is devoted to the activity in question and the people who engage in it. Consequently, they feel that others are more interested in them and that, perhaps, their problems are in some sense better understood, regardless of whether this understanding is objectively real or leads to specific consequences for the pattern of decisions. Thus agency people felt good at being able to educate their departmental superiors. Top departmental officials believed that the zero-base approach helped agency people see their work in perspective. Through being compelled to justify the existence of their agency's programs, they would see how it fit into the total operations carried out by the Department of Agriculture. This line of reasoning may help explain why many officials were certain that the zero-base approach had helped people at other levels in the hierarchy, even if they were unable to suggest any way in which it had helped them.

POLITICAL USE OF BUDGET

Our analysis would not be complete without noting that the zero-base method of budgeting—whose advocates present it as a means of focusing on costs and benefits rather than on political maneuvering—was used for strategic purposes, thereby enhancing its appeal to some officials. They felt that the zero-base procedure was useful in dealing with the Bureau of the Budget and the appropriations committees. "We've examined these requests from the ground up," they would say in justifying their requests as "solid" and not subject to cuts. By stating that the desirability of changes had emerged from the zero-base analysis, several officials had the opportunity to call attention to changes they had wanted in previous years. In this way one agency was able' to get approval for building funds denied the previous year. In general, the zero-base experiment helped those who had previously decided they wanted to review a program by providing them with an excellent reason for not delaying the review. Resistance to providing essential information was overcome to some extent because top agency officials "were armed with weapons which forced . . . the disgorging of the information they needed to get. . . . This is often like pulling teeth." And having proposed the change they had in mind, the responsible officials could use the belief that the zero-base approach was more rational to make their colleagues more amenable to the change.

ATTITUDE TOWARD ANNUAL ZERO-BASE BUDGET

No one suggested that the zero-base approach be followed every year. Among those who felt that the experiment should be repeated, the most common suggestions were: "not every year periodically," "at intervals, every few years," or "every five years or so." Since new officials would stand to benefit the most, such officials reasoned, a zero-base budget would be useful only with changes in administration. Another view was that budgets changed little from year to year, so that an annual zero-base budget would result in "duplicating the same pages." The authors were cautioned to "remember that the budgetary process is not the only decision-making process for setting policy. Parts of operations are considered through other channels all the time." The general conclusion was that the zero-base method might be useful every five years "for a reference document," or "to find out where you are now," or so "we'll have a more recent base." It is apparent that even those who found some use for the zero-base approach began to assimilate it to the more familiar incremental method. They would use it from time to time to "take inventory," as one put it, and then take their bearings for the immediate future from that date.

RECOMMENDATIONS

No one, least of all the authors, would claim that an innovation like zero-base budgeting, which was confined to a single department for a single year, can be conclusively evaluated on the basis of this experience alone. Since this was the only experiment of its kind, however, it seems desirable to attempt at least a tentative appraisal. The first conclusion would be that comprehensive budgeting vastly overestimates man's limited ability to calculate and grossly underestimates the importance of political and technological constraints. The required calculations could not be made and would not have led to substantial changes. As a result, a great deal of effort went into zero-base budgeting with few specific changes attributable to this costly method.[19]

Had much more time been available, it might have been possible for the department to develop work-load measures for more programs. With more time and experience, the initial confusion might also have been overcome; but the basic problem of the zero-base budget still would not have been solved. In order to compare activities on a department-wide basis under a zero-base budget, the top officials would have had to develop categories cutting across agency programs, together with methods of relating their costs and benefits. Present methods of calculation are not equal to this task.

Failure to consider the contributions of the existing budgetary process toward calculation distorts the magnitude of the problem. New programs and substantial increases and decreases in old programs do receive close attention. The political system opens up subjects to special scrutiny as interest groups, politicians, or bureaucrats, demand an investigation. What escapes scrutiny is not the whole but only certain parts, which carry on much as before. The fact that certain activities do not receive intensive scrutiny is hardly reason for repeating everything every year. Indeed, we would argue that attempts to do everything are not only self-defeating, they are inefficient in diverting resources from tasks which can be managed and give promise of some results.

We advocate following an incremental approach, making use of the division of labor in government. Attention may be focused on those activities which do not change much from year to year, since these are the ones that may escape periodic review. Since they do not alter radically, a thorough review every four of five years ought to be sufficient. Nor need any one organization do it all. Department budget offices, the bureaus themselves, the Bureau of the Budget, and the House and Senate appropriations subcommittees and their investigating staffs, might use sampling techniques so that they review a few programs of this kind every year.[20] The results could then be used to see if more activity was warranted the next year. In this way a large part of the problem may be met while adding a little to the burden of calculation for any one participant.

Narrowing, fragmenting, and dispersing these budgetary reviews has considerable advantages from the viewpoint of encouraging experimentation and innovation. Because no participant is overburdened, the most thorough analysis is facilitated. More active participation by high-level officials is encouraged because the material to be considered at a given time is not overwhelming. As the knowledge and interest of top officials is fed back down the line, the significance of the activity and the importance of those who engage in it is likely to be enhanced. If these reviews can be freed from the peak periods of the formal budgetary cycle, the absence of immediate deadlines may encourage speculation and experimentation, while the increased probability of hierarchical superiors having time to listen would give promise that the efforts might lead to tangible results. The variety of organizations involved should also lead to consideration of a broad range of values and perspectives.

Although it may be useful at times to compel alterations in customary modes of analysis, there are possibilities other than comprehensive budgeting. One could move in the opposite direction and try a more radical version of incremental budgeting.[21] Instead of doing even a minimum amount of budgeting for programs that change little from year to year, these programs might be neglected for several years and efforts of the agency might be devoted to only a few major programs at a time. By shifting the emphasis every few years, it would be possible to direct the agency's efforts toward those programs that are undergoing the greatest amount of change and in which it is feasible to effect changes. Attention would thus be directed at those parts of the agency's budget which promise the greatest results from intensive analysis.

NOTES

[1]We would like to thank the many officials in the Department of Agri-

culture whose generosity, time, and knowledge made this study possible. Thanks are also due to Rufus Browning, Jesse Burkhead, Tom Blaisdell, Richard Fenno, Irving Fox, Frederick Mosher, Nelson Polsby, Allen Schick, and Larry Wade for criticizing various drafts of the manuscript, but we alone are responsible for the work presented here. The work was done while the senior author was a research fellow at Resources for the Future in Washington, D.C. The term "agency" refers to bureaus and other sub-units in the Department of Agriculture.

[2]See Wildavsky, "Calculations" in *The Politics of the Budgetary Process* (Boston: Little, Brown, 1964), ch. ii, pp. 6–62.

[3]See, for example, W. F. Willoughby, *The Problem of a National Budget* (New York: D. Appleton, 1918); A. E. Buck, *Public Budgeting* (New York: Harper, 1929); Commission on the Organization of the Executive Branch of the Government, *Budgeting and Accounting* (Washington, D.C.: U.S. Gov't. Printing Office, 1949); Jesse Burkhead, *Government Budgeting* (New York: Wiley, 1956); Arthur Smithies, *The Budgetary Process in the United States* (New York: McGraw-Hill, 1955); and Edward A. Kolodziez, "Congressional Responsibility for the Common Defense: The Money Problem," *The Western Political Quarterly*, 16 (March 1963), p. 149–160.

[4]"Quoted with evident approval by A. E. Buck in *The Budget in Governments of Today* (New York: Macmillan, 1934), p. 172.

[5]"Some Shortcomings of Present Budgetary Practice," *Toward Better Budgeting* (Detroit: Governmental Research Association, 1941), p. 6.

[6]*Op. Cit.,* p. 16.

[7]U. S. Senate, Committee on Government Operations, Subcommittee on National Policy Machinery, *Hearings Organizing for National Security; The Budget and the Policy Process*, 87th Congress, 1st. Session, 1961, p. 1107.

[8]David Braybrooke and Charles E. Lindblom, *A Strategy of Decision* (New York: The Free Press, 1963); also Lindblom's "Decision-Making in Taxation and Expenditure," in *Public Finances: Needs, Sources, Utilization* (Princeton: National Bureau of Economic Research, 1961), pp. 295–336.

[9]See Patricia L. Kendall and Katherine M. Wolf, "The Two Purposes of Deviant Case Analyses," in P. F. Lazarsfeld and Morris Rosenberg, *The Language of Social Research* (Glencoe, Ill.: The Free Press, 1955), pp. 167–170. For excellent examples of the insight to be derived from an unusual case, see Herbert A. Simon, "Birth of an Organization: The Economic Cooperation Administration," *Public Administration Review*, 13 (1953), 227–236, and S. M. Lipset, M. A. Trow, and J. S. Coleman, *Union Democracy* (Glencoe, Ill.: The Free Press, 1956).

[10]Thomas Flinn, *Governor Freeman and the Minnesota Budget,* Inter-University Case Program. No. 60 (University of Alabama, 1961).

[11]It should be clearly understood that this approach was being tried only at the Department of Agriculture and not in the Budget Bureau or Congress. As the "Instructions" pointed out, "Since it is anticipated that the Department Estimates for 1964 will be submitted to the Budget Bureau in accordance with existing . . . instructions, the justifications . . . will be primarily in terms of changes from 1963." Thus a list of "Increases and Decreases, 1964, Compared with Latest Estimate, 1963," was also requested of each agency.

[12]An official at the department level writes that this "sentence . . . appears to . . . contain an erroneous conclusion. As the author of the sentence referred to, I can clearly recall that at the time we very explicitly rejected the proposition that zero-base budgeting as such necessarily had to take place without regard to over-all limitations on financial resources. I felt then, and still feel, that the 'ceiling' technique and zero-base budget development and justification are logically compatible. As the article points out, the zero-base budget approach that was used involved not only the question of whether or not work should be done but also the amount of work proposed and the price tags. Each of these aspects is logically a variable but can be adjusted within a program or between programs in the light of over-all available resources. The reason the sentence was included in the instructions (and in a sense it was superfluous) was merely to make it very explicit to the agencies that we were not making the assumption that the budget-decision making system would suddenly tolerate all 'justifiable' expenditures merely by virtue of a change in the technique of presenting the budget, and that the Secretary in fact had an over-all objective that he wished to attain with respect to the department as a whole. The sentence, of course, was not intended to mean, and did not mean, that the objective applied to each individual program and activity separately."

[13]The secretary and his staff, the six assistant secretaries and their staff assistants, and the Director of Budget and Finance and his staff.

[14]See the statement to this effect by the late William A. Jump, a noted budget officer in the Department of Agriculture, quoted in Wildavsky, *op. cit.,* pp. 23–24.

[15]Wildavsky, "Deciding How Much to Ask For," in *op. cit.* pp. 21–31. Despite our stress on the political aspects of budgeting, more than one official wrote: "Greater emphasis perhaps could also have been placed on the importance of the political imperative on the budgetary process.

At the point that budgeting begins, i.e., gathering of base information, there is often only meager guidance on economic and other assumptions on which to base estimates which are compatible with sound practices. This guidance consists of admonitions to be economy-minded—guidance which may become meaningless if interest in program emphasis suddenly increases."

[16]See Robert K. Merton, "Manifest and Latent Functions," in *Social Theory and Social Structure* (Glencoe, Ill.: The Free Press, 1957), pp. 19–04. We have avoided use of Merton's "manifest and latent function" because functional analysis has some inappropriate implications for this paper.

[17]The reassurance function of the zero-base budget is clear from two quotations. A newcomer said:

"Coming into a big department like this you need landmarks on which to justify your own opinions of the budget. This is difficult when the budget this year is based on last year which is based on the year before. You sometimes had the feeling that they were building it like a sort of poor skyscraper, piling on more and more steel, without knowing where the building was headed. [After the zero-base budget] you had the feeling that you understood the programs better . . . and had more confidence in the value of the services being performed."

An old-timer in the department confirmed this view and gave it a special twist in terms of the functions performed for the agencies:

"When new administrators come in, they see things they didn't know the Department of Agriculture was doing. They figure this is just the top of the iceberg and get worried. If you take the whole iceberg out of the water and drop it on their desks, and they're too overwhelmed to look at it, they don't have an excuse to nag you anymore. This is the major benefit from the agency point of view: to the extent that their superiors looked at the stuff they were reassured; to the extent they didn't, they no longer have an excuse to nag them [the agencies]."

[18]Elton Mayo, *The Social Problems of an Industrial Civilization* (Cambridge: Graduate School of Business Administration, Harvard University, 1945); Fritz Roethlisberger, *Management and Morale* (Cambridge: Harvard, 1941).

[19]If one makes the conservative estimate that at least 1,000 administrators above the level of clerk-typist and messenger were involved in bringing together parts of the zero-base budget throughout the Department of Agriculture and its many field offices, and that they spent an average of thirty hours a week for six weeks preparing the data, above

and beyond their usual budgetary work, then at least 180,000 man-hours may be charged directly to this activity. With the generous estimate that $200,000 worth of changes (without going into their desirability) can be attributed to the zero-base budget, it appears that the government achieved a return of something more than one dollar per hour (leaving out the cost of facilities, paper, clerical help, and depreciation of human talent). Nor do we know what these officials missed in terms of opportunities foregone during the time they worked on the zero-base budget. The point is not that the reader should place too much credence in these estimates (respondents differ as to whether we are too high or too low) but rather that according to any reasonable estimate the return to the government would be very small. Had anything like the same amount of effort been devoted to studies of filing, the flow of paper, or similar operations, much greater returns might have been achieved. Since half of these men were not usually involved in budgeting, however, there might well have been important intangible benefits that we have not taken into account.

One respondent went further and wrote: "The author might find it advisable or worthwhile to really set about analyzing the present cost of budget preparation and justification throughout its entire process. While this is an important activity, there is little written evidence as [to] the resources going into the preparation and justification of agency budgets within the Department, the Bureau of the Budget, and the Congress of the United States. A careful analysis might reveal that possible shorter steps or involvement by fewer people would be in order."

[20]"It has been my experience during 27 years of government employment," an official writes, "that what you propose is frequently and regularly taking place in Department budget offices and in the bureaus . . . whether or not [it is] recognized and with little publicity."

[21]See Wildavsky, "Toward a Radical Incrementalism: A Proposal to Aid Congress in Reform of the Budgetary Process" (Mimeo, 1965).

IV.
THE PPB APPROACH
TO BUDGETING

8.
Program Budgeting—
Applying Economic Analysis
to Government Expenditure Decisions*

MURRAY L. WEIDENBAUM

A fundamental shift is occurring in the focus of *public finance*. As recently as the early 1950's, the textbooks in the field primarily dealt with taxation; a few chapters were devoted to debt and fiscal policy and perhaps a section described the mechanics of governmental budgeting.

The pendulum now appears to be swinging sharply. Recently the emphasis in public finance has been on the expenditure side in attempting to apply economic analysis to governmental expenditure decisions. Benefit/cost comparisons, cost/effectiveness analysis, and *program budgeting* all have become important manifestations of this shift. The most recent and ambitious operational effort along these lines is the Planning-Programming-Budgeting System of the federal government which may, in retrospect, represent a major advance in the application of economic analysis to public sector decision-making.

This article deals mainly with this new development, but in doing so the antecedent efforts will be related to the current budget reform movement. And possible future changes will also be indicated.

On August 25, 1965, President Johnson announced

. . . a very new and very revolutionary system of planning and programming and budgeting throughout the vast federal government—so that through the tools of modern management the full promise of a finer life can be brought to every American at the lowest possible cost.[1]

---

*Reprinted from Murray L. Weidenbaum, "Program Budgeting—Applying Economic Analysis to Government Expenditure Decisions," *Business and Government Review*, 7:4 (July-August, 1966), 22–31, by permission of the author and publisher. Murray L. Weidenbaum is chairman of the Department of Economics at Washington University, St. Louis, Missouri.

Before evaluating this governmental innovation, it may be useful to see how earlier developments in the economic analysis of governmental expenditure decisions relate to it. We may then be in a better position to evaluate the "new" and "revolutionary" aspects of the Planning-Programming-Budget System, or PPBS, as it is commonly called.

ANTECEDENTS OF PPBS

Economists have long been interested in identifying policies that would promote economic welfare, specifically by improving the efficiency with which a society uses its resources. Governmental budgeting provides one important example of this concern.

For a good many years benefit/cost analysis has been applied by a few federal agencies, particularly the Corps of Engineers and the Bureau of Reclamation, to the evaluation of prospective projects. Despite important operational difficulties, such as choosing an appropriate discount rate which would correspond to a realistic estimate of the social cost of capital, the use of benefit/cost analysis has improved the allocation of government resources.

It has served as a partial screening device to eliminate obviously unec-

Table 1
TYPICAL B/C ANALYSIS
Water Resource Development Project

	Amortization Period	
	50 yrs.	100 yrs.
	(Thous.)	
Investments		
Total	$3,100	$3,100
Annual Costs		
Interest & amortization	$123.4	$101.6
Operation, maintenance, etc.	25.4	25.9
Total	$148.8	$127.5
Annual Benefits		
Flood damage reduction	$168.0	$206.0
Fish, wildlife, & recreation	32.8	35.5
Total	$200.8	$241.5
Benefit-Cost Ratio		
Ratio	1.4	1.9

onomical projects—those whose prospective gains are less than estimated costs. It also has provided some basis for ranking and comparing projects and choosing among alternatives.[2] Perhaps the overriding value of benefit/cost analysis has been in demonstrating the importance of making fairly objective economic analyses of proposed essentially political actions and perhaps narrowing the area in which political forces may operate.

New Pentagon Program

A related development has been the application of cost/effectiveness or cost/utility analysis to military budget decision-making. Much of the development effort was performed at the Rand Corporation under Air Force auspices.[3] For military programs, ordinarily the benefits or results cannot be expressed in dollar terms. However, the end objective, such as the capability to destroy X number of enemy targets under stipulated conditions, can be expressed in quantitative terms. And, more important, the alternative methods of achieving the objective—Y bombers versus Z missiles or some combination—can be priced out and a *least cost* solution arrived at.

This approach has been at the heart of the Planning-Programming-Budgeting System introduced in the Pentagon so successfully by Secretary McNamara and economists Hitch, Enthoven and their associates. It clearly has been the success of the McNamara approach which has led to adoption of a government-wide PPBS effort.

Table 2 illustrates the fundamental shift that has occurred in military resource allocation. Under the old or pre-McNamara system, each service competed for a larger share of the defense budget and, within the service totals, strategic weapons such as ICBM's competed for funds with tactical programs. Under the new system, close substitutes for performing the same or similar mission are compared with each other, such as ICBM's and submarine launched strategic missiles, although different services are involved.

Performance Budgeting

One other development needs to be acknowledged, in sketching out the origin of the current program budgeting effort, and that is the work on performance budgeting encouraged by the two Hoover Commissions and implemented in part by the United States Bureau of the Budget. By a performance budget the Hoover Commission meant " . . . a budget based upon functions, activities, and projects. . . ." Such an ap-

Table 2

SHIFT IN MILITARY RESOURCE ALLOCATION

Old Budget System	New Planning-Budgeting System
Navy	*Strategic forces*
Polaris	Polaris
Marine Corps	ICBM's
Carrier task forces	Long range bombers
Air Force	*General purpose forces*
ICBM's	Marine Corps
Tactical aircraft	Armored divisions
Air defense aircraft	Tactical aircraft
Long range bombers	Carrier task forces
Army	*Continental defense forces*
Air defense missiles	Air defense aircraft
Armored divisions	Air defense missiles

proach, it was contended, would focus attention on the general character and relative importance of the work to be done, rather than upon the things to be acquired.[4] Although it may not appear so, this was a fundamental shift in budgetary thinking at the federal level. Less of the budgetary detail was to be devoted to changes in numbers and types of clerical personnel and office supply usage and more attention given to the activities to be performed. However, implementation was slow and only partial.

The current emphasis on program budgeting may represent the delayed fulfillment of the Hoover Commission recommendation. As we will see, cost/benefit and cost/effectiveness analysis also play important parts in this new budgetary approach.

MECHANICS OF PPBS

The Planning-Programming-Budgeting System which each major federal department and agency is now setting up, in response to the directive from President Johnson, is patterned on the Pentagon approach. It is being developed by the Bureau of the Budget working with the various federal departments and agencies charged with implementation. The entire system is new and its structure has barely been developed or put into operation. Hence, it should be recognized that it is somewhat hazardous to attempt a description, much less an evaluation now.

PPBS is based, according to the Bureau of the Budget, on the introduction of three major concepts into federal government operations:[5]

1. *The development in each government agency of an analytical capability to examine in depth both agency objectives and the various programs to meet these objectives.*

   This is hardly the traditional "green-eye-shade" type of approach to financial management and may be far more difficult to accomplish. However, this does widen the frame of reference of governmental management officials and sets the stage for the next steps.

2. *The formation of a five-year planning and programming process coupled with a sophisticated management information system.*

   This should yield an improved basis for decision-making by department heads and the President in that it is designed to provide a comprehensive framework for acting on the myriad of questions that face the management of an organization, public or private.

3. *The last and perhaps fundamental concept to be introduced is the creation of an improved budgeting mechanism which can take broad program decisions,*

Figure 1

THE FEDERAL BUDGET ANNUAL CYCLE

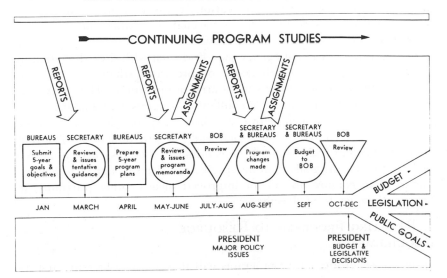

translate them into more refined decisions in a budgetary context, and present the results for Presidential and congressional action.

This may be more of a statement of ultimate desire and long-term objective to be achieved.

Through the combined planning and budgeting process, it is hoped that broad national goals will be reduced to specific program operations and the most economical method of carrying them out identified. Four major steps have been identified which will need to be taken to accomplish this rather tall order.

1. IDENTIFYING NATIONAL GOALS

The specific goals which are deemed proper and appropriate for the federal government to be seeking will somehow have to be selected in the light of a comprehensive evaluation of national needs and objectives. This is now beginning to get underway in each major department and agency; and there is little indication of the formal methodology, if any, which is employed or available at this step of the process.

2. RELATING BROAD GOALS TO SPECIFIC PROGRAMS

Specific alternative programs which may help to achieve the broad national goals and objectives will then be examined. The ones that appear to be most promising, given the various constraints under which the government operates, will have to be selected. The subject of constraints is not one to be passed over too quickly.

The typical government agency may find itself with little discretion in selecting the optimum combination of programs which can assist in achieving broad national goals in its area of operations. They may well find that there is little, vague, or conflicting congressional guidance as to the goals to be attained. However, there may be clear and precise congressional directive as to which specific programs—and in what amounts and particulars—are to be conducted. The task here may well be both to infer the goals from the specific programs Congress authorized and then to conjure up new or improved means (other programs) to achieve these goals or objectives.

3. RELATING PROGRAMS TO RESOURCE REQUIREMENTS

Specific costs of alternative programs will then need to be estimated (in terms of total resources they would require) in order to compare their efficiency in achieving the goals. To those acquainted with benefit/cost or cost/utility analysis, this will be no mean achievement in many illusive program areas. All sorts of specific techniques come to mind here, as well as more informal examinations with less quantification.

In view of the many theoretical and operational shortcomings of these tools, the user will need to keep in mind that the basic purpose of any of these techniques is the carrying out of broad systems analyses in which alternative programs are compared, with respect to both the costs to be incurred and the gains to be achieved. Recent attempts to apply benefit/cost analysis to fields other than water resources (such as health, education, transportation, and research) reveal the host of pitfalls and shortcomings of available techniques and methodology.

4. RELATING THE RESOURCE INPUTS TO BUDGET DOLLARS

Finally, the manpower, facilities, and other source requirements will need to be translated into budget dollars—all projected several years ahead—so that the costs of the programs can be analyzed over a meaningful period and decisions made to implement the PPBS results. This sounds much easier than it is likely to be in practice. To cite one among numerous possibilities, one may wonder as to how the externalities involved—especially non-federal costs—will be handled. Nevertheless, this four-step procedure sounds both necessary and desirable.

Perhaps the most essential ingredient—and one not prominently mentioned in the available materials on PPBS—is the acceptance, at each line and staff level, of the value of, and need for, the tremendous amount of detail and effort being imposed.[6] To some degree this is inherently both subjective and circular. The better the quality of input into the system, the greater the likelihood of good results. But it will be the value of the results that justify the substantial expenditure (perhaps investment is a more appropriate term) in time and effort involved.

The parallel here, to the introduction of PPBS at the Pentagon, may not be complete. The persons involved in that operation had spent many years at such organizations as Rand where they became intimately knowledgeable of military concepts, organization, requirements, and constraints. They had:

Developed specific methodology for making military systems analysis.
Identified the key points of budgetary decision-making (the selection of weapon systems).

Developed specific formats and concepts for making comparisons among alternative systems, including a sophisticated methodology for costing out alternatives.

One may wonder where the civilian government counterparts of these defense PPBS personnel will come from. The answer is neither obvious nor clear.

FRAMEWORK OF THE SYSTEM

The main product of PPBS is designed to be a comprehensive multi-year program and financial plan for each government agency, which will be updated periodically and systematically. An early and essential step is determining for each the output-oriented categories which cover its total work and area of responsibility.[7] Such a mission-oriented or objectives-oriented program format would be in sharp contrast with present practice—which focuses on the increase in funds over the previous year's budget required to meet rises in the annual expenses of the agency. Thus the present budget review is oriented to organizational units and to inputs such as wages, travel costs, and office equipment.

The *first* level of detail or breakdown in preparing the program and financial plan is termed Program Categories, which are groupings of a department's activities serving the same broad objective or mission. For example, one such broad program objective may be considered to be improvement of higher education. This program category might contain such federal programs as aid to undergraduate, graduate, and vocational education, as well as such auxiliary activities as library support and research assistance.

The *second* level of information is the program sub-categories. These combine activities on the basis of somewhat narrower objectives contributing directly to the broad purposes of the program category as a whole. Thus, expansion of engineering and science training could be a program sub-category within the program category, "improvement of higher education."

The *third* level of detail is the program element, which is the basic building block of the PPBS structure. An element may be a specific product that contributes to the program's objectives. An element could include personnel as well as equipment and facilities. An example of a program element expressed in terms of the objectives served would be the number of teachers to be trained in using the new mathematics as a part of "improvement of elementary education."

OUTPUT MEASUREMENT PROBLEMS

Many difficulties are involved in selecting the measurement of output or performance of a program. Conceptually, only the end-product should be measured rather than intermediate outputs. For example, in the Post Office Department, the end product might reflect the number of letters delivered, and not the number of times these letters were handled at the various stages of their journey.

Similarly, in the case of hospital programs, it may be possible to look at output in terms of patient-days. However, the mission of a hospital might be described better as proper treatment of patients rather than the generation of a number of patient-days. Within a broader framework, the mission of a health program might be viewed as promotion and maintenance of good health and the output measure might reflect prevention of diseases as well as treatment.[8] Legend has it that in better days Chinese patients paid their doctors in times of health and not of illness—a high mark of *output* rather than *input* orientation.

The Bureau of the Budget (the official custodian of PPBS) itself on occasion may mistake the nature of governmental output. In the February 21, 1966 supplement to the PPBS directive, it lists "training *costs* per worker" (italics supplied) as a possible means of measuring output!

The agencies are encouraged to consider comparisons and possible trade-offs among program elements which are close substitutes, even though the activities may be conducted in different bureaus. This attempt to introduce some element of competition is designed to achieve greater effectiveness from the limited budgetary resources utilized for a given program category or sub-category.

EXTENDING THE TIME HORIZON

In sharp contrast to historical budgeting for the next twelve-month fiscal period, PPBS is intended to extend usually five years into the future. In some cases, such as timber production and multiple-purpose water resource projects, longer time-spans may be more appropriate.

Table 3 is a hypothetical sketch of this new approach. Transportation is a good example of a major program category which consists of a variety of activities in different departments, with little attention to gaps or overlapping functions or conflicting objectives.

Major agencies involved are the Bureau of Public Roads and the Maritime Administration in the Department of Commerce, the Federal Avia-

Table 3
ILLUSTRATIVE OUTLINE*
Of a National Transportation Program

Elements

GENERAL INTER-CITY TRANSPORT

Interstate Highways

Interstate Highway Program
Primary System Highways

Domestic Water Transport

Inland Waterways Facilities
Maritime Programs

Aviation

CAB Subsidies to Airlines
FAA and NASA Aircraft Technology

URBAN COMMUTER TRANSPORTATION

Urban Highway Systems
Urban Transit Systems

RURAL ACCESS

Secondary System—Roads
Forest, Public Lands, National Parks Roads
Aid to Local Service Aviation

MILITARY STANDBY TRANSPORTATION

*Columns are provided on the right of the form for fiscal years 1967, 68, 69, 70, 71, 72.

tion Agency, the Corps of Engineers in the Department of the Army, the Forest Service in the Department of Agriculture, the National Park Service in the Department of the Interior, the mass transit assistance program in the Department of Housing and Urban Development, plus a number of regulatory operations, such as the ICC, CAB, Federal Maritime Board, and the Coast Guard among others. Significantly, only a few of these agencies are scheduled to be absorbed by the proposed Federal Department of Transportation.

Table 4 illustrates the possible specific elements which might comprise one of the transportation sub-categories—urban commuter transportation. These elements may vary from the number of miles of way placed under construction (a measure of capital investment) to the number of ton-miles of freight carried (a measure of utilization).

I would doubt whether, in its initial stages, the Planning-Programming-Budgeting System is able to do much toward rationalizing the whole gamut of federal transportation programs. Presumably the current em-

Table 4

COMMUTER TRANSPORTATION
Illustrated Elements of a Transportation
Program Category

	Data
Urban Highways	
Passenger-miles carried	*
Ton-miles of freight carried	*
Miles of way completed	*
Miles of way placed under construction	*
Urban transit system	
Passenger-miles carried	*
Ton-miles of freight carried	*
Miles of way completed	*
Miles of way placed under construction	*

From the above information, comparisons could be made between urban highways and urban transit systems in terms of:
1. Capital cost per mile of way.
2. Operating cost per mile of way.
3. Average commuter travel time per mile of way.

phasis is on improving the "building blocks," the difficult task of evaluating the individual components. Nevertheless, tables 3 and 4 are indicative of the broader horizons of the new breed of budgeteers and represents an initial small step along a relatively new path in governmental resource allocation.

LONG-TERM IMPACTS

Assuming that some aspects of PPBS do increasingly become operational—at the departmental, then bureau, and then program level—the decision-making process in the government ultimately may undergo substantial change. With the introduction of sophisticated managerial tools such as benefit/cost, cost/utility, and systems analysis generally, there will be a reduced tendency for decisions on authorizing and financing individual government programs to be made in isolation and solely on the basis of subjective, intuitive judgments. Of course, the computers will not replace managers in making decisions, nor will staff analysts replace line management.

Changes may well occur both in the types of government officials hired and promoted and in the kinds of considerations and information they need to deal with. Nevertheless, even after the implementation of PPBS at the congressional level—which is proceeding at a much slower pace than in the Executive Branch—political consideration will continue to play key roles.

GREATER ECONOMIC RETURN

It is possible that the composition of the federal budget will shift substantially as a result. On the basis of preliminary work, it appears that benefit/cost and similar analyses increasingly will show that certain government programs yield a greater economic return (dollar benefit to the nation) than do others.

Federal expenditures for education, training and retraining, and health —so-called investments in "human" resources—are likely to yield estimated benefits substantially in excess of total costs. In contrast, some more traditional construction-oriented activities, notably irrigation, power and other multipurpose water resource projects, are likely to show up far less favorably in this regard. Hence, some shifts from "physical" to "human" capital investment are likely to take place in the federal budget, as PPBS enfolds its long-term influence on the government and the economy.[9]

Also, a *demonstration effect* on state and local governments, and on private companies, will occur as expertise is demonstrated by federal civilian agencies in putting into successful practice these planning concepts and techniques. The initial impact may be transmitted via grant-in-aid programs to states and localities and traditional procurement contracts with business firms.

PROSPECTS FOR PPBS

In testimony before a congressional committee shortly after the presidential announcement of PPBS, Budget Director Schultze stated that he did

. . . not want to leave anybody with the idea that what we are doing is some revolutionary change. It really is an improvement in what we are doing now, a systemization and routinization, if you will . . .[10]

Perhaps the revolutionary has become routine in the Great Society.

As almost every knowledgeable person who has examined the usual budgetary process has concluded, major shortcomings are apparent and fundamental improvements needed.[11] For example, there has been little interest in focusing on the goals and objectives of government spending programs or, as a result, on alternative and more effective ways of achieving them. The future costs of present decisions are often ignored. Hence, it is not surprising that formal planning and systems analysis has had limited effect on budget decisions.

The PPBS approach obviously is designed to help remedy these shortcomings. If it succeeds in only a limited way, it will represent a major advance in application of economic analysis to the allocation of public resources. Some initial shortcomings—such as the lack of public availability of the results of the analyses—may be overcome in time.

POSSIBLE DIFFICULTIES

It obviously is premature to judge the liklihood of PPBS succeeding in what it is attempting to do. Will the vast system of reports generate into a wheel-spinning operation, or will the results become a significant factor in public policy formulation? From one viewpoint, it is too ambitious, in that it is attempting to apply economic and systems analysis to all of the vast gamut of civilian government operations simultaneously. Perhaps some pilot studies, or a few test cases in civilian agency work, would have provided a sounder basis on which to proceed.

From another viewpoint, however, the PPBS approach may be failing to come to grips with the larger choices in allocating federal funds among different agencies and programs. "Would a dollar be more wisely spent for education or for public works?" This fundamental question is not raised anywhere in the budgetary process at the present time—nor is it likely to be answered or even raised under the sub-optimizing approach of PPBS.

This apparent satisfaction with sub-optimization is also evident in the historical experience in the two areas where program budgeting and benefit/cost analysis have been most widely used—national defense and water resource development. For example, much effort has gone into comparing proposed ICBM systems with long range bombers as alternative means of fulfilling a strategic (or general war) requirement. Little, if any, attention has been devoted to determining the optimum allocation of the defense budget between strategic forces and limited war (or general purpose) forces. Yet the latter kind of choice may be the critical or fundamental decision in preparing the defense budget.

FUNDAMENTAL QUESTIONS RAISED

Nevertheless, such questions dealing with fundamentals are being raised, in a general way and at the highest levels during the present period of attempting to reduce some expenditures, in order to offset the inflationary impacts of the Viet Nam military buildup. In a recent statement to the National League of Cities, President Johnson urged the mayors to defer or stretch out construction outlays—"I am simply asking you to put first things first." One newspaper commented on this as follows:

What then should be put first? More NASA blast-offs at Cape Kennedy or more youngsters in Head Start and The Job Corps? Better food and better housing or questionable research and development projects?[12]

Perhaps it is inevitable that the formal budget process will continue to fail to come to grips with these basic, but perhaps too elusive, questions. The rule of thumb of budget preparation which I reported to a congressional committee a few years ago still appears to be holding—the smaller and smaller the item the more and more attention is lavished upon it.

In any event, the application of a formalized planning and programming and budgeting mechanism augurs well for extending the use of economic analysis in making governmental expenditure decisions. From one sub-optimization viewpoint, it already has worked wondrously well. The institution of PPBS has resulted in a very brisk labor market in Washington for economists, systems analysts, and possessors of related skills.

NOTES

[1]President Lyndon B. Johnson, announced at a news conference of August 25, 1965 (as reproduced in the *N. Y. Times* of Thursday, August 26, 1965, "Transcript of the President's News Conference on Foreign and Domestic Matters.")

[2]Otto Eckstein, *Water Resource Development: The Economics of Project Evaluation* (Cambridge: Harvard University Press, 1958); John D. Krutilla and Otto Eckstein, *Multiple Purpose River Development* (Baltimore: Johns Hopkins Press, 1958); Roland N. McKean, *Efficiency in Government Through Systems Analysis,* (New York: John Wiley & Sons, 1958).

[3]Charles J. Hitch and Roland N. McKean, *The Economics of Defense in the Nuclear Age* (Cambridge: Harvard University Press, 1960); E. E. Quade, (ed.), *Analysis for Military Decisions* (New York: Rand McNally, 1964).

[4]U. S. Commission on the Organization of the Executive Branch of the Government, *Budgeting and Accounting* (Washington, D.C.: U. S. Government Printing Office, February 1949), pp. 7–12.

[5]This section is drawn from statements by Budget Director Charles J. Schultze in Joint Economic Committee, *Fiscal Policy Issues of the Coming Decade,* Hearings before the Subcommittee on Fiscal Policy, July 1965, pp. 59–96 and Joint Committee on the Organization of the Congress, *Organization of Congress,* Part 12, August–September 1965, pp. 1775–1835.

[6]Cf. David Novick, (ed.), *Program Budgeting* (Cambridge: Harvard University Press, 1965), especially Part III: Implementation and Operation; George A. Steiner, "Program Budgeting, Business Contribution to Government Management," *California Management Review,* Spring 1965, pp. 43–51.

[7]U. S. Bureau of the Budget, *Planning-Programming-Budgeting* (Bulletin No. 66–3, October 12, 1965 and Supplement to Bulletin No. 66–3, February 21, 1966).

[8]Nestor Terleckyj, "Measurement of Output of Federal Government Programs," Lecture at the U.S. Naval Post-Graduate School, Monterey, California, October 29, 1965, p. 7.

[9]Some indications may be obtained from comparing results of benefit/cost and return on investment studies in these respective areas. Cf. Robert H. Haveman, *Water Resource Investment and the Public Interest* (Nashville: Vanderbilt University Press, 1965); Eckstein *op. cit.;* Krutilla and Eckstein, *op. cit.;* Robert Dorfman, (ed.), *Measuring Benefits of Government Investments* (Washington, D.C.: Brookings Institution, 1965); Howard G. Schaller, ed., *Public Expenditure Decisions in the Urban*

Community (Baltimore: Johns Hopkins Press, 1962); Theodore W. Schultz, "Reflections on Investment in Man," *Journal of Political Economy,* October 1962, Part 2, pp. 1-8; Selma J. Mushkin, (ed.), *Economics of Higher Education* (Washington, D.C.: U. S. Department of Health, Education, and Welfare, 1962); Gary Becker, "Underinvestment in College Education?", *American Economic Review,* May 1960.

[10]Statement of Charles J. Schultze, "U.S. Congress, Joint Committee on the Organization of Congress," *Organization of Congress,* Part 12, p. 1799.

[11]Arthur Smithies, *The Budgetary Process in the United States* (New York: McGraw-Hill, 1955); Jesse Burkhead, *Government Budgeting* (New York: John Wiley, 1956); Aaron Wildavsky, *The Politics of the Budgetary Process* (New York: Little, Brown & Co., 1964); Murray L. Weidenbaum and John Saloma, *Congress and the Federal Budget* (Washington, D.C.: American Enterprise Institute, 1965).

[12]"Deflating the Great Society," editorial in *St. Louis Post Dispatch,* April 6, 1966, p. 2B.

9.
The Role of Cost-Utility Analysis in Program Budgeting*

GENE H. FISHER

It may be inferred that program budgeting involves several essential considerations. The primary ones may be summarized under three main headings: structural (or format) aspects, analytical process considerations, and data or information system considerations to support the first two items.

The *structural* aspects of program budgeting are concerned with establishing a set of categories oriented primarily toward "end-product" or "end-objective" activities that are meaningful from a long-range-planning point of view.[1] In such a context emphasis is placed on provision for an extended time horizon—some five, even ten or more, years into the future. These characteristics are in marked contrast to conventional governmental budgeting, which stresses functional and/or object class categories and a very short time horizon.

Analytical process considerations pertain to various study activities conducted as an integral part of the program-budgeting process. The primary objective of this type of analytical effort is to systematically examine alternative courses of action in terms of utility and cost, with a view to clarifying the relevant choices (and their implications) open to the decision-makers in a certain problem area.

Information system considerations are aimed at support of the first two items. There are several senses in which this is important, the primary ones being (1) progress reporting and control and (2) providing data and information to serve as a basis for the analytical process—especially

---

*Reprinted by permission of the publishers from David Novick (ed.), *Program Budgeting: Program Analysis and the Federal Government* (Cambridge, Mass.: Harvard University Press, Copyright by RAND Corporation, 1965), pp. 61–78. Gene H. Fisher is on the staff of The RAND Corporation.

to facilitate the development of estimating relationships that will permit making estimates of benefits and costs of alternative future courses of action.

The present chapter is concerned primarily with the second of the items listed above: analytical process considerations. That an analytical effort is an important part of program budgeting (at least as practiced in the Department of Defense) is made clear in a recent statement by Secretary of Defense McNamara:

As I have pointed out in previous appearances before this committee, in adding to a defense program as large as the one we now have, we soon encounter the law of diminishing returns, where each additional increment of resources used produces a proportionately smaller increment of overall defense capability. While the benefits to be gained from each additional increment cannot be measured with precision, careful cost/effectiveness analyses can greatly assist in eliminating those program proposals which clearly contribute little to our military strength in terms of the costs involved.

This principle is just as applicable to qualitative improvements in weapons systems as it is to quantitative increases in our forces. The relevant question is not only, "Do we want the very best for our military force?", but also, "Is the additional capability truly required and, if so, is this the least costly way of attaining it?"

Let me give you one hypothetical example to illustrate the point. Suppose we have two tactical fighter aircraft which are identical in every important measure of performance, except one—Aircraft A can fly ten miles per hour faster than Aircraft B. However, Aircraft A costs $10,000 more per unit than Aircraft B. Thus, if we need about 1,000 aircraft, the total additional cost would be $10 million.

If we approach this problem from the viewpoint of a given amount of resources, the additional combat effectiveness represented by the greater speed of Aircraft A would have to be weighed against the additional combat effectiveness which the same $10 million could produce if applied to other defense purposes—more Aircraft B, more or better aircraft munitions, or more ships, or even more military family housing. And if we approach the problem from the point of view of a given amount of combat capability, we would have to determine whether that given amount could be achieved at less cost by buying, for example, more of Aircraft B or more aircraft munitions or better munitions, or perhaps surface-to-surface missiles. Thus, the fact that Aircraft A flies ten miles per hour faster than Aircraft B is not conclusive. We still have to determine whether the greater speed is worth the greater cost. This kind of determination is the heart of the planning-programming-budgeting or resources allocation problem within the Defense Department [roman supplied].[2]

Numerous analytical approaches may be used to support the total program-budgeting process. Here we shall focus on one of them: cost-utility analysis. Before turning to this subject, however, a few of the other types of analysis should be noted briefly.

In terms of the types of problems encountered in the total program-budgeting process, perhaps one might think of a wide spectrum going all the way from the most major allocative decisions on the one hand, to progress reporting and control on the other. Major allocative decisions involve such questions as: Should more resources be employed in national security in the future, or in national health programs, or in preservation and development of natural resources, etc.?[3] Ideally, the decision-makers would like to plan to allocate resources in the future so that for a given budget, for example, the estimated marginal return (or utility) in each major area of application would be equal. But this is more easily said than done; and at the current state of analytical art, no one really knows with any precision how the "grand optimum" might be attained. In the main, the analytical tools now available—particularly the quantitative ones—are just not very helpful in dealing directly with such problems. Intuition and judgment are paramount.

At the other end of the spectrum—progress reporting and control—the main problem is to keep track of programs where the major decisions have *already been made,* to try to detect impending difficulties as programs are being implemented, and to initiate remedial actions through a feedback mechanism when programs are deemed likely to get out of control in the future. Numerous techniques are available for dealing with these types of program-management problems. Examples are the following: financial and management accounting techniques;[4] network-type systems for planning, scheduling, progress reporting, and control;[5] critical-path methods (within the framework of a network-type system);[6] Gantt chart techniques for program planning and control;[7] and various program-management reporting and control schemes developed in recent years in the Department of Defense to help program managers in the management of complex weapon system development and production programs.[8]

The area between the ends of the spectrum is a broad and varied one, offering the opportunity for applying a variety of analytical techniques. These techniques are focused primarily on problem areas short of dealing with determination of the "grand optimum," although they can be of real assistance in sharpening the intuition and judgment of decision-makers in grappling with the very broad allocative questions. Technically, this is called "sub-optimization," and it is here that the analytical efforts are likely to have the highest payoff.[9]

In cases where a wide range of alternative future courses of action needs to be examined in a broad sub-optimization context, the main subject of this chapter, cost-utility analysis,[10] may well be the most useful analytical tool. However, in other cases where the sub-optimization context is much narrower and a wide range of alternatives is not available, the problem may be one of examining relatively minor variations *within* an essentially prescribed future course of action. The sub-optimization context may be relatively narrow for numerous reasons—severe political constraints, lack of new technology to provide the basis for a wide range of alternatives, etc. Here, something akin to capital budgeting[11] techniques may be most appropriate.

In many instances, the above mentioned techniques may have to be supplemented by other methods. For example, in numerous major decision problems it is not sufficient to deal only with the *direct* economic consequences of proposed alternative future courses of action, ignoring their possible indirect or spillover effects. In such instances, it may well be vitally important to consider indirect economic effects either on the economy as a whole or on specified regions or sectors of the total economic system. Certain transportation problems involve considerations of this type.[12] Also, in the case of certain national security and space decisions, especially in the higher echelons of the decision hierarchy, it is often necessary to consider possible regional or industry sector economic impacts associated with alternative weapon system development and procurement choices.[13] One way to deal with such problems is through the use of macro-economic models that attempt to take into account key interactions among important components of the economic system: for example, inter-industry (input-output) models for the economy as a whole,[14] and various types of regional models dealing w th parts of the total national economy.[15]

Thus it is clear that numerous analytical methods and techniques exist that may be used to support various facets of the total program-budgeting process. We have dealt with this point at some length to emphasize that the subject of this chapter, cost-utility analysis, is not the only analytical tool that might be used in program budgeting. Let us now turn to our central theme.

WHAT IS COST-UTILITY ANALYSIS?

Attempting to define cost-utility analysis poses somewhat of a semantics problem. Numerous terms in current use convey the same general meaning but have important different meanings to different people:

"cost-benefit analysis," "cost-effectiveness analysis," "systems analysis," "operations research," "operations analysis," etc. Because of such terminological confusion, in this chapter all of these terms are rejected and "cost-utility analysis" is employed instead.

Cost-utility analysis, as envisioned here, may be distinguished by the following major characteristics:

1. A most fundamental characteristic is the systematic examination and comparison of alternative courses of action that might be taken to achieve specified objectives for some future time period. Not only is it important to systematically examine all of the relevant alternatives that can be identified initially, but also to *design additional ones* if those examined are found wanting.[16] Finally, the analysis, particularly if thoroughly and imaginatively done, may at times result in modifications of the initially specified objectives.

2. Critical examination of alternatives typically involves numerous considerations; but the two main ones are assessment of the cost (in the sense of economic resource cost) and the utility (the benefits or gains) pertaining to each of the alternatives being compared to attain the stipulated objectives.

3. The time context is the future (often the distant future—five, ten, or more years).

4. Because of the extended time horizon, the environment is one of uncertainty (very often great uncertainty). Since uncertainty is an important facet of the problem, it should be faced up to and treated explicitly in the analysis. This means, among other things, that wherever possible the analyst should avoid the use of simple expected value models.

5. Usually the context in which the analysis takes place is broad (often very broad) and the environment very complex, with numerous interactions among the key variables in the problem. This means that simple, straightforward solutions are the exception rather than the rule.

6. While quantitative methods of analysis should be used as much as possible, because of items 4 and 5 above,[17] purely quantitative work must often be heavily supplemented by qualitative analysis. In fact, we stress the importance of *good* qualitative work and of using an appropriate combination of quantitative and qualitative methods.

7. Usually the focus is on research and development and/or investment-type decision problems, although operational decisions are sometimes encountered. This does not mean, of course, that operational considerations are ignored in dealing with R&D and investment-type problems.

8. Timeliness is important. A careful, thorough analysis that comes six

months after the critical time of decision may be worth essentially zero, while a less thorough—but thoughtfully done—analysis completed on time may be worth a great deal.

THE PRIMARY PURPOSE OF COST-UTILITY ANALYSIS

In the context being considered in this chapter, let us be very clear about what the main purpose of analysis in general, and cost-utility analysis in particular, really is. Contrary to what some of the more enthusiastic advocates of quantitative analysis may think, we visualize cost-utility analysis as playing a somewhat modest, though very significant, role in the over-all decision-making process. In reality, most major long-range-planning decision problems must ultimately be resolved primarily on the basis of intuition and judgment. We suggest that the main role of analysis should be to try to *sharpen* this intuition and judgment. In practically no case should it be assumed that the results of the analysis will *make* the decision. The really interesting problems are just too difficult, and there are too many intangible (e.g., political, psychological, and sociological) considerations that cannot be taken into account in the analytical process, especially in a quantitative sense. In sum, the analytical process should be directed toward assisting the decision-maker in such a way that (hopefully!) his intuition and judgment are better than it would be without the results of the analysis.[18]

Viewing the objective of cost-utility analysis in this way is likely to put the analyst in a frame of mind that will permit him to be much more useful to the decision-maker than if he takes a more hard-core view. There are two extremes here. On the one hand, it might be argued that the types of long-range-planning decision problems considered in this chapter are just too complex for the current state of analytical art to handle. Therefore, decisions must be made purely on the basis of intuition, judgment, and experience—i.e., the zero analysis position. At the other extreme are those who (naively) think that all problems should be tackled in a purely quantitative fashion, with a view essentially to making the decision. Such a view implies explicit (usually meaning quantitative) calculations of cost and utility for all the alternatives under consideration. This may be possible, at times, for very narrowly defined, low-level sub-optimization problems; but even this is questionable.

More generally, in dealing with major decision problems of choice, if the analyst approaches his task in an inflexible hard-core frame of mind, he is likely to be in for trouble. For example, he may soon give up in complete frustration; or he may wind up with such a simplified model that the resulting calculations are essentially meaningless; or his conclusions may not be ready for presentation until two years after the critical decision time and would therefore be useless to the decision-maker.

The viewpoint taken here is that in most cases the relevant range is between the extremes mentioned above, and that in such a context there is a wide scope of analytical effort that can be useful. Furthermore, even when only a relatively incomplete set of quantitative calculations of cost and utility can be made (probably the general situation), much can be done to assist the decision-maker in the sense that the term "assistance" is used in this chapter. To repeat: The objective is to *sharpen* intuition and judgment. It is conceivable that even a small amount of sharpening may on occasion have a high payoff.

One other point seems relevant. In that rare circumstance when a fairly complete set of calculations of cost and utility is possible and a resulting conclusion about a preferred alternative is reached, it may well be that the conclusion itself is not the most useful thing to the decision-maker. For one thing, as pointed out earlier, the analysis usually cannot take everything into account—particularly some of the nebulous non-quantitative considerations. The decision-maker has to allow for these himself. But more important, most high-level decision-makers are very busy men who do not have time to structure a particular problem, think up the relevant alternatives (especially the *subtle* ones), trace out the key interactions among variables in the problem, etc. This the analyst, if he is competent, can do, and should do. And it is precisely this sort of contribution that may be most useful to the decision-maker. The fact that the analysis reaches a firm conclusion about a preferred alternative may in many instances be of secondary importance.

SOME OF THE MAJOR CONSIDERATIONS INVOLVED IN DOING COST-UTILITY ANALYSIS

At this point, one might logically expect the title to be "How To Do Cost-Utility Analysis"—a cookbook, so to speak. We avoid this for two main reasons: (1) If such a treatise were attempted it would take an entire book; but, more important, (2) it is doubtful that even a book on the subject is possible. At the current stage of development of analytical methods, cost-utility analysis is an art rather than a science. The really significant problems to be tackled are each in a sense unique, with the result that it is not possible to give a definitive set of rules on how to do an appropriate analysis. All that can be done is to give some guidelines, principles, and illustrative examples. But books, or major parts of books, have been written on this subject.[19] Here the treatment must of necessity be more limited.

Some important guidelines to be followed in carrying out a cost-utility analysis (not necessarily in order of relative importance) are discussed in the following paragraphs.[20]

PROPER STRUCTURING OF THE PROBLEM AND DESIGN OF THE ANALYSIS

This is by far the most important of the guidelines. Given an incredibly complex environment, that which is relevant to the problem at hand must be included, and that which is irrelevant excluded. There are no formal rules to guide us. The experience, skill, imagination, and intuition of the analyst are paramount. It is at this point—the *design* of the analysis—that most cost-utility studies either flounder hopelessly or move ahead toward success. In sum, if we can structure the problem so that the *right questions* are being asked, we shall be well on the way toward a good analysis. This sounds trite, but it really is not. The author has seen all too many instances of large amounts of effort being expended on an analytical exercise addressed to the wrong questions.[21]

Another point is that typically the problem and the design of the analysis may well have to be *re*structured several times. Considerations that were initially thought to be important may, after some preliminary work, turn out to be relatively unimportant, and vice versa. Finally, in the process of doing some of the analytical work new questions and new alternatives may come to mind.

THE CONCEPTUAL FRAMEWORK

In general there are two principal conceptual approaches:[22]

1. *Fixed utility approach.* For a specified level of utility to be attained in the accomplishment of some given objective, the analysis attempts to determine that alternative (or feasible combination of alternatives) likely to achieve the specified level of utility at the lowest economic cost.

2. *Fixed budget approach.* For a specified budget level to be used in the attainment of some given objective, the analysis attempts to determine that alternative (or feasible combination of alternatives) likely to produce the highest utility for the given budget level.

Either (or both) of these approaches may be used, depending on the context of the problem at hand. In any event, the objective is to permit *comparisons* to be made among alternatives, and for this purpose something has to be made fixed.

At this point a comment on the use of ratios (e.g., utility-to-cost ratios) seems in order. Very often such ratios are used to evaluate alternatives. The use of ratios usually poses no problem as long as the analysis is conducted in the framework outlined above (i.e., with the level of either utility or cost fixed). However, the author has on occasion seen studies where this was not done, with the result that the comparisons were essentially meaningless. For example, consider the following hypothetical illustration:

	Utility (U)	*Cost (C)*	*U/C*
Alternative A	20	10	2
Alternative B	200	100	2

If the analyst is preoccupied with ratios, the implication of the above example is a state of indifference regarding the choice between A and B. But *should* the analyst be indifferent? Most probably not, because of the wide difference in scale between A and B. In fact, with such a great difference in scale, the analyst might not even be comparing relevant alternatives at all.[23]

BUILDING THE MODEL

Here the term "model" is used in a broad sense. Depending on the nature of the problem at hand, the model used in the analysis may be formal or informal, very mathematical or not so mathematical, heavily computerized or only moderately so, etc. However, the main point is that the model need not be highly formal and mathematical to be useful. In any event, the following are some important points to keep in mind:

1. Model building is an art, not a science. It is often an experimental process.
2. The main thing is to try to include and highlight those factors that are relevant to the problem at hand, and to suppress (judiciously!) those that are relatively unimportant. Unless the latter is done, the model is likely to be unmanageable.
3. The main purpose in designing the model is to develop a meaningful *set of relationships* among objectives, the relevant alternatives available for attaining the objectives, the estimated cost of the alternatives, and the estimated utility for each of the alternatives.

4. Provision must be made for explicit treatment of uncertainty. (There will be more on this later.)
5. Since by definition a model is an abstraction from reality, the model must be built on a set of assumptions. These assumptions must be made *explicit*. If they are not, this is to be regarded as a defect of the model design.

TREATMENT OF UNCERTAINTY

Since most really interesting and important decision problems involve major elements of uncertainty, a cost-utility analysis of such problems must provide for explicit treatment of uncertainty. This may be done in numerous ways.

For purposes of discussion, two main types of uncertainty may be distinguished:

1. Uncertainty about the state of the world in the future. In a national security context, major factors are technological uncertainty, strategic uncertainty,[24] and uncertainty about the enemy and his reactions.
2. Statistical uncertainty. This type of uncertainty stems from chance elements in the real world. It would exist even if uncertainties of the first type were zero.

Type 2 uncertainties are usually the least troublesome to handle in cost-utility studies. When necessary, Monte Carlo[25] and/or other techniques may be used to deal with statistical fluctuations; but these perturbations are usually swamped by Type 1 uncertainties, which are dominant in most long-range planning problems. The use of elaborate techniques to treat statistical uncertainties in such problems is likely to be expensive window-dressing.[26]

Type 1 uncertainties are typically present in most long-range decision problems, and they are most difficult to take into account in a cost-utility analysis. Techniques that are often used are sensitivity analysis, contingency analysis, and *a fortiori* analysis.[27]

Sensitivity Analysis. Suppose in a given analysis there are a few key parameters about which the analyst is very uncertain. Instead of using "expected values" for these parameters, the analyst may use several values (say, high, medium, and low) in an attempt to see how sensitive the results (the ranking of the alternatives being considered) are to variations in the uncertain parameters.[28]

Contingency Analysis. This type of analysis investigates how the ranking of the alternatives under consideration holds up when a relevant change in criteria for evaluating the alternatives is postulated, or a major change in the general environment is assumed. (For example, in a military context, the enemy is assumed to be countries A and B. We might then want to investigate what would happen if C joins the A and B coalition.)

A Fortiori Analysis. Suppose that in a particular planning-decision problem the generally accepted intuitive judgment strongly favors alternative X. However, the analyst feels that X might be a poor choice and that alternative Y might be preferred. In performing an analysis of X versus Y, the analyst may choose deliberately to resolve the major uncertainties in favor of X and see how Y compares under these adverse conditions. If Y still looks good, the analyst has a very strong case in favor of Y.

Creation of a New Alternative. Although the three techniques listed above may be useful in a direct analytical sense, they may also contribute indirectly. For example, through sensitivity and contingency analyses the analyst may gain a good understanding of the really critical uncertainties in a given problem area. On the basis of this knowledge he might then be able to come up with a newly designed alternative that will provide a reasonably good hedge against a *range* of the more significant uncertainties. This is often difficult to do; but when it can be accomplished, it may offer one of the best ways to compensate for uncertainty.

TREATMENT OF PROBLEMS ASSOCIATED WITH TIME

More likely than not, the particular problem at hand will be posed in a dynamic context; or at least the problem will have some dynamic aspects to it. While a "static" type analysis can go a long way toward providing the decision-maker with useful information, very often this has to be supplemented by analytical work that takes time into account explicitly.

A case in point is with respect to the treatment of the estimated *costs* of the alternatives for a fixed level of utility.[29] The nature of the problem may be such that the costs have to be time-phased, resulting in cost streams through time for each of the alternatives. The question then arises whether the decision-maker is or is not indifferent to the time impact of the costs. If he is not indifferent about time preference, then the cost streams have to be "discounted" through time, using an appropriate rate of discount.[30] Determining specifically what rate to use can be a problem; but it is usually manageable.[31] If it is not, an upper bound rate and a lower bound rate may be used to see whether it really makes any difference in the final conclusions of the problem.

It should be pointed out that the analyst pays a price for introducing time explicitly into an analysis:[32]

1. It complicates the analysis by increasing the number of variables and hence the number of calculations. If we put time in, we may have to take something else out.
2. As implied above, it complicates the selection of a criterion for evaluating alternatives: solution X may be better for 1966 and worse for 1970; solution Y may be just the reverse.

VALIDITY CHECKING

In the preceding paragraphs we have discussed building the analytical model, "exercising" the model (sensitivity and contingency analysis), etc. Another important consideration—often relatively neglected—is checking the validity of the model. Since the model is only a *representation* of reality, it is desirable to do some sort of checking to see if the analytical procedure used is a reasonably good representation, within the context of the problem at hand. This is difficult to do, especially in dealing with problems having a time horizon five, ten, or more years into the future.

In general, we cannot test models of this type by methods of "controlled experiment." However, the analyst might try to answer the following questions:[33]

1. Can the model describe known facts and situations reasonably well?
2. When the principal parameters involved are varied, do the results remain consistent and plausible?
3. Can it handle special cases where we already have some indication as to what the outcome should be?
4. Can it assign causes to known effects?

QUALITATIVE SUPPLEMENTATION

We have already stressed the importance of qualitative considerations in cost-utility analysis—particularly qualitative *supplementation* of the quantitative work. Introduction of qualitative considerations may take several forms:

1. Qualitative analysis *per se,* as an integral part of the total analytical effort.

2. Interpretation of the quantitative work.
3. Discussion of relevant non-quantitative considerations that could not be taken into account in the "formal" analysis.

The latter item can be particularly important in presenting the results of a study to the decision-maker. The idea is to present the results of the formal quantitative work, interpret these results, and then say that this is as far as the formal quantitative analysis per se will permit us to go. However, there are important *qualitative* considerations that you (the decision-maker) should try to take into account; and here they are (list them). Finally, relevant questions about each of the qualitative items can be raised and important interrelations among them discussed.

SUMMARY COMMENTS

We stress again that the discussion above pertains to a long-range planning context, with emphasis on specifying, clarifying, and comparing the relevant alternatives. Since comparative analysis is the prime focus, it is vitally important to continually emphasize *consistency* in the analytical concepts, methods, and techniques used. That is, instead of trying for a high degree of accuracy in an *absolute* sense (which is usually unattainable anyway), the analyst should stress development and use of procedures that will treat the alternatives being considered in an unbiased, consistent manner.

The main points presented in this chapter may be summarized as follows:

1. An analytical activity is an important part of the total program-budgeting process.

2. Cost-utility analysis pertains to the systematic examination and comparison of alternative courses of action that might be taken to achieve specified objectives for some future time period. Not only is it important to examine all relevant alternatives that can be identified initially but it is also important to design additional ones if those examined are found wanting.

3. The primary purpose of cost-utility analysis is usually not to *make* the decision, but rather to *sharpen* the intuition and judgment of the decision-makers. Identification of the relevant alternatives and clarification of their respective implications are of prime importance.

4. In a long-range planning context, the following are some of the major considerations involved in a cost-utility analysis:

(a) Proper structuring of the problem is all important. The analysis must be addressed to the right questions.

(b) In making comparisons, an appropriate analytical framework must be used. For example, for a specified level of utility to be attained in the accomplishment of some given objective, the alternatives may be compared on the basis of their estimated economic resource impact; or (vice versa), for a given budget level, the alternatives may be compared on the basis of their estimated utility.

(c) It is usually necessary to construct a model (either formal or informal) to be used in the analytical process. Here the main purpose is to develop a set of relationships among objectives, the relevant alternatives available for attaining the objectives, the estimated cost of the alternatives, and the estimated utility for each of the alternatives.

(d) Uncertainty must be faced explicitly in the analysis. Sensitivity analysis, contingency analysis, and *a fortiori* analysis' are three possible techniques that may be used in dealing with the problem of uncertainty.

(e) Although it complicates the analysis because of an increase in the number of variables, very often *time-phasing* of the impacts of the various alternatives is a requirement. If the decision-makers are not indifferent to time preference, the estimates of time-phased impacts must be "equalized" over time through the use of a "discounting" procedure.

(f) Since the model is only a representation of reality, it is desirable to do some validity checking of the analytical procedure; e.g., can the model describe known facts and situations reasonably well?

(g) Although cost-utility analysis stresses the use of quantitative methods, the analyst should not hesitate to supplement his quantitative work with appropriate *qualitative* analyses.

NOTES:

[1] In many instances, end products may in fact be *intermediate* products, especially from the point of view of the next higher level in the decision hierarchy.

[2] From the introduction of the Statement of Secretary of Defense Robert S. McNamara before the Committee on Armed Services on the Fiscal Year 1965–1969 Defense Program and 1965 Defense Budget, January

27, 1964, *Hearings on Military Posture* and H.R. 9637, House of Representatives, 88th Cong., 2d Sess. (Washington, D.C.: U.S. Government Printing Office, 1964).

[3]For example, see Arthur Smithies, *Government Decision-Making and the Theory of Choice,* P-2960 (Santa Monica, Calif.: The RAND Corporation, October 1964).

[4]See Robert N. Anthony, *Management Accounting* (Homewood, Ill.: Richard D. Irwin, Inc., 1960), Chaps. 13–15.

[5]One example is the so-called PERT system. For a description, see *USAF PERT, Volume I, PERT Time System Description Manual,* September 1963 and *USAF PERT, Volume III, PERT Cost System Description Manual,* December 1963 (Washington, D.C.: Headquarters, Air Force Systems Command, Andrews Air Force Base, 1963).

[6]See James E. Kelly and Morgan R. Walker, "Critical-Path Planning and Scheduling," *Proceedings of the Eastern Joint Computer Conference* (Ft. Washington, Pa.: Manchly Associates, Inc., 1959), pp. 160–173; and F. K. Levy, G. L. Thompson, and J. D. Wiest, *Mathematical Basis of the Critical Path Method,* Office of Naval Research, Research Memorandum No. 86 (Pittsburgh, Pa.: Carnegie Institute of Technology, May 30, 1962).

[7]L. P. Alford and John R. Bangs, *Production Handbook* (New York: Ronald Press, 1947), pp. 216–229.

[8]For a good example, see *Systems Data Presentation and Reporting Procedures* (Rainbow Report), November 1, 1961 (with revisions as of March 9, 1962), Program Management Instruction 1–5 (Washington, D.C.: Headquarters, Air Force Systems Command, Andrews Air Force Base 1962).

[9]For a discussion of suboptimization, see Charles Hitch, "Suboptimization in Operations Problems," *Journal of the Operations Research Society of America,* Vol. 1, No. 3, May 1953, pp. 87–99; and Charles J. Hitch and Roland N. McKean, *The Economics of Defense in the Nuclear Age* (Cambridge, Mass.: Harvard University Press, 1960), pp. 396–402.

[10]Sometimes called "systems analysis"; e.g., see Roland N. McKean, *Efficiency in Government Through Systems Analysis* (New York: John Wiley & Sons, Inc., 1958).

[11]For example, see Joel Dean, *Capital Budgeting* (New York: Columbia University Press, 1951); Harold Bierman, Jr., and Seymour Smidt, *The Capital Budgeting Decision* (New York: The Macmillan Co., 1960); and Elwood S. Buffa, *Models for Production and Operations Management* (New York: John Wiley & Sons, Inc., 1963), Chaps. 13 and 14.

[12]For example, see Brian V. Martin and Charles B. Warden, "Trans-

portation Planning in Developing Countries," *Traffic Quarterly,* January 1965, pp. 59–75.

[13]See *Convertibility of Space and Defense Resources to Civilian Needs: A Search for New Employment Potentials,* compiled for the Subcommittee on Employment and Manpower of the Committee on Labor and Public Welfare, Senate, 88th Cong., 2d Sess. (Washington, D.C.: U.S. Government Printing Office, 1964). Note especially Part III, "National Adjustments to Shifts in Defense Planning," and Part IV, "Studies in Regional Adjustment to Shifts in Defense Spending."

[14]W. W. Leontief *et al., Studies in the Structure of the American Economy* (New York: Oxford University Press, 1953).

[15]For example, see Walter Isard *et al., Methods of Regional Analysis: An Introduction to Regional Science* (Boston and New York: Technology Press of Massachusetts Institute of Technology and John Wiley & Sons, Inc., 1960).

[16]E. S. Quade, *Military Systems Analysis,* RM-3452-PR (Santa Monica, Calif.: The RAND Corporation, January 1963), p. 1.

[17]And also because of inadequate data and information sources.

[18]Apparently this view is held by Alain C. Enthoven, Deputy Assistant Secretary for Systems Analysis, Department of Defense. He writes:

Where does this leave us? What is operations research or systems analysis at the Defense policy level all about? I think that it can best be described as a continuing dialogue between the policy-maker and the systems analyst, in which the policy-maker asks for alternative solutions to his problems, makes decisions to exclude some, and makes value judgments and policy decisions, while the analyst attempts to clarify the conceptual framework in which decisions must be made, to define alternative possible objectives and criteria, and to explore in as clear terms as possible (and quantitatively) the cost and effectiveness of alternative courses of action.

The analyst at this level is not computing optimum solutions or making decisions. In fact, computation is not his most important contribution. And he is helping someone else to make decisions. His job is to ask and find answers to the questions: "What are we trying to do?" "What are the alternative ways of achieving it?" "What would they cost, and how effective would they be?" "What does the decision-maker need to know in order to make a choice?" And to collect and organize this information for those who are responsible for deciding what the Defense program ought to be.

(Alain C. Enthoven, "Decision Theory and Systems Analysis," *The Armed Forces Comptroller,* Vol. IX, No. 1, (March 1964), 39.

[19]For example, see Hitch and McKean, *op. cit.*, especially Part II; and McKean, *op. cit.*

[20]Observance of these guidelines will not in itself produce a good analysis, but it will most surely help. Many of the points listed here are based on Quade, *Military Systems Analysis*, pp. 8–24.

[21]Incredible as it may seem, there have been studies that started out by asking questions about which alternative would maximize gain and at the same time minimize cost—clearly an impossible situation.

[22]The fixed level of utility or budget is usually specified by someone "outside the analysis"; i.e., it is usually a datum given to the analyst. Very often the analyst will use several levels (e.g., high, medium, and low) to investigate the sensitivity of the ranking of the alternatives to the utility or budget level.

[23]For a further discussion of the possible pitfalls of using ratios, see McKean, *op. cit.*, pp. 34–37, 107–113.

[24]For example: Will there be a war in the future? If so, when? General or local? With what political constraints? Who will be our enemies? Our allies? See C. J. Hitch, *An Appreciation of Systems Analysis*, P-699 (Santa Monica, Calif.: The RAND Corporation, August 18, 1955), p. 6.

[25]For a discussion of Monte Carlo techniques, see Herman Kahn and Irwin Mann, *Monte Carlo*, P-1165 (Santa Monica, Calif.: The RAND Corporation, July 30, 1957); and E. S. Quade, *Analysis for Military Decisions*, R-387-PR (Santa Monica, Calif.: The RAND Corporation, November, 1964), pp. 407–414.

[26]Hitch, *Appreciation of Systems Analysis*, p. 7.

[27]Quade, *Military Systems Analysis*, pp. 23–24.

[28]Enthoven, *op. cit.*, pp. 16–17, talks about sensitivity analysis in the following way:

If it is a question of uncertainties about quantitative matters such as operational factors, it is generally useful to examine the available evidences and determine the bounds of the uncertainty. In many of our analyses for the Secretary of Defense, we carry three estimates through the calculations: an "optimistic," a "pessimistic," and a "best" or single most likely estimate. Although it is usually sensible to design the defense posture primarily on the basis of the best estimates, the prudent decision-maker will keep asking himself, "Would the outcome be acceptable if the worst possible happened, i.e., if all the pessimistic estimates were borne out?" Carrying three numbers through all of the calculations can increase the work load greatly. For this reason, a certain amount of judgment has to be used as to when the best guesses are satisfactory and when the full range of uncertainty needs to be explored.

If there are uncertainties about context, at least one can run the calculations on the basis of several alternative assumptions so that the decision-maker can see how the outcome varies with the assumptions.

[29]Maintaining a fixed level of utility *through time* is often a tricky problem in itself. We cannot go into this matter in the present limited discussion.

[30]One may raise the question regarding under what conditions the decision-maker *would* be indifferent. Economic theorists might argue that there probably should not be any such condition. However, in practice, decision-makers often find themselves in an institutional setting (such as the Department of Defense, for example) where it is customary to be indifferent regarding time preference; hence discounting of cost streams through time is not done. This is not to say that the decision-makers are correct in principle.

It should be emphasized that the type of discounting under discussion here is purely to equalize cost streams through time with respect to time preference—not to compensate for risk.

[31]For example, see E. B. Berman, *The Normative Interest Rate*, P-1796 (Santa Monica, Calif.: The RAND Corporation, September 15, 1959).

[32]Hitch, *Appreciation of Systems Analysis*, pp. 11–12.

[33]Quade, *Military Systems Analysis*, p. 20.

10.
Costs and Benefits
from Different Viewpoints*
ROLAND N. McKEAN

When people live in groups or even have any significant contacts with each other, it is clear that they have to do some planning—that is, they have to think about the implications of alternative rules and arrangements and choose among them. People may devise rules that permit considerable decentralization and individual choice, or they may have rules under which most issues are settled by authority or tradition, leaving less scope for individual choice. In any case, these rules constitute planning: they are not chosen at random but are the result of some sort of political process in which various persons did some thinking (and also a good deal of compromising). In an urban area, the existing complex of laws, ordinances, and institutions for governing constitute a kind of "urban plan"—usually a rather helter-skelter one but nonetheless the result of human planning as we know it.

All too often this process—indeed the exercise of central authority in general—has led to planning of the people, by the few, and for the few. Also, urban plans in the formal sense have too often been chosen in terms of narrow partial criteria—efficiency in carrying out one function regardless of undesirable effects elsewhere, esthetics alone without regard for other consequences, or the betterment of one group regardless of the implications for others.

It is reasonable to believe that we can do better, and in recent years, there has been growing interest in the use of broader criteria for the

*Reprinted from Roland N. McKean, "Costs and Benefits from Different Viewpoints," in Howard G. Schaller (ed.), *Public Expenditure Decisions in the Urban Community* (Washington, D.C.: Resources for the Future, Inc., 1963), pp. 147–163, by permission of the author and publisher. Roland N. McKean is professor of economics at the University of California, Los Angeles.

analysis of city plans. There has been growing recognition that criteria used in the past have included only *part* of the things desired and part of the sacrifices entailed. Hope has sprung up of using cost-benefit analyses that take into account more of the costs and more of the benefits of alternative institutional arrangements.[1] Of course, we shall never be able to include, at least quantitatively, *all* of the relevant costs and gains. For example, we cannot measure adequately the significance of a plan's impact on the range of individual choice or on the probability of maintaining individual rights. But we can hope to measure more of the costs and gains than were considered in the past and measure them more accurately than in the past, making final evaluations easier (though still not easy by any means).

In devising and evaluating rules for social organizations, the forces that raise the major problems are the discrepancies between individual costs (or benefits) and our conceptions of total costs (or benefits). If no discrepancies existed, each individual could do whatever he pleased, and we would have no objection. These discrepancies are the main reason we have police departments, zoning ordinances, or any form of urban planning. They are also the reason for wanting relatively broad analyses of alternative city plans, because fairly comprehensive cost-benefit analyses are necessary to reveal the indirect effects as well as the direct ones, the costs and gains in total as well as to selected groups or individuals. The basic difficulty is that the costs and gains felt by one group are different from those perceived by another group. The cost and gains felt by the mayor are quite different from those felt by citizen A or B and still different from our conceptions of *total* costs and gains.

But our problems would not be solved even if cost-benefit analyses could reveal the plan that in the abstract would yield the greatest total benefit (net of costs). The problems would not all be solved because these same divergences between individual interest and total costs and gains are likely to thwart the implementation of many plans. In trying to put rules or plans into effect, we must think very carefully about ways to cope with the resulting pressures. Moreover, in many instances we should apply a "degradation factor" to the net gains promised by a plan to allow for the ways in which the results would go awry because of these discrepancies between individual interests and the aims of the plan. In fact the measures that seem second or third best in terms of straightforward cost-benefit analysis may appear to be best when one reflects on how the various proposals would actually turn out.

These statements are simple propositions about human behavior and political realities, but there is danger of losing sight of them as analyses become more sophisticated and more dependent upon the skills of physical scientists, economists, architects, and others who are not always vividly aware of the nature of political processes. Because of such danger, it is worthwhile to examine the reasons that these simple propositions are so important.

SELF-INTEREST AND THE IMPLEMENTATION OF URBAN PLANS

When people appraise proposals for government action, they often have extremely misleading models of political and administrative behavior in mind. Some persons assume that every politician or official is vicious, having as his primary aim the achievement of evil. More persons are at the other extreme, I would guess; they slip into assuming that anyone paid by the public will act in the interests of the public— that any activity placed in the public sphere will automatically be conducted in the public interest. Yet a little reflection ought to remind us that this is not necessarily so. Consider the following comment on an activity well below the policy-making level:

At first sight there hardly seems to be a problem here. If we employ a man to direct activities at a playground, of course *he will spend his time each day from nine to five at the playground;* of course *he will organize and direct play activities there;* of course *he will carry out the policies formulated by the directors of the organization who are responsible for planning its program. Only the many instances of organization failure—instances where an organization does not carry out its task or where it succeeds at an excessive economic and human cost—warn us that there is really nothing automatic about the process.*[2]

The two extreme models of government officials' behavior—that government action is always evil and that public activities are automatically conducted in the public interest—are dangerously unrealistic. No model of behavior can be 100 per cent realistic, of course, but these extremes are too far from the mark for them to serve us usefully. Actually, government officials and politicians are much like business employees and administrators. They are not a random sample of the population, for they have above average ability and ambition, but they are not a separate breed. As for other citizens and voters, who also play vital roles in political processes, their motivation is fairly understandable. None of these groups is ceaselessly trying to do evil, on the one hand, or to secure the maximum total benefit for the nation, on the other.

In general terms, an individual is moved to act by anticipated costs and gains *as he feels them.* Sometimes the terms "deprivations" and "gratifications" or "sacrifices" and "satisfactions" are used instead of costs and gains, but the idea is the same. In this general form, this kind of proposition is a tautology. It is like saying that a man acts because of the things that make him act. But discussions of behavior can start out with this framework and lead to significant propositions. With the aid of any insight into what factors cause individuals to feel gratification or deprivation, one can arrive at a predictive model rather than an empty tautology.[3]

What *are* the principal items that affect the gains and costs felt by an individual? Material comfort for himself and his family is clearly a major item. Some persons believe that economists regard material gain or loss as the only factor motivating man. They believe this because economists have talked a good deal about "economic man." This term does suggest a person with a one-track mind, but in point of fact it has usually meant "rational man"[4] as distinguished from "neurotic man." It has not referred to a person who pursues only material wealth.

Material wealth and comfort, then, is one of the *desiderata,* but there are many others.[5] Just where to draw the line, nobody knows, but one surely gets more insight into average behavior by confining the list to major and rather obvious driving forces—such as the desires for prestige, material gain, power, security, and avoidance of difficult decisions and inconveniences—and by ignoring the minor or bizarre factors that may be operative. By the same token, we would do well for the most part to neglect completely neurotic behavior in trying to predict performance (though we should certainly keep the *threat* of neurotic behavior in mind when appraising plans for cities or other social organizations).

We should keep in mind too that probability of success figures importantly in calculating the expected reward from undertaking some action. No matter how much a government official values personal promotion or civil rights, he will not be moved to take an action to further those aims if the action has a near-zero probability of achieving those ends. Each of us has an enormous stake in preventing thermonuclear war, but few of us put in several hours per day in an effort to prevent it. Why? Because we know that individual efforts of ordinary persons can have almost no influence on the outcome. This is another reason why many motives that might be called "noble" ones play so small a role in shaping our actions.

One major question about costs and rewards is the following: For *whom* does a person want increased gratifications and decreased deprivations? If he wants good things for everyone with equal fervor, then propositions about his motivation became very general again, and can explain any sort of action but predict none. It is fairly clear, however, that most persons want the desirable things primarily for themselves and their immediate families. To a lesser yet significant extent, they are concerned about the well being of close friends. If we look outside this circle, the amount of genuine concern falls off rapidly. (Anonymous philanthropists do exist, but they are the exception rather than the rule). Once more, we do not know just where to draw the line. But I submit that we get considerable insight into behavior if we adopt a sort of "cookie-cutter technique"—if we assume that each individual is concerned about himself, his immediate family circle, and a few close friends, and neglect whatever concern he may feel for other living persons or for unborn generations. (We get no insight at all if we make the cookie-cutter embrace everyone.)

To be sure, each of us identifies with various groups such as the department or organization where we work. A gain for the Republican party is a gain to the individual members. A blow to the firm is a blow to the employee. Even so, these loyalties stem in large part from the fact that the individual has tied his personal prospects, at least for the moment, to that group or organization. Typically, one's loyalties and attitudes shift quickly when he accepts a job with a different firm or moves from one government department to another.

The assumption here is, then, that officials, employees, and voters will fairly consistently act in their own self-interest *rather narrowly conceived.* That is, each will try to increase gains and reduce costs—in terms of wealth, prestige, power, security, and convenience of working and living —for himself, his family, and to a lesser extent his close friends.[6] This assumption is by no means photographically realistic. People *are* concerned to some extent with unknown persons and abstract principles. Some devote their lives to such causes, and in crises numerous individuals have risked death to save total strangers from tragedy. Most of the time, though, the rather narrow self-interest assumption does not depart wildly from reality, and I believe it is the kind of abstraction from reality that is useful, the kind of model of human behavior that we would do well to keep in mind.

DISCREPANCIES BETWEEN INDIVIDUAL
AND TOTAL COSTS AND GAINS

We must recognize too that ordinarily there are serious discrepancies between the self-interest of the individual voter, employee, or official and the interest of the whole group. That is, there are important divergences between the costs and gains felt by each individual alone and the total effects that cost-benefit analysis seeks to measure. Discrepancies between individual and total costs or gains in the private sector of the economy have been discussed for many years. These are sometimes entitled "external economies or diseconomies" or, perhaps more graphically, "spillover effects." Wherever these effects are important, we try to rig the costs and rewards to individuals so as to induce them to take these spillovers into account. But some persons damn the whole private enterprise system on the grounds that these external effects are too pervasive.

We must not forget, however, that analogous phenomena are present in the public sector of the economy. It is probably even harder there to bring self-interest into line with community interest. One reason is that many governmental functions are placed in that sector precisely because external effects of those activities are particularly serious, making it difficult for the private enterprise system to handle them properly. Another reason is that it is in any event difficult in government to utilize markets and voluntary exchange, or any other devices to *reveal* costs and rewards explicitly. It is also difficult to make use of competition and bargaining in such a way as to make the right costs and rewards *felt*, even if they are revealed. Whatever the reasons, though, the governing process is shot through and through with discrepancies between self-interests, other group interests, and total community interest.[7]

Good examples are provided in connection with government proposals to deal with water problems in the Washington, D.C., area. Apparently Falls Church, Virginia, has tapped some of the best sources of water in the vicinity and is reselling the water at a tidy profit to various cities in Fairfax County. Now the county officials are greatly upset because they must get water from costlier sources than those that would be available if Falls Church had not already tapped them.[8] Another example concerns what is literally a spillover from an anti-pollution proposal:

Today I am speaking on behalf of the Accokeek Citizens Association, the Accokeek Democratic Club, the Accokeek PTA, the Moyaone organization, the Piscataway Co. . . .

We have joined together in the Potomac Tidewater Council. . . . This council has one purpose; that is, to reaffirm to this committee that the river does not end at 14th Street.

All the comprehensive plans prior to this committee's studies, work their way down from the headwaters to 14th Street. . . .

The Army engineers in their report did a little better than some. They promised, if we would support their upper river work, to float the sewage down to us a little faster. "Get your sewage while it's fresh, fellows," seemed to be their slogan.[9]

What kind of trouble can arise because of the differences between the self-interest of individuals and the community interest? In general terms the trouble is that wrong actions and policies are undertaken. An individual will take steps that look good from his standpoint even if those actions inflict damages on others. (Unless he has to compensate the others, in which case he is made to feel those costs by "buying" those deprivations from others.) Or, an individual will not take steps that do not look good from his viewpoint even if those actions would bestow significant gains on others. (Unless he is allowed to feel those gains by "selling" those benefits to the recipients.)

In urban planning the result can be inaction if few of the community gains are felt by officials or if officials encounter personal sacrifices that are not real costs from the community's standpoint. Suppose a subsidy is currently being paid to owners of tenements (or any other industry), and an urban plan that looks good in terms of comprehensive cost-benefit analysis calls, among other things, for removal of that subsidy. Council members may feel the gains, e.g., pressure from taxpayers and affected groups, very slightly, but feel the sacrifices (loss of the support of some highly articulate and influential groups) very keenly. The result may be no action at all. The thing to be stressed is that the persons involved need not be acting in any malevolent or anomalous fashion. Most of us, if placed in any of these roles, would behave in much the same way. Costs and rewards from one person's standpoint are different from the costs and gains that are perceived by another, and these costs and rewards are like the strings on marionettes—they keep pulling and affecting behavior in rather predictable ways.

Or, if it is not inaction, the result may be a highly distorted set of measures instead of the recommended plan, or unanticipated responses that lead to results quite different from those planned. These are common outcomes that need no elaboration or illustration. Nearly every city's history reflects the many slips between planning and doing. Again there is little use in abusing the marionettes. The thing to do is to work on the strings to see if we can bring about more desirable outcomes. Sometimes, to be sure, there are despicable individuals and actions involved. The power of self-interest often induces officials to step outside the law, and there is illegal or immoral behavior, rather than merely inequitable, inefficient, or frustrated urban planning. Even in the case of corruption, however, we should recognize it as a product mainly of the cost-reward structure, and we should try to re-rig the strings rather than merely hope for better marionettes. Too often we look upon "the shame of our cities" as a product of bad luck or declining morality and try to use the weak strings of exhortation alone to manipulate the participants.

One key actor whose behavior is often gauged badly is the ordinary citizen affected by urban planning. When laws are made or altered, he will adjust wherever possible so as to reap benefits and avoid losses. He will not usually forego available gains or incur unnecessary losses just to further community objectives or improve the lot of other groups. We must not expect producers or voters or officials to act regularly against their own interests narrowly conceived. We must not expect the farmer facing an acreage limitation to refrain voluntarily from farming his land more intensively. We must not expect citizens to move to locations where they do not wish to live. We must not expect the voter to inform himself and get to the polls when the costs of doing so exceed the gains.[10] (Unless he has a special stake in an issue, the man who votes sacrifices time yet gains only an infinitesimal probability of affecting the outcome.)

There are analogous divergences between individual and total interest at national and international levels. In the relationship among nations, in fact, these discrepancies can and probably will lead to disaster. The total net gains from avoiding thermonuclear war are tremendous. Yet each national leader must look at the gains and costs of alternative defense policies from his own nation's standpoint. And since he cannot control the other nation's behavior, his country may suffer more if he does not run a high risk of war than if he does. The resulting cost-reward pattern as each nation sees it is vastly different from the total costs and gains associated with alternative policies. To reduce the chances of catastrophe, we must assess those cost-gain patterns carefully—e.g., the costs to an enemy of striking first versus the expected costs to him of not striking first, or, as another example, the cost to the U.S.S.R. of permitting suitable inspection arrangements. Furthermore, we must then influence those cost-reward patterns, perhaps through unilateral action or perhaps through enforceable multilateral agreements. We cannot hope for much if we rely on exhortation or mere replacement of the marionettes.

Now, emphasis on conflicting political pressures is nothing new (in either urban planning or planning for peace). Nonetheless, I think it needs to be further emphasized that these pressures stem mainly from the cost-gain patterns that confront each decision-maker, that self-interest rather narrowly conceived is a powerful force, and that to a considerable extent the social organization must try to harness rather than override individual self-interest (or at least recognize rather than ignore its implications).

COSTS AND BENEFITS FROM DIFFERENT STANDPOINTS

To see more vividly how the gains and costs of alternative decisions must appear to various officials, let us review two cases pertaining to urban planning measures.

PUBLIC HOUSING IN CHICAGO

Consider first public housing decisions in Chicago during the late 1940's. The background and influences at work have been described in some detail by Martin Meyerson and Edward C. Banfield.[11] How did decisions about public housing proposals look to, say, an alderman from a middle-class residential section of the city? To survive and perhaps advance in local politics, he had to please a majority of his constituents, not on each and every issue, but on enough issues to keep their support. Also he had to secure the co-operation of many aldermen, particularly the more influential ones who were chairmen of important committees, for the Council could ruin him if it really wanted to do so. The Council could do this by withholding patronage or campaign funds, by letting public services in the ward deteriorate, by encouraging investigations or other actions that would embarrass the alderman, and so on. The alderman was dependent upon the Council for many things that were provided to him and his constituents.

Since he received only $5,000 per year in salary, he usually had outside interests, such as an insurance or real estate business. Often, therefore, he was especially concerned about keeping the favor of those politicians or constituents who brought business and outside income to him. He was dependent in some degree upon the mayor, other city officials, ward committeemen (where they were not the same persons as the alderman), state politicians, the press, and perhaps particular ethnic or religious groups. Typically there were things the alderman could do for these persons, and in turn he was partially dependent upon them.[12]

The chain of interdependence was usually a long and complicated one—A would be in some degree dependent upon B because B had some leverage over C, who had some leverage over D, who had some influence with group E, which could threaten or reward A. The existence of these relationships—of the costs and gains confronting A—did not have to be reaffirmed each time an issue arose. Indeed they did not have to be stated explicitly at any time. If A was reasonably intelligent, he automatically asked himself: "What are the pleasant and unpleasant consequences for me if I take a particular action?" If he was fairly astute, he could answer the question well enough to survive and advance.[13]

In these circumstances how did the gains and costs of public housing decisions appear to our hypothetical alderman? Consider, for instance, the costs and gains of voting against a public housing proposal that included one site in his own ward (we shall call this "Proposal X").

EFFECTS ON ALDERMAN A OF OPPOSING PROPOSAL X

Costs	*Benefits*
Loss of support of some aldermen and (maybe) of the mayor.	Gain of many constituents' favor. Residents opposed having site in that ward, because public housing believed to lower values of middle-class properties.
(1) Some felt the general pressure for city to get housing largely at expense of federal government.	Gain of certain key aldermen's support (they opposed the proposal for their own reasons).
(2) Several aldermen favored public housing, especially if site were not in their wards.	Retention of insurance business from pleased constituents and politicians.
(3) Deadline for getting federal money was close.	Protection of value of alderman's own properties in his ward.
Loss of good will of certain state and federal officials who want-	

ed the program expanded—
good will that was valuable to
the Council and might be
valuable some day if not at
that moment to the alderman.

Loss of support and insurance
business from contractors in
ward who would help build
public housing project.

Loss of good relationship with
Chicago Housing Authority
(but this would not cost the
alderman much).

Loss of personal satisfaction in
seeing the program materialize
(here we assume that this alderman favored public housing
in principle).

Loss of support he might otherwise gain from occupants of
public housing project (but
where their support would go
was really quite doubtful).

Avoidance of possible racial
conflicts and troublesome issues in his ward.

Possible gain of support of city
transportation officials, who
wanted the site for freeway access roads, etc.

These are just a few of the costs and gains as seen by the alderman,
but the list includes several of the most significant ones. Note that the
most important costs and benefits from the nation's standpoint (or the
city's standpoint) are not on the list—for example, the resource costs of
using the sites and building the project, the worth of the improved housing to the probable occupants, or the long-run impact on racial integration. In other words, there may be huge discrepancies between the public interest and the official's interest. Note too that personal principles
were probably relatively minor considerations—if the alderman had
strong wishes to survive in politics and in his business activities. Personal
views can play a larger role, of course, if the alderman (or other official)
is independently wealthy or can shift to another occupation *with little
sacrifice.*

Suppose we turn now to the costs and gains of opposing Proposal X
from the mayor's standpoint. The consequences with which he had to be
concerned were somewhat different.

EFFECTS ON MAYOR OF OPPOSING PROPOSAL X

Costs	*Benefits*
Loss of support of many voters (1) Voters, businessmen who would profit directly from the project. (2) Voters who felt the advantages of getting project mostly at federal expense. Loss of good will of certain state and federal officials who wanted the program expanded—good will that could affect patronage, campaign funds and support, political prospects of the mayor. Loss of harmony in Council, support for mayor's programs, backing of certain ward committeemen in next election. Loss of good relationship with Chicago Housing Authority, through which Chicago had to work if the city was to receive federal funds.	Gain of support of voters and ward committeemen who opposed project, mainly in wards containing proposed sites. Gain of firmer support from key aldermen in whose wards sites had been selected; and these aldermen might be strong enough to keep Council pretty much in line. Avoidance, or postponement, of extending areas of racial conflicts. Net gain of newspaper support, because the largest newspapers opposed public housing for their own reasons (though some newspapers were campaigning strongly for the project). The interdependence of influences, and the net effects, are very uncertain here.

Some of the costs and gains as viewed by the mayor are similar in nature to those felt by the alderman. Yet the weights attached to them were no doubt quite different. Moreover, other effects on the mayor were quite different from those on the alderman. In both instances, however, the considerations obviously diverged greatly from costs and benefits from the community's standpoint, and the latter diverged sharply from costs and benefits from the nation's viewpoint. In general, the criterion of good policy used by each participant in the political process, though tempered and constrained by the influences of other participants, differs greatly from the criteria used in cost-benefit analyses.[14]

Transportation in Washington

Transportation proposals for Washington, D.C., provide another case that reminds us of the hurdles that planning must take into account. Although Washington, D.C. may not be a typical metropolitan area, it is a good subject of study in one respect: there are voluminous hearings on its problems conducted by congressional committees. These hearings bring out rather vividly some of the divergences between costs and benefits as viewed by various officials and individuals, though here also many influences are felt by officials without any explicit testimony about those considerations being given.

Recent hearings pertained to a specific proposal to improve urban transportation in the Washington area.[15] Many citizens' groups opposed the use of freeways and cloverleafs because of the properties that would have to be taken over for rights of way, because of noise and other impacts on their neighborhoods, and because of beliefs that the equivalent job could be done less expensively by more effective use of existing streetcar and railroad tracks.[16] For some groups, however, there were opportunities for large monetary gains. It was alleged, incidentally, that General Motors, Firestone, Phillips Petroleum, and Standard Oil of California have financed National City Lines and that NCL buys control of local street railways with the understanding that they will substitute buses for streetcars.[17] (Sometimes firms are formed to buy up unprofitable transit companies and resell them at a big profit to a newly organized municipal authority.) Such activities, which supposedly run counter to the public interest, need not be illegal or immoral; they come about because cost-reward structures induce public officials to co-operate with these proposals when reaching decisions.

Another interest group comprised the existing local transit companies. Their main concern was survival, and they were worried primarily about the organization of the central transportation authority, because such authorities sometimes set up competing bus lines in such a way as to bankrupt the private companies.[18] Another interest was that of Lockheed, which proposed a monorail system.[19] Existing transit companies and many others took a dim view of this plan. Testimony of another group, the Bureau of Public Roads, seemed to be in favor of freeways. On one point all local groups seemed to be in agreement—namely, that the larger the share of the burden assumed by the federal government, the better the proposal (other things being equal).

The major costs and gains as seen by the adjacent states are easy to figure out. Representative Lankford of Maryland thought the plan (as modified after the first hearings) (1) did not allow for (encourage?) enough growth in portions of Maryland, (2) did not make efficient use of existing track and rail facilities, and (3) did not give the states enough voice in future transportation decisions.[20]

The point to be stressed here is that the divergent pulls exerted by cost-reward structures are omnipresent, not immoral or abnormal or exceptional. As we all know, sometimes cost-reward structures lead to graft and corruption.[21] But our concern here is not with violations of the law. It is usually true, as Blanshard wrote about New York City, that: "The great majority of the city's employees are honest, industrious, and faithful. But the faithfulness of these employees rarely receives the headlines, whereas the exposure of one black sheep is featured in all the newspapers."[22] This still leaves the wrong impression, however, for it sounds as though corruption is the only thing that should cause us concern. But for every instance of corruption, there must be a hundred instances of distorted, inefficient, or completely frustrated programs produced by the cost-reward structures that confront municipal leaders.[23]

Cost-Gain Patterns

This bargaining process, which undoubtedly leads to more satisfactory results with some institutional arrangements than with others, is a pervasive phenomenon. "Even in totalitarian societies, where the opportunities for ordinary citizens to assert their demands and to organize to press for them without the sanction of the ruling cliques are tightly circumscribed, there are some evidences that this bargaining process occurs."[24] It certainly does occur in totalitarian societies—the differences between those societies and others are mainly in the amounts and kinds of influence possessed by various participants. Brute force, for instance, may be a major influence. In other words, the differences between institutional arrangements manifest themselves in the cost-gain structures that face various officials and individuals.

Note how decisions change when cost-reward structures change. If the cost of something goes up, a business or individual consumer usually buys fewer units. If the cost of any action goes up, an individual is deterred from taking that action to a greater extent than before. If the worth of some item to a person goes up, he finds himself willing to pay more for it. If the value of some action rises, an individual is more anxious than before to take that action.

Often in politics, circumstances gradually alter the cost-reward structures confronting officials. Prior to the construction of the Idlewild air-field, the value to various groups of having more airport facilities gradu-ally rose, and officials clearly felt the shifting cost-gain patterns from their own standpoints.[25] In Philadelphia, when support for two Republican leaders became almost evenly divided in 1956, the value of acquiring the support of a few more ward leaders soared, and "large bribes were reportedly offered to wavering ward leaders, and it is said that several of them were threatened with physical violence."[26] To mention another example, as the probability of success declined for the Republican party in Philadelphia, the expected value of contributing financial and other support fell also, and therefore the amount of support given to the party declined.[27] Shifts in cost-reward patterns are frequently introduced de-liberately. When the federal government offers to pay 90 per cent of the cost of certain freeway projects, it makes the net gains to the local community almost irresistible. When Mayor La Guardia of New York began to get action in his campaign against corruption, he made cer-tain illegal activities more costly than they had been. When costs and rewards change, decisions and actions change until a new temporary equilibrium is achieved. The bargaining process leads to a balancing of these forces somewhat as marbles seek a position when they are poured into a bowl, and further shifts in decision-making occur somewhat as the marbles alter positions whenever the bowl is tilted.

IMPLICATIONS FOR URBAN PLANNING AND COST-BENEFIT ANALYSIS

It is of growing importance for urban planners and cost-benefit ana-lysts to keep these political realities in mind. We read repeatedly of the inability of planning agencies to accomplish much.[28] Would the exis-tence of sound cost-benefit analyses really have affected the outcomes (without concomitant institutional changes)? Probably not. Many of us have seen fairly convincing cost-benefit or economic analyses have little or no impact on decisions. What should urban planners and cost-benefit analysts do?

One possible course of action is for them simply to lower their sights and be less dissatisfied with the imperfections of urban living. If our aspirations are too far ahead of our capacities, it is supposed to be healthy to relax a little. Besides, the present bargaining apparatus in American cities, even with all its shortcomings, does have virtues. It seeks to compromise among various pressures and allots at least *some* weight to most of the important interests. The outcome is not random, nor is it completely perverse. The results are better than we could expect from an extreme form of hierarchy.[29] If the urban planner simply lowers his sights, cost-benefit analysis should perhaps be used to compare marginal modifications of municipal policies or modest plans that have a reasonable chance of acceptance under present political arrangements.

To some extent, this sort of life adjustment is no doubt in order. But it is not very satisfying, because we know that it is *sometimes* possible to effect relatively large changes in urban conditions. We should not completely rule out more ambitious actions; the relevant alternatives surely include inducing conditions to adjust as well as adjusting ourselves to conditions. Moreover, there is a whole spectrum of bargaining arrangements, even in American cities, and some work better than others. At minimum, then, urban planners can reasonably seek (1) marginal modification of cities within present urban political frameworks and (2) changes in political frameworks that might produce improved bargaining processes.

In other words they can seek ways of manipulating the cost-reward patterns that confront various participants. One method is by seeking modified institutional arrangements, as political scientists and public administration experts have done for a long time. Occasionally these modifications have been discussed explicitly as ways of altering costs and rewards.[30] This is surely the fruitful way to consider planning proposals or institutional changes—for example, to ask what a strong mayor form of government or a smaller Council does to the cost-gain structure that faces the various officials and groups. If the mayor can be made less dependent upon others, he may find the adoption of "rational" urban plans more rewarding but he may also find that being concerned about small minority groups is less rewarding than before. In any event, the way to analyze the effects of changes in the framework is in the light of impacts on cost-reward structures.

Another method of manipulating costs and rewards that needs cautious consideration is getting the federal government to use overt subsidies and penalties more frequently. These devices are extremely effective in shaping local cost-benefit patterns—they can make a freeway or a housing project or a pension plan exceedingly attractive to state or local governments. Moreover, extension of the use of federal subsidies appears to be politically feasible, for taxpayers across the country object surprisingly little to small payments per taxpayer for the benefit of particular areas or groups. But this technique is also a dangerous one to encourage. It sacrifices important advantages of the local bargaining process—the ability of small minority groups to exert at least a little influence, and the avoidance of extremes that the usual frustrating bargaining process insures. Having the central government shape local cost-reward patterns can be a powerful force for good—or for evil.

Still another way of influencing costs and rewards, though it is a weak one, is to develop and publicize good cost-benefit analyses pertaining to the principal alternative plans to be considered. If sound, such analyses can to some extent increase the costs to officials of pursuing "bad" policies.[31] If no one can see which action is better than another, in terms of community costs and benefits, then community interest is not directly and explicitly considered at all. If officials and voters can see a relatively sound and convincing case for one action, then it is at least slightly embarrassing (i.e., expensive) to ignore such evidence. One must admit, though, that this impact on cost-reward patterns is extremely weak. Since the general public as well as various political factions are hard put to decide whether or not an analysis is sound, no group can turn it into much of a weapon. Besides, very few persons are trying to maximize net community benefit.

There is another technique for influencing cost-reward patterns that deserves more exploration—the greater use, by urban governmental units themselves, of tax and compensation provisions to bring individual interests and the public interest closer into line. This is what we often attempt to do where there are wide discrepancies between private and total costs—e.g., tax the user of soft coal when it imposes heavy costs on others, subsidize or shelter inventors since their activity produces external benefits for which they are not compensated. Federal subsidies for freeways are attempts to bring local and national interests closer together, but, as mentioned before, extension of this technique poses serious problems. But urban areas themselves may be able to make greater use of this method. Advocates of urban planning measures might propose ways of charging more of the principal beneficiaries and compensating more of the principal losers instead of trying to sell a plan that distributes free windfalls to some officials and citizens and forces heavy costs upon others.

One way or another, the major opposition has to be compensated when actions are taken in a voluntaristic society. At present the compensation takes the form of intricate horse-trading or log-rolling which produces many bad side-effects or reaches an impasse that blocks further action. I am suggesting that it is sometimes feasible to charge the gainers and pay off the losers overtly and that where feasible this method can produce more rational planning. If an urban plan produces net community gains, it should be possible in principle to compensate the opposition. In practice it should be possible to move a little further in this direction. Maybe we can rig costs and rewards so as to bring self-interests more nearly into harmony with community interest. Perhaps we can move a bit closer to institutions such ". . . that a decision which is (subjectively) rational from the standpoint of the deciding individual, will remain rational when reassessed from the standpoint of the group."[32]

To mention a simple example, the cost-reward structures facing aldermen and municipal officials can often be improved simply by raising their salaries. This change makes their official duties less costly in terms of sacrificing their business interests and makes it less urgent for them to have their official actions pay off personally. If the effects of cost-reward patterns are explained more vividly to the public (instead of letting them believe that moral decay accounts for most bad decisions), voters may be willing to incur the costs of higher salaries. Still more important, though, would be influencing officials' costs and rewards by affecting constituents' views. Here especially is where tax and compensation policies might be effective. People who will gain from a project will not be turned against it even if they must give up part of the gains. People who will lose are not as violently opposed to a project if they are at least partially compensated.

Already, of course, we charge for easily identifiable benefits (e.g., water for irrigation or power for households) and compensate for easily identifiable damages (such as buildings and sites destroyed or used for freeways). It is time to consider going further. Maybe we can charge a crude (and conservative) approximation of the benefits from control of floods or water-pollution. Perhaps we can award rough (and again conservative) compensations for expected declines in property values due to re-zoning or other changes. If such taxes and compensations were incorporated into planning proposals in a realistic fashion, more voters' interests would coincide with net community benefits, and as a consequence the interests of aldermen and city officials would also more nearly coincide with community interests.

To explore these possibilities of rigging costs and rewards, we would have to examine costs and benefits from the standpoint of major factions as well as from the community's standpoint. Estimates of such costs and benefits are not new. Opponents of legislation often present evidence to show how much they would be damaged. Newspapers sometimes point out the windfalls that would be bestowed on other groups.

But we need to examine these costs and benefits to particular factions more systematically, to give them the attention and emphasis that they deserve. And we must try to perceive what kinds of pressures are felt by aldermen and other officials as a result of these costs and benefits and of the political framework.

It would be impossible, of course, to determine gains and costs of an urban plan from the viewpoint of each individual affected, but we might be able to see the major impacts on certain categories of persons. Past experience with re-zoning, freeways, and control of water pollution gives some information about the gains in property values attributable to these actions. Past experience also tells us something about which groups would get hurt. Many such effects used to be measured and labelled "secondary benefits." If recognized as benefits (and costs) from the standpoint of particular groups rather than as net community benefits (and costs), such estimates might yet serve a valuable purpose.

We need these analyses of cost-reward patterns, it seems to me, whichever strategy urban planners or cost-benefit analysts adopt. We need to know more about costs and gains from various groups' viewpoints if we are to explore the extended use of charges and compensations to implement urban planning. We need this knowledge if we are to recognize what urban plans have a chance of being implemented under present political institutions—i.e., if we are to design cost-benefit analyses that compare politically feasible urban plans. We need such knowledge too if we are merely to understand the possibilities of urban planning better—if we are to understand the strengths, weaknesses, and dangers of alternative institutional arrangements in municipal planning.

NOTES:

[1]Nathaniel Lichfield, "Cost-Benefit Analysis in City Planning," *Journal of the American Institute of Planners,* November, 1960, pp. 273–79. See also Lichfield's *Economics of Planned Development* (London: Estates Gazette, 1956).

Harvey S. Perloff traces the way urban planning has evolved in *Education for Planning; City, State and Regional* (Baltimore: The Johns Hopkins Press, 1957), especially pp. 9–24.

[2]Herbert A. Simon, Donald W. Smithburg, and Victor A. Thompson, *Public Administration* (New York: Alfred A. Knopf, 1950), p. 55 (italics in original).

[3]A number of persons have contributed extremely useful analyses or discussions. For example, see James G. March and Herbert A. Simon,

Organizations (New York: Wiley & Sons, 1958), especially pp. 9–11 and 83–111; Robert A. Dahl and Charles E. Lindblom, *Politics, Economics, and Welfare* (New York: Harper & Brothers, 1953), pp. 93–117; and Anthony Downs, "An Economic Theory of Political Action in a Democracy, *"Journal of Political Economy,* April, 1957, pp. 135–50.

[4]Note that there are severe limits to a man's ability to know and to choose wisely, however. Rationality has to mean, not omniscience and optimal choice, but something like trying to do the best one can in the circumstances.

[5]For a detailed discussion of the influences on behavior, see Simon, Smithburg, and Thompson, *op. cit.* (footnote 2), pp. 55–91.

[6]For public officials, as will be seen, this involves trying to survive or advance in the political-administrative hierarchy, which imposes many constraints on the official's behavior. The pursuit of self-interest does not imply that constraints or costs will be ignored.

[7]See Herbert A. Simon, *Administrative Behavior* (2nd ed.) (New York: Macmillan Co., 1961), pp. 63–64, 186–88, 198–217.

[8]*Washington Metropolitan Area Water Problems,* Hearings before the Joint Committee on Washington Metropolitan Problems, Congress of the United States, 85th Congress, 2nd Session (Washington: U.S. Government Printing Office, 1958), pp. 559–63.

[9]*Ibid.,* p. 338.

[10]Downs, *op. cit.* (footnote 3), pp. 135–50.

[11]See their book entitled *Politics, Planning, and the Public Interest* (Glencoe, Ill.: The Free Press, 1955).

[12]Most books on public administration give the reader some feeling for these interrelationships. A systematic discussion of influences on municipal decisions is presented in Wallace S. Sayre and Herbert Kaufman, *Governing New York City,* Parts 2 and 3 on "Strategies of the Contestants" (New York: Russell Sage Foundation, 1960), pp. 121–708.

[13]The subtle ways in which influences are felt and the fact that interest groups often need no overt representation when decisions are being reached are well known. For instance, see David B. Truman, *The Governmental Process* (New York: Alfred A. Knopf, 1951), p. 449.

[14]John Krutilla has pointed out that it is advisable to distinguish between (1) public outlays to make economically efficient investments, such as transportation aids or water-pollution controls, and (2) those avowedly intended to redistribute wealth. As Krutilla has stressed, the appropriate cost-benefit measurements from a community standpoint

depend upon the purposes of each proposal. This distinction is a relevant and an important one; though I believe that cost-reward structures, unless bargaining arrangements are just right, can distort either type of project—e.g., proposals conceived originally as ways of helping impoverished farmers as well as those intended as conventional investments.

[15]*Transportation Plan for the National Capital Region,* Hearings before the Joint Committee on Washington Metropolitan Problems, Congress of the United States, 86th Congress, 1st Session (Washington, D.C.: U.S. Government Printing Office, 1960).

[16]*Ibid.,* especially pp. 793–823, 873, 901–53, 981–89.

[17]*Ibid.,* p. 983.

[18]*Ibid.,* pp. 594–694.

[19]*Ibid,* pp. 605–606.

[20]*National Capital Transportation Act of 1960,* Hearings before the Joint Committee on Washington Metropolitan Problems, Congress of the United States, 86th Congress, 2nd Session (Washington: U.S. Government Printing Office, 1960), p. 5.

[21]See, for example, Paul Blanshard, *Investigating City Government in the La Guardia Administration,* A Report of the Activities of the Department of Investigation and Accounts, 1934–1937 [no publisher indicated], 1937, and James Reichley, *The Art of Government: Reform and Organizational Politics in Philadelphia,* A Report to the Fund for the Republic, reprinted from *Greater Philadelphia Magazine,* Philadelphia, Pa., [no date shown but probably appeared in 1959], pp. 1–38. Earlier, of course, there was the muckraking era during which Lincoln Steffens wrote his famous exposés.

[22]Blanshard, *op. cit.* (footnote 21), p. 61.

[23]For additional cases and discussions that are especially pertinent to these matters, see Edward C. Banfield, *Political Influence* (New York: Free Press, 1961).

[24]Sayre and Kaufman, *op. cit.* (footnote 12), pp. 88–89.

[25]See Harold Stein (ed.), "Gotham in the Air Age" in *Public Administration and Policy Development* (New York: Harcourt, Brace and Co., 1952), pp. 145–97.

[26]Reichley, *op. cit.* (footnote 21), p. 14.

[27]*Ibid.,* p. 18.

[28]As an illustration, see William A. Robson, *The Government and Mis-Government of London* (London: George Allen & Unwin, 1939), pp. 186–91.

[29]Charles E. Lindblom, "Bargaining: The Hidden Hand in Government," RAND RM-1434-RC, *The RAND Corporation*, Santa Monica, Calif., (1955), pp. 1–44.
[30]Simon, Smithburg, and Thompson, *op. cit.* (footnote 2), pp. 451–87.
[31]John Krutilla has suggested two important points here: Such analyses can increase these costs to officials further if the analyses are (1) better insulated from the political process, freeing the studies from political judgments and fixing more clearly the responsibility of decision-makers, and (2) more timely so that they can be brought to bear in time.
[32]Simon, *op. cit.* (footnote 7), p. 243.

11.
Benefit-Cost Analysis:
Its Relevance to Public Investment Decisions*

ARTHUR MAASS

The United States government has for some time used benefit-cost analysis in the design and justification of dams and other waters resources improvements. Currently the government is trying to adapt the technique to other public investment programs. At the request of the Bureau of the Budget, the Brookings Institution held a major conference on the topic in November 1963 with papers on applying benefit-cost analysis to urban highways, urban renewal, outdoor recreation, civil aviation, government research and development, and public health.[1] In 1965 the Bureau of the Budget established a special unit to adapt and apply benefit-cost and cost-effectiveness studies to a broad range of government programs. It is appropriate, therefore, to examine and evaluate this important branch of welfare economics.

WHAT IS THE PROBLEM?

The major limitation of benefit-cost analysis, as it has been applied to public investments in the United States, is that it ranks projects and programs in terms only of economic efficiency. (At the national level this means that projects and programs are judged by the amount that they increase the national product.) But the objective of most public programs is not simply, not even principally, economic efficiency. The redistribution of income to classes or to regions is an important objective in government plans—witness the Appalachia Program; and there are

*Reprinted by permission of the author and publisher from Arthur Maass, "Benefit-Cost Analysis: Its Relevance to Public Investment Decisions," in *Quarterly Journal of Economics*, Vol. 80, No. 2 (May, 1966), 208–226, copyright by the President and fellows of Harvard College. Arthur Maass is professor of government at Harvard University.

other objectives, too, the promotion of national self-sufficiency, for example.

In other words, the objective functions of most government programs are complex; yet benefit-cost analysis has been adapted to only a single objective—economic efficiency. Thus, benefit-cost analysis may be largely irrelevant, or relevant to only a small part of the problem of evaluating public projects and programs. We should not settle for the current state of benefit-cost analysis, but rather find ways to make it applicable to the real issues of public investment.

Now in all complex objective functions for government programs, economic efficiency will be one term. A second is frequently income redistribution, as we have noted, to classes (e.g., the poor) or to regions (e.g., depressed areas). These two objectives may be complementary in some ways; a program designed to transfer income from the rest of the nation to Appalachia or from the wealthy to the poor may also increase national product.[2] But a government program that maximizes efficiency will not necessarily, indeed is not likely, to achieve a specified high level of income redistribution. Thus, a planner who is responsible for developing a program or project for both purposes will need to know the relative weights to assign to efficiency and income redistribution.

Assume that the problem is to design an irrigation project on an Indian reservation so as to increase the income of the Indians as a group and to increase food production for the nation as a whole. The relation between income for the Indians (income redistribution) and food production (national economic efficiency) in this case can be stated in any one of three ways as follows:[3]

(1) Maximize net income to the Indians, subject to a constraint that the ratio of efficiency benefits to efficiency costs is at least 1.0 to 1.0, or 0.9 to 1.0, or some other.

(2) Maximize net benefits from food production in national terms— i.e., economic efficiency—subject to a constraint that the Indians net $X thousand per year.

(3) Maximize a weighted sum of net benefits from economic efficiency and income redistribution in which $1 of income to the Indians is valued at $(1 \times X)$ of efficiency. (In this case the X can be called a shadow premium on redistribution benefits.)

With proper values these three statements will be equivalent. Any constraint can be converted into a shadow price and any shadow price, into a constraint.

The efficiency benefits and costs of this two-term objective function can be measured fairly well by the art of benefit-cost analysis in its present state. There are problems, to be sure, resulting from such factors as the collective character of the benefits of many public programs, the need to measure costs in terms of resource displacements rather than market prices where these two measures diverge, the selection of an appropriate discount rate, various so-called external effects; but great progress has been made on these in recent years.[4] Thus, all that is needed to solve the maximization equation is to specify the trade-off ratio between efficiency and income redistribution. If there is a way of finding this ratio, the maximization problem can be solved in any of its three forms, and we can design projects and programs that are responsive to a realistic two-factor objective function.

There is a way to determine the trade-off—through the political process. For the federal government my studies indicate that there is a capacity in the legislative process to make the trade-off decisions that can then govern the design of projects and programs. The President initiates the legislative process; the Congress examines the President's proposals in the light of alternatives and accepts, modifies, or rejects them. Thus, the experts in the executive departments need to develop data that show the effects on the design of programs and projects of different trade-off ratios. This the executive can do. The President needs to select one or a range of these ratios and thereby initiate formally the legislative process. This the President can do. And finally, the Congress, when presented with such data and such a presidential initiative, needs to and can, as we shall see, respond in order.

Ironically but understandably, the field of public investment for which the present benefit-cost technique is most advanced, water resources, is the field for which the political technique for determining trade-offs among efficiency and other objectives is most primitive. The legislative process for water resources consists principally of omnibus bills that authorize individual projects, rather than of legislation that sets standards and criteria. In the housing and urban renewal area, by contrast, standards and criteria, based on both income redistribution and economic efficiency, are determined in the legislative process, and benefit-cost analysis is primitive.

The problem is to combine the advanced state of the art of efficiency benefit-cost analysis, as found in water resources planning, with an equally sophisticated technique for relating efficiency benefits and costs to those stemming from other objectives.

HAVE BENEFITS BEEN OVERESTIMATED?

In this context it is interesting to examine the arguments over so-called secondary benefits and how they should be included, if at all, in project analyses. There is no such thing as a secondary benefit. A secondary benefit, as the phrase has been used in the benefit-cost literature, is in fact a benefit in support of an objective other than efficiency.[5] The word benefit (and the word cost, too) has no meaning by itself, but only in association with an objective; there are efficiency benefits, income redistribution benefits, and others. Thus, if the objective function for a public program involves more than economic efficiency—and it will in most cases—there is no legitimate reason for holding that the efficiency benefits are primary and should be included in the benefit-cost analysis whereas benefits in support of other objectives are secondary and should be mentioned, if at all, in separate subsidiary paragraphs of the survey report. Using the curent language and current standards, most of the benefits to the Indians in the Indian irrigation project are secondary benefits. How silly!

In this context it is interesting also to examine the conclusion of many non-governmental studies of government planning for water resources projects, namely, that benefits have been overestimated. Professor Hubert Marshall recently recited the evidences of chronic overestimation in a major address before the Western Resources Conference at Fort Collins.[6] The principal cause of such benefit "overestimation" is, I believe, the unreal restrictions placed on the analysis of projects by the unreal but virtual standard that the relation of efficiency benefits to efficiency costs is the indicator of a project's worth, when in fact the project is conceived and planned for objectives in addition to efficiency. In such an incongruous circumstance one might expect project planners to use a broad definition of efficiency benefits. The critics, either not understanding or unsympathetic to the planners' plight, have judged them by a more rigorous definition of efficiency.[7]

HOW DID WE GET TO WHERE WE ARE?

Why has benefit-cost analysis developed in this way? Certainly not because of any myopia on the part of the Congress, though executive officers are frequently quick to blame Congress for their ills. To be sure, we do not have adequate legislative objectives, standards, or trade-off ratios for the design and evaluation of water resources projects, but this is because the President has failed to initiate the legislative process, not because of a lack of receptivity to such initiatives by Congress. In fact certain committees of Congress, impatient with the President for not proposing legislation to set standards, have tried to initiate the legislative process themselves; but without cooperation from the executive they have failed, understandably.[8] The task of assembling and analyzing data, the necessary first step in the legislative process, is beyond the capacity of the Congress and its staffs in complex areas like this one. Insofar as there is a general standard for the design of water projects that has been approved by Congress in legislation, it is a thirty-year-old statement that "the benefits to whomsoever they may accrue should exceed the costs."[9] This standard, you will note, does not specify efficiency benefits, but "benefits to whomsoever they may accrue."

The executive agencies have painted themselves into the efficiency box. In 1950 the Subcommittee on Benefits and Costs of the Federal Inter-Agency River Basin Committee gave overwhelming emphasis to the efficiency ranking function in its now well-known "Green Book" report.[10] In 1952 the Bureau of the Budget, in a Budget Circular that neither required nor invited formal review and approval by the Congress, nailed this emphasis into national policy, adopting it as the standard by which the bureau would review agency projects to determine their standing in the President's program.[11] And soon thereafter agency planning manuals were revised, where necessary, to reflect this Budget Circular. In this way benefits to all became virtually restricted to benefits that increase national product.

The federal bureaucrats, it should be noted, were not acting in a vacuum; they were reflecting the doctrines of the new welfare economics which has focused entirely on economic efficiency. Non-efficiency considerations have been held to be outside the domain of the welfare economist. They have been called by such loaded names as inefficient, value-laden, altruistic, merit wants, uneconomical.[12]

WHAT CHANGES IN WELFARE ECONOMICS THEORY ARE NEEDED?

From a practical point of view the new welfare economics has dealt exclusively with efficiency because for it, and not for other objectives, benefit and cost data are provided automatically by the market, though market prices sometimes have to be doctored. Theoretically, however, the preoccupation of present-day welfare economics, and its branch of benefit-cost analysis, with economic efficiency results from its very basic assumptions, and two of these in my view can and should be abandoned.

First is indifference to the distribution of income generated by a government program or project—the assumption that each dollar of income from the program is of equal social value regardless of who receives it. In benefit-cost analysis that maximizes efficiency, an extra dollar to a Texas oil man is as desirable socially as one to an Arkansas tenant farmer, and an additional dollar of benefits for Appalachia, West Virginia is no more worthwhile than one for Grosse Pointe, Michigan.

Few welfare economists support the social implications of this basic assumption, and they would compensate for them in one of two ways. Some hold that the professional planners should design projects and programs for economic efficiency, for which benefit-cost analysis can provide the necessary ranking function; and that thereafter these project designs can be doctored and modified by a political process to account for any "uneconomic" objectives.[13] But this response is unsatisfactory for reasons already given. Where government programs are intended for complex objectives they should be designed, where this is possible, for such objectives, not designed for one objective, which may not be the most important, and subsequently modified in an effort to account for others. Almost inevitably economic efficiency will be overweighted in such a scheme. How relevant is this type of planning for our Indian irrigation project? Furthermore, such a planning process calls on political institutions to perform a task for which they are not well equipped. Where the approval and modification of individual projects, rather than a debate on objectives and standards for designing projects in the first place, is the *principal* activity of the legislative process, decision-making for the nation can disintegrate into project-trading. In the legislature, for example, the voices of the whole house and of committees are muted at the expense of those of individual members, each making decisions for projects in his district and accepting reciprocally the decisions of his colleagues. Nor does the executive under these circumstances play a more general or high-minded role. The public investment decision process can be organized, hopefully, to play to the strengths rather than to the weaknesses of political institutions.

An alternative response of some welfare economists to the inequitable social consequences of the basic assumption of indifference to income distribution is as follows. It is more efficient to redistribute income directly from one group of individuals to another, through government programs of taxation and subsidies, than to do so indirectly through government investment programs that are designed also to increase national product. If the government's objectives are, for example, to increase both national food production and income of the Indians, it should plan to accomplish these by two programs rather than by a single one. Government planners should design the most efficient program for increasing food production, which may mean additional irrigation facilities in the Imperial Valley of California where there are no Indians. Then, with taxes collected from the irrigators that represent their willingness to pay for their new benefits, the government should make subsidy payments to the Indians. In this way, so goes the argument, the government can achieve the best of both worlds. Best in this context means efficient, however, and there is no reason why a community need prefer the most efficient method for redistributing income, especially if it requires transferring cash from one group to another. As Marglin points out in his treatment of this subject, the means by which a desired distribution of income is achieved may be of great importance to the community.[14] In our example, the community would probably be willing to give up some efficiency to see the living standard of the Indians improved by their own labors rather than by the dole. In short, the community may quite properly want to realize multiple purposes through public investment projects and programs, and if benefit-cost analysis is to be of great use in planning these activities, then the basic assumption of indifference to their distributive consequences must be abandoned.

It should be noted, however, that where, as in the case of the Indian irrigation project, a government program produces benefits that can be sold or otherwise charged for, a desired redistribution of income can be achieved by both the quantity of benefits produced and the prices charged for them. For any given quantity of irrigation water, the smaller the repayment required from the Indians, the greater the income they will receive. Thus, when the agency men prepare data showing the effects on public programs of alternative trade-offs between economic efficiency and income redistribution, these alternatives should include different repayment possibilities.

The second basic assumption of the new welfare economics and of benefit-cost analysis that needs to be challenged is consumers' sovereignty—reliance solely on market-exhibited preferences of individuals. This assumption, to be sure, provides normative significance for the familiar prescriptions of welfare economics on which the efficiency calculus is based—for example, that price ought to equal marginal costs. Nonetheless, it is not relevant to all public investment decisions, for an individual's market preference is a response in terms of what he believes to be good for his own economic interest, not for the community.

Each individual plays a number of roles in his life—social science literature is filled with studies of role differentiation—and each role can lead him to a unique response to a given choice situation. Thus an individual has the capacity to respond in a given case, to formulate his preferences, in several ways, including these two: (1) what he believes to be good for himself—largely his economic self-interest, and (2) what he believes to be good for the political community. The difference between these two can be defined in terms of breadth of view. To the extent that an individual's response is community- rather than privately-oriented, it places greater emphasis on the individual's estimate of the consequences of his choice for the larger community.

Now, the response that an individual gives in any choice situation will depend in significant part on how the question is asked of him, and this means not simply the way a question is worded, but the total environment in which it is put and discussed. This can be illustrated by a small group experiment. Questions with relevance for the church (e.g., should birth control information be provided to married individuals who desire it?) were asked of Catholic students randomly divided into two groups. One group met in a small room where they were made aware of their common religious membership. The other group met in a large auditorium, along with hundreds of other students of many religions, where no effort was made to establish awareness of common religious beliefs. Although all of the students were instructed to respond with their "own personal opinions," there was a significant difference between the replies of the group that were aware of their common religious membership and the unaware group, the former approximating more closely the orthodox Catholic position against birth control.[15]

An individual's response depends, then, on the institutional environment in which the question is asked. Since the relevant response for public investment analysis is a community- not privately- oriented one, the great challenge for welfare economics is to frame questions in such a way as to elicit from individuals community-oriented answers. The market is an institution designed to elicit privately-oriented responses from individuals and to relate these responses to each other. For the federal government the electoral, legislative, and administrative processes together constitute the institution designed to elicit community-oriented responses. The Maass-Cooper model describes these processes within such a context.[16]

Although several welfare economists have recognized explicitly that individuals play several roles and that these roles influence preferences, they go on to say that in making decisions relating to social welfare each individual uses a composite utility function, a total net position representing a balance of all of his roles.[17] This last hypothesis, which is not supported by experimental evidence, is unfortunate. It misses the point that an individual will respond differently depending on how the question is asked of him, and it fails to give proper emphasis to the differentiation of institutions for putting the question—e.g., the market institution to elicit private-oriented responses and political institutions for those which are community-oriented.

Ideally we want the community, not market, responses of individuals with respect to both factors in our complex objective function—economic efficiency and income redistribution. Fortunately, however, market-determined prices are a fairly good surrogate for the economic efficiency factor, providing adjustments are made for so-called externalities and the like.[18] This is opportune. Were it not for the propriety of using market-related prices for efficiency benefits and costs, benefit-cost analysis for public projects and programs would be beyond the capacity of available economic techniques and of political institutions as they operate today.

Some day, I am confident, we shall be able to use institutions that elicit community-oriented responses to measure all factors in a complex objective function—efficiency, income redistribution, and others. The very recent search by a few economists, inspired largely by the work of Kenneth Arrow, for a new criterion of social welfare may contribute to this end.[19] The more modest proposal of this article is that we use political institutions to measure the trade-off ratio between a basically market-determined efficiency and the single most important non-efficiency objective of a government program, which is likely to be income redistribution but may be some other.

WHAT IS THE EVIDENCE THAT TRADE-OFFS CAN BE DETERMINED?

It remains to be demonstrated that there is a capacity in the legislative process to select trade-off ratios in a way that will be useful for the design of government programs and projects. As stated earlier, the legislative process involves three steps. First, the officials in the executive departments prepare data showing what would be the effects on programs and projects of alternative trade-offs between economic efficiency and another objective; second, the President, with these data in hand, selects a trade-off ratio and proposes it to Congress as the legislative standard; and third, Congress examines the President's proposal, in the light of the alternatives developed in the departments and of others that may come from outside sources, and accepts, rejects, or modifies it.

The first step should not involve great difficulties, especially in water resources where analysis of the efficiency factor is well advanced, although there will be obvious problems in areas where economic efficiency analysis is primitive. For continuing programs, the data necessary to initiate the legislative process need not relate to projects and programs being designed or to be designed; they can be drawn from projects already in operation and in some cases from hypothetical or prototype projects. Agency men can re-examine complete projects and programs and estimate how differently they would have been built and would have operated with different trade-offs among objectives. At the same time they can reflect in the data that they prepare for new investment programs information generated during previous planning periods, thereby using a sequential planning process.[20]

It is at the final, or congressional, stage that doubters will raise most questions, and it is, of course, this stage that is most difficult to prove, because in the water resources area, for which the legislative initiative could be taken most clearly, the President has failed to act. To demonstrate Congress' capacity we must, therefore, turn to public investment programs for which standards have been set in legislation, and these are ones for which efficiency benefit-cost analysis is so rudimentary that it is necessary to examine the record very carefully for implicit evidence of a concern for trade-offs between efficiency and other objectives.

Legislation authorizing the National System of Interstate Highways, principally the Act of 1956, furnishes one example.[21] The legislation provides that the system should consist of 41,000 miles of roads which are identified generally as to location, and it sets design criteria for these roads. The criteria depart from those of earlier highway legislation in three important respects, apart from the taxing methods for financing the federal government's share of the costs. First, roads are to be designed for predicted traffic volumes of 1975, and the monetary authorizations are calculated from this standard.[22] Second, the federal-state matching ratio is changed from 50:50 to 90:10. Third, the formula for apportioning funds among the states is changed. The earlier formula for the primary system of roads was one-third on the basis of each of the following ratios: a state's population to the total U.S. population, a state's area to the total U.S. land area, a state's rural delivery and star routes to the total U.S. mileage of such roads. The new formula provides a single ratio: the estimated cost of completing the Interstate System within the borders of a state to the total estimated cost of completing the entire system by a fixed date, 1972.[23] This last criterion was agreed to after considerable discussion involving numerous alternatives, but principally two: the one adopted and one that would continue to give considerable weight to a state's area and its population. As Major has shown, these alternatives represent respectively economic efficiency, or more properly a surrogate for efficiency, and income redistribution. Given the requirement of completing a given mileage, by a given date, to a given capacity (1975 traffic volume), an apportionment based on cost of completion would be efficient; and one based on such factors as a state's area would introduce other objectives into the program, namely, redistribution of income (largely federal construction funds) to rural states where traffic volumes and highway construction costs per mile are typically lower. This is especially true because the alternative provided that if a state received more funds than necessary to complete its portion of the Interstate System, it could divert a percentage of the excess for use on its other federally-aided roads.

A study of the legislative process in which these new program criteria, especially the third one, were adopted has some useful lessons for our inquiry. There was a vigorous and effective executive initiative of the process. The concept of uniform completion of an Interstate System in all states at approximately the same time appears to have been recommended first by a non-federal entity, the American Association of State Highway Officials. Thereafter the Bureau of Public Roads made a detailed factual study of the costs of building an Interstate System. The President, in an address before the 1954 Governors' Conference, proposed that the nation develop a new master plan for highways, and he appointed an Advisory Committee on a National Highway Program, chaired by General Lucius Clay, to prepare one. The Clay Committee used the Bureau of Public Roads report as its empirical base. It recommended the three design standards that were finally adopted, presenting them in the context of alternatives about which debate in the legislative process could and did revolve.[24] Both the BPR and the Clay reports were sent to the Congress, along with a Presidential recommendation. The discussion in Congress, in committee and on the floor, was informed and extensive. Information was available on the expected consequences in terms of investment of choosing alternative standards, the participants were aware of the nature of the choices they had to make, and their debate was rich in relevant arguments pro and con on the alternatives, especially on apportionment formulae.

What we have called economic efficiency in this case—i.e., the most efficient way to satisfying a fixed requirement—is of course quite different from economic efficiency as an objective in benefit-cost analysis for water resources, where it means to maximize the contribution of a project to national product. The latter concept played no part in setting the standards for the highway program. The art of efficiency benefit-cost analysis is much less well developed for public investments in highways than in water resources developments, and this was even more true ten years ago than it is today. It is not unreasonable to suggest, from the record of the legislative process for the Interstate Highway System, that had data been available on real economic efficiency and on alternative trade-offs between it and income redistribution, these would have been used intelligently in setting standards.

Comparing the legislative processes for the Interstate Highway System and water resources, the former is less concerned with authorizing individual projects that have been designed and more concerned with setting standards for project design. To be sure, the highway act authorized 41,000 miles of roads and fixed their general locations. Design of the roads, including definite locations for them, was left, however, for administrative action insofar as the federal government was concerned.

In federal programs for housing and urban renewal, standards and design criteria have been set in the legislative process, and the recent legislative history of the rent supplement program is an instructive example.[25] In his Housing Message of 1965, President Johnson described a proposed program for rent supplement payments as "the most crucial new instrument in our effort to improve the American city." The federal government was to guarantee to certain private builders the payment of a significant part of the rent for housing units built for occupancy by moderate-income families. These are families with incomes below the level necessary to obtain standard housing at area market prices, but above the level required for admission to publicly-owned low-rent housing units. The rent payments were to be the difference between 20 per cent of a family's income (the proportion of income that a moderate-income family is expected to allocate to housing) and the fair-market rental of the standard housing to be built. The President proposed an authorization of $200 million over four years which was designed to encourage the construction of 500,000 new housing units in this period.

The housing supported in this way would constitute some but not all of the rental units in new housing projects.

The Housing Act of 1961 had also included a program designed specifically for moderate-income families, but this program had encountered certain problems that slowed its expected impact. Section 221d(3) of the 1961 Act provided for 100 per cent loans to qualified private builders at below-market interest rates. The low interest rates were to keep rents within the reach of moderate-income families. The law provided, however, that the interest rate was to be the average rate on all outstanding marketable federal obligations. This was 3⅛ per cent when the program began, but it had risen to approximately 4⅛ per cent by mid-1965. This meant that rents would be significantly higher and beyond the capacity of most moderate-income families. Another problem with the 1961 program was that the low interest mortgages constituted a heavy drain on the special assistance funds of the Federal National Mortgage Association (FNMA), the federal housing credit agency that purchased them. Because these mortgages were below market rates, FNMA could not issue against them debentures for sale in private capital markets, and they remained a 100 per cent charge on federal funds. Nonetheless, the administration recommended in 1965 that the 221d(3) program be continued for four years with a mortgage authorization of $1.5 billion, for about 125,000 new housing units. But this program was to be phased out if the rent supplement proposal worked as its backers hoped that it would.

The Administration had three principal objectives in proposing rent supplements. The first was to increase the number of housing starts. This derived from a desire to expand the national housing stock and a concern about the possibly failing health of the housing industry and the industry's impact on the national economy. We can equate this objective roughly with increasing national product, or economic efficiency. The government's housing experts found that there was a large untapped market for new housing among moderate-income families, and that rent supplements for them would stimulate the rapid construction of substantial amounts of new housing.

The second principal objective of the Administration in recommending a rent supplement program was to give direct assistance to a large group of families with incomes above the public housing level but below the level needed to obtain standard housing at market prices. This objective we can equate with income redistribution—to moderate-income families.

As for direct assistance to low-income families, the Administration bill would authorize additional public housing units. Over a four-year period 140,000 new units were to be built and 100,000 units purchased or leased from private owners and rehabilitated. Using the trickle down theory, the Administration could claim that all other housing programs that increased the national stock of standard housing would ultimately improve the housing of the poor, but certainly the primary and direct impact of the rent supplement program, insofar as its objective was income redistribution, favored moderate-income families.

The Administration's rent supplement program contained, then, as one design criterion, a trade-off ratio relating the objectives of efficiency and income redistribution and as a second, a specification of the group to be favored by the redistribution. The second criterion was explicit in the Administration's legislative initiative, though the first was largely implicit.

The Administration's third principal objective for the rent supplement program was "economic integration." Families being aided by the government would live in projects with families who would pay normal market rentals for their housing. In this respect the new program differed from most other federal housing programs for disadvantaged groups, for the latter promoted economic segregation. Only the poor live in public housing; all units in 221d(3) projects are for occupancy by designated groups. To encourage economic integration even where local authorities may oppose it, the Administration proposed that in certain cases projects supported by rent supplements need not conform to locally approved "workable programs" for housing development.

After hearings, debates, and conferences, Congress modified drastically the Administration's design criteria for a rent supplement program. Briefly, the supplements are to be given for standard housing units that are to be occupied by low-income families. As a result, both the trade-off ratio between efficiency and income redistribution and the impact of the redistribution itself have been changed.

The relative contributions of the program to increasing national product and to redistributing income have been altered because, with a given authorization or appropriation, there will be fewer housing starts if rents of low-, rather than moderate-, income families are supplemented. The unit costs of standard housing are the same in either case, but the supplement required to make up the difference between what the family can pay and what is needed to support the new housing varies greatly. The new law authorizes $150 million for rent supplements (rather than the $200 million proposed by the President). Ac-

cording to current (December 1965) estimates of housing experts, this
$150 million would result in 350–375,000 housing starts over four years
if it were available for the Administration's program of aiding moderate-
income families. As rent supplements for low-income families, the same
money will induce only 250–300,000 starts.[26]

As for the criterion that governs the group to be benefited, the relative
impacts on low-and moderate-income families of the original and revised
programs for rent supplements and closely related activities are shown in
Table I.

TABLE I.

IMPACT ON LOW AND MODERATE INCOME FAMILIES OF CERTAIN
PROVISIONS OF 1965 HOUSING ACT

Program	Administration Proposal	Congressional Action
(all figures are thousands of housing units over four year)		
Low income		
Public housing	240	240
Trickle down from all programs that increase national stock of standard housing	ok	ok
Rent supplement program	zero	250–300
Moderate income		
Rent supplements	467–500	zero
221d(3)	125 (*but* problems in achieving this because of high interest rate and drain on FNMA funds)	125 (*and* this likely to be achieved because interest rate fixed at 3% and provision made for tapping private capital)

The impact of Congress' revisions on the Administration's third objective of economic integration is not so clear. Insofar as it is poor rather
than moderate-income families who are enabled to live in housing developments along with families that are able to pay normal rents, a
more dramatic integration can be achieved. On the other hand, it is
clear from the legislative history that Congress does not intend that the

housing agency exempt any rent supplement projects from the "workable plan" requirement, which means that local controls will continue.

The housing case study, like that of the highway program, shows that there is a capacity in the legislative process to discuss and adopt standards and criteria to control the design of public projects and programs; that the Congress is prepared to focus its efforts on such standards and forego authorization of the projects themselves—public works for housing, urban renewal, and community facilities are not individually authorized by law; and that the legislative process for setting standards can be used to select trade-off ratios where a program has two objectives. On this latter point, the rent supplement case is a bit weak, to be sure. The Administration in its legislative initiative did not make sufficiently explicit the trade-off between economic efficiency and income redistribution that was involved in its proposal for approximately 500,000 new housing starts for the benefit of moderate-income families. Administration witnesses failed to give a clear statement of how the two objectives were related and how the program would differ if alternative trade-off ratios were assumed. One reason for this failure is that efficiency benefit-cost analysis has not been perfected for housing programs as it has for water resources. Nonetheless, the Congress, in reviewing the President's program, managed to focus on the relevant design criteria and, after extensive consideration, including some confused debate, revised them in a way that apparently was consistent with its policy preferences. Also, the executive now has a legislated standard that it can use in redesigning the relevant housing programs. How much better the process would have been if the initiative had been better prepared!

THE LESSON

To those in the executive departments of the United States government, the lessons of this article should be clear. If the subject is water resources, initiate a legislative proposal for setting a trade-off value between economic efficiency and the most important non-efficiency objective that is relevant to your agency's program. Once this is approved, you can forget about secondary benefits, probably be relieved from the repetitive and profession-wise insulting charges that you persistently overestimate benefits, and you can design projects that are more in accord with the nation's objectives. If the subject is highways, or housing, or most other public investment programs, perfect the efficiency benefit-cost technique for your agency's program. Once this is done, there should be no difficulty in deriving through the legislative process a trade-off between efficiency and another objective. As a result, the design and selection of projects will be more intelligent and the program should be more convincing to those who judge it.

After the agencies have learned how to work with two-term objective functions, they can try to solve a more complex one. For the time being, however, purposes other than efficiency and the most important non-efficiency objective will need to be treated descriptively in the familiar "additional paragraphs" of program and project reports.

NOTES:

This article results from several studies of the public investment decision process by members of the Harvard Water Program. The program has been supported by the United States Army Engineers, Resources For the Future, Inc., and the United States Public Health Service.

[1] Robert Dorfman (ed.) *Measuring Benefits of Government Investments* (Washington: The Brookings Institution, 1965).

[2] For conditions under which regional redistribution in the United States can be achieved without any significant loss in economic efficiency, see Koichi Mera, "Efficiency and Equalization in Interregional Economic Development," unpublished Ph.D. thesis, Harvard University, 1965. For a more general statement of the relations between economic efficiency and income distribution, see Stephen A. Marglin, "Objectives of Water-Resource Development: A General Statement," in Arthur Maass, Maynard M. Hufschmidt, Robert Dorfman, Harold A. Thomas, Jr., Stephen A. Marglin, and Gordon Maskew Fair, *Design of Water-Resource Systems* (Cambridge: Harvard University Press, 1962), pp. 63–67.

[3] This example is adapted from Marglin, "Objectives of Water-Resource Development," *op. cit.*

[4] For a discussion of these problems as of 1961, see Chaps. 2 (Marglin), 3 (Dorfman), 4 (Marglin) in Maass, Hufschmidt, *et al., Design of Water-Resource Systems, op. cit.;* and Maynard M. Hufschmidt, John Krutilla, and Julius Margolis, with assistance of Stephen A. Marglin, "Report of Panel of Consultants to the Bureau of the Budget on Standards and Criteria for Formulating and Evaluating Federal Water Resources Developments" (Washington, June 30, 1961), mimeo. For examples of more recent developments see Peter O. Steiner, "The Role of Alternative Cost in Project Design and Selection," this *Journal,* LXXIX (Aug. 1965), 417–30, and Kenneth J. Arrow, "Discounting and Public Investment Criteria," paper presented at Water Resources Conference, Fort Collins, Colorado, July 6, 1965.

[5]The term has been used also to describe a small class of *efficiency* benefits that are *induced* rather than *produced* directly, by the public investment, but this distinction is of questionable utility.

[6]Hubert Marshall, "Politics and Efficiency in Water Development," Fort Collins, Colorado, July 7, 1965.

[7]There are causes, in addition to what I consider to be the principal cause, for so-called benefit overestimation, and these, but not the principal cause, are given in Marshall's Fort Collins paper, *op. cit.*

[8]Arthur Maass, "System Design and the Political Process: A General Statement," in Maass, Hufschmidt, *et. al., Design of Water-Resource Systems, op. cit.,* p. 588.

[9]The origin of this provision of the Flood Control Act of 1936 (49 Stat. 1570) did not, incidentally, come from a presidential initiative.

[10]U.S. Federal Inter-Agency River Basin Committee, Subcommittee on Benefits and Costs, *Proposed Practices for Economic Analysis of River Basin Projects* (May 1950).

[11]U.S. Bureau of the Budget, *Circular A-47,* Dec. 31, 1952.

[12]See for an example Richard A. Musgrave, *The Theory of Public Finance* (New York: McGraw Hill, 1959). The first of these labels is perhaps correct technically, but even this cannot be said of the others, for efficiency is not necessarily either less or more value laden, or altruistic, or meritorious than other objectives.

[13]In essence this is what Dorfman proposes for West Pakistan. Robert Dorfman, "An Economic Strategy for West Pakistan," *Asian Survey,* III (May 1963), 217–23.

[14]Stephen A. Marglin, "Objectives of Water-Resource Development," *op. cit.,* pp. 17–18, 62–67. Jan Tinbergen, *On the Theory of Economic Policy* (Amsterdam: North Holland, 1952), observes that in the normal case n programs (or instruments) are required to maximize a welfare function that includes n objectives (or targets). But for his normal case Tinbergen assumes that only the results of the programs, not their qualitative characteristics, affect welfare and that planners are free to select that level of achievement of each objective that maximizes the over-all welfare function. This freedom is theirs only if n programs are available to the planners. Our discussion, on the other hand, proceeds from the assumptions that the qualitative characteristics of the program affect welfare, and that the number of acceptable programs may be fewer than the number of objectives, which necessitates the trade-off among objectives. This would be an abnormal case in Tinbergen's formulation.

[15]W. W. Charters, Jr. and Theordore M. Newcomb, "Some Attitudinal

Effects of Experimentally Increased Salience of a Membership Group," in Eleanor E. Maccoby, Theodore M. Newcomb, and Eugene L. Hartley, *Readings in Social Psychology* (New York: Henry Holt, 1958), pp. 276–81.

[16]Arthur Maass, "System Design and the Political Process: A General Statement," *op. cit.*

[17]Anthony Downs, "The Public Interest: Its Meaning in a Democracy," *Social Research,* Vol. 29 (Spring 1962), 18–20, 27–32; Gerhard Colm, "The Public Interest: Essential Key to Public Policy," in C. J. Friedrich (cd.), *The Public Interest* (New York: Atherton, 1962), p. 121; Jerome Rothenberg, *The Measurement of Social Welfare* (Englewood Cliffs, N.J.: Prentice-Hall, 1961), pp. 296–97.

[18]Marglin's 1962 analysis, *op. cit.,* is one demonstration of this.

[19]For an excellent summary of this research see Rothenberg, *op. cit.*

[20]See Stephen A. Marglin, *Public Investment Criteria* (London: Allen and Unwin, 1966).

[21]My data are taken from David C. Major, "Decision Making for Public Investment in Water Resource Development in the United States," unpublished, Ph.D. thesis, Harvard University, 1965, Chap. 5. See this thesis for citations of statutes and reports referred to here.

[22]This design standard was amended in 1963 to provide for predicted traffic volumes twenty years from date of approval of project plans.

[23]The Act of 1956 contemplated completion by fiscal year 1969, but both estimated costs and year of completion were later amended.

[24]The Clay report's proposals on tax policy and accounting procedures for financing the road system, which we do not discuss here, were altered significantly in the legislative process.

[25]Except where otherwise noted, the facts of this case are derived from legislative documents relating to the Housing and Urban Development Act of 1965: President's Message (H. Doc. 89–99); Hearings before Subcommittees on Housing of the House and Senate Committees on Banking and Currency (Mar.–Apr. 1965); Reports of House and Senate Committees on Banking and Currency (H. Report 89–365, S. Report. 89–378); Debate in House and Senate (*Cong. Rec.* for June 28–30 and July 14–15); Conference Report (H. Report 89–679; Debate in House and Senate on adoption of Conference Report (*Cong. Rec.* for July 26–27). Dr. David C. Major has assisted in developing the facts and interpretation of this case.

[26]Under the Administration bill the rent supplement would be the difference between rent for standard housing and 20 per cent of a moderate-

income family's income. Under the act as approved, the rent supplement is the difference between the same rent and *25* per cent of a *low*-income family's income. The two changes made by Congress work in opposite directions, but they do not offset each other.

12.
Quality of Government Services*
WERNER Z. HIRSCH[1]

Interest in the quality of urban government services comes from a number of directions. First, demand and cost analysis requires that quality be made explicit. For example, either a cost or demand function of public education is not very useful where education is an unknown mixture of various shades of poor, mediocre and excellent qualities. A second interest relates to the need for performance comparison of different governments offering a given service. Government policy with respect to service quality is a third issue. Unlike price policy, quality policy is multi-dimensional and an urban government operating on a given budget should seek efficient ways to render maximum amounts of each of the various service qualities. Finally, there is interest in better understanding temporal quality changes, if for no other reason than to adjust production and price indices for quality changes.

An understanding of the quality aspects of government services requires consideration of what and how government produces and an examination of the uses to which its products are put. Government outputs are difficult to appraise and once estimates have been obtained, their meaning often cannot be readily interpreted. Let us illustrate these points by an example. Between 1902 and 1958, total current expenditures for local and state government services increased by 3,700 per cent. During the same period, similar expenditures for sanitation increased by 2,300 per cent, and expenditures for health and hospitals, 5,400 per cent. About the same relationship prevailed for capital outlays, with total capital expenditures for local and state government services

*Reprinted from Werner Z. Hirsch, "Quality of Government Services," in Howard G. Schaller (ed.), *Public Expenditure Decisions in The Urban Community* (Washington, D.C.: Resources for the Future, Inc., 1963), pp. 163–179, by permission of the author and publisher. Werner Z. Hirsch is professor of economics and director of the Institute of Government and Public Affairs at the University of California, Los Angeles.

increasing by 7,600 per cent, while those for sanitation went up 2,700 per cent, and those for health and hospitals, 20,700 per cent.[2] Do we have a series of output estimates? Do these figures imply that the service with the largest relative increase improved in quality more than the others? Specifically, does this mean that the quality of public health and hospital services during 1902–1958 improved more, relatively, than the quality of all government services? And were the quality increases of sanitation during this period relatively lower than those of other government services? These are important questions on which we hope to shed some light in this paper.

My plan is first to examine the work economists have done so far in defining and measuring quality of goods and services in general and of urban government services in particular. This appears appropriate since the quality issue has been somewhat neglected in the literature. I intend, next, to present an approach to the problem, which will then be examined in some detail with regard to two services—refuse collection and public education. Finally, the issue of measuring temporal quality changes will be considered.

QUALITY—THE ECONOMIST'S STEPCHILD

Economists in the past have shown little awareness or interest in quality as an economic parameter, in spite of the fact that Adam Smith already realized that "the time spent in different sorts of work will not always alone determine this proportion (between two quantities of labor). The different degrees of hardship endured, and the ingenuity exercised must likewise be taken into account." But Smith had also realized that "it is not easy to find any accurate measure either of hardship or ingenuity."[3]

Alfred Marshall recognized the existence of quality differences, but explicitly disregarded them, assuming "for the sake of simplicity, that all the corn in the market is of the same quality."[4] Simplicity was well served by this assumption! But in all fairness it must be stated that by disregarding qualities, great complications were avoided. Technical and economic conditions of bygone days rendered this simplification somewhat more legitimate than those of today's world. In the eras of Adam Smith and even of Alfred Marshall, product and service inputs were technologically simple and changed relatively slowly. Product differentiation was minor and government services were relatively few. Thus the operation of the market which then, more than ever since, conformed to the purely competitive model of Marshall, may have handled quality differences quite well by assigning corresponding prices to them.

Perhaps the first major attempts to define and measure quality more clearly were made by a group of agricultural economists in the late 1920's. They applied empirical methods in order to relate produce prices to quality.[5]

A few years thereafter, Edward H. Chamberlin took a careful look at the quality dimension and concluded that " . . . In the quality of the product itself [we may refer to] technical changes, a new design, or better materials; it may mean a new package or container; it may mean more prompt or courteous service, . . . a different location." He considered quality changes as resulting in distinctly different products, i.e., "'product' variations are in their essence qualitative, rather than quantitative; they cannot, therefore, be measured along an axis and displayed in a single diagram. Resort must be had, instead, to the somewhat clumsy expedient of imagining a series of diagrams, one for each variety of 'product.'"[6]

To Lawrence Abbott, quality has been "a multi-dimensional variable— a compound of numerous elements (e.g., in a necktie: size, shape, type of construction, color fastness), each of which is variable."[7]

In the early 1950's, concern with income elasticities of consumer goods led H. Theil and H. S. Houthakker to look into the quality problem.[8] Theil defined "a quality as a perfectly homogeneous good . . . [and] a commodity as a set of qualities."[9] He stipulated that a set of qualities is a commodity only if the prices have a certain functional relationship to each other during the period considered. Using this concept and finding that the prices of butter and oleomargarine are highly correlated, he looked upon them as a single commodity.

Houthakker introduced qualities as separate variables, which are determined by the consumer no less than is quantity.[10] Thus the consumption of the ith commodity is described by physical quantity X_i and quality V_i. The latter number indicates the quality bought and is defined as the price per unit under some basic price system. The total revenue from the sale of X_i units of quality V_i will then be $X_i V_i$. This is the simplified case, which is followed by one more complex in which the quality of a commodity is described by multiple quality variables. Thus, he stated, "If we are speaking of an overcoat we may, e.g., give quantitative expressions for its size, weight, colour, warmth, etc. The consumer will then be supposed to have preferences for various combinations of those characteristics, rather than for overcoats which are only described by their price. On the other hand, the price of the coat will also depend on these characteristics, since they are produced by different factor inputs."[11]

The differentiation between the cost of creating quality and its value was earlier introduced by Hans Brems. He pointed to the two different meanings of the term quality as a parameter of action, i.e., " . . . what the consumer gets from the product . . . [and] what the producer puts into it."[12] Brems thus advocated the use of consumers' and producers' criteria in defining and evaluating quality, surmising that these two coincide only in a few cases.

In the last few years emphasis on quality has come from a new source, i.e., from concern that production and price indices fail to reflect changes in quality adequately. In recognition of this issue efforts were initiated to develop a quality index that could be used to deflate production or price indices, principally by Richard Stone, Erland von Hofsten, Edward F. Denison, Richard and Nancy Ruggles, Frank de Leeuw, and Irma Adelman and Zvi Griliches.[13]

Very little research on the quality of public services has been carried out so far. In the 1930's, Clarence E. Ridley and Herbert A. Simon began a major investigation of measurement of municipal activities.[14]

While this study had a primarily conceptual orientation, another major effort, by the National Board of Fire Underwriters, has been mainly concerned with specific measurement in the field of fire protection. With the aid of the board, a set of standards has been developed to provide an equitable basis for appraising the potential conflagration hazard of cities and for judging the adequacy of all phases of municipal fire protection.[15] These standards were arrived at with the aid of engineering principles and they take into consideration characteristics of the fire department, water supply, fire alarm system, police department, structural conditions in business districts, and enforcement ordinances relating to building construction and fire prevention. The final grading involves an engineering evaluation of the physical properties and manpower of a fire-defense system from the standpoint of effective fire-fighting and prevention. Grading has been carried out for most cities in the United States.

In the field of public primary and secondary education, a most ambitious quality measurement project has been initiated by the State of New York Education Department. Efforts are being made to develop workable school quality criteria, together with empirical studies to attempt actual measurements.[16]

In addition, certain benefit-cost analyses of urban government services that directly bear on this problem have been undertaken in recent years.[17] Furthermore the author has attempted to measure the quality of education, fire protection, police protection, refuse collection and street services.[18]

Henry D. Lytton, in a path-breaking study, has attempted to measure the output of certain federal government departments, including the Post Office, Veterans Administration and Internal Revenue Service.[19] Output measurements have mainly been made in terms of the number of such items handled as papers and letters. As the author recognizes, these measures tend to neglect the quality factor.

Henry J. Schmandt and G. Ross Stephens have used the number of municipal sub-functions performed as an indication of service quality level.[20] For example, they utilized data collected by the Citizen's Governmental Research Bureau of Milwaukee, which breaks down police protection into sixty-five categories, including such activities as foot and motorcycle patrol, criminal investigation, youth aid bureau, ambulance and pulmotor service, school crossing guards, radio communication, radar speed units, etc. They assume that the more sub-functions performed, the higher is the service quality. This approach has some serious shortcomings. For example, it takes into account neither the relative importance of a sub-function nor its quality.

All this work can provide a helpful point of departure for an analysis of the quality aspects of urban government services and their measurement.

SOME GENERAL CONSIDERATIONS

In our effort to gain better insight into the quality phenomenon and to attempt measurements, the following general outlook will prevail. Products of outputs of government, not unlike those of private enterprise, are considered to have both quantitative and qualitative aspects. The line is blurred for quite a few urban government services and in virtually all cases, identification and evaluation of quality characteristics is difficult. It is a key characteristic of most public as well as private services that they do not conform to such clearly defined units of output as do wheat and corn, commonly used as examples by the classical economists.

Defining and measuring output units of government services does not necessarily offer unique difficulties, although they tend to be more pervasive than those of private goods. At the same time, defining social want-satisfying units appears more urgent than in the case of private goods, since the market mechanism that helps define private goods in money terms, and thus facilitates proper allocation, cannot be counted on with regard to public services.

Quality determination of urban government services can proceed in three distinct steps:

Definition of service unit;

Identification of quality characteristics of service unit;

Estimation of the money-value and money-cost, respectively, of quality characteristics.

These steps will now be examined in turn.

Efforts to define a basic urban government service unit cannot draw on tradition or usage. It becomes a matter of explicit analytical choice. The rendering of a service is an activity which has both demand and cost aspects, not unlike the production and distribution of a commodity. A government service, no less than any tangible commodity, can be viewed as having a variety of quality dimensions—both from the views of producer and consumer. As Brems has already intimated, there can be cases in which those who produce a service and those who consume it might want to argue in terms of different physical units. However, such a practice would at best be cumbersome and unworkable, since it would not permit internally consistent cost and demand analyses. Instead, it is essential that the same service unit be applied on both the cost and demand sides.

Defining a useful, basic service unit involves discovery of a high level of abstraction to which major qualities of concern to producers and users can be attached successfully. Where there is a choice of abstraction, the issue is one of value judgment. Thus, in our opinion, the basic government service unit should be defined in such a way as to be a unit of contribution to the successful pursuit of the aims of the government activity. In virtually all cases this will favor the consumer. But there is a further reason that induces us to prefer the demand side. Technological changes, including substitution of one type of service for another, can greatly modify the production process, yet the output continues to satisfy the same desires. For example, the evolution from a horse-drawn street car to a cable car, to a bus, and finally to a high speed electric train—perhaps a monorail—involves distinctly different processes which all, however, are designed to meet the urbanite's need to move rapidly and conveniently from one part of town to another. Even good highways, allowing private cars to travel fast and safely, are in a sense substitutes. Thus, to define the basic service unit as a certain technological process, or type of input, is not appropriate, since with the passage of time new processes will appear that will have different quality characteristics; they will usually defy comparison. However, regardless of improvements and changes, consumer preferences can often be judged by the same criteria involving virtually unchanged quality characteristics on the demand side.

Thus, the ideal basic service unit should be flexible and should accommodate the largest possible horizon of existing or potential quality dimensions. It should be defined in real terms and if a choice must be made between the demand and cost sides, the former should dominate.[21]

Identifying service units is a major undertaking and a few examples are in order. Let us start with residential refuse collection. The amount of refuse can be stated in pounds, cubic feet, or even number of containers. The refuse collection service provides a household (or person) with an average weekly pickup of a given number of pounds (or cubic feet, or containers). Thus, refuse collection and disposal per household (or per capita) per week in pounds is a useful basic service unit.

In the case of water supply, the basic service unit is a cubic foot of water delivered to the place of use. The basic unit of street cleaning is a square foot of street cleaned, and that of street lighting, a mile of street lit.

For some urban government services, defining the basic service unit in terms of consumer preference is more complex. For hospital services, the unit might be a patient-day in the hospital; for police protection, a city block protected from crime; for fire protection, a city block protected from fire; and for schools, the education accruing to a pupil per day or year.

Once the service unit is defined, its relevant quality dimensions must be identified and ultimately measured. In these attempts it is helpful to remember that many government departments perform a service in a manner quite similar to a vertically integrated firm. In some cases the service unit involves a tangible product, which is produced by government and then delivered to users. Under such circumstances, the product itself can have quality dimensions, as can the delivery process.

Water supply is a good example. A cubic foot of water has important inherent quality characteristics in terms of its physical, chemical, and biological attributes. Among the major features are hardness, turbidity, temperature, color, taste, odor, mineral content, bacteria count, etc. But a municipal water department involves a high degree of vertical integration in that it not only produces water, but also wholesales and retails it. There are various quality characteristics distinctive of water in the delivery process—water pressure, reliable supply, rapid repair, courteous and correct metering, etc.

A similar situation prevails with regard to library service, where a book is the basic unit. Selection and physical condition are important quality characteristics of the books themselves. Availability of books when requested, good reading room facilities, help to children in selecting books, reference service, and location of library, are all auxiliary quality characteristics of serving patrons.

In the case of refuse collection, discussed below, virtually all quality issues relate to the delivery process; the service is delivering residents from their refuse.

After defining relevant quality dimensions, measurements must be devised and two separate criteria are indicated. One should mainly reflect the hardship and ingenuity involved in rendering the service, already pointed to by Adam Smith. In short, we must measure the technical input factors, i.e., the cost side. The second measure should reflect consumer preferences and benefits, i.e., the demand side. For the sake of comparability, it is desirable that the quality characteristics of the service unit be translated into money-value on the demand side, and into money-cost, on the cost side.

An understanding of quality dimensions from the demand side, and the estimation of money-value, can be facilitated by identifying beneficiaries and types of benefits that are likely to accrue. For many urban government services, direct benefits are much more substantial and weighty than indirect. Unless our main concern is to facilitate efficient resource allocation, which requires equating marginal social benefits and costs and thus inclusion of as many indirect benefits as possible, the emphasis can be on direct benefits.[22]

Estimates of money-value of quality characteristics will usually require a benefit analysis. However, this is complicated by the fact that many quality characteristics are interdependent and interact in an intricate manner, a difficulty which also exists in relation to the money-cost determination. Estimates of money-cost of quality characteristics can be made either with the aid of engineering cost functions or *ex post* empirical regression studies.

We will now turn to two examples, close to the ends of the spectrum of urban government services, and explore their quality aspects and measurements in some detail. Residential refuse collection has reasonably definable and measurable physical units and quality characteristics. The other example, public education, is perhaps the most intricate urban government service of them all, and many of its quality aspects presently defy measurement.

QUALITY MEASUREMENT OF RESIDENTIAL REFUSE COLLECTION

As previously noted, a useful basic service unit is refuse collection and disposal per household (or per capita) per week in pounds. However, such a unit can be associated with different service qualities. To determine significant quality dimensions, it is useful to ask who the possible beneficiaries of residential refuse collection are and how they are likely to benefit. In brief, it can be stated that refuse collection can affect the person at whose residence the pickup is made; those who live near the disposal site; those who are near streets used by pickup trucks; and the community at large, since refuse collection combats many health hazards. With regard to each type of beneficiary, various activities of varying quality can take place.

From the resident's view, the manner in which refuse removal is made, and especially its frequency, bear on the elimination of both odors and the breeding of insects and rodents; disease prevention; and cleanliness and beauty of the neighborhood. Quality differences are based mainly on the number of weekly pickups; care and reliability of the removal services; and cleanliness, noiselessness and courtesy of the collection crew. Quality differences also affect the effort the constituent must make, which is the convenience factor.

Thus, from the resident's view, the quality of residential refuse collection can be assessed mainly in the following terms:

Number of weekly pickups.

Proximity of pickup location to building.

Nature of pickups, i.e., whether separation of refuse into garbage and trash is required.

Based on these characteristics, eight different qualities of refuse collection can be identified. They are:

1. Separate, once a week curb collection.
2. Combined, once a week curb collection.
3. Separate, twice a week curb collection.
4. Combined, twice a week curb collection.
5. Separate, once a week rear-of-house collection.
6. Combined, once a week rear-of-house collection.
7. Separate, twice a week rear-of-house collection.
8. Combined, twice a week rear-of-house collection.

Similarly, refuse collection can be analyzed in relation to those who live near the disposal site. Modern incinerators will benefit this group more than city dumps or open land fills. Finally, transportation of refuse is less annoying and hazardous if it is made in specialized refuse collection equipment rather than in open trucks. Both items can be included in the specification of refuse collection quality, thus giving us five major quality dimensions.

Now let us turn to the measurement of some of these quality dimensions. On the cost side, each must be studied in terms of its technical factor inputs and their cost implications. While in theory many quality dimensions involve continuous data which can assume an infinitely large number of values, the alternatives are relatively few in the case of refuse collection service. For example, residential collection frequency is basically once or twice a week. Three collections are most unusual and represent the maximum. Likewise, pickup locations are either on the curb or behind the house. Pickups are primarily on a combined trash and garbage, or separate, basis. Thus, in this case, we mainly face sets of dichotomies. We would like to estimate the effect of either quality alternative on costs. Care must be exercised to isolate net relationships.

Let us look at an example. A field study of refuse collection and disposal operations in thirteen California cities made in 1950 and 1951 by the Sanitary Engineering Research Project of the University of California can help provide cost information on three quality dimensions, although the findings are mainly in terms of labor requirements.[23] It indicates that collection frequency is a major cost factor. For example, twice a week collection generally resulted in substantially greater quantities of refuse from each household each week than once a week collection. Specifically, the increase amounted to about 47 per cent. In addition, time studies of the effect of collection frequency on labor requirements of the pickup operation showed that twice a week collection required approximately 55 per cent more manpower per ton of refuse than once a week collection, assuming that about equal amounts are collected from each household each week. Therefore, twice a week collection may increase labor requirements by about 128 per cent. Since disposal and administration costs are affected to only a minor extent by collection frequency, and labor costs tend to comprise about 80 per cent of all costs, it might be possible to conclude that twice a week collection is about twice as costly as once a week. Once per week collection required an average of about 2.3 man-minutes per household per week and twice a week collection, an average of about 4.6 man-minutes.

Proximity of pickup location to building is a further quality dimension and there have been at least two empirical investigations into its cost. A study of the 1955–56 operations of a number of municipal and private refuse collectors in the St. Louis area revealed that in-street collection was about 35 per cent, and in-alley collection about 40 per cent, less expensive than rear-of-dwelling collection. The California field study indicated that the "approximate manpower requirements for pickup operation (time required to load the refuse on the collection vehicle) varied rather consistently from an average of 100 man-minutes per ton for 100 per cent alley or curb collection to 165 man-minutes per ton for 100 per cent, rear-of-house collection."[24] By making similar assumptions to those above, one might conclude from these two studies that rear-of-house collection may be about 50 per cent more costly than alley or curb collection.

No detailed empirical study known to us has addressed itself to measuring the cost differential of separate versus combined collection. But the California study looked into the cost of specialized collection equipment. It found that "the use of mechanical compaction type refuse vehicles requires approximately 10 per cent more manpower to pick up a unit of refuse than is required for open-body type trucks."[25] Such equipment is also more expensive and has fewer uses and may therefore be assumed to increase general costs by about 10 per cent.

If this information is applied to a simplified case where refuse collection has only two quality dimensions—collection frequency and pickup location—and the lowest quality case, once a week curb collection, is given the value 1, the following quality valuation, from the cost side, results:

Refuse, once a week, curb collection	1.0
Refuse, once a week, rear-of-house collection	1.5
Refuse, twice a week, curb collection	2.0
Refuse, twice a week, rear-of-house collection	3.0

On the demand side, the money-value of given quality characteristics of weekly household refuse collection and disposal must be estimated. The benefits associated with frequency, proximity, and nature of the refuse collection service, as well as the disposal and hauling method, are mainly in terms of disease prevention, convenience and beautification. In the United States, only when collection and disposal practices are very poor can the health factor be assumed to play the major role.

Assessing the value of convenience and beauty is a task we will not attempt.

In a few instances the market mechanism might help. There may be some communities in which households have a choice of buying other service qualities from private contractors, but even under such circumstances, price is unlikely to reflect quality differences significantly.[26]

QUALITY MEASUREMENT OF EDUCATION

In the area of public primary and secondary education, the relevant service unit is not entirely obvious. However, the education accruing to a pupil attending public school per day (or year) appears to be a useful measure. He is the direct beneficiary and although we also recognize that his present and future family, his employer, as well as society at large, are potential beneficiaries, we are tempted to neglect this issue here.

The education that accrues to a pupil in primary and secondary schools per day (or year) has a variety of quality dimensions. Kershaw and McKean[27] have grouped these dimensions as follows:

Knowledge in standard subjects.
Knowledge in special and optional subjects.
Ability to reason.
Intellectual curiosity.
"Creativity."
Social Poise.
Emotional stability.
Physical health.

Obviously these items are highly interrelated and often a school activity that affects one has a bearing on others. From this viewpoint, the money-cost (and money-value) of quality needs to be estimated jointly for all of these items. A more selective approach will be discussed later.

The quality of public education in general, and the acquisition of knowledge in standard subjects in particular, appear to be affected by many more factors than is the case in refuse collection. Empirical efforts toward their appraisal are further complicated by the fact that most of them are continuous variables. The following seem to be the most significant inputs:

1. *Caliber of teaching staff and teaching load:*
   Important characteristics are per cent of experienced teachers, per cent of teachers who are graduates of strong liberal arts colleges

with majors in the field in which they teach; number of outside-the-area candidates interviewed for each teacher hired; number of students per counselor, librarian and other specialists; number of college hours the average teacher has taken; and per cent of teachers with more than ten years' teaching experience. Average teacher salary is likely to reflect some of these factors. Teaching load is another indicator. In many schools, twenty hours a week of teaching, and dealing with about 175 students, is considered normal. One measure would be the average teaching load of a given school in relation to the national average.

2. *Caliber of school administration:*
The leadership and ability of the school superintendent and his principals cannot be neglected. Number of superintendents, principals and consultants per 100 pupils could prove a useful measure.

3. *Grouping and class size:*
Many educators maintain that within limits good education requires students of common ability and interest to be grouped together.[28] The result is small classes, which generally indicate a more intensive educational effort that can thus be measured by the pupil-teacher ratio.[29]

4. *Teaching program:*
The scope and quality of the teaching program can be measured in terms of the number of high school instruction units offered by the school. Other measures might be per cent of college bound students who carry four courses a year in English, mathematics, science, history or foreign languages; per cent of students who take mathematics courses beyond a second year of algebra and one year of plane geometry, or four years of foreign languages.

5. *Length of school year and day:*
Schools differ in the number of hours in a given year in which a child participates in formal education.

These characteristics combine in various ways and result in many different qualities of public education from the cost side. Basically, the estimation of the money-cost of the quality of education calls for determining the cost of various combinations of factors in the five main categories. For example, the cost implication of (a) the organizational structure of a school district, i.e., its use of an elementary and high school system (the 8–4 system) or the elementary, junior and senior schools (the 6–3–3 system); (b) its additional administrative and supplementary specialists; (c) its average class size; and (d) its average salary costs, can be readily appreciated from the sample district of Table 1. These ninety-six alternative per-pupil school costs indicate the wide range of variability in quality associated only with select members of a district's professional staff.

The base quality represented in Table 1 is Case 1, in which the district employs an 8–4 system with two schools for its 3,000 elementary

Table 1. Cost implications of alternative organizational plans, size of elementary schools, professional staff and classes, and salary scales for a hypothetical school district of 4,000 pupils

Case	Type of organizational plan 8–4	6–3–3	Number of Elem. Schools 2	6	Asst. Principals Elem. 0	Elem. 1	Jr. & Sr. HS. 1	Jr. & Sr. HS. 2	Librarians per school 0	1	Teacher/pupil ratios Elem. 1/35 / Jr.&Sr.HS. 1/30	Elem. 1/20 / Jr.&Sr.HS. 1/15	Cost per pupil ($) Salary Scale * I	II	III
1	x		x		x		x		x		x		99	146	248
2		x	x		x		x		x		x		104	154	258
3	x			x	x		x		x		x		104	153	259
4		x		x	x		x		x		x		109	161	272
5	x		x			x		x	x		x		102	151	255
6		x	x			x		x	x		x		108	160	268
7	x			x		x		x	x		x		111	163	274
8		x		x		x		x	x		x		117	173	290
9	x		x		x		x			x	x		102	150	254
10		x	x		x		x			x	x		108	160	267
11	x			x	x		x			x	x		110	162	273
12		x		x	x		x			x	x		116	172	289
13	x		x			x		x		x	x		105	155	261
14		x	x			x		x		x	x		112	166	276
15	x			x		x		x		x	x		117	172	289
16		x		x		x		x		x	x		124	183	307
17	x		x		x		x		x			x	178	262	444
18		x	x		x		x		x			x	191	282	475
19	x			x	x		x		x			x	183	269	455
20		x		x	x		x		x			x	196	289	489
21	x		x			x		x	x			x	181	266	451
22		x	x			x		x	x			x	195	288	485
23	x			x		x		x	x			x	189	278	471
24		x		x		x		x	x			x	203	301	507
25	x		x		x		x			x		x	181	266	451
26		x	x		x		x			x		x	184	288	484
27	x			x	x		x			x		x	189	278	470
28		x		x	x		x			x		x	203	300	506
29	x		x			x		x		x		x	184	270	457
30		x	x			x		x		x		x	198	293	493
31	x			x		x		x		x		x	196	287	485
32		x		x		x		x		x		x	210	311	526

* Position	Salary scale ($ per year) I	II	III
Principal, High School	5,800	9,000	17,000
Principal, Jr. High School	5,100	8,000	14,000
Principal, Elementary School	4,900	7,000	11,000
Assistant Principal, High School	4,500	6,500	10,000
Assistant Principal, Junior High School	4,000	6,000	9,200
Assistant Principal, Elementary School	3,700	5,500	8,700
Librarian, High School	4,200	6,000	9,200
Librarian, Junior High School	3,800	5,500	8,500
Librarian, Elementary School	3,500	5,000	8,100
Teacher, High School	3,600	5,100	9,000
Teacher, Junior High School	3,200	4,800	8,100
Teacher, Elementary School	3,000	4,500	7,500

grade pupils. Only the high school principal has an assistant and no professional librarian is employed. Students, in this case, are in relatively large classes—thirty-five and thirty students per teacher on the elementary and high school levels, respectively. The district which pays the lowest salaries (scale I) will spend $99 per pupil annually for professional services, while one that is able to bid for somewhat better personnel (scale II), will have annual costs of $146 per pupil; and one that pays salaries competitive with private enterprise for skilled administrators and with private academies and colleges for highly qualified teachers (scale III), will incur annual costs of $248 per pupil. The highest quality represented in Table 1 is Case 32. Here the district uses a junior high school for improved student grouping, small elementary schools for improved teacher supervision, and smaller classes for closer pupil-teacher relationships. Principals in the six elementary schools have assistants and the junior and senior high school principals each have two. Each school has a trained librarian. The costs of this quality level are over 110 per cent higher than the base quality of Case 1 and there is a 432 per cent difference in costs between the lowest quality-lowest salary scale and the highest quality-highest salary scale.

In some cases, extreme paucity of data leaves the investigator either with the alternative of abandoning an attempt at quality estimation or of utilizing partial factor input information, which appears reasonably well correlated with over-all service money-costs. Under such circumstances, the author used the number of principals, superintendents and consultants, per 1,000 pupils in average daily attendance, as a service quality measure for primary and secondary public education for selected years from 1900–1958.[30]

Next, the money-value of the quality of education will be considered. The pupil benefits from education depending to no small extent upon the earlier mentioned quality factors—caliber of teaching staff and school administration, grouping and class size, teaching program, and length of school year. Perhaps the single best way to estimate the money-value of different qualities of education is in terms of the resultant lifetime earnings. While estimates of the effects of elementary high school and college education on lifetime earnings have been made, we are not aware of studies that have attempted to relate the earlier discussed qualities to lifetime earnings.[31] Such studies appear feasible and should be undertaken, keeping in mind that not all earning increases are likely to have resulted from quality variation, but are also likely to be associated with the pupil's inherent ability and informal education in the home.

For this reason it appears desirable to adjust earning results according to at least three factors in addition to educational quality—native ability or inherent intelligence, home environment, and motivation or ambition to learn.[32]

An evaluation of quality dimensions of public education can also proceed on a more restricted basis. It can be in non-monetary terms, which can then ultimately be translated into money-value terms.

Of the eight principal dimensions of education referred to earlier, there appears to be general agreement that a most important, perhaps the most important single item, is the acquisition of knowledge in standard subjects. Educational achievement in the basic subjects is measured with the aid of achievement tests. While the scores on batteries of standardized achievement tests are far from perfect indicators of output (they do not cover all of the worthwhile aspects of learning in the subject area), nevertheless it is possible that a comprehensive battery, like the Iowa Test, is sufficiently sensitive to produce a fairly good measure of the average academic achievement. Thus it is possible to use the scores of achievement tests, taken in senior high school, to reflect, in a major degree, quality dimensions of primary and secondary education, from the demand side.

At present, unfortunately, various school systems use different achievements tests and results are not directly comparable. Under these circumstances some makeshift methods could be employed to compare test scores. For example, the national average of test scores of a number of different achievement tests could be used as a norm. The corresponding figure of a particular school district could be compared to this norm. Thus, for example, while 30 per cent of all students who took achievement tests had a test score of a given value, different percentage figures would prevail for specific school districts. The larger the percentage above the norm, the higher would be the quality level of the school district, from the pupil's viewpoint.

Since a pupil's performance is not only the result of the quality of education to which he has been exposed, adjustments must be made similar to those suggested with respect to the lifetime earnings measure, i.e., native ability, home environment, and motivation.

A study along some of these general lines was recently completed by James H. Crandall.[33] It covered 6,000 children from grades 4 through 8 in sixteen California elementary school districts. Approximately one-half of these children were from eight school districts included in the top 10 per cent based on expenditures for instruction for all elementary school districts of 1,000 to 4,000 average daily attendance in California, over a four-year period. The other half of the group were from eight school districts of similar size, but included in the bottom 10 per cent in expenditures for instruction during the same period. Each individual child had remained in the same school district for the full four years and had taken the same standardized intelligence and achievement tests. To avoid comparison of variations in achievement possibly resulting from differences in the intelligence of the children, all achievement test scores were considered in terms of their IQ. Expenditures on eleven items were related to academic achievement—administration, supervisors, principals, teachers, librarians, school clerks, instructional supplies, textbooks, all visual aids, workbooks, and health services. Significantly, higher academic achievement was separately associated with higher expenditures, both in terms of dollars and per cent of total expenditures for instruction, in each of the following categories—administration, principals, instructional supplies, workbooks, clerks, and health services. The study found that in all areas of academic achievement, districts high in expenditure for administration ranged from three to nine months above those school systems low in expenditure in this classification. These differences in average achievement were, in general, statistically significant at the 5 per cent level. They occurred between school districts which on the average, over a four-year period, spent $18.12 and $9.48, respectively, per pupil for administration. An even more consistently significant relationship of all areas examined occurred between academic achievement and expenditure rate for principals. The top four districts in this class of expenditure averaged both six months higher in academic achievement, and $10.30 more per pupil, than did school systems which spent the least money for principals.[34]

While achievement test scores tend to measure quality in non-monetary terms, it should be possible to relate a pupil's test scores to lifetime earnings after adjusting for the other factors that can affect his earnings, as was discussed above.

MEASURING TEMPORAL QUALITY CHANGES

Only measures which pertain to a single time period have been discussed so far, with one minor exception. Often, however, temporal comparisons are required. For example, it would be very helpful to initiate a quality series to adjust the United States Department of Commerce's implicit deflators for the state and local government sector of gross national product. Thus, Richard and Nancy D. Ruggles are convinced that the implicit price deflators do not properly allow for quality and efficiency improvements. They note that "the price of Government services as measured by the pay of Government employees" rose by an average of over 5 per cent a year from 1946 to 1957 and add, "there is a good reason to believe, however, that the productivity of Government workers has increased substantially in this period."[35]

In theory, we could use any of the measures that were discussed in the earlier section, make estimates for successive years, adjust them for price level changes, and so obtain estimates of temporal service level changes. Paucity of data appears to make such a step difficult, if not impossible. There are two additional methods for measuring temporal changes in service quality, as viewed from the cost side.

An effort could be made, for example, to decompose an expenditure series of an urban government service into two major components—polygenetic cost changes (those that are independent of service quality changes) and cost changes that result from changed service quality. Emphasis should rest upon obtaining good estimates of polygenetic cost changes. This figure should be subtracted from total cost changes and the residual would indicate service quality related cost changes.[36]

This method appears to offer little advantage, however, for services whose inputs are mainly in the form of labor or have greatly benefited from capital improvements during the period under analysis. It might, for example, prove useful for the assessment of service quality changes of municipal water departments and sewage disposal systems. For instance, chemicals and electricity are the major current costs of a municipal water department and neither element has undergone major quality change during the last few years.

Most urban government services, however, mainly use labor as input. For such services, a method might be developed that relies principally on wage increase comparisons. The assumption could be made that the government unit that pays higher than competitive wages and salaries is likely to procure higher than average quality labor, and that high quality labor also produces high quality output. Thus, if unit costs of a particular government unit have not changed over time, or have changed less than wages, and yet wage rates have increased more than in an industry which actively competes for the labor, the service quality might be expected to have improved over the competing industry's.[37]

Such a method, for example, might be applied to public and private education. On the average, whichever of the two pays better salaries is likely to acquire better teachers, superintendents, principals, and consultants. Assuming the same ratio of teachers, superintendents, etc., to students, the system that pays higher wages is likely to offer a higher quality of education.

In summary, it is apparent that efforts to measure the quality of urban government services offer exciting challenges and prospects. Much more work is needed along three key lines of inquiry—defining service units in real terms, identifying their major quality characteristics, and estimating the money-value and money-cost of these characteristics.

NOTES:

[1]The author is very much indebted to Professors Harold J. Barnett, Jesse Burkhead, and Jerry Miner; Drs. Selma Mushkin, Norman Breckner, and Norman Townshend-Zellner; Messrs. Elbert Segelhorst and Morton Marcus, for numerous helpful suggestions and criticism. Needless to say, all are accorded full discharge from responsibility.

[2]Special computations in co-operation with Data Classification and Research Branch of the U. S. Bureau of the Census.

[3]Adam Smith, *The Wealth of Nations,* Modern Library Edition (New York: Random House, 1937), Book 1, chap. 5, p. 31.

[4]Alfred Marshall, *Principles of Economics,* 8th Edition (London: Macmillan & Co., 1920), Book 5, chap. 2, p. 332.

[5]Frederick V. Waugh, *Quality as a Determinant of Vegetable Prices* (New York: Columbia University Press, 1929); W. S. Kuhrt, "A Study of Farmer Elevator Operation in the Spring Wheat Area," Pt. 2, U. S. Department of Agriculture, *Preliminary Reports,* Washington, D.C., October, 1926, and October, 1927; Claude L. Benner and Harry S. Gabriel, "Marketing of Delaware Eggs," Delaware Agriculture Experiment Station *Bulletin,* No. 150, 1927.

[6]E. H. Chamberlin, *The Theory of Monopolistic Competition,* 5th Edition (Cambridge: Harvard University Press, 1946), p. 71, pp. 78–79.

[7]Lawrence Abbott, "Vertical Equilibrium Under Pure Quality Competition," *The American Economic Review,* X/43 (December, 1953), 827.

[8]H. Theil, "Qualities, Prices and Budget Enquiries," *Review of Economic Studies,* Vol. 19 (3), No. 50 (1952–53), 129–47, and H. S. Houthakker, "Compensated Changes in Quantities and Qualities Consumed," *Review of Economic Studies,* Vol. 19 (3), No. 50 (1952–53), 155–64.

[9]Theil, *op. cit.,* (footnote 8), p. 129.

[10]Houthakker, *op. cit.* (footnote 8), p. 156.

[11]*Ibid.*, p. 163.

[12]Hans Brems, *Product Equilibrium Under Monopolistic Competition* (Cambridge: Harvard University Press, 1951), p. 18.

[13]Richard Stone, *Quantity and Price Indexes in National Accounts* (Paris: Organization for European Economic Cooperation, 1956); Erland von Hofsten, *Price Indexes and Quality Changes* (Stockholm: Bokforlaget Forum, 1952), 135 pp.; Edward F. Denison, "Theoretical Aspects of Quality Change, Capital Consumption, and Net Capital Formation," *Problems of Capital Formation* (Princeton: Princeton University Press, 1957), pp. 215–61; Richard Ruggles and Nancy D. Ruggles, "Prices, Costs, Demand, and Output in the United States 1947–57," in *Relationship of Prices to Economic Stability and Growth,* Joint Economic Committee, 85th Congress, Second Session, March 31, 1958, pp. 297–308; Frank de Leeuw, "The Measurement of Quality Changes," *Proceedings of the Business and Economic Statistics Section, American Statistical Association,* 1958, pp. 174–83; Irma Adelman and Zvi Griliches, "On an Index of Quality Change," *Journal of the American Statistical Association* (56) (September, 1961), 535–48.

[14]Clarence E. Ridley and Herbert A. Simon, *Measuring Municipal Activities* (Chicago: Chicago International City Managers' Association, 1938).

[15]League of California Cities, *The Fire Protection Grading Process as Related to the Economics of Fire Protection* (Los Angeles: League of California Cities, April, 1961), p. 65.

[16]Samuel M. Goodman, *The Assessment of School Quality* (Albany: The University of the State of New York, 1959), 65 pp.; and William D. Firman *et al., Procedures in School Quality Evaluation* (Albany: The University of the State of New York, 1961).

[17]Examples are Nathaniel Lichfield, *Cost-Benefit Analysis in Urban Redevelopment* (Berkeley: University of California, 1962), 52 pp.; Peter O. Steiner, "Choosing Among Alternative Public Investment in the Water Resource Field," *American Economic Review,* 49 (December, 1959), 893–916; Marion Clawson, *Methods of Measuring the Demand for and Value of Outdoor Recreation* (Washington: Resources for the Future, Inc., 1959), 36 pp.; John V. Krutilla and Otto Eckstein, *Multiple Purpose River Development: Studies in Applied Economic Analysis* (Baltimore: The Johns Hopkins Press, 1958), 301 pp.; Herbert Mohring, "Land Values and the Measurement of Highway Benefits," *Journal of Political Economy,* 69 (June, 1961), 236–49; Julius Margolis, "Secondary Benefits, External Economies, and the Justification of Public Investment," *Review of Economics & Statistics,* 39 (August, 1957), 284–91; Otto A. Davis and Andrew B.

Whinston, "The Economics of Urban Renewal," *Law and Contemporary Problems*, 24, No. 1 (Winter, 1961).

[18]Werner Z. Hirsch, "Determinants of Public Education Expenditures," *National Tax Journal* (13) (March, 1960), 29–40; and *Measuring Factors Affecting Expenditure Levels for Local Government Services* (St. Louis: Metropolitan St. Louis Survey, 1957), mimeographed.

[19]Henry D. Lytton, "Recent Productivity Trends in the Federal Government: An Exploratory Study," *Review of Economics and Statistics* (41) (November, 1959), 341–59.

[20]Henry J. Schmandt and G. Ross Stephens, "Measuring Municipal Output," *National Tax Journal* (13) (December, 1960), 369–75; and Harvey Shapiro, "Measuring Local Government Output: A Comment," *National Tax Journal* (14) (December, 1961), pp. 394–97.

[21]The discourse of the service unit issue has benefited greatly from points made with great precision by Professor Richard A. Musgrave in his discussion of an earlier version of this paper and from discussions with Dr. Norman Townshend-Zellner.

[22]This point was eloquently made by Professor Richard A. Musgrave in formal discussion of an earlier version of this paper.

[23]Sanitary Engineering Research Project, *An Analysis of Refuse Collection and Sanitary Landfill Disposal* (Richmond, Calif.: University of California, 1952), 133 pp.

[24]*Ibid.*, p. 2.

[25]*Ibid.*, p. 2.

[26]Some thought might be given to the possibility of using a game device, to permit a sample of refuse-collection users to express preferences and indicate their value. The gaming could benefit from the experience Robert L. Wilson gained when he applied a simple game to the determination of service quality preferences in Greensboro and Durham, North Carolina. See Robert L. Wilson, "Livability of the City: Attitudes and Urban Development," *Urban Growth Dynamics* (New York: Wiley & Sons, 1962), pp. 387–99.

[27]J. A. Kershaw and R. N. McKean, *Systems Analysis and Education* (Santa Monica: The RAND Corporation, 1959), pp. 8–9.

[28]See James B. Conant, *The American High School Today* (New York: McGraw-Hill, 1959), 140 pp.

[29]Like any other average, this ratio conceals much detail and should be separately given for primary and secondary education. Also the number of teacher aids should be considered.

[30]The use of this input measure assumes that the number of principals, superintendents and consultants contribute significantly to the school's

service level, and that superior school districts not only hire more specialists than do inferior, but they are also of higher caliber. In general, it assumes that superior districts are rational and approximate a marginal calculus, i.e., the quantity and quality of all of the inputs that comprise good education satisfy the usual economic efficiency conditions, in which factors are employed to the point where the ratios of their marginal productivities equal the ratios of their prices. Werner Z. Hirsch, *Analysis of the Rising Costs of Public Education,* Study Paper #4 of the Joint Economic Committee of the Congress of the United States, 1959, 40 pp.

[31]On the relation between educational attainment and earnings, see: G. Becker, "Underinvestment in College Education?" *American Economic Review, Papers and Proceedings,* Vol. 50 (May, 1960), 346–54; H. S. Houthakker, "Education and Income," *Review of Economics and Statistics,* Vol. 41 (February, 1959), 24–27; H. P. Miller, "Annual and Lifetime Income in Relation to Education: 1939–1959," *American Economic Review,* Vol. 50 (December, 1960), 962–86; E. F. Renshaw, "Estimating the Returns to Education," *Review of Economics and Statistics,* Vol. 42 (August, 1960), 318–24.

[32]No fool-proof information is available for these factors. However, the first factor might be approximated by IQ test scores, and the second, by the number of books read by the parents in a year. Adjustment for these factors can be made with the aid of co-variance or regression analysis. Martin David, Harvey Brazer, James Morgan and Wilbur Cohn, *Educational Achievement—Its Causes and Effects* (Ann Arbor: Survey Research Center, 1961), 158 pp.

[33]James H. Crandall, "A Study of Academic Achievement and Expenditures for Instruction" (unpublished doctoral dissertation, University of California, Berkeley, 1961), pp. 1–33.

[34]This study validates to some degree the appropriateness of selecting number of principals, superintendents, and consultants, per 1,000 pupils in ADA, as an important quality measure, as was done in Hirsch, *Analysis of the Rising Cost of Public Education, op. cit.* (footnote 30).

[35]Ruggles and Ruggles, *op. cit.* (footnote 13), p. 299.

[36]For a general discussion of this approach to measuring quality changes of private goods, see Adelman and Griliches, *op. cit.* (footnote 13).

[37]It would be useful to have information on quality changes in the industry which competes for labor. This industry could be producing a private good and such estimates might be possible. On this basis, the service quality change could be further tied to the quality change in the private good.

V.
THE SYSTEMS BASE
OF PPB

13.
Systems Analysis and the Navy*
ALAIN ENTHOVEN

The past eighteen months have seen a great increase in the amount and quality of weapon systems analysis in the Navy, and in the range of problems studied. The Navy's efforts have been successful in clarifying the issues and in laying the foundations for further progress. The work that has been completed has been good for the Navy and good for the United States. It has made it possible to obtain a more effective Navy and to do so at less cost than would otherwise be necessary. Some of the best studies yielded the added return of greatly improved mutual understanding between the Navy and the Office of the Secretary of Defense about force and resource requirements for the Navy. Gloomy predictions that the systematic application of analysis would prove to be disastrous to the Navy were shown to be untrue.

What is systems analysis? I have not been able to produce a good brief definition. I would describe the art, as it has evolved in the Department of Defense, as a reasoned approach to problems of decision. Some have defined it as "quantitative common sense." Alternatively, it is the application of methods of quantitative economic analysis and scientific method, in the broadest sense, to the problems of choice of weapon systems and strategy. It is a systematic attempt to provide decision-makers with a full, accurate, and meaningful summary of the information relevant to clearly defined issues and alternatives.

Systems analysis is not synonymous with the application of computers. There is no essential connection between the two. Certainly the development or utility of the former in no way depends on the latter. Some researchers, working within the limits of the systems analysis ap-

*Reprinted from Alain Enthoven, *Naval Review 1965,* copyright 1964 by United States Naval Institute, Annapolis, Maryland, by permission of the author and publisher. Alain Enthoven is Assistant Secretary of Defense for Systems Analysis.

proach, try to do their analyses by means of large-scale computer simu-
lations, and sometimes this causes the uninformed to identify systems
analysis with computers. Actually, the computer simulation approach so
far has not been particularly fruitful as a method of weapon systems
analysis. However, the potential advantages offered by high-speed electronic computers are sufficiently great that I would not want to suggest
that systems analysts will never make them useful servants of informed
judgment. When that day comes, I may be persuaded to modify my
preference for the slide rule and "back of the envelope."

Moreover, systems analysis is not arcane, mysterious or occult. It is
not performed with the help of a mysterious black box. Stories that
speak of "slashing equations and whirring computers" are fiction, and
poor fiction, at that. A good systems analyst should be able to give a
clear non-technical explanation of his methods and results to the responsible decision-makers.

APPLIED ECONOMICS

The systems analysis approach, as it is being applied today in the office
of the Secretary of Defense, is a systematic attempt to bring to bear on
the problem of planning the defense program many relevant disciplines,
and to do so in an integrated way. The list includes traditional military
planning, economics, political science and other social sciences, applied
mathematics, and the physical sciences. Perhaps because I am an economist by professional training, I like to emphasize systems analysis as applied economic analysis. What does that mean?

Economics is the science of the allocation of limited resources; the
study of both how our economic system actually allocates limited resources
and how it might be done more efficiently. Thus, economics is not concerned merely with money. It is concerned with limited resources of all
kinds. Economists give particular attention to money simply because it
is the common denominator our society uses to measure the relative value of material things.

What does economics have to do with weapon systems, strategies, and
military requirements? Many people say the answer to that question is
"nothing"; that our military security, which is one of the foundations of
our freedom, is so important that one should not put a price tag on it;
that no price is too high to pay for freedom. Another view concedes that
economics and military requirements are related in peacetime, but holds
that in wartime, when military budgets are "unlimited," economics is irrelevant. These views are wrong.

Whether we like it or not, we have only a limited amount of goods and services available at any one time. Our gross national product, though large, is limited. We have only a finite number of man-hours available for all forms of productive activity. Moreover, there are other needs besides defense: feeding, clothing, and housing our population, educating our children, cultivating our minds, fighting disease, and so on. Therefore, in peace or in war, only a limited amount of resources is available for defense. And if we wish to assure our freedom, it is important that we use those resources well.

A lack of understanding of these fundamental facts shows up often in discussions of practical problems. For example, CVA-67 will cost about $280 million to build. Had it been decided to make her nuclear-powered, she would have cost over $400 million. For roughly $400 million, one can buy either a nuclear-powered carrier or a conventionally powered carrier plus four 3,500-ton destroyer escorts. Responsible defense officials must face the choice between the alternative ways of spending the 400 million. People may disagree on which is the better way to spend that money, but there should be no disagreement that it is necessary and correct to pose the problem in this fashion.

Unfortunately, there is such disagreement. Some argue that we should buy the "best" carrier available, regardless of cost, and then, if they are needed, buy the four destroyer escorts also. This argument is usually combined with exhortations about "nothing but the best" which ignore the crucial difference between "best, given our limited resources," and "best, assuming hypothetically that there is no limitation on resources." Or, it is combined with attacks on "arbitrary budget ceilings." But the man who wants a nuclear carrier plus four destroyer escorts cannot escape the fact that for the same cost one could have a conventional carrier and eight destroyer escorts. Therefore, he cannot escape the question: "Which is the best way to spend the money?"

The difficulty arises out of a confusion between budget *level* and the *allocation* of any given budget. The nuclear power issue is primarily a budget allocation question: How should we spend four billion dollars per year (or whatever figure one might choose) on attack carrier forces? The question cannot be avoided by arguing that we should add $120 million to the shipbuilding budget to make the carrier nuclear-powered, unless one is prepared also to argue that the extra money is better spent on nuclear power than on the four extra DES, or on some other $120 million program.

I emphasize the inescapability of the limitation of resources, and the resulting necessity for choice, because it is the basis for the relevance of economics to weapon system choice. Out of this limitation of resources stems the need for systematic thought on the problem of getting the most out of them.

What are the principles of economics? I cannot condense all of the elements into a few pages. But it is possible to indicate briefly some of the fundamental notions that are relevant to systems analysis.

First, in the economist's world there are always alternatives, alternative ways of using resources or alternative ways of doing a job. His theories are built on that assumption, and clearly it is a good one. Thus, if an economist hears that it is required that an airplane be able to fly at Mach 2, he naturally thinks, almost in spite of himself, "I wonder whether Mach 1.9 or Mach 2.2 would be better." Or, if he is told "400 missiles are required to destroy the targets," he instinctively thinks about 350 and 450, and other alternatives. A great deal of economic theory is concerned with the comparison of alternatives.

Of particular interest to economists is the *marginal comparison;* for example, a comparison between the costs and target destruction capabilities of a force of 400 missiles and one of 399 missiles, or some other number not far from 400. The reason for this is that it is often possible to derive a clue as to whether 400 is a sensible force level from a comparison of forces of 399 and 400 missiles.

Let me illustrate. Suppose that, all operational factors considered, our missiles each have a 50 percent chance of destroying a target, and that we must commit all of our missiles to their targets before the firing begins. Suppose there are 100 targets. How many missiles are "required" to destroy the targets?

One approach is to assume, arbitrarily, that we must be able, on the average, to destroy, for example, 90 per cent of the targets. Then determining the "required number" becomes a simple arithmetic matter. If we program one missile per target, on the average we can expect to destroy 50 targets (50 per cent of 100 targets). If we program two missiles per target, we can expect to destroy 75, and so forth.[1] On the average, a force of 340 missiles can be expected to destroy 90 targets. The answer seems simple and clear enough.

But if one considers the force of 340 missiles in the context of a range of alternative forces, some deeper questions emerge. The following table shows the average number of targets destroyed for several different forces.

Number of Missiles	Average Number of Targets Destroyed
200	75
300	87.5
308	88
324	89
340	90
356	91
380	92.5
400	93.75

The question immediately arises, "Why 90 per cent?" Is it worth the price of sixteen extra missiles to raise the average number of targets destroyed from eighty-nine to ninety; or of 140 extra missiles to raise the average number of targets destroyed from seventy-five to ninety? If we keep ninety as our objective, *on the average,* it costs us 3.4 missiles per target aimed at, and nearly 3.8 missiles per target destroyed. But *at the margin,* raising the required average number of targets destroyed by one costs us sixteen missiles. This concept, *marginal cost,* is one of the fundamental notions of economic theory. Its twin is *marginal product:* the 341st missile will add one-sixteenth of one target to the average number of targets destroyed.

Armed with these concepts, the economist will seek out marginal costs and marginal products and describe them for the decision-maker. Of course, the fact that raising the required damage level from eighty-nine to ninety targets costs sixteen missiles carries no necessary implication that we should not do it. It is up to the responsible officials charged with making such decisions, that is, the Secretary of Defense, the service secretaries, and those to whom they have delegated the authority to make such decisions, to weigh the marginal costs and marginal products and to judge at what point the extra target destruction caused by more missiles is no longer worth the extra cost. Having drawn out what the costs of the various alternatives really are, economic analysis has nothing more to contribute to the problem. It becomes a matter of judgment. But the distinction between *marginal* and *average* costs is important. If it were not made, a responsible official might be misled into thinking that because, on the average, 340 missiles destroy ninety of the 100 targets, whence about 3.8 missiles must be expended for each target destroyed, the ninetieth target also costs 3.8 missiles to destroy.

This example is a particularly simple one. Few requirements problems in the Defense Department can be described in such simple terms. Still, the example does furnish an important insight that does have application even in the most complicated of problems. If one plots the curve relating effectiveness, which is measured in targets destroyed in this example, and cost, which is measured in number of missiles in this example, one very frequently finds a curve with the following characteristic shape:

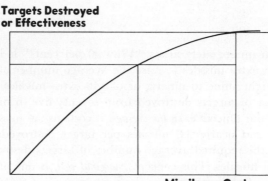
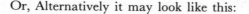

**Targets Destroyed
or Effectiveness**

Missiles or Cost

Or, Alternatively it may look like this:

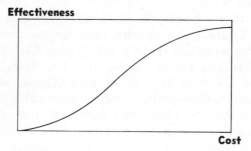

Effectiveness

Cost

These curves illustrate the widespread phenomenon of *diminishing marginal returns.* That is, as the resources devoted to a mission are increased, after a point the marginal products of additional resources generally decline, or, put another way, the marginal costs of extra effectiveness rise. An understanding of this point is important because it is the key to the sensible resolution of many requirements issues. Rather than viewing the problem of military requirements determination as one of calculation of the forces required to achieve an arbitrarily selected objective or level of effectiveness, it is often sensible to reduce the problem to one of judging at what point the extra effectiveness resulting from more forces—the marginal product—is no longer worth the extra effort—the marginal cost. Alternatively, many requirements issues have been resolved by observing that, at some point, more forces would put us "out on the flat of the curve," that is, they would put us in the position of paying large sums of money for small increases in effectiveness. For these reasons, I have not been able to resist facetiously calling this simple diagram "the single all-purpose cost-effectiveness curve."

Much economic theory is an analysis of what we often refer to in the Defense Department as "balance." What are balanced forces? Or, to put the question into the economist's jargon, how does one determine an efficient mix of forces? Suppose that our problem is one of determining the efficient mix of tactical air and ground forces; that is, for example, the combination of wings and divisions that will permit us to achieve a stipulated military objective at least cost.

Number of Wings

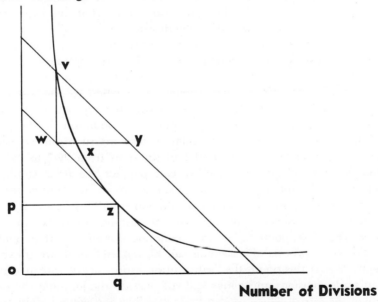

Number of Divisions

First, we must determine the substitution or trade-off possibilities. Suppose that CINCSTRIKE advises us that the objective can be achieved with equal probability or margin of safety by any of a number of combinations of wings and divisions, and that these combinations all lie on the curve shown in the diagram above. This curve then represents the substitution possibilities between wings and divisions. Its slope at any point represents the number of wings we can give up in exchange for one more division, or vice versa, and still just be able to accomplish the objective. For example, if we are at point "v", we can trade the number of wings represented by the distance between points "v" and "w" for the number of divisions represented by the distance between points "w" and "x" and still be able to accomplish the objective. The ratio of those numbers, i.e., the ratio of the distances "v" to "w" and "w" to "x", might be called the "substitution ratio," or the ratio at which we should be just willing to substitute wings for divisions at the wing strength represented by point "v". The shape of the curve reflects diminishing marginal returns. The fewer wings we have, the more divisions are required to compensate us for the loss of another wing.

Now, where is the optimum point on the curve? That depends on the relative costs of wings and divisions. Suppose that the relative costs of a wing and a division are in the ratio of the distances "v" to "w" and "w" to "y"; that is, the cost ratio is such that one can trade the number of wings represented by the distance "v" to "w" for the number of divisions represented by the distance "w" to "y" with no change in the total cost. Then consider point "v". Is it the optimum, or can we do better? Well, we have already observed first, that from point "v" we can give up the number of wings represented by the distance "v" to "w" in exchange for the number of divisions represented by the distance "w" to "x", thus moving to point "x", and still do the job. But we have also observed that the relative costs are such that we can give up wings from "v" to "w" and add divisions from "w" to "y" at no change in total cost. Thus, if we can pay for the force combination represented by point "v", we have the alternative, at the same total cost, of moving to point "x", which does the job equally well, and having the number of divisions represented by the distance from "x" to "y" left over. Therefore, point "x" is more economical or efficient than point "v."

The same process of reasoning can be repeated until we converge at point "z." At this point, the "substitution ratio," or the rate at which we can trade divisions and wings and still just do the job, and the cost ratio, or the rate at which we can trade divisions and wings within any given total budget, are equal. And that is the point that corresponds to the combination of wings and divisions that just does the job at minimum total cost. Thus, for this particular situation and these relative costs, the combination "p" wings and "q" divisions represents a "balanced force."

The same logic can be applied to many problems of allocation of resources; for example, the problem of choice between numbers and quality. One often hears arguments for more numbers at the expense of quality or performance, or for higher performance at the expense of numbers, and the arguments are often in the abstract, independent of the shape of the substitution curves and the relative costs. The important thing is that one cannot decide such matters in the abstract. In the diagram, instead of wings read number of aircraft, and instead of divisions, read individual aircraft performance. Let the job to be done be the destruction of a given set of targets. Then, to determine the optimum combination, one must examine the trade-off curve and the relative costs. At some points like "v," the performance is too low and it would be better to sacrifice numbers to get higher performance. At points below "z," numbers are too low, and performance should be sacrificed to get more numbers. Of course, many other relevant considerations, some of them intangible, must be brought to bear before a final decision can properly be made. One important example would be the safety of the pilots and the impact on morale of heavy loss of life. That is why such problems are matters of decision, i.e., judgments to be made by the Secretary of Defense, the service secretaries, and those to whom they have delegated authority for such decisions, and not simply matters of calculation to be resolved by the systems analysts.

The issue here is not whether the country should spend more money to get more performance. The level of the budget is a separate question. The point is that one should seek the combination of numbers and performance that would get the most effectiveness out of any given budget. To do otherwise would be wasteful.

CONSTRUCTION OF PARTIAL ORDERINGS

In the discussion of diminishing marginal returns, I mentioned effectiveness but did not define it. What is military effectiveness and how is it measured? That is a very complicated question and there is no generally satisfactory answer. A great deal of analysis must be done before we begin to get a reliable grip on that elusive concept "military effectiveness." But a part of the work of systems analysis is to develop criteria that will permit us to rank alternative mixes of forces in terms of their military effectiveness.

Let me illustrate with an example. The designer of the guidance system for Polaris can make a variety of trade-offs between accuracy, cost, reliability, and weight. On what basis can he choose one combination of these characteristics over another? If he chooses accuracy as his measure of effectiveness, he might make a choice in favor of maximum accuracy, but at a great cost in terms of the other characteristics. He might pursue accuracy to the point that he is "out on the flat of the curve." Therefore, he needs criteria that will help him to make a good compromise between accuracy and other characteristics. To get them, he must study the purposes of the Polaris system as a whole.

The Polaris system is a part of our Strategic Retaliatory Forces whose purposes include making nuclear war unlikely by deterring direct attack against us, and should that fail, helping to limit the damage caused to ourselves and our allies by destroying as many as possible of the enemy's forces before they are launched. The extent to which our Strategic Retaliatory Forces can be effective in achieving the second purpose depends on the circumstances of outbreak of the war, that is, on the relative timing of the launching of enemy forces and our own. However, because of "rate of fire" limitations on bombers and some kinds of missile systems, we may expect, even in circumstances in which we are striking second, to be able to destroy a substantial part of the enemy's nuclear delivery forces on the ground. Both of these purposes involve an ability to destroy targets, though different kinds of targets. Thus, the designer of the Polaris guidance system can begin to derive information on good mixes of accuracy, reliability, weight, cost, and other matters, by looking at the targets. For any particular target, the preferred mix of characteristics can be derived from its hardness, its extent, the desired probability of destruction, and so on. If the objective were to destroy as many as possible of an unlimited list of identical targets, the problem would end here.

But, there are more fundamental objectives underlying target destruction. The deterrence objective is served by an ability to destroy, in a second strike (i.e., after the enemy has attacked our forces), things the enemy values. At least in terms of present-day strategic concepts, this means enemy cities, which are soft, extensive targets. The damage-limiting objective is served by an ability to destroy, under various conditions, bomber bases, missile sites, and other military targets, which are more or less blast resistant "point targets."

Thus, the preferred mix of accuracy, reliability, weight, and cost will depend on which targets the Polaris will be used to attack, and therefore on our strategy and on the availability of other weapon systems. For example, a strategy that emphasizes counterforce targeting would increase the requirement for accuracy; the availability of large numbers of highly accurate Minuteman missiles would lessen the requirement for accuracy in Polaris.

The extent to which a large investment in a counterforce posture makes sense depends on the effectiveness of our forces in limiting the damage to ourselves and our allies. Under any given set of assumptions about circumstances of outbreak, war plans, and so forth, this effectiveness can be measured by the difference between the damage that could be caused by the enemy forces if not attacked by our own, and the damage that could be caused us in spite of our attacks on the enemy forces.

Of course, each of our weapon systems and forces has particular advantages and disadvantages that are measured in other ways than by surviving population and wealth. For example, it is argued by some that a large-scale civil defense program in this country would have significant effects on national psychology and attitudes. Our anti-aircraft defense system controls our airspace against peacetime intruders, as well as helping to limit damage in wartime. An anti-missile defense could protect our cities from isolated accidental missile firings, or from blackmail by small powers. All of these factors should enter into judgments made about our choice of weapon systems and strategies.

Thus, to do a good job of measuring the effectiveness of the Polaris guidance system, it is necessary to develop a complete analysis of the effectiveness of our whole posture under a variety of assumed conditions. Such an analysis permits us to translate accuracy, reliability, weight, and number of missiles (which depends on costs) into target destruction, and to translate target destruction into surviving military forces, population, and wealth.

For several reasons, it is important to put each weapon system problem in the context of the other problems that surround it, and of the broader problems of which it is a part. First, the test of whether a particular set of criteria is a good one is its relevance to the broader objectives which the system is intended to serve. For example, accuracy alone is not a good criterion for the Polaris guidance system; the objective of target destruction might be better served by larger numbers of more reliable missiles even at some cost in accuracy. Second, developing such a hierarchy of criteria makes it possible to aggregate a large number of detailed measures of performance into a few broad criteria of over-all effectiveness that are more meaningful to top level officials who have to deal with so many problems that they cannot consider every accuracy-reliability choice in detail. In the example cited above, the Secretary of Defense and the Joint Chiefs should not have to worry about the weight of the Polaris guidance package. They will want to concentrate their attention on prospective damage to U.S., allied, and enemy populations and military forces under a range of possible wars, and on many important intangible factors about which they must make the key judgments. A good analysis will leave them free to do that.

Moreover, putting each problem in its larger context helps the analyst and the decision-maker to see the full range of alternatives. Putting Polaris in the context of the Strategic Retaliatory Forces helps one to see that one alternative to greater Polaris accuracy is to have more Minuteman ICBMs. Another alternative is to have more bombers. Considering the Strategic Retaliatory Forces in the context of our whole posture for general nuclear war helps one to see that, in addition to the foregoing, the alternatives to more Polaris accuracy or to more Strategic Retaliatory Forces include Continental Air and Missile Defense, Civil Defense, and anti-submarine forces. To take but one of these, unless we can easily and surely destroy enemy ICBMs on the ground, perhaps it would be better to plan to destroy their warheads in the air.

Viewing each problem of analysis and decision in this way also helps one to understand the important fact that ends and means interact. Too often, analyses of military requirements will be limited to determining one feasible way, or perhaps the best way of achieving a particular objective. The problem is that whether any particular military objective is worth pursuing will depend on how much it costs to achieve it, because there are almost always alternative ways of achieving the broader or higher objective.

For example, it would be extremely difficult to find and destroy a substantial number of enemy missile submarines in the few minutes between the outbreak of a nuclear war and the time by which they could fire most of their missiles. One approach to the problem of ASW force requirements for this mission is to insist on ever larger forces, even though the ones we now have would not be able to destroy very many submarines before they had launched their missiles, and even though a large expansion in the forces would not make us appreciably better off. Proponents of this approach ignore the fact that we have alternative ways of keeping those missiles off our cities: these include active anti-missile defenses, better Strategic Retaliatory Forces to improve our deterrent to nuclear attack, and improved conventional forces to deter limited aggressions or at least keep them from escalating into nuclear war.

A frequent but mistaken view of the determination of strategy and force requirements is that the complete process if one of starting at the top with broad national objectives and then deriving a strategy, and from the strategy, force requirements, and from the force requirements, a budget. It is mistaken because the costs must be considered in choosing strategies and objectives. There are alternative objectives and alternative strategies. And it may be that the advantages of a somewhat more ambitious strategy are worth its somewhat greater cost. And, of course, the cost and effectiveness of each strategy will depend on the cost and effectiveness of the weapon systems used. Thus, the line of causation should not be thought of as running one way, from the strategy to the forces, or, for that matter, from the budget to the strategy. Rather our objectives, strategy, forces, and weapon systems should be thought of as interdependent. And a "requirement" for a particular force level or weapon system cannot be established independently of its cost.

Important as it is to develop a hierarchy of criteria for ordering alternative mixes of weapon systems and forces, it is clear that the best we can ever hope for is a partial ordering. For example, it seems doubtful that we can ever develop criteria that will permit the effectiveness of Polaris and airlift to be measured in the same terms. In fact, the criteria of damage to population and wealth that we use to compare alternative Strategic Retaliatory and Continental Air and Missile Defense Forces cannot establish a complete ordering. Each kind of force will offer a number of "by-products" that cannot be measured in these terms. For example, suppose two postures offer exactly the same number of United States and allied survivors in a particular set of circumstances, but one posture does it by a larger Strategic Retaliatory Force and no anti-missile defenses, while the other contains an anti-missile defense but fewer Strategic Retaliatory Forces. Although the two forces may be identical in terms of prospective damage to the alliance in a thermo-nuclear war, they would have important differences. Presumably, the one with larger Strategic Retaliatory Forces would offer a stronger deterrent to deliberate attack, while the one with the anti-missile defenses would offer some peacetime protection against accidental missile firings. Thus, we cannot and should not expect ever to be able to develop a complete set of numerical criteria to measure "military effectiveness" in general.

SCIENTIFIC METHOD

The art of weapon systems analysis is an application of scientific method, using that term in its broadest sense. I hesitate to say "scientific" to naval or military readers for several reasons. First, some may mistakenly interpret this as a reference to the narrower methods of the physical sciences, whereas I wish to refer to the philosophy of science. Second, many mistakes have been advertised as scientific. I can appreciate that it would be tiresome, to say the least, for an experienced naval or military officer to be told that we need a "scientific" approach to war or to the proper development of amphibious forces. Warfare is, after all, more an art than a science, combining such critical but intangible factors as training, morale, and leadership. Third, one risks suggesting that scientists are the leading experts. One sees some nuclear physicists advertised as experts on thermonuclear war, despite the fact that they have not studied war empirically or systematically and know nothing about it, and this also must be tiresome to a military or naval person. But, the point is not the authority of science or of scientists. Rather, it is the *method* of science.

What are the relevant characteristics of scientific method as applied to the problem of choosing strategies and selecting weapon systems? There are several. First, the method of science is open, explicit, verifiable, and self-correcting. It combines logic and empirical evidence. The method and tradition of science require that scientific results be openly arrived at, so that any other scientist can retrace the same steps and get the same result. Applying this to weapon systems and to strategy would require that all calculations, assumptions, empirical data, and judgments be described in the analysis in such a way that they can be subjected to checking, testing, criticism, debate, discussion, and possible refutation. Of course, neither science nor systems analysis is infallible. Chemists used to believe in the phlogiston theory of combustion. Some biologists still claim to believe in the inheritance of acquired traits. I have seen many systems analyses containing equally questionable conclusions. But infallibility is not being claimed; it would be worse than unscientific to do so. However, scientific method does have a self-correcting character that helps to guard science from persistence in error.

Second, scientific method is objective. Although personalities doubtless play an important part in the life of the physics profession, the science itself does not depend upon personalities or vested interests. The truth of a scientific proposition is established by logical and empirical methods common to the profession as a whole. The young and inexperienced scientist can challenge the results of an older and more experienced one, or an obscure scientist can challenge the findings of a Nobel Prize winner, and the profession will evaluate the results on the basis of methods quite independent of the authority of the contenders, and will establish what is the correct conclusion. In other words, the result is established on the objective quality of the physics and not on the reputations of the persons involved. Doubtless, some would scoff at the challenger, and the odds would favor the Nobel Prize winner. But, the physics profession is not likely to harbor incorrect hypotheses for long just because of the authority of their originators.

Third, in scientific method in the broadest sense, each hypothesis is tested and verified by methods appropriate to it. Some are tested and verified logically, some experimentally, some historically, and some in still other ways. Some sciences, of course, lend themselves to inexpensive experimentation and, where this is so, experiments tend to be emphasized. This is notably the case with the physical sciences. In others, particularly some branches of medicine and the social sciences, one cannot experiment as readily, and detailed analysis of available historical data may be more appropriate. In this respect, the latter closely resemble military science. In choosing weapon systems, some experimentation is possible but a great deal of analysis is also required. In fact, the development of weapon systems analysis is more handicapped than most of the sciences, because fully realistic tests come only at infrequent intervals in war, while the development of new weapon systems takes place in peacetime also. This points to the need for better analysis and more heavy reliance on analysis where fully relevant experience is not generally available.

Fourth, quantitative aspects are treated quantitatively. This is not to say that all matters can be reduced to numbers, or even that most can be, or that the most important aspects can be. It is merely to say that the appropriate method for dealing with some aspects of problems of choice of weapon systems and strategies requires numbers. Non-quantitative judgment is simply not enough.

What is at issue here is not numbers or computers versus words or judgment. The real issue is one of clarity of understanding and expression. Take, for example, the statement; "Nuclear power for surface ships offers a major increase in effectiveness." Precisely what does that mean? Does it mean 10 per cent better or 100 per cent better? When that sort of question is asked, a frequent answer is, "It can't be expressed in numbers." But, it has to be expressed with the help of numbers. Budgets are expressed in dollars, and nuclear power costs more dollars than conventional power. If nuclear power costs, say 33 per cent more for a certain ship type, all factors considered, then, no matter what the budget level, the Navy and the Secretary of Defense must choose whether to put the nation's resources into four conventional or three nuclear ships, or for a larger budget, eight conventional or six nuclear ships. Therefore it is important to know whether by "major increase in effectiveness" is meant more than 33 per cent, about 33 per cent, or less than 33 per cent. Because the Secretary of Defense has to make the decision in these terms, the statement "major increase" is not particularly helpful. It must be replaced by a quantitative analysis of the performance of various missions, leading to a conclusion such as: "Nuclear power for surface ships offers something between 'X' and 'Y' per cent more effectiveness per ship. Therefore, one billion dollars spent on nuclear-powered ships will provide a force somewhere between 'A' and 'B' per cent more or less effective than the same dollars spent on conventionally-powered ships."

Numbers are a part of our language. Where a quantitative matter is being discussed, the greatest clarity of thought is achieved by using numbers, not by avoiding them, *even when uncertainties are present.* This is not to rule out judgment and insight. Rather, it is to say, that judgments and insights need, like everything else, to be expressed with clarity if they are to be useful.

Let me emphasize the point about uncertainties. Many people seem to feel that quantitative analysis is not possible if there are any uncertainties. Of course, if this were strictly true, I suppose we would have no such science as physics. But this view is incorrect. In fact, there is substantial literature on the logic of decision-making under uncertainty going back at least as far as Pascal, Bernoulli, and Bayes in the seventeenth and eighteenth centuries. Moreover, there are simple practical techniques for dealing with uncertainty which make it possible to do analyses that point up the uncertainties for the decision-maker and indicate their significance. In fact, rather than conceal uncertainties, a good analysis will bring them out and clarify them.

ASSUMPTIONS AND UNCERTAINTIES

In order to calculate or analyze a problem, one generally must make assumptions about a variety of factors, some of which will involve substantial uncertainties. Critics of the systems analysis approach like to point out that the results are no better than the underlying assumptions. Though true for any individual calculation, this statement may not be true of a complete study. Good systems analysts have acquired some wisdom in dealing with this problem over the years.

As to assumptions in general, let me make two observations. First, a good systems analyst will do sensitivity tests on his assumptions in order to identify which ones really affect the outcome, and by how much. This will enable him to isolate for further research and evaluation those assumptions that prove to be the most important, and to call them to the attention of the responsible decision-maker.

Second, generally speaking, there is no single "right" set of assumptions. There is often a variety of sets of relevant assumptions, each more or less equally defensible. It is unfortunately the case that this important point is not widely understood. Far too many people keep looking for the "right" set of assumptions the way ancient alchemists looked for the philosophers' stone. Their prospects for success are no better. This is unfortunate, because some people find a set of assumptions that leads to the conclusion they believed all along or hoped would emerge, and they then put forward their conclusions as soundly established, not realizing that the opposite conclusion could have been derived from equally defensible but different assumptions. A good systems analysis will describe the significant alternative sets of assumptions and their implications in such a way that the responsible decision-maker can make his judgment based on the full range of relevant assumptions.

This point was well illustrated by the controversy over the comparative costs of a nuclear-powered and conventionally-powered aircraft carrier. It might seem that comparing the costs of a CVA and a CVAN ought to be a straightforward matter; that one should be able simply to add up the costs of each and compare them. But, in fact, in order to make a cost comparison, one must first make assumptions about a number of relevant factors, each debatable, and each liable to have a noticeable effect on the outcome.

For example, should one include the costs of the escort ships, or not? I have heard senior naval officers argue reasonably on both sides of this question, though the balance of the judgment seems to favor including them. It matters because the relative cost increase associated with using nuclear power in the smaller escort ships is much greater than it is for the carrier.

Should one make the comparison on the basis of estimates of the costs of two wholly new task forces identical in all respects but propulsive power? It would seem reasonable to do so. But that would bias the comparison in favor of nuclear power because, at the moment, we have all or most of the conventional major fleet escort ships we need. One could argue that the nuclear force should have to bear the costs of both construction and operation of its nuclear-powered escorts while the conventional force should be charged only with operating costs of the conventional escorts. That, in turn, would be "unfair" to nuclear power because eventually the conventional escorts will have to be replaced. But "eventually" now seems off in the uncertain future. Therefore, although we know that they should lie between these two extremes, good sets of assumptions seem difficult to identify.

Moreover, the assumptions made about the "scenarios" in which the carrier forces are to be used can influence the cost comparison by influencing the fleet support requirements. For example, a cold war deployment involving a long, high-speed transit, little flying, and no consumption of ordnance, will favor the nuclear task force because fleet logistic support requirements will be minimal. If oil is not required, the task force will be able to operate without replenishment for a relatively long time. On the other hand, in a limited war situation involving heavy flying and delivery of ordnance, the advantage of not requiring black oil will be considerably reduced; both nuclear and conventional forces will require substantial re-supply. Which is the "right" assumption? Neither by itself would be completely "right" or "fair." A good systems analysis will describe the situation for the decision-maker, and provide him with whatever information is available that might help him to make a judgment as to the frequency and value of both types of mission in the future.

I mentioned earlier that rather than conceal uncertainties, a good analysis will bring them out and clarify them. This is important. A best guess is not the same as certain knowledge. If it is a question of uncertainties about quantitative matters such as operational factors, or uncertainty about enemy strategies, it is desirable to examine the available evidence and determine the bounds of uncertainty. In many of our analyses for the Secretary of Defense, we carry three estimates through the calculations: a "best" or single most likely estimate, an "optimistic," and a "pessimistic" estimate. One admiral calls this procedure "bop (for best, optimistic, pessimistic) estimates."

"Bop" estimates have produced some unexpected benefits. For one thing, the concept of "bop" estimates has led to some valuable clarity of thought on the whole question of comparing our forces to those of our opponents. There has been a widespread belief that, in cases of doubt, the safe thing to do is to pick from the high end of the range of uncertainty in estimating one's opponent's capabilities and to pick from the low end in estimating one's own. If uncertain about the reliability of the enemy's missiles and ours, according to this belief, one should be sure not to underestimate the enemy's or to overestimate ours. This might be a conservative or safe approach if we did not have limited resources. But, in fact, we have learned that it can be just as dangerous to overestimate the enemy's capabilities relative to our own as it is to underestimate them. Overestimates do not necessarily lead to insurance and safety. They are just as likely to lead to despair, to pricing important capabilities out of the market, and to strategies of desperation.

Perhaps the best example of this has been the persistent gross overestimates of the effectiveness of the Soviet Army. In the United States we get sixteen combat-ready divisions (plus a variety of other units) out of an army of about 960,000. Under existing concepts of organization and existing missions and commitments (e.g., Continental Air Defense, Vietnam, to name but two), we could probably get the equivalent of about eighteen divisions out of a 1,000,000-man army. It is generally agreed that the Soviet Union has an army of roughly 2,000,000 men. Yet one often hears and reads statements to the effect that the Soviets have over 100 divisions, each one presumably as effective as one of ours. In fact, numbers like 160 and 175 still appear in print. How can this be? Unless the United States Army is very inefficient in its use of manpower (which it is not), surely the Soviets could not get from their army of 2,000,000 a great deal more than the equivalent of twice the eighteen divisions we could get out of a 1,000,000-man army. The overestimate can be traced to the omission of two key factors: first, the important distinction between combat-ready units and units of low readiness; and second, the fact that our divisions, with their non-divisional combat support, such as engineers and heavy artillery, have about twice as many men as their Soviet counterparts. The main reason for the overestimate is doubtless the widespread belief that no harm could come from overstating the strength of the Soviets. But the plain fact is that these overestimates have led to an attitude of hopelessness about the prospects for a successful non-nuclear defense against non-nuclear attacks in the NATO area, and to an unnecessary and excessive reliance on the early first use of nuclear weapons by NATO. Yet, without an adequate non-nuclear force, we could be forced by Communist aggression into the horrible dilemma of suicide or surrender.

Another benefit of the use of "bop" estimates has been a greater measure of agreement in joint requirements studies. It may well be impossible for two officers from different services and with different points of view, to agree on a single estimate of an uncertain magnitude, or on a single "right" set of assumptions when in fact such does not exist. In the past, such failure to agree has sometimes been erroneously labeled as parochialism. But failure to agree is not surprising when one realizes that there are genuine uncertainties—cases in which we simply do not know where a magnitude will fall between certain limits—and that there often is no single "fair" or right set of assumptions. We have found that an approach that acknowledges that there can be alternative assumptions saves a great deal of otherwise wasted time.

Systems Analysis and Operations Research

It may be helpful to an understanding of the systems analysis approach to have it contrasted with the discipline traditionally known as operations research. The Navy has a strong tradition in operations research and has every right to be proud of it. But sometimes I fear that when I talk to Navy men about the need for more systematic quantitative analysis, some may interpret this to mean more operations research. There are significant differences between the two. Of course, in reality there is a continuum between them, just as there is between physiology and medicine and between physics and engineering. One necessarily must artificially divide a continuous spectrum into discreet segments in order to define the different disciplines. However, I do think it would be useful further to clarify the sense of the systems analysis approach.

In doing this, I would not want for a moment to suggest that systems analysis is in any sense, intellectually or otherwise, superior to operations research. That would be like suggesting that medicine is superior or inferior to biology. Both have their place. I am reminded of a statement contained in the Carnegie report on excellence to the effect that if a society does not respect both its plumbers and its philosophers, neither its pipes nor its theories will hold water.

Let me contrast operations research and systems analysis in several ways.

Operations research techniques are applicable to problems such as calculations of optimum inventory levels for spare parts for an SSBN, calculation of the optimum search pattern for ASW forces seeking a submarine in a given area, calculation of the most efficient blend of aviation gasoline, and the like. Systems analysis, on the other hand, is an

approach to broader problems such as determining the preferred characteristics for a new attack aircraft, the design of the Polaris system, a determination of how many Polaris submarines are required, or the study
of the number of anti-submarine ships or the number of attack carriers
that should be included in the Navy force structure.

Generally speaking, operations research accepts specified objectives
and given assumptions about the circumstances, the hardware, and the
like, and then attempts to compute an optimum solution, usually maximizing or minimizing some objective, given the available resources. Operations research attempts to do an optimization in the small. It may be
necessary for the operations researcher first to define the problem, but
the operations research techniques themselves are intended for the solution of well defined problems, that is, problems in which all of the relevant relationships can be specified. Operations research then attempts to
select an optimum solution from a predetermined range of alternatives.

Systems analysis, on the other hand, has a broader orientation. It ana-
lyzes alternative objectives and explores their implications. It is focused
more on exploring the implications of alternative assumptions than on
analyzing in extensive detail the implications of a single set of assumptions. Systems analysis ordinarily is not concerned with computing an
optimum solution. If there is optimization involved, it is optimization in
the large, rather than in the small. Systems analysis is concerned with
avoiding gross error and with giving the decision-maker a range of
choices representing different mixes of effectiveness and cost so that he can
make his choice. It is part of systems analysis to question the objectives.

Systems analysis takes problems that are not defined and attempts to
define them. If the problem cannot be well defined, that is, specified in
all its aspects, systems analysis techniques are still useful in helping the
decision-maker by attempting to define those aspects of the problem
that can be defined and quantified. Systems analysis emphasizes design
of new solutions and widening of the range of alternatives, rather than
selecting the best alternative from among a predetermined range. Rather than trying to select a precise maximum or minimum, a motto of the
Systems Analysis Office in the Office of the Secretary of Defense is: "It
is better to be roughly right than exactly wrong."

The epistemology of operations research is the epistemology of the exact sciences; that is, operations research assumes that the empirical data
are accurate, at least accurate enough to make refined and precise calculations worthwhile. On the other hand, the epistemology of systems analysis is the epistemology of the inexact sciences. Statistics may be used,

although in most major weapon system problems the uncertainties are greater than the statistical variations, so that extensive use of mathematical statistical techniques is not likely to produce useful results. Systems analysis emphasizes techniques for dealing with uncertainty, such as sensitivity tests, the use of ranges, alternative scenarios, and the like.

Operations research technique emphasizes applied mathematics, such as linear programming, queueing theory, search theory, and inventory theory; that is, a collection of mathematical techniques for maximizing or minimizing something subject to constraints. Also operations research emphasizes the use of computers because its emphasis is largely on efficient and accurate computation of optimum solutions. In effect, operations research is oriented toward problems in which the element of calculation is dominant, and therefore in which mathematics can be thought of as a substitute for rather than as an aid to judgment.

Systems analysis, on the other hand, emphasizes basic economic concepts, mostly the simple concepts of marginal product and marginal cost. The systems analysis approach has developed a variety of techniques for analyzing complex problems of decision in such a way as to make calculation the servant of informed judgment. It has, therefore, made use of calculation, but it puts much less emphasis on it than does operations research.

Who, then, are systems analysts? I am unable to hazard a satisfactory definition of them as a group. There are few courses and no degrees in the subject, and that is doubtless a good thing because it helps to minimize appeals to authority. The main attributes of a good systems analyst, other than those, such as good character and imagination, that are valuable in most professions, are an understanding of scientific method, economic intuition, some facility with mathematics, which is the language of science, and an appreciation of the limitations as well as the capabilities of his methods. Some very effective systems analysts are officers, some are civilians. No one professional background has proved itself to be best. Representation from a variety of professions and disciplines is clearly beneficial.

LIMITATIONS AND BIASES

What is wrong with systems analysis? What are its particular limitations and biases? One criticism I have heard is that emphasis on quantitative analysis risks ignoring those factors that cannot be reduced to numbers, or at least overemphasizing those that can.

Suppose, for example, that the problem is to choose between two alternative ways of destroying a certain set of targets. The less costly way is to base short-range missiles on the territory of an ally; the most costly way is to cover the targets with long-range missiles based in the United States. But suppose basing the missiles on the ally's territory would lead to political difficulties, to the embarrassment and possible fall of a friendly government. How does one take account of such political aspects in a quantitative analysis? The answer is that one does not. There is no way of "grinding in" the potential political difficulties of an ally. The most the analysis can do is make clear to the decision-maker the differences in cost and effectiveness between the two approaches so that he can make an informed judgment about their weight in relation to the political problems.

I would not want to deny that there is potential danger here, even though there is nothing about the systems analysis approach that prevents an assessment of the political or other non-quantitative factors from being included in the staff work. I am confident that the top-level leaders of the Department of Defense who use systems analyses as one of their sources of information are careful to give balanced consideration to all factors, whether quantitative or not.

Another criticism sometimes made is that application of the "flat of the curve" argument to force or performance requirements may lead people to ignore the decisiveness of a narrow edge in superior performance. There is a danger here if an unwary analyst confuses *performance* and *effectiveness*. There is no question but that, in some cases, a narrow edge in performance may have a very great impact on effectiveness. The performance advantage of the Japanese Zero fighter over American aircraft at the beginning of World War II is a good case in point. But there are other cases in which even a substantial increase in performance, purchased at a high price, may have a small impact on effectiveness. For example, many Navy aviators believe that under today's conditions, a substantial speed advantage in attack aircraft may mean rather little in terms of increased effectiveness. It is easy to confuse performance and effectiveness. But this mistake is clearly not peculiar to the systems analysis approach. The only way to avoid it, and to relate performance to effectiveness properly, is with the help of good analysis. The "single all-purpose cost-effectiveness curve" I drew earlier has effectiveness and not performance on the vertical axis.

Next, it is argued that the systems analysis approach may be biased against the new and in favor of the old. I am sometimes concerned that our analyses may be subject to such bias, but I think that the method of open explicit analysis is much less likely to be so biased than is reliance on judgment or intuition or experience unsupported by analysis. The reason for the bias is that we all tend to compare the old and the new in the current mission that happens to have been optimized for the old. For example, in comparing the effectiveness of the conventional- and nuclear-powered carriers, there is a danger that the studies may, in effect, by trying to answer the question: "How well can the nuclear-powered carrier do the conventional carrier's job?" The answer to that question is likely to understate the gain in effectiveness associated with nuclear power.

A similar argument has it that cost-effectiveness analysis is biased against new systems to replace those already in operation because the new system is charged with its initial investment as well as operating cost, while the old system is charged only with its operating cost. I would plead guilty to this accusation but insist that this is not an unfair bias. Rather, it is the correct procedure for a rational equipment replacement policy. The point is that our objective, in selecting the rate of replacement of weapons and ships, should not be to maximize the degree of newness in the forces. It should be to maximize the total effectiveness we get out of the resources available for defense. And sometimes that objective is best served by replacing the old with new; sometimes by continuing to operate the old. The "break-even point" comes when the new system, in relation to its costs including initial investment costs, is more effective than the old, in relation to its operating costs. Part of the proof that the cost-effectiveness approach is not biased against modernization is that the past three years have seen a rate of modernization in our armed forces unprecedented in peacetime, and it has generally been justified on cost-effectiveness grounds.

Finally, sometimes it is said that systems analyses oversimplify complex problems. Of course, we have to simplify the complex problems we face; no one could possibly understand most problems of modern weapon systems and strategy in all their complexity. And it is a natural human failing to oversimplify. But I believe the facts are that the systems analysis approach is much less prone to oversimplification than any alternative approach. For it is part of systems analysis to bring to bear all of the best of modern analytical techniques for organizing data and summarizing clearly its most relevant aspects. Moreover, reliance on the method of open, explicit analysis is our best guarantee against persistence in harmful oversimplification. For if I must lay out clearly all of my assumptions, objectives, factors, and calculations, my critics can see what I have done and point out where I have oversimplified, if indeed I have done so. But if I am allowed to keep it all in my head and appeal to experience or judgment, others have no way of knowing whether or not I have oversimplified the problem.

SYSTEMS ANALYSIS AND THE NAVY

Some people have feared that the systems analysis approach would do violence to the Navy because of the latter's multi-purpose and flexible character and because of the subtlety and complexity of many of the missions of naval forces. Some predicted that the growth of systems analysis would lead to the decline of the Navy.

This pessimistic view has proved to be wrong. Systems analysis has been beneficial to the Navy, and the Navy's top leadership has given it strong support. Systems analysis done by the Navy, in collaboration with the Office of the Secretary of Defense, have identified and substantiated requirements for an improved light attack aircraft, for accelerated modernization of the amphibious fleet, for development of a new surface-to-air missile system, for more anti-submarine destroyer escorts, and many other improvements in our naval forces.

Systems analysis will prove beneficial to the Navy for another reason also. Many of the traditional reasons for maintaining a large surface Navy do not fit today's conditions. There is no major enemy surface navy for ours to fight. For this reason, one of the main original missions of the attack carrier no longer exists. Nor is the carrier an efficient competitor for the Minuteman and Polaris systems in the strategic retaliatory mission. But an important part of systems analysis is relating our various military forces to our broad national security objectives. Systems analysis can help and is helping the Navy to find new ways of using our sea power to protect American security, to define new missions best performed by naval forces, and to help navy men articulate the reasons for maintaining a modern, effective navy.

Rapid change is a major characteristic of our times. There is rapid change in technology, weapon systems, and the relationships between nations. As these conditions change, the relationship between our military forces and our broad national security objectives, that is, our military strategy, must change. If the Navy is to continue to make a vital contribution to American security, it must keep re-thinking its purposes, re-defining its missions, and re-shaping its forces. To do this well, it needs rational procedures of analysis. Therefore, Navy men should welcome and encourage the growth of systems analysis in the Navy.

As for the complex multi-purpose character of naval forces, rather than acting as a barrier to systems analysis, it has been an intellectual challenge, a problem clearly worthy of the best efforts of our most talented analysts, both officers and civilians. Many important problems remain unsolved. The criterion problem for those forces we refer to as "Anti-submarine Warfare, Ocean Surveillance and Control Forces" is an example. We have not so far been able to develop completely satisfactory quantitative standards of adequacy. That is, we do not yet know how, in principle, to answer the question: "What is the right amount?" But it would be hard to find a more interesting problem.

Because the systems analysis approach tries to relate military force to our broad national security objectives, it quite naturally leads to emphasis on *usable* military force. By that I mean force that can be applied in a selective and controlled way to achieve those limited objectives necessary to preserve our freedom and that of our allies, without causing unnecessary damage or loss of life and while holding to a minimum the risk of escalation to a more destructive level of conflict. Put alternatively, military force is usable if it can reasonably be expected to bring about a better rather than a worse situation; peace and freedom rather than widespread destruction. Thus, in the past three years, systems analysis has contributed to a shift in United States military strategy away from reliance on the "trip wire" and "massive retaliation" to a strategy that emphasizes flexibility, options, deliberation, and control. At the nuclear level, this has meant a requirement for Strategic Retaliatory Forces that can be used with deliberation and control. Polaris has proved to be an ideal weapon system for this strategy. But even more important, the shift in strategy has led to a build-up in conventional or non-nuclear forces that can be used selectively and with control to bring military force to bear against a wide range of aggressions and crises on the Sino-Soviet periphery and elsewhere. President Kennedy's response to the Cuban missile crisis in October 1962 provides an excellent illustration of this concept. And it is clear that a description of this strategy is a good description of many of the qualities of the Navy-Marine Corps team.

NOTE:

[1] If we fire two missiles at a target, there are four possible results, each

equally probable: (1) both missiles hit the target, (2) the first hits and the second misses, (3) the first misses and the second hits, and (4) both miss. Only if both miss, an event whose probability is 25 per cent, will the target survive. In the other three cases, with a combined probability of 75 per cent, the target is destroyed.

14.
Systems Analysis Techniques for Planning–Programming–Budgeting*
E. S. QUADE

INTRODUCTION

Broadly speaking, any orderly analytic study designed to help a decision-maker identify a preferred course of action from among possible alternatives might be termed a systems analysis. As commonly used in the defense community, the phrase "systems analysis" refers to formal inquiries intended to advise a decision-maker on the policy choices involved in such matters as weapon development, force posture design, or the determination of strategic objectives. A typical analysis might tackle the question of what might be the possible characteristics of a new strategic bomber and whether one should be developed; whether tactical air wings, carrier task forces, or neither could be substituted for United States ground divisions in Europe; or whether we should modify the test-ban treaty now that the Chinese Communists have nuclear weapons and, if so, how. Systems analysis represents an approach to, or way of looking at, complex problems of choice under uncertainty that should have utility in the Planning–Programming–Budgeting (PPB) process. Our purpose is to discuss the question of extending military systems analysis to the civilian activities of the government, to point out some of the limitations of analysis in this role, and to call attention to techniques that seem likely to be particularly useful. I will interpret the term "technique" broadly enough to range from proven mathematical algo-

---

* Reprinted from E.S. Quade, "Systems Analysis Techniques for Planning–Programming–Budgeting," Report P-3322 (Santa Monica, California: The RAND Corporation, March, 1966). E. S. Quade is a member of the staff at the RAND Corporation.

rithms to certain broad principles that seem to be often associated with successful analysis.

Some fifteen years ago a similar extension raised quite some doubt. When weapons system analysts (particularly those at The RAND Corporation) began to include the formulation of national security policy and strategy as part of their field of interest, experienced "military analysts" in the Pentagon and elsewhere were not encouraging. They held that the tools, techniques, and concepts of operations analysis, as practiced in World War II, or of weapons system optimization and selection —in which analysts had been reasonably successful—would not carry over, that strategy and policy planning were arts and would remain so.

Fortunately, these skeptics were only partially right. It is true that additional concepts and methodologies significantly different from those of earlier analysis had to be developed. But there has been substantial progress, and the years since 1961 have seen a marked increase in the extent to which analyses of policy and strategy have influenced decision-makers on the broadest issues of national defense.

Today's contemplated extension to PPB is long overdue and possibly even more radical. Systems analysis has barely entered the domain of the social sciences. Here, in urban planning, in education, in welfare, and in other non-military activities, as Olaf Helmer remarks in his perceptive essay:

. . . *we are faced with an abundance of challenges: how to keep the peace, how to alleviate the hardships of social change, how to provide food and comfort for the inaffluent, how to improve the social institutions and the values of the affluent, how to cope with revolutionary innovations, and so on.*[1]

Since systems analysis represents an approach to, or way of looking at, any problem of choice under uncertainty, it should be able to help with these problems.

Actually, systematic analysis of *routine* operations is widespread throughout the civil government as well as in commerce, industry, and the military. Here analysis takes its most mathematical form and, in a certain sense, its most fruitful role. For example, it may help to determine how Post Office pick-up trucks should be routed to collect mail from deposit boxes, or whether computers should be rented or purchased to handle warehouse inventories, or what type of all-weather landing system should be installed in new commercial aircraft. Such problems are typically an attempt to increase the efficiency of a man-machine system in a situation where it is clear what "more efficient" means. The analysis can often be reduced to the application of a well understood mathematical discipline such as linear programming or queuing theory to a generic "model," which, by a specification of its parameters, can be made to fit a wide variety of operations. An "optimum" solution is then obtained by means of a systematic computational routine. The queuing model, for example, is relevant to many aspects of the operations of the Post Office, airports, service facilities, maintenance shops, and so on. In many instances such models may actually tell the client what his decision or plan ought to be. Analysis of this type is usually called operations research or management science rather than systems analysis, however.

There are, however, other decisions or problems, civilian as well as military, where computational techniques can help only with sub-problems. Typical decisions of this latter type might be the determination of how much of the federal budget should be allocated to economic development and what fraction of that should be spent on South America; or whether the needs of interstate transportation are better served by improved high speed rail transport or by higher performance highway turnpikes; or if there is some legislative action that might end the growth of juvenile delinquency. Such problems will normally involve more than the efficient allocation of resources among alternative uses; they are not "solvable" in the same sense as efficiency problems in which one can maximize some "pay-off" function that clearly expresses what one is trying to accomplish. Here, rather, the objectives or goals of the action to be taken must be determined first. Decision problems associated with program budgeting are mainly of this type—where the difficulty lies in deciding what ought to be done as well as in how to do it, where it is not clear what "more efficient" means, and where many of the factors in the problem elude quantification. The final program recommendation will thus remain in part a matter of faith and judgment. Studies to help with these problems are systems analyses rather than operations research.[2]

Every systems analysis involves, at one stage, a comparison of alternative courses of action in terms of their costs and their effectiveness in attaining a specified objective. Usually this comparison takes the form of an attempt to designate the alternative that will minimize the costs, subject to some fixed performance requirement (something like reduce unemployment to less than 2 per cent in two years, or add a certain number of miles to the interstate highway system); or conversely, it is an attempt to maximize some physical measure of performance subject to a budget constraint. Such evaluations are called cost-effectiveness analyses.[3] Since they often receive the lion's share of attention, the entire study also is frequently called a cost-effectiveness analysis. But this label puts too much emphasis on just one aspect of the decision process. In analyses designed to furnish broad policy advice, other facets of the problem are of greater significance than the comparison of alternatives: the specification of sensible objectives, the determination of a satisfactory way to measure performance, the influence of considerations that cannot be quantified, or the design of better alternatives.

THE ESSENCE OF THE METHOD

What is there about the analytic approach that makes it better or more useful than other ways to furnish advice—than, say, an expert or a committee? In areas such as urban redevelopment or welfare planning, where there is no accepted theoretical foundation, advice obtained from experts working individually or as a committee must depend largely on judgment and intuition. *So must the advice from systems anlysis.* But the virtue of such analysis is that it permits the judgment and intuition of the experts in relevant fields to be combined systematically and efficiently. The essence of the method is to construct and operate within a "model," a simplified abstraction of the real situation appropriate to the question. Such a model, which may take such varied forms as a computer simulation, an operational game, or even a purely verbal "scenario," introduces a precise structure and terminology that serve primarily as an effective means of communication, enabling the participants in the study to exercise their judgment and intuition in a concrete context and in proper relation to others. Moreover, through feedback from the model (the results of computation, the countermoves in the game, or the critique of the scenario), the experts have a chance to revise early judgments and thus arrive at a clearer understanding of the problem and its context, and perhaps of their subject matter.[4]

THE PROCESS OF ANALYSIS

The fundamental importance of the model is seen in its relation to the other elements of analysis.[5] There are five all told, and each is present in every analysis of choice and should always be explicitly identified.

1. *The objective (or objectives).* Systems analysis is undertaken primarily to help choose a policy or course of action. The first and most important task of the analyst is to discover what the decision-maker's objectives are (or should be) and then how to measure the extent to which these objec-

tives are, in fact, attained by various choices. This done, strategies, policies, or possible actions can be examined, compared, and recommended on the basis of how well and how cheaply they can accomplish these objectives.

2. *The alternatives.* The alternatives are the means by which it is hoped the objectives can be attained. They may be policies or strategies or specific actions or instrumentalities and they need not be obvious substitutes for each other or perform the same specific function. Thus, education, anti-poverty measures, police protection, and slum clearance may all be alternatives in combating juvenile delinquency.

3. *The costs.* The choice of a particular alternative for accomplishing the objectives implies that certain specific resources can no longer be used for other purposes. These are the costs. For a future time period, most costs can be measured in money, but their true measure is in terms of the opportunities they preclude. Thus, if the goal is to lower traffic fatalities, the irritation and delay caused to motorists by schemes that lower automobile speed in a particular location must be considered as costs, for such irritation and delay may cause more speeding elsewhere.

4. *A model (or models).* A model is a simplified, stylized representation of the real world that abstracts the cause-and-effect relationships essential to the question studied. The means of representation may range from a set of mathematical equations or a computer program to a purely verbal description of the situation, in which intuition alone is used to predict the consequences of various choices. In systems analysis (or any

Figure 1:
THE STRUCTURE OF ANALYSIS

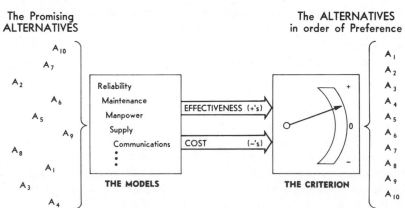

analysis of choice, the role of the model, (or models, for it may be inappropriate or absurd to attempt to incorporate all the aspects of a problem in a single formulation) is to estimate for each alternative the costs that would be incurred and the extent to which the objectives would be attained.

5. *A criterion.* A criterion is a rule or standard by which to rank the alternatives in order of desirability. It provides a means for weighing cost against effectiveness.

The process of analysis takes place in three overlapping stages. In the first, the formulation stage, the issues are clarified, the extent of the inquiry limited, and the elements identified. In the second, the search stage, information is gathered and alternatives generated. The third stage is evaluation.

To start the process of evaluation or comparison (see Fig. 1), the various *alternatives* (which may have to be discovered or invented as part of the analysis) are examined by means of the *models*. The models tell us what consequences or outcomes can be expected to follow from each alternative; that is, what the *costs* are and the extent to which each *objective* is attained. A *criterion* can then be used to weigh the costs against performance, and thus the alternatives can be arranged in the order of preference.

Unfortunately, things are seldom tidy: too often the objectives are multiple, conflicting, and obscure; alternatives are not adequate to attain the objectives; the measures of effectiveness do not really measure the extent to which the objectives are attained; the predictions from the model are full of uncertainties; and other criteria that look almost as plausible as the one chosen may lead to a different order of preference. When this happens, we must take another approach. A single attempt or pass at a problem is seldom enough. (See Fig. 2.) The key of successful analysis is a continuous cycle of formulating the problem, selecting objectives, designing alternatives, collecting data, building models, weighing cost against performance, testing for sensitivity, questioning assumptions and data, re-examining the objectives, opening new alternatives, building better models, and so on, until satisfaction is obtained or time or money force a cut-off.

In brief, a systems analysis attempts to look at the entire problem and look at it in its proper context. Characteristically, it will involve a systematic investigation of the decision-maker's objectives and of the relevant criteria; a comparison—quantitative insofar as possible—of the cost, effectiveness, risk, and timing associated with each alternative policy or

Figure 2:
THE KEY TO ANALYSIS

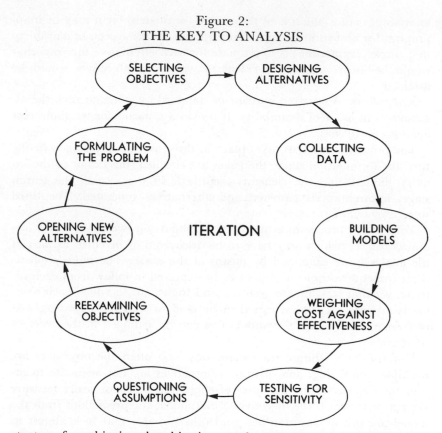

strategy for achieving the objectives; and an attempt to design better alternatives and select other goals if those examined are found wanting.

Note that there is nothing really new about the procedures I have just sketched. They have been used, more or less successfully, by managers throughout government and industry since ancient times. The need for considering cost relative to performance must have occurred to the earliest planner. Systems analysis is thus not a catchword to suggest we are doing something new; at most, we are doing something better. What may be novel though, is that this sort of analysis is an attempt to look at the entire problem systematically with emphasis on explicitness, on quantification, and on the recognition of uncertainty. Also novel are the schemes or models used to explore the consequences of various choices and to eliminate inferior action in situations where the relationships cannot be represented adequately by a mathematical model.

Note that there is nothing in these procedures that guarantees the advice from the analysis to be good. They do not preclude the possibility that we are addressing the wrong problem or have allowed our personal biases to bar a better solution from consideration. When a study is a poor one it is rarely because the computer was not powerful enough or because the methods of optimization were not sufficiently sophisticated, but because it had the wrong objective or poor criteria. There are some characteristics of a study, however, that seem to be associated with good analysis. Let me identify some of these.

PRINCIPLES OF GOOD ANALYSIS

1. It is all important to tackle the "right" problem. A large part of the investigators' efforts must be invested in thinking about the problem, exploring its proper breadth, and trying to discover the appropriate objectives and to search out good criteria for choice. If we have not chosen the best set of alternatives to compare we will not discover the best solution. But if we have chosen the wrong objective then we might find a solution to the wrong problem. Getting an accurate answer to the wrong question is likely to be far less helpful than an incomplete answer to the right question.

2. The analysis must be systems oriented. Rather than isolating a part of the problem by neglecting its interactions with other parts, an effort should be made to extend the boundaries of the inquiry as far as required for the problem at hand, to find what interdependencies are important, and to study the entire complex system. This should be done even if it requires the use of purely intuitive judgment.

An interdisciplinary team of persons having a variety of knowledge and skills is helpful here. This is not so merely because a complex problem is likely to involve many diverse factors that cannot be handled by a single discipline. More importantly, a problem looks different to an economist, an engineer, a political scientist, or a professional bureaucrat, and their different approaches may contribute to finding a solution.

3. The presence of uncertainty should be recognized, and an attempt made to take it into account. Most important decisions are fraught with uncertainty. In planning urban redevelopment we are uncertain about city growth patterns, about the extent to which freeways or rapid transit systems will be used, about costs, about tax revenues, about the demand for services. For many of these things, there is no way to say with confidence that a given estimate is correct. The analyst attempts to identify these uncertainties and evaluate their impact. Often he can say

the value of a parameter will be more than A but less than B. Some-times it is possible to indicate how the uncertainty can be reduced by further testing and how long that will take. Most important, the analy-sis should determine the effect of uncertainty on the answers. This is done by a sensitivity analysis that shows the answers change in response to changes in assumptions and estimates.[6]

The study report should include the presentation of a contingency table showing the effectiveness and cost associated with each significant alternative for various future environments and for each set of assump-tions about the uncertainties.

4. The analysis attempts to discover new alternatives as well as to im-prove the obvious ones. The invention of new alternatives can be much more valuable than an exhaustive comparison of given alternatives, none of which may be very satisfactory.

5. While in problems of public policy or national security, the scientific method of controlled repeated experiment cannot be used, the analysis should strive to attain the standards traditional to science. These are (1) intersubjectivity: results obtained by processes that can be duplicated by others to attain the same results; (2) explicitness: use of calculations, assumptions, data, and judgments that are subject to checking, criticism, and disagreement; and (3) objectivity: conclusions do not depend on personalities, reputations, or vested interests; where possible these con-clusions should be in quantitative and experimental terms.

THE MODELS

As mentioned earlier, systems analysis is flexible in the models it uses. Indeed, it has to be. Mathematics and computing machines, while ex-tremely useful, are limited in the aid they can give in broad policy ques-tions. If the important aspects of the problem can be completely formu-lated mathematically or represented numerically, techniques such as dynamic programming, game theory, queuing theory, or computer simu-lation may be the means of providing the best solution. But in most policy analyses, computations and computers are often more valuable for the aid they provide to intuition and understanding, rather than for the results they supply.

While a computer can solve only the problems that the analyst knows conceptually how to solve himself, it can help with many others. The objection that one cannot use results which depend on many uncertain parameters represents a lack of understanding of how systems analysis can help a decision-maker. For a study to be useful it must indicate the *relative* merit of the various alternatives and identify the critical parameters. The great advantage of a computerized model is that it gives the analyst the capability to do numerous excursions, parametric investigations, and sensitivity analyses and thus to investigate the ranking of alternatives under a host of assumptions. This may be of more practical value to the decision-maker than the ability to say with high confidence that a given alternative will have such and such a rank in a very narrowly defined situation.

The type of model appropriate to a problem depends on the problem and what we know or think we know about it.

For example, suppose we are concerned with long-range economic forecasting or decisions about the development of a national economy. The type of model to use will depend on the particular economy and on the kind of questions that must be answered. If the questions were about the United States, the model might be mathematical and possibly programmed for a computer because of its size and complexity. (By a mathematical model I mean one in which the relationships between the variables and parameters are represented by mathematical equations.) In the case of the United States, because of the vast amount of data available in the form of economic and demographic time series regarding just about every conceivable aspect of economic life, numerous mathematical and computer models have been formulated and used with more or less success.

If we are not able to abstract the situation to a series of equations or a mathematical model, some other way to represent the consequences that follow from particular choices must be found. Simulation may work. Here, instead of describing the situation directly, each element making up the real situation may be simulated by a physical object or, most often, by a digital computer using sets of random numbers, and its behavior analyzed by operating with the representation. For example, we might use computer simulation to study the economy of some Latin American country. The distinction between a computer simulation and the use of a computer to analyze a mathematical model is often a fuzzy one, but the fundamental difference is that in simulation the over-all behavior of the model is studied through a case-by-case approach.

For studying the economy of a newly emerging nation such as is found in Africa, where the situation is even more poorly structured and where we have little firm knowledge of existing facts and relationships, a possible approach would be through the direct involvement of experts who have knowledge of the problem.

Ordinarily, we would like to have the judgment of more than one expert, even though their advice usually differs. There are several ways to try for a consensus; the traditional way has been to assemble the experts in one place, to let them discuss the problem freely, and to require that they arrive at a joint answer. They could also be put to work individually, letting others seek methods for the best combined use of their findings. Or they could be asked to work in a group exercise—ranging from a simple structured discussion to a sophisticated simulation or an "operational game"—to obtain judgments from the group as a whole.

This latter approach is a laboratory simulation involving role-playing by human subjects who simulate real-world decision-makers. To study the economy of an underdeveloped country the various sectors of the economy might be simulated by specialized experts.[7] They would be expected, in acting out their roles, not so much to play a competitive game against one another, but to use their intuition as experts to simulate as best they could the attitudes and consequent decisions of their real-life counterparts. For instance, a player simulating a goods-producing sector of the economy might, within constraints, shut down or expand manufacturing facilities, modernize, change raw material and labor inputs, vary prices and so on. There would also need to be government players who could introduce new fiscal or monetary policies and regulations (taxes, subsidies, tariffs, price ceilings, etc.) as well as social and political innovations with only indirect economic implications (social security, education, appeals to patriotism, universal military service, etc). In laying down the rules governing the players' options and constraints and the actions taken within these rules, expert judgement is essential. It is also clear that for this problem political and sociological experts will be needed, as well as economists.

There is, of course, no guarantee that the projections obtained from such a model would be reliable. But the participating experts might gain a great deal of insight. Here the game structure—again a model—furnishes the participants with an artificial, simulated environment within which they can jointly and simultaneously experiment, acquiring through feedback the insights necessary to make successful predictions within the gaming context and thus indirectly about the real world.

Another useful technique is one that military systems analysts call "scenario writing." This is an effort to show how, starting with the present, a future state might evolve out of the present one. The idea is to show how this might happen plausibly by exhibiting a reasonable chain of events. A scenario is thus a primitive model. A collection of scenarios provides an insight on how future trends can depend on factors under our control and suggests policy options to us.

Another type of group action, somewhat less structured than the operational game, attempts to improve the panel or committee approach by subjecting the views of individual experts to each other's criticism without actual confrontation and its possible psychological shortcomings. In this approach, called the Delphi method, direct debate is replaced by the interchange of information and opinion through a carefully designed sequence of questionnaires. At each successive interrogation, the participants are given new refined information, and opinion feedback is derived by computing consensus from the earlier part of the program. The process continues until either a consensus is reached, or the conflicting views are documented fully.[8]

It should be emphasized that in many important problems it is not possible to build really quantitative models. The primary function of a model is "explanatory," to organize our thinking. As I have already stated, the essence of systems analysis is not mathematical techniques or procedures, and its recommendations need not follow from computation. What counts is the effort to compare alternatives systematically, in quantitative terms when possible, using a logical sequence of steps that can be retraced and verified by others.

THE VIRTUES

In spite of many limitations, the decision-makers who have made use of systems analysis find it extremely useful. In fact, for some questions of national defense, analysis is essential. Without calculation there is no way to discover how many missiles may be needed to destroy a target system, or how arms control may affect security. It may be essential in other areas also; one cannot experiment radically with the national economy or even change the traffic patterns in a large city without running the risk of chaos. Analysis offers an alternative to "muddling through" or to settling national problems by yielding to the strongest pressure group. It forces the devotees of a program to make explicit their lines of argument, to calculate the resources their programs will require as well as the advantages they might produce.

It is easy, unfortunately, to exaggerate the degree of assistance that systems analysis can offer the policy-maker. At most, it can help him understand the relevant alternatives and the key interactions by providing an estimate of the costs, risks, pay-offs and the time-span associated with each course of action. It may lead him to consider new and better alternatives. It may sharpen the decision-maker's intuition and will certainly broaden his basis for judgment, thus helping him make a better decision. But value judgments, imprecise knowledge, intuitive estimates, and uncertainties about nature and the actions of others mean that a study can do little more than assess some of the implications of choosing one alternative over another. In practically no case, therefore, should the decision-maker expect the analysis to demonstrate that, beyond all reasonable doubt, a particular course of action is best.

THE LIMITATIONS

Every systems analysis has defects. Some of these are limitations inherent in all analysis of choice. Others are a consequence of the difficulties and complexities of the question. Still others are blunders or errors in thinking, which hopefully will disappear as we learn to do better and more complete analyses.

The alternatives to analysis also have their defects. One alternative is pure intuition. This is in no sense analytic, since no effort is made to structure the problem or to establish cause-and-effect relationships and operate on them to arrive at a solution. The intuitive process is to learn everything possible about the problem, to "live with it," and to let the subconscious provide the solution.

Between pure intuition, on one hand, and systems analysis, on the other, other sources of advice can, in a sense, be considered to employ analysis, although ordinarily of a less systematic, explicit, and quantitative kind. One can turn to an expert. His opinion may, in fact, be very helpful if it results from a reasonable and impartial examination of the facts, with due allowance for uncertainty, and if his assumptions and chain of logic are made *explicit*. Only then can others use his information to form their own considered opinions. But an expert, particularly an unbiased expert, may be hard to find.

Another way to handle a problem is to turn it over to a committee. Committees, however, are much less likely than experts to make their reasoning explicit, since their findings are usually obtained by bargaining. This is not to imply that a look by a "blue ribbon" committee into such problems as poverty or the allocation of funds for foreign aid might not be useful, but a committee's greatest usefulness is likely to be in the critique of analysis done by others.

However, no matter whether the advice is supplied by an expert, a committee, or a formal study group, the analysis of a problem of choice involves the same five elements and basic structure we discussed earlier.

It is important to remember that all policy analysis falls short of being scientific research. No matter how we strive to maintain standards of scientific inquiry or how closely we attempt to follow scientific methods, we cannot turn systems analysis into science. Such analysis is designed primarily to recommend—or at least to suggest—a course of action, rather than merely to understand and predict. Like engineering, the aim is to use the results of science to do things well and cheaply. Yet, when applied to national problems, the difference from ordinary engineering is apparent in the enormous responsibility involved in the unusual difficulty of appraising—or even discovering—a value system applicable to the problems, and in the absence of ways to test the validity of the analysis.

Except for this inability to verify, systems analysis may still look like a purely rational approach to decision-making, a coldly objective, scientific method free from preconceived ideas, partisan bias, judgment and intuition.

It really is not. Judgment and intuition are used in designing the models; in deciding what alternatives to consider, what factors are relevant, what the interrelations between these factors are, and what criteria to choose; and in interpreting the results of the analysis. This fact—that judgment and intuition permeate all analysis—should be remembered when we examine the apparently precise results that seem to come with such high-precision analysis.

Many flaws are the results of pitfalls faced by the analyst. It is all too easy for him to begin to believe his own assumptions and to attach undue significance to his calculations, especially if they involve bitter arguments and extended computations. The most dangerous pitfall or source of defects is an unconscious adherence to a "party line." This is frequently caused by a cherished belief or an *attention bias.* All organizations foster one to some extent; RAND, the military services, and the civilian agencies of the government are no exception. The party line is "the most important single reason for the tremendous miscalculations that are made in foreseeing and preparing for technical advances or changes in the strategic situation."[9] Examples are plentiful: the political adviser whose aim is so fixed on maintaining peace that he completely disregards what might happen should deterrence fail; the weaponeer who is so fascinated by the startling new weapons that he has invented that he assumes the politician will allow them to be used; the union leader whose attention is so fixed on current employment that he rejects an automatic device that can spread his craft into scores of new areas. In fact, this failure to realize the vital interdependence of political purpose, diplomacy, military posture, economics, and technical feasibility is the typical flaw in most practitioners' approach to national security analysis.

There are also pitfalls for the bureaucrat who commissions a study or gives inputs to it. For instance, he may specify assumptions and limit the problem arbitrarily. When a problem is first observed in one part of an organization, there is a tendency to seek a solution completely contained in that part. An administrator is thus likely to pose his problems in such a way as to bar from consideration alternatives or criteria that do not fit into his idea of the way things should be done; for example, he may not think of using ships for some tasks now being done by aircraft. Also, to act wisely on the basis of someone else's analysis one should, at the very least, understand the important and fundamental principles involved. One danger associated with analysis is that it may be employed by an administrator who is unaware of or unwilling to accept its limitations.

Pitfalls are one thing, but the inherent limitations of analysis itself are another. These limitations confine analysis to an advisory role. Three are commented on here: analysis is necessarily incomplete; measures of effectiveness are inevitably approximate; and ways to predict the future are lacking.

ANALYSIS IS NECESSARILY INCOMPLETE

Time and money costs obviously place sharp limits on how far any inquiry can be carried. The very fact that time moves on means that a correct choice at a given time may soon be outdated by events and that goals set down at the start may not be final. The need for reporting almost always forces a cut-off. Time considerations are particularly important in military analysis, for the decision-maker can wait only so long for an answer. Other costs are important here, too. For instance, we would like to find out what the Chinese Communists would do if we put an end to all military aid to Southeast Asia. One way to get this information would be to stop such aid. But while this would clearly be cheap in immediate dollar costs, the likelihood of other later costs precludes this type of investigation.

Still more important, however, is the general fact that, even with no limitations of time and money, analysis can never treat all the considerations that may be relevant. Some are too intangible—for example, how some unilateral United States action will affect NATO solidarity, or whether Congress will accept economies that disrupt cherished institutions such as the National Guard or radically change the pattern of domestic military spending. Considerations of this type should play as important a role in the recommendation of alternative policies as any idealized cost-effectiveness calculations. But ways to measure these considerations even approximately do not exist today, and they must be handled intuitively. Other immeasurable considerations involve moral judgments—for example, whether national security is better served by an increase in the budget for defense or for welfare, or under what circumstances the preservation of an immediate advantage is worth the compromise of fundamental principles. The analyst can apply his and others' judgment and intuition to these considerations, thus making them part of the study; but *bringing them to the attention of the decision-maker*, the man with the responsibility, is extremely important.

MEASURES OF EFFECTIVENESS ARE APPROXIMATE

In military comparisons, measures of effectiveness are at best reasonably satisfactory approximations for indicating the attainment of such vaguely defined objectives as deterrence or victory. Sometimes the best that can be done is to find measures that point in the right direction. Consider deterrence, for instance. It exists only in the mind—and in the enemy's mind at that. We cannot, therefore, measure the effectiveness of alternatives we hope will lead to deterrence by some scale of deterrence, but must use instead such approximations as to the potential mortalities that we might inflict or the roof cover we might destroy. Consequently, even if a comparison of two systems indicated that one could inflict 50 per cent more casualties on the enemy than the other, we could not conclude that this means the system supplies 50 per cent more deterrence. In fact, since in some circumstances it may be important *not* to look too dangerous, we encounter arguments that the system threatening the greatest number of casualties may provide the *least* deterrence!

Similarly, consider the objective of United States government expenditures for health. A usual measure of effectiveness is the dollar value of increased labor force participation. But, this is clearly inadequate; medical services are more often in demand because of a desire to reduce the every day aches and pains of life. Moreover, we cannot be very confident about the accuracy of our estimates. For example, one recent and authoritative source estimates the yearly cost of cancer to the United States at $11 billion, while another, equally authoritative, estimates $2.6 billion.[10]

No Satisfactory Way To Predict the Future Exists

While it is possible to forecast events in the sense of mapping out possible futures, there is no satisfactory way to predict a single future for which we can work out the best system or determine an optimum policy. Consequently, we must consider a range of possible futures or contingencies. In any one of these we may be able to designate a preferred course of action, but we have no way to determine such action for the entire range of possibilities. We can design a force structure for a particular war in a particular place, but we have no way to work out a structure that is good for the entire spectrum of future wars in all the places they may occur.

Consequently, defense planning is rich in the kind of analysis that tells what damage could be done to the United States given a particular enemy force structure; but it is poor in the kinds of analyses that evaluate how we will actually stand in relation to the Soviets in years to come.

In spite of these limitations, it is not sensible to formulate policy or action without careful consideration of whatever relevant numbers can be discovered. In current Department of Defense practice, quantitative estimates of various kinds are used extensively. Many people, however, are vaguely uneasy about the particular way these estimates are made and their increasingly important role not only in military planning but elsewhere throughout the government.

Some skepticism may be justified, for the analytical work may not always be done competently or used with its limitations in mind. There may indeed be some dangers in relying on systems analysis, or on any similar approach to broad decisions. For one thing, since many factors fundamental to problems of federal policy are not readily amenable to quantitative treatment, they may possibly be neglected, or deliberately set aside for later consideration and then forgotten, or improperly weighed in the analysis itself, or in the decision based on such analysis. For another, a study may, on the surface, appear so scientific and quantitative that it may be assigned a validity not justified by the many subjective judgments involved. In other words, we may be so mesmerized by the beauty and precision of the numbers that we overlook the simplifications made to achieve this precision, neglect analysis of the qualitative factors, and overemphasize the importance of idealized calculations in the decision process. But without analysis we face even greater dangers in neglect of considerations and in the assignment of improper weights!

THE FUTURE

And finally, what of the future? Resistance by the military to the use of systems analysis in broad problems of strategy has gradually broken down. Both government and military planning and strategy have always involved more art than science; what is happening is that the art form is changing from an ad hoc, seat-of-the-pants approach based on intuition to one based on analysis *supported by* intuition and experience. This change may come more slowly in the non-military aspects of government. For one thing, the civilian employees of the government are not so closely controlled "from the top" as those in the military; also the goals in these areas are just as vague and even more likely to be conflicting.[11] The requirements of the integrated Planning–Programming–Budgeting System will do much to speed the acceptance of analysis for other tasks, however.

With the acceptance of analysis, the computer is becoming increasingly significant—as an automaton, a process-controller, an information processor, and a decision aid. Its usefulness in serving these ends can be expected to grow. But at the same time, it is important to note that even the best computer is no more than a tool to expedite analysis. Even in the narrowest decisions, considerations not subject to any sort of quantitative analysis can always be present. Big decisions, therefore, cannot be the *automatic* consequence of a computer program or of any application of mathematical models.

For broad studies, intuitive, subjective, even *ad hoc* study schemes must continue to be used—but supplemented to an increasing extent by systems analysis. The ingredients of this analysis must include not only an increasing use of computer-based models for those problems where they are appropriate, but for treatment of the non-quantifiable aspects, a greater use of techniques for better employment of judgment, intuition, and experience. These techniques—operational gaming, "scenario" writing, and the systematic interrogation of experts—are on the way to becoming an integral part of systems analysis.

CONCLUDING REMARKS

And now to review. A systems analysis is an analytic study designed to help a decision-maker identify a preferred choice among possible alternatives. It is characterized by a systematic and rational approach, with assumptions made explicit, objectives and criteria clearly defined, and alternative courses of action compared in the light of their possible consequences. An effort is made to use quantitative methods, but computers are not essential. What is essential is a model that enables expert intuition and judgment to be applied efficiently. The method provides its answer by processes that are accessible to critical examination, capable of duplication by others, and, more or less, readily modified as new information becomes available. And, in contrast to other aids to decision-making, which share the same limitations, it extracts everything possible from scientific methods, and therefore its virtues are the virtues of those methods. At its narrowest, systems analysis has offered a way to choose the numerical quantities related to a weapon system so that they are logically consistent with each other, with an assumed objective, and with the calculator's expectation of the future. At its broadest, through providing the analytic backup for the plans, programs, and budgets of the various executive departments and establishments of the federal government, it can help guide national policy. But, even within the Department of Defense, its capabilities have yet to be fully exploited.

NOTES:

Any views expressed in this paper are those of the author. They should not be interpreted as reflecting the views of The RAND Corporation or the official opinion or policy of any of its governmental or private research sponsors. Papers are reproduced by The RAND Corporation as a courtesy to members of its staff.

A condensed version of this paper was presented in the course Executive Orientation in Planning, Programming, and Budgeting, sponsored by U.S. Bureau of the Budget and the U.S. Civil Service Commission, Washington, D.C., February 24–25, 1966.

[1]Helmer, O., *Social Technology,* The RAND Corporation, P-3063, February 1965; presented at the Futuribles Conference in Paris, April 1965.

[2]For a further discussion of this distinction, see Schlesinger, J. R., "Quantitative Analysis and National Security," *World Politics,* Vol. XV, No. 2 (January 1963), 295–315.

[3]Or, alternatively, cost-utility and cost-benefit analysis.

[4]C. J. Hitch in Quade, E. S., (ed.), *Analysis for Military Decisions,* (Chicago: Rand McNally, 1964), p. 23, states: "Systems analyses should be looked upon not as the antithesis of judgment but as a framework which permits the judgment of experts in numerous subfields to be utilized—to yield results which transcend any individual judgment. This is its aim and opportunity."

[5]Olaf Helmer, *op. cit.,* p. 7, puts it this way: "The advantage of employ-

ing a model lies in forcing the analyst to make explicit what elements of a situation he is taking into consideration and in imposing upon him the discipline of clarifying the concepts he is using. The model thus serves the important purpose of establishing unambiguous intersubjective communication about the subject matter at hand. Whatever intrinsic uncertainties may becloud the area of investigation, they are thus less likely to be further compounded by uncertainties due to disparate subjective interpretations."

[6]See, for example, Fort, Donald M., *Systems Analysis as an Aid in Air Transportation Planning*, The RAND Corporation, P-3293, January 1966, pp. 12–14.

[7]Helmer, O., and E. S. Quade, "An Approach to the Study of a Developing Economy by Operational Gaming," in *Recherche Operationnelle et Problèmes du Tiers-Monde*, Colloquium organized by the French Society of Operational Research, with the participation of the Institute of Management Sciences, Operations Research Society of America (Paris: Dunod, 1964), pp. 43–54.

[8]Helmer, O., and Norman C. Dalkey, "An Experimental Application of the Delphi Method to the Use of Experts," *Management Sciences*, Vol. 9, No. 3 (April 1963), 458–467; and Helmer, O., and Nicholas Rescher, "On the Epistemology of the Inexact Sciences," *Management Sciences*, Vol. 6, No. 1 (October 1959), 25–52.

[9]*Ibid.*

[10]Kahn, H., and I. Mann, *Ten Common Pitfalls*, (Santa Monica, Calif.: The RAND Corporation, RM-1937, July 17, 1957.)

[11]James R. Schlesinger, *op. cit.*, has a slightly different view: "Thus the mere uncovering of ways to increase efficiency is not sufficient. Even where a decision is clear to the disinterested observer, it is difficult to persuade committed men that their programs or activities should be reduced or abandoned. The price of enthusiasm is that those who have a commitment will be 'sold' on their specialty and are incapable of viewing it in cold analytical terms. This may be especially true of the military establishment, where the concepts of duty, honor, and country *when particularized* lead to a certain inflexibility in adjusting to technological change and the new claims of efficiency. But it is also true in the civilian world: for conservationists, foresters, water resource specialists, businessmen, union leaders, or agrarians, some aspects of their value-systems run directly counter to the claims of efficiency. The economic view strikes them all as immoral as well as misleading. (After all, is it not a value judgment on the part of economists that efficiency calculations are important?).

"Even in the case of fairly low-level decisions, if they are political, systematic quantitative analysis does not necessarily solve problems. It will not convince ardent supporters that their program is submarginal. Nevertheless, quantitative analysis remains most useful. For certain operational decisions, it either provides the decisionmaker with the justification he may desire for cutting off a project or forces him to come up with a nonnumerical rationalization. It eliminates the purely subjective approach on the part of devotees of a program and forces them to change their lines of argument. They must talk about reality rather than morality. Operational research creates a bridge to budgetary problems over which planners, who previously could assume resources were free, are forced, willingly or unwillingly, to walk."

Other References

Marshall, A. W., *Cost/Benefit Analysis in Health*, (Santa Monica, Calif.: The RAND Corporation, P-3274, December 1965).

McKean, R. N., *Efficiency in Government Through Systems Analysis*, (New York: John Wiley & Sons, Inc., 1958).

Hitch, C. J., and R. N. McKean, *The Economics of Defense in the Nuclear Age*, (Cambridge, Mass.: Harvard University Press, 1960).

Peck, M. J., and F. M. Scherer, *The Weapons Acquisition Process: An Economic Analysis*, (Cambridge, Mass.: Harvard University Press, 1962).

Ellis, J. W., Jr., and T. E. Greene, "The Contextual Study: A Structured Approach to the Study of Limited War," *Operations Research*, Vol. 8, No. 5 (September–October 1960), 639–651.

Novick, D., (ed.), *Program Budgeting: Program Analysis and the Federal Budget*, (Washington, D.C.: Government Printing Office, 1965); (Cambridge, Mass.: Harvard University Press, 1965).

Mood, Alex M., "Diversification of Operations Research," *Operations Research*, Vol. 13, No. 2 (March–April 1965), 169–178.

Dorfman, Robert, (ed.), *Measuring Benefits of Government Investments*, (Washington, D.C.: The Brookings Institution, 1965).

Fisher, G. H., *The World of Program Budgeting*, (Santa Monica, Calif.: The RAND Corporation, P-3361, May 1966).

15.
Guaranteed Income Maintenance: A Public Welfare Systems Model*
HELEN O. NICOL

This article is concerned with an approach to poverty through the design of a public welfare systems model which incorporates a guaranteed minimum income for the poor as well as the provision of various social services to all in need.

In discussing current income maintenance programs, the Council of Economic Advisers in its Economic Report to the President, January 1966,[1] emphasized the inadequacy of these programs: About half of the poor do not receive public transfer income. There are large gaps in coverage under existing public assistance programs: About 26,000,000 poor persons were not receiving such aid in June 1965.[2] This figure included 11.5 million poor children, their 7,000,000 parents, about 3.5 million needy aged, and some 4,000,000 adults without dependent children in the eighteen to sixty-four age group. Moreover, the benefits paid to most public assistance recipients were not enough to enable them to live at even a minimum subsistence level. The council stated: "Increasing concern about these problems is producing a variety of new income-maintenance proposals. One approach would make public assistance coverage more comprehensive and assure all recipients more adequate benefit levels."

Another approach to poverty which the council suggested is concerned with an income maintenance system integrated with the existing federal personal income tax system, usually referred to as the negative income tax. In a previous article, in *Welfare in Review,*[3] the author sum-

*Reprinted from Helen O. Nicol, "Guaranteed Income Maintenance: A Public Welfare Systems Model," *Welfare in Review,* 4:9 (November, 1966), 1–12. Helen O. Nicol is a welfare economist in the Welfare Administration, Department of Health, Education, and Welfare.

marized the proposals of the four most prominent advocates of the negative income tax.

A broad reform of the public assistance system was recommended in detail to the Secretary of Health, Education, and Welfare by the Advisory Council on Public Welfare in June of this year.[4] This council was appointed by congressional directive to review the administration of the public assistance and child welfare services programs and to make recommendations for their improvement.

In this article a new methodology, systems analysis, is used as the conceptual tool to design a public welfare model which fulfills the requirements of a broadened public welfare mechanism as envisaged by both the Council of Economic Advisers and the Advisory Council on Public Welfare. The emphasis is on identifying problems for decision-making and no attempt is made to indicate prescriptive solutions.

The discussion will proceed as follows: The principles of systems analysis will be explained and the schema for a public welfare systems model will be developed, its parameters defined in terms of attributes, objectives, and performance criteria. In addition a sub-system will be constructed which explicates the relationships between the problems of the poor in a low income community and the strategies and tactics that could be employed in a multi-purpose neighborhood social service center to deliver effectively a comprehensive service program to the poor where they live.

The negative income tax approach to poverty rests on the implied hypothesis that, given money, the social functioning of the poor would be assured. In its simplest formulation, this hypothesis implies that the only thing distinguishing the poor from the non-poor is lack of money and if that were given them (in the form of a negative income tax allowance), everything else could be expected to follow, the assumptions being: they would escape poverty once and for all; they would enter the mainstream of American middle-class society; they would have full opportunity to develop in this new environment; and their children, no longer poor, would adopt the aspirations and values of middle-class life.

This hypothesis needs testing. Certainly, a minimum guaranteed income would go a long way in lifting the poor above the level of the most desperate, grinding, and debasing poverty. And, certainly, it would help those temporarily in need as well as some of the more resourceful poor to raise themselves above the poverty line. But for the majority of the poorest of the poor the premise that years, if not generations, of necessary adaptation to a poverty style of life have left neither damage nor scars that money alone cannot cure seems highly doubtful. Would a minimum income floor, by itself, solve the many-layered problems of the millions of educationally, socially, physically, and psychologically deprived? Would it relieve the pressures on distressed mothers burdened by too many, too closely spaced children? Would it salvage children denied parental support and supervision, or redeem troubled aimless young people, unmotivated to prepare for work or seek work? Would it relieve the social isolation of the aged or improve the social functioning of the sick, the disabled and the mentally retarded? Would a minimum income floor alone decrease the dependency of multi-problem poor families in multi-problem crowded ghettos?

AN INTELLECTUAL TOOL: SYSTEMS ANALYSIS

SYSTEMS ANALYSIS EXPLAINED

An analysis of public welfare programs presents a special problem: while the negative income tax approach to alleviating poverty can to some extent be evaluated in quantifiable terms—income expressed in dollars is the measure of success—the results of providing social, medical, and facilitative services cannot be measured in equally exact terms and can only be postulated in relative rather than absolute values. To approximate this problem, but not to solve it, we shall resort to an oversimplification by using the conceptual tool of systems analysis.[5]

Systems analysis furnishes the methodology for identifying the essential features of complex problems and the areas for investigation. It is part of the family of analytical techniques known as "simulation," which refers to the construction and manipulation of an operating model of a process.[6] Systems analysis permits experimentation on this model by manipulating the variables of the model and their interrelationships through the use of computers. As applied to the problem, systems analysis will help maintain the general field of vision and keep some nuances in approach in proper perspective. It can make possible the formalized structuring of alternative paths of action and alternative sets of objectives in instances where the problem is incompletely stated, where different ways of realizing objectives are possible, where objectives are stated in non-quantifiable terms, and where several solutions are possible—depending on the number of objectives to be attained.

Systems analysis has been used with varying degrees of success in solving military, production, engineering, and business problems. Its application to many problems in the social sciences, however, is still experimental, largely because systems models have not been sufficiently tested in an area of inquiry where inter-relationships are fluid, where many data are not quantifiable, and where there is lack of consensus on criteria for value judgments of qualitative data.[7] Our system model will, therefore, not be rigorous. But it will provide a simplified conceptual framework for analysis.

Essentials of a System

The schema for a simple and limited system, such as a public welfare system would represent, is shown in Figure 1. It is a limited anti-poverty

Figure 1:
SCHEMA OF A SYSTEM

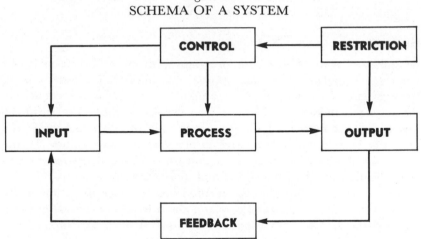

system to the extent that public welfare in our society represents only one, though the most fundamental, approach to poverty. The basic parameters of this system (that is, the arbitrary characteristics of its components) consist of:

(1) *Input,* which generates the process. It can be conceived for our purposes as the resources. For a public welfare system, these would be: dollars, personnel, facilities, and the poor to be served. Input can be varied. The poor, for example, could be classified by demographic categories.

(2) *Process,* which represents the transformation or conversion of the input into the output. In the system under discussion the process would

consist of the provision of financial and/or other assistance in the form of a guaranteed minimum income and services to the poor. The process can be broken up into segments and restructured in terms of sub-systems.

(3) *Output,* which is the result of a process. In a public welfare system it is identical with objectives—improving the income levels of the poor, or improving their social functioning, or whatever other objectives we postulate as representing policy. There are no restrictions on the number of outputs that may result from a process, as the output represents the rationale for bringing together objects, attributes, and relationships in the system. Output can, in turn, be used as input in a sub-system. For example, some of the employable poor may become input in labor force systems.

(4) *Feedback,* which is one of the special characteristics of the system. It is that process which measures the quality of the output. It represents a control sub-system which permits a comparison of the output with system performance criteria. If the criteria of performance in the system are effectiveness and efficiency in raising the financial and social status of the poor, feedback will show the results achieved in relation to the inputs. Feedback can be structured as a sub-system to which cost-benefit analysis can be applied.[8]

In addition to the four parameters defined above, two additional parameters, restriction and control, are necessary to complete the system.

(5) *Restriction* refers to the exogenous boundaries or limitations of a system. In an economic or social conceptualization these limitations would be stated in the form of assumptions. Here they form part of the system and refer to legislative and budgetary limitations.

(6) *Control* refers to a different type of restriction—an endogenous restriction, one that is inherent in the operation of the system. Its purpose is to maintain or improve or set the standards for performance. Here control consists of the income and needs test and the standards of performance.

Out of these six "building blocks" it is now possible to construct the system.

Further analysis reveals both the advantages and the difficulties inherent in this type of formal presentation. The elements of the input parameter present no problem as long as "the poor," in numbers, are related to a standard for eligibility, such as an income-needs test (control). The output parameter, on the other hand, presents problems for special analysis. What are the criteria for evaluating the objectives? Output is stated in terms of the objectives in a most general way, but these could be specified in a sub-system. It is possible that the outcome may have characteristics not necessarily anticipated. In a less formal representation, outcome characteristics would be conceptualized. For example, a guaranteed minimum income given to poor young people may lead to earlier family formation. Or it may change the housing habits of older people as they may move out of their children's homes to homes of their own or to nursing homes. Or, if all the poor in a poverty ghetto receive a guaranteed minimum income, the societal outcome characteristics might be to transform the ghetto into a lower middle-class community. The simplified system discussed here makes it impossible to evaluate the variety of changes that may result.

In the feedback parameter, "adequacy of coverage" has reference to the universe of the poor that is to receive a guaranteed minimum income and the universe that is to receive social services. Were these people properly identified and reached? "Adequacy of assistance" has reference to the dollar amounts to which they were entitled and the type of services they needed. A further criterion of adequacy, but outside the framework of this system, would be whether the guaranteed income was sufficient to move the poor out of poverty (up to the poverty line). This we do not know as we do not indicate in this system how the controls should be spelled out in terms of the size of the poverty gap to be filled (50 per cent or less; 100 per cent?). "Timing of assistance" has reference to the time period elapsing between the day the poor apply for assistance and the day they receive help. The criterion of performance for the guaranteed minimum income, for example, would require that waiting time be as short as possible and that in emergency situations help be immediate.

These are the elements of one type of public welfare system, but not the only possible type. A public welfare system could be designed as a sub-system of a larger system—a comprehensive social welfare system, for example—which would include among its parameters all programs, public and private, offering both financial aid and services, which have the purpose of improving the well being of people. Alternatively, public welfare could form part of a public income-maintenance system which would encompass those government programs providing an income floor and which are transfer payments.

There are thus different ways that systems analysis can be used to construct models which define problems organizationally, functionally, and operationally.

DESIGN FOR A PUBLIC
WELFARE MODEL

We shall now proceed to design a public welfare systems model which incorporates a guaranteed minimum income based on an objective income test. (Figure 2) The design will identify problems for decision-making that are open to debate and discussion. This system would have the following attributes:

1. It would serve universally all those identified as in need.
2. It would provide financial assistance in the form of a guaranteed minimum income.
3. It would provide preventive, supportive, and rehabilitative social services to those in need of them.
4. It would be administratively and organizationally efficient in operation.
5. Its cost to the economy would be the minimum compatible with national standards of adequacy of assistance.

Figure 2:
A PUBLIC WELFARE SYSTEM

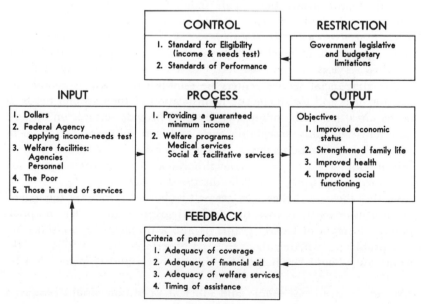

These features will be discussed. "Serving all in need" requires that the poor be identified by a universal and uniform, nationally determined income test that is related to a federal government standard separating the poor from the non-poor, where need is the sole criterion. This standard could vary according to geographic cost-of-living (consumer price) index or state per capita income differentials. The poor would be classified according to income level which might vary according to their family circumstances, such as family size and composition, rural or urban residence, and the like.

The question arises, what would be the decision points? The identification of the poor is one of the problems for decision and how "income" for this purpose should be defined is another.

Providing a guaranteed minimum income requires not only that the poor receive sufficient money to raise them up to whatever predetermined level of adequacy is established but also that they receive this financial support promptly, regularly, and with certainty for as long as they need it. Whether this will mean closing the poverty income gap entirely or only partially is one of the problems for decision. Another problem is whether this guaranteed minimum income shall be paid to them directly by the federal government, or through the intermediary of state and local jurisdictions with federal financing, or federal-state financing, and whether it shall be paid on an annual, monthly, or other basis.

Providing those in need with preventive, supportive, and rehabilitative social services, as well as referral to available community facilities, requires that social service centers be established to which people can come for help and for diagnostic identification of their special needs. It also requires that such community facilities provide services on an adequate and nationally acceptable basis and that sufficient personnel be available to staff these facilities. How this can be accomplished presents problems for decision. (How a neighborhood multi-purpose social service center might function will be discussed later.)

Whether the cost of these services will be borne entirely by the federal government or partially by state and local governments under an apportionment formula of federal grants, is also a problem for decision. Another problem is whether those in need of services, but not poor by the income test, should be charged for those services and if so by what fee structure.

An administratively simple and efficient operation would require a well organized federal-state-local jurisdictional organization with clear-cut lines of authority and procedurally arranged steps at different levels of responsibility. This also presents problems for decision.

The amount of transfer payments required to finance such a public welfare system which would be compatible with standards of income need and need for facilitative social services, poses still more problems for decision. In this area the parameters for judgment consist of rates of economic growth, levels of gross national product, and the fiscal tools and resources available to the federal government, the states, and the local jurisdictions.

The federal government has the task of balancing competing economic interests subject to the overriding national goal of achieving sustained growth of the economy at stable prices and high employment levels. Within the broader context of social welfare, public welfare is only one area of interest to which the government must respond and its responsiveness may vary depending on whether the economy is prosperous or in a recession, and it may also vary depending on the degree of urgency of public demand for such a measure. During prosperity, of course, the nation can "afford" to give sufficient financial aid to its needy to assure them at least minimum standards of food, housing, clothing, and physical health and sufficient services to develop their social participation. During times of recession, with the numbers of needy increasing, the nation cannot afford to do less, even if the government's power to tax is weakened and its power to borrow must be invoked.[9] The particular policy decisions to be made, as they relate to fiscal planning, will affect all the people, at all income levels.[10] Economic costs, therefore, represent the over-all limiting restriction for a public welfare system. What these costs can be at any particular point of time and how they can be allocated is a problem for economic and political decision-making; what they should be is a problem of value judgment.

We have now established that every parameter of a public welfare model indicates problems for decision-making. It is also apparent that for many of these problems alternative formulations will be possible, yet the only relevant ones must be politically and fiscally possible to achieve, considering that they would cut across and impinge on jurisdictional levels of authority and responsibility.

Our system differs from the current welfare mechanism mainly in two respects: (1) it is designed to address itself to a universe of the poor selected by an objective income-needs test, and (2) it is designed to incorporate a guaranteed minimum income for those in need. Significantly, this system would continue the traditional welfare function of providing medical, social, and facilitative services, but it would provide these services to a much larger population of the poor than the current mechanism—including people in need of services but not necessarily poor according to the poverty standard.

A NEIGHBORHOOD MULTI-PURPOSE SOCIAL SERVICE CENTER

The systems analysis approach is particularly adaptable to the designing of sub-systems for the identification of crucial relationships in special areas. From our objectives-oriented over-all public welfare model, we move now to a sub-system which could be useful for planning a neighborhood multi-purpose social service center to serve in a community of substantial and enduring poverty. This model is intended to clarify the process of intervention with reference to the manifold problems of a risk population requiring a solution strategy and the manifold tactics (programs) through which objectives may be reached.

The model of a simple process-oriented sub-system is shown in Figure 3. Its three basic parameters can be conceptualized as steps toward solving three basic poverty issues: lack of money, lack of good health, and inability to work because of age, disability, or lack of skill, or to obtain (or keep) a job which would provide an adequate level of living.

The sustained poverty of the population in this community represents the problem that needs solution. This problem can be broken down into the special problems of the individually poor. For example, the risk population in this poverty community might comprise: (1) all families with adults of low education and skill level that have potential for self-support,

Figure 3:
SCHEMA OF A PROCESS–ORIENTED SUBSYSTEM

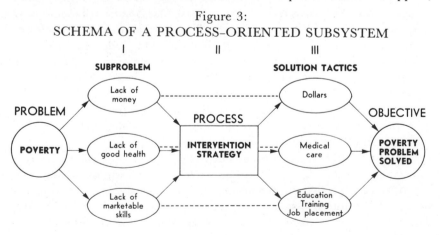

(2) all unmarried mothers and their children; (3) all families disrupted by death or desertion of the main breadwinner; (4) all children and youth with health, educational, or emotional problems and children and youth in need of protection and care; (5) all aged, blind, disabled, or handicapped persons; (6) all other individuals with problems of self-support and self-care, and (7) all those with other special problems affecting their social functioning and adjustment.

The objectives-parameter for this sub-system indicates how the problems would be answered in terms of the goals: solving or alleviating the special problems of people in a poverty community. This parameter could be further developed in an objectives-oriented sub-system. The objectives could be analyzed in terms of: (1) those obtained by the social service centers in preventing or reducing some dependency in the target neighborhood; (2) those obtained for the individual poor in improving their potential for self-support, self-care, and social and family adjustment; and (3) those obtained by the greater community and by society at large in obtaining an improvement in the economic and social functioning of a risk population in blighted urban centers.

A sub-system of a neighborhood multi-purpose social service center is outlined in Figure 4. This model shows the main relationships between the problems that may exist and the strategy and tactics that could be used to attack these problems. Because this is a simplified presentation, not every possible problem nor every possible program is designed into the model. For example, a complete model would indicate cross-over relationships—multiple tactics of approaching one or more problems or multiple problems solved by one or more tactics. "Financial assistance" might be one of the solution tactics for several types of problems, and "medical care" or "legal aid" might be one of the solution tactics applicable to several different problems.

A separate feedback evaluation sub-system could be designed to measure efficiency in giving help and the effectiveness of service programs. Ideally, these should be measured in terms of costs and benefits, but this is one area of analysis where value judgments may largely have to substitute for a dollars-and-cents approach.

Any particular neighborhood service center can be seen as a contributing sub-system of a total system. Both total systems as well as their sub-systems may differ from place to place on a nation-wide basis. A neighborhood service center of a relatively simple first-stop diagnosis and referral type, for example, may form a satellite center in a constellation of other such satellite centers, each an outpost of a single com-

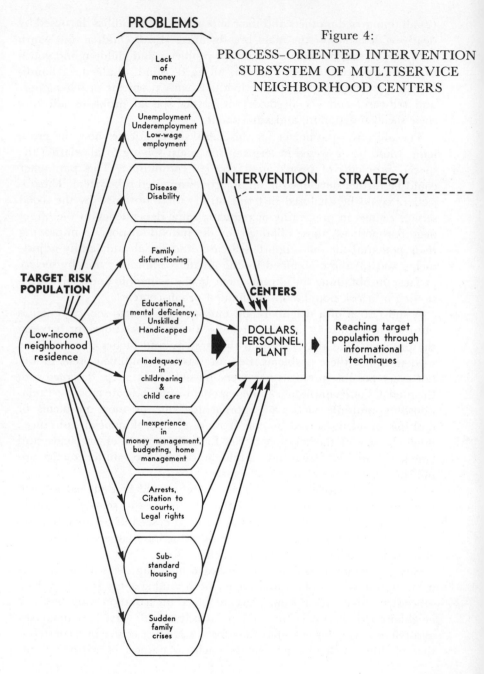

PROBLEMS

Figure 4:

PROCESS–ORIENTED INTERVENTION
SUBSYSTEM OF MULTISERVICE
NEIGHBORHOOD CENTERS

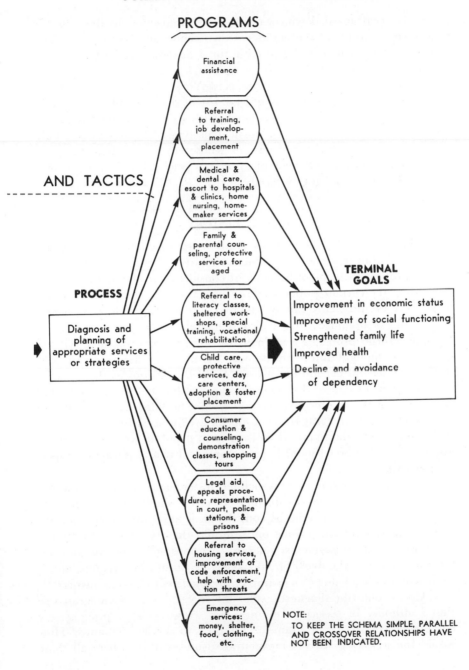

PROGRAMS

AND TACTICS

PROCESS

Diagnosis and planning of appropriate services or strategies

Financial assistance

Referral to training, job development, placement

Medical & dental care, escort to hospitals & clinics, home nursing, homemaker services

Family & parental counseling, protective services for aged

Referral to literacy classes, sheltered workshops, special training, vocational rehabilitation

Child care, protective services, day care centers, adoption & foster placement

Consumer education & counseling, demonstration classes, shopping tours

Legal aid, appeals procedure; representation in court, police stations, & prisons

Referral to housing services, improvement of code enforcement, help with eviction threats

Emergency services: money, shelter, food, clothing, etc.

TERMINAL GOALS

Improvement in economic status
Improvement of social functioning
Strengthened family life
Improved health
Decline and avoidance of dependency

NOTE:
TO KEEP THE SCHEMA SIMPLE, PARALLEL AND CROSSOVER RELATIONSHIPS HAVE NOT BEEN INDICATED.

prehensive centralized downtown public welfare center. In this case the total system consists of the one downtown center and its satellites. This type of arrangement may be suitable for a medium-sized city with dispersed poverty pockets.

In a megalopolis, such as greater New York or Los Angeles, on the other hand, the total system might consist of a cluster of several comprehensive public welfare centers, each with its own satellite neighborhood centers in several parts of town. This type of arrangement would permit adaptation to risk populations whose ethnic or other characteristics require different methods of approach (such as a required knowledge of foreign languages by service staff).

CONCLUSION

We have seen that the systems analysis approach tends to abstract from reality, but it makes it possible to isolate both the general and the special problems which confront us in consideration of broadening and expanding the current public welfare mechanism. It also indicates how some of these problems can be divided into manageable components that would be organized into a format for solution.

Many crucial problems remain to be solved. Some of these will require much thought and study because the ultimate design for a public welfare model will depend on answers to such questions as these:

1. At what income level should the poverty line be drawn, and what percentage of the income-poverty gap should be filled by a guaranteed minimum income integrated into a public welfare system?

2. How should the financial costs of such a public welfare system be apportioned, and how should federal-state-local relationships be properly restructured?

3. How should eligibility be re-defined in terms of an income test and what accounting period for income received should be established? (Should only current income be considered or also past income and future income? If current income only, should the definition include contributory insurance payments, veterans' pensions, gifts, income and services in kind, and the like?) Should assets be taken into account, and if so, at what dollar value (for example, imputed rent of home owners)?[11]

4. How should the diagnostic steps for service needs be integrated so that continuity of service is maintained? How could a progressively comprehensive service program be adapted to service demands? How would the services gradually move toward universality, where all those

who need and want services can have them? Should the principle of a "fee for services rendered" be applied and if so should the non-poor who avail themselves of services be charged according to a schedule of user fees?

5. How should the family unit be defined? Should the definition be based on current household relationships (including sub-families and related individuals living together)? Would young people spin off the family unit and establish separate households and if so would they qualify for a guaranteed minimum income? Would a guaranteed minimum income encourage family formation?

6. Should the computation of family income needs be based on family size and composition by age—in other words, should the negative income tax philosophy of deductions and exemptions be introduced in this instance, such as inclusion of double deductions for the aged and blind?

7. What work-incentive formula should be structured into the system for the working poor? (Alternatively, what current work disincentive features should be avoided?) How should the critical income area be handled where the guaranteed minimum income plus allowable retained earnings approach the poverty line or overlap with the incomes of the not-quite-so-poor?

8. Should geographical cost-of-living differentials be taken into consideration, as also differentials between urban and rural residence, and if so by what criteria?

9. Should urgent needs of applicants for financial aid be satisfied immediately? How can that be done effectively? How should adjustments be made in case of overpayment when a longer—possibly annual—income period is considered? And how can a guaranteed minimum income be adjusted for people with intermittent employment patterns?

The answers to these questions will largely determine to what extent a broadly expanded public welfare system will operate with maximum effectiveness and efficiency on a nation-wide basis. Hopefully, such a system would provide considerably more assistance in terms of financial aid and services to more needy people than the current mechanism is able to do. (This assumes also that the facilities for such an expanded public welfare system will be established and that sufficient personnel to staff them will be forthcoming.) Hopefully, organizing energies will also be mobilized and the total social service resources of communities will be concentrated in the areas most urgently in need of public welfare— the poverty islands of our central cities.

But, even at best, for all that it may be able to achieve, such a public welfare system cannot be expected to accomplish what it never was designed to do. It cannot eradicate once and for all time the multi-faceted, multi-causation poverty problems of our society.[12] Public welfare is only one system in a constellation of integrated systems that affect the social welfare of all the people. For its own best functioning it depends on the concerted and efficient functioning of the other systems that help shape our society.

Thus, business and industy—our productive, income-creating system—must be able to provide jobs for the potentially employable at adequate wage rates. Our educational system, at all levels, must be able to prepare young people for a lifetime of work and contribution to society. Our medical system must be geared to provide health and hospital care to all those in need. Our contributory insurance systems must be able to provide sufficient income maintenance through their programs. Public and private poverty programs must be able to work successfully in their own special areas of concern. The church—a powerful system for spiritual guidance—must persevere in inculcating in men faith and hope and good will toward their fellowmen.

In a balanced society, where each of these systems works effectively and bears its own share of responsibilities, the public welfare system can best fulfill its own particular mission and by working together with the other systems help in improving human welfare.

NOTES

[1]*Economic Report of the President, together with the Annual Report of the Council of Economic Advisors* transmitted to the Congress January, 1966.

[2]*Ibid.*, p. 114.

[3]"Guaranteed Income Maintenance—A Discussion of Negative Income Tax Plans," *Welfare in Review* (April 1966), pp. 1–10.

[4]"Having the Power, We have the Duty." The Advisory Council on Public Welfare. Report to the Secretary of Health, Education, and Welfare. (U.S. Department of Health, Education, and Welfare. Welfare Administration, Washington, D.C. June 29, 1966.) The report was prepared in accordance with Section 11114 of the Social Security Act, amended in 1962.

[5]The general systems schema has been adapted from Stanford L. Optner, *Systems Analysis for Business and Industrial Problem Solving*, Prentice-Hall International Series in Industrial Engineering and Management Science (Englewood Cliffs, N.J.: Prentice Hall, Inc., 1965). See also Harold

Guetzkow, (ed.), *Simulation in social Science—Readings* (Englewood Cliffs, N.J.: Prentice Hall, Inc., 1962); and Guy H. Orcutt, M. Greenberger, J. Korbel, and A. Rivlin, *Microanalysis of Socioeconomic Systems—A Simulation Study* (New York: Harper and Bros., 1961); and Arthur D. Hall, *A Methodology for Systems Engineering* (Princeton, N.J.: D. Van Nostrand Co., Inc. 1962).

[6]For an application of simulation to AFDC programs, see Abraham S. Levine, "Cost Benefit Analysis of the Work Experience Program: Research Strategy," *Welfare in Review* (August–September, 1966).

[7]See also Abram Bergson, *Essays in Normative Economics* (Cambridge, Mass.: The Belknap Press of Harvard University, 1966), *passim.*

[8]For an application of cost-benefit analysis to welfare problems, see Abraham S. Levine, "Cost-Benefit Analysis and Social Welfare," *Welfare in Review* (February, 1966), pp. 1–11.

[9]The suggestion has been made that expenditures for social welfare be related to the level of GNP (Gross National Product) by a stated percentage. This general measurement might set a useful benchmark and it permits comparison with other countries.

[10]Public decision-making might be facilitated by creation of a system of social accounts which would permit the balancing of social benefits against social costs. The difficulty with this approach is that social accounts are considered mainly in areas where aggregate statistics are available. Much work will need to be done before "performance budgets" could be applied in the area of social welfare. (*Technology and the American Economy*, Report by the National Commission on Technology. Automation, and Economic Progress, Vol. I February 1966, pp. 96–138).

[11]An "income test" is still a means test and it still sets the poor apart from the non-poor, but it is a test that has the virtue of being universally applied by an objective standard, thus conforming to the concept of equity.

[12]See also Ben B. Seligman, (ed.), *Poverty as a Public Issue* (New York: The Free Press, 1965); Leonard A. Lecht, *Goals, Priorities, and Dollars— The Next Decade* (New York: The Free Press, 1966), Chapter V: Social Welfare; and Leonard H. Goodman, (ed.), *Economic Progress and Social Welfare* (New York: Columbia University Press, published for the National Conference on Social Welfare, 1966).

16.
Cybernetics*

MAGOROH MARUYAMA

Western man has traditionally thought of the physical world in terms of cause and effect going in one direction. That is, if A causes B, B cannot cause A. The reason for this assumption is that event order has been confused with logical order; Western man has assumed that because "circular argument" was prohibited in the logic, there cannot be circular causal relationships in the natural or social events.

But not everyone has thought this way. Many tribes in Africa, peoples in pre-Communist China, and some American Indian tribes, especially the Navajos, have seen the universe as a mutual process of various spirits or influences in harmony and occasionally disturbed harmony—in complementary balance rather than in vertical hierarchy. These people have seen the universe in terms of *events* in mutual interaction, rather than in terms of *beings* classified into categories.

Cybernetics, a science of processes by mutual interaction between components of a system, has not been imported from these cultures, however. It was independently developed by radio engineers and discovered by economists several decades ago. Radio engineers used *positive feedback* to generate radio waves, and economists knew of the vicious circle of the poor getting poorer and the rich getting richer.

Mutual interaction between components may work in two ways. They may reinforce one another's change, or they may counteract one another's change. Such mutual interactions exist in many biological, ecological and social processes. But Western science has been slow in recognizing the principle of mutuality in such processes. A kind of taboo against thinking in terms of mutuality prevailed in many fields, though there were some rudimentary inventions which in retrospect can be

*This article is the author's revision of his earlier "Cybernetics," NEA Journal, 53:9 (December 1964), 51–54. Inclusion and revision of the article is made with permission of the author and publisher. Magoroh Maruyama is associate professor of psychology at San Francisco State College.

called precursors of cybernetic ideas: the thermostat, for example, and the mechanism for steering a ship automatically. These devices work on the principle that a deviation from the desired equilibrium activates a mechanism which counteracts the deviation. The signal which activates the counteracting mechanism is called *negative feedback*.

Development of cybernetics as a science came about during the Second World War, when radar was hooked up to anti-aircraft artillery for the purpose of automatically taking into consideration the course, speed and altitude of a moving target and to trace the deviation of the projectile from the target.

Soon scientists realized that similar complicated processes go on in animals' activities—for example, in the interplay of brain and muscles when a cat pounces on a fast-moving mouse. And a science of automatic control in machines and in animals based on feedback was created. This was the first cybernetics. Norbert Wiener, Arturo Rosenblueth, and Warren McCulloch were among the main contributors during this period. Since then, the first cybernetics has expanded as electronic computers grew, and automation has come into being.

It should be emphasized at this point that the relationship between the feedback and the action of the machine often cannot be broken down into a series of alternating, unidirectional causal processes. Instead, this reciprocal relationship has to be mathematically solved simultaneously and continuously.

The concept of feedback was a major challenge to the traditional thinking, as it involved a circular relationship. But still a trace of the traditional thinking lingered in the concept of feedback. For example, although the thermostat is in a causal loop with the room temperature, it is subordinated to the room temperature. There remains the traditional logical and teleological hierarchy.

Meanwhile, biologists were becoming increasingly aware of *mutual* interactions between cells which generated complex structures in organisms. Recognizing a principle of mutual causality in biological pattern generation, I proposed to call it "the Second Cybernetics." In the first cybernetics, feedback counteracts deviation. In the second cybernetics, mutual interaction amplifies deviation and generates patterns. In biological processes we find interactions which are truly mutual, without logical or teleological priority on any components.

To understand pattern generation by mutual interaction, let us take for an example the growth of a city in an agricultural plain. In the beginning, the plain was homogeneous as to its potentiality for agriculture; that is, no one spot was any more likely to become a farm than any other. Then, by some chance, a man starts a farm at a certain spot on the plain. This farmer's action is the initial deviation, or the initial "kick."

Several farmers follow him. Someone opens a tool shop. A village is created. There is a mutual deviation-amplification between the population and the number of people moving into the place: the greater the population, the greater the number of people attracted to the place and moving in; on the other hand, the greater the number of people moving in, the greater the population becomes.

Gradually a city grows, and the presence of this city prevents another city from rising too close, because each city needs an agricultural background. Within the new city, schools and factories grow with some spacing between them. Thus, patterns are generated within the city. Many cities on the plain may also make a pattern.

This process is simple enough, but there are a few important theoretical implications that may not be immediately obvious. For example, the farmer could have chosen any spot on the plain, since the plain was homogeneous. But once he has chosen a spot, the plain loses its homogeneity. Further, this departure from homogeneity increases as time goes on.

If a historian should try to find a geographical "cause"—a reason why this spot became a city rather than some other spot—he will fail to find it. There was no "cause" in the initial condition. Nor can the first farmer be credited for the establishment of the city. The secret is in the process of mutual deviation-amplification as we have seen.

In traditional thinking, similar conditions produce similar results. Consequently, dissimilar results are attributed to supposedly proportionally dissimilar conditions. It does not occur to the traditional thinker to examine deviation-amplification, because mutual causality is not considered.

Another implication of pattern generation is as follows: Not only can mutual interaction generate patterns, but also it became apparent that *simple* rules of interaction can generate *complex* patterns. This discovery has a profound implication in genetics and embryology: the genes may achieve economy of information by not storing a coded blueprint of the adult but by storing a set of rules for interaction between the parts. Hans Spemann was a precursor in this way of thinking, which was more recently expanded by Curt Stern and others.

As we have seen, mutual causal processes have two aspects: deviation-counteracting and deviation-amplifying. On page 334 is a diagram showing some mutual relationships that might exist in a city.

The arrows in the diagram indicate the direction of influences. The plus signs indicate that the changes occur in the same direction, but not necessarily positively. For example, the plus sign between G and B indicates that an increase in the amount of garbage per an area, say a city block, causes an increase in the number of bacteria per the same area. But at the same time it indicates that a decrease in the amount of garbage per area causes a decrease in the number of bacteria per area.

The minus between S and B indicates that an increase in sanitation facilities causes a decrease in the number of bacteria per area. But at the same time it indicates that a decrease in sanitation facilities causes an increase in the number of bacteria per area.

As you can see, some of the arrows form loops. For example, there is a loop from P to M, M to C, and C back to P. A loop indicates mutual causal relationships.

In a loop, the influence of an element comes back to itself through other elements. For example, in the loop of P-M-C-P, an increase in the number of people causes an increase in modernization, which in turn increases migration into the city, which in turn increases the number of people in the city.

In short, an increase in population causes a further increase in population. On the other hand, a decrease in population causes a further decrease in population through decreased modernization and decreased immigration. Regardless of whether a decrease or an increase is involved, the deviation is amplified.

We can also start the same loop from M, and call it an M-C-P-M loop. Then we see that a deviation of M amplifies itself through C and P.

Now let us look at loop P-G-B-D-P. This loop contains a negative influence from D to P. Step-by-step analysis will show that an increase in population causes a decrease in population through garbage, bacteria, and diseases. If we start the loop from G, we also see that its deviation counteracts itself. This loop is deviation-counteracting. Such a deviation-counteracting loop may result in stabilization or oscillation, depending on the time lag involved in the counteraction and the size of counteraction.

Let us further consider the loop P-M-S-D-P. This loop has two negative influences. A step-by-step analysis will show that this loop is deviation-amplifying. Two negative influences cancel each other. In general, a loop with an even number of negative influences is deviation-amplifying, and a loop with an odd number of negative influences is deviation-counteracting or oscillating.

The diagram contains several loops. Whether the system as a whole

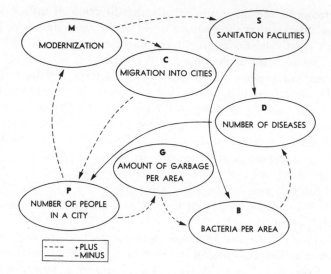

is deviation-amplifying or deviation-counteracting depends on the strength of each loop and its relationship to one another.

This way of looking at relationships is useful in many fields. Today, the influence of the second cybernetics is gradually reaching sociology and psychology.

Sociologists and psychologists pioneered in a method of research called *multivariate analysis.* This method was designed to discover relationships between many variables which change simultaneously.

Those sociologists and psychologists were the first to break the traditional rule of science that only one variable should be changed at one time. Physicists, too, are beginning to realize that multivariate analysis can be useful for studying such complex physical events as weather or the scattering of radio waves in the sky.

But multivariate analysis, as it is used today, is still based on the assumption of unidirectional, though multiple, causality. A one-way causal direction is still sought. While the computational procedure is not designed to discover the causal direction, the analyst is expected to supply the direction himself.

Cybernetic analysis looks for mutual causality. The mathematics of the first cybernetics is well developed. But the mathematics of the second cybernetics is only at its beginning stage. As for application of the second cybernetics, it has not even started in most fields. Its development belongs to the coming generation.

VI.
APPLICATION AND CRITIQUE
OF PPB

17.
Limitations, Risks, and Problems*

ROLAND N. McKEAN AND
MELVIN ANSHEN

The type of program budget recommended in this article is not a simple proposal for improvement in public administration, easily designed, readily installed, promptly effective in operation. On the contrary, from initial concept to final implementation the project raises difficult and important problems. Unless these problems are recognized at the outset, the recommended innovation may invite over-enthusiastic acceptance. This is likely to be followed by the discovery of deficiencies and limitations that could destroy confidence in the entire undertaking. Therefore, the purpose of this chapter is to report frankly on the problems, limitations, and risks of a program budget, and to suggest ways and means of alleviating some and removing others.

This discussion should emphasize one significant point. The purpose of the program budget proposal is to redesign a basic management tool so that the quality and grasp of decision-making in the federal government can be improved. The proposal does not open the gates to a public administration utopia, nor does it contemplate the displacement of managerial imagination, judgment, or experience. The hard choices that are inevitably present in any effort to allocate scarce resources among competing claims will remain. Hopefully, they will be aided by a more appropriate and operationally meaningful organization of information on inputs and outputs, above all with information structured in relation to planning, decision, and implementation, rather than, as is now generally the case, to assure integrity in the use of appropriated funds.

*Reprinted by permission of the publishers from David Novick (ed.), *Program Budgeting: Program Analysis and the Federal Government* (Cambridge, Mass.: Harvard University Press, copyright by The RAND Corporation, 1965), 285–307. Roland N. McKean is professor of economics at the University of California, Los Angeles. Melvin Anshen is professor of economics at Columbia University.

Difficulties in the program budget will be examined under three headings: *conceptual*—those encountered in designing the program budget and relating it to the decision-making requirements of the executive and legislative branches of the government; *operational*—those related to managerial implementation of the program budget, particularly in the period immediately following its adoption; and *institutional*—those encouraged by bureaucratic or political pressures that are unavoidably present in any organizational setting, public or private. The description and assessment of problems, limitations, and risks will. be followed by suggestions for coping with them and, at least, minimizing their impact and significance.

CONCEPTUAL PROBLEMS OF THE PROGRAM BUDGET

The meaning of the term "program budget" has not become standardized through general use. To some it suggests no more than a restructuring of budget exhibits, accumulating costs in more meaningful categories. This would suggest a budget organized in terms of categories that are closer to being true outputs than the older categories, which, as we see them in the current budget array, are generally inputs with some mixture of ill-related outputs, all heavily influenced by administrative and organization history. Those who hold this view judge such categories to be more useful because they contribute to better assessment of the implications of incremental changes to established programs.

To other people, a program budget implies a budget that employs a longer time horizon than is commonly found in the present federal budget with its forward projection limited to one year. Within the one-year horizon public officials commit themselves to purchase on the installment plan while examining only the size of the down payment. With the longer time horizon the full cost implications of alternative choices are less likely to be neglected (either inadvertently or deliberately).

To still others, the concept of program budgeting includes, in addition, the use of cost-utility analysis, a logical and measuring relation of inputs to outputs. Here the emphasis is on the analytical contributions of the program budgeting process, and the consequent increased rationality and efficiency in the use of scarce resources.

Finally, there are those who understand the term to imply all the foregoing plus one significant addition—arrangements for enforcing the allocative decisions through appropriate implementation provisions. Such arrangements might, for example, include institutional reorganization to bring relevant administrative functions under the jurisdiction of the authority making the final program decisions. With or without reorganization, there would be information reporting systems and shifts in the power structure to the extent necessary to secure compliance with program decisions by the agencies responsible for their execution.

The program budgeting concept adopted in this study embraces all four of the items listed above. In other words we are interested in the organization of information for decision-making and our view of decision-making is one that continues through implementation. To say this by way of description is not to solve the conceptual problem, however. In fact, it does not even fully define the problem. At best, it does little more than indicate the general approach.

What concept of program array constitutes an efficient design? How many programs should there be? What should their content be? What type of relationship to the decision process should the program structure embody? The central issue to which these questions lead is no less than the definition of the ultimate objectives of the federal government to be implemented through resource allocations. The framers of the Constitution did their architectural work in a similar context, of course, although the objectives they held in view were as much political as economic and, where economic, of a philosophic rather than a managerial or operational character. The decision-making structure came later and, as we have observed before, under the influence of objectives other than rationality of choice.

Beneath what may be termed the technical problem of designing a new programming-budgetary array composed of a specific set of programs that are in some sense end objectives for the achievement of which resources are assigned, lies a conceptual problem. Its nature may be suggested by the question: What is the government trying to accomplish? When this question was asked in the Department of Defense, in the design stage of its program budget in 1961, a viable and acceptable answer was found in such categories as Strategic Retaliatory Forces, Continental Air and Missile Defense Forces, Airlift and Sealift Forces, and Research and Development. Within these categories it seemed meaningful to identify further breakdowns into such compartments as types of aircraft, unique missile systems, and discrete military or support activities. It is by no means clear that comparable acceptable answers are readily forthcoming for the rest of the federal government. As the political campaign in progress in the fall of 1964 suggested, "What is government for?" can be a question of philosophy about which strong disagreements boil. The government is, to be sure, concerned with education, welfare, transportation, research, and other familiar ends. But the nature of its concern must be defined in terms of rational decision contexts as well as political-philosophical considerations.

To take one example as a key to the puzzle, it is not just education that the government is concerned with. It is certain kinds of education, certain levels of education, certain educational clients, certain educational methods. The character of the decision process must be influenced by the requirements created by these rather specific concerns. And it would then follow that the program budget design most efficiently responsive to the needs of that decision process is one that organizes information in a manner that is relevant to the decision process. After all, the main advantage claimed for the program budget process over that of the present budget is that it is designed in relation to the decision process and helps to make it more effective by clearly defining the alternatives among which choices must be made, and creating an information system that permits analytical appraisal of costs in relation to expected benefits. To bring this about, one must come to grips with such conceptual issues as whether educational activities within an anti-poverty program (such as skill training) should be dealt with in the decision context of relief for the unemployed, or in the context of the more familiar framework of most types of educational activities not tied to a special class of clients or a special kind of instruction. Above all, it must be recognized that this is not a problem to be resolved by Solomonic wisdom. If there is a "right" answer, it will be discovered only through study of the logics and logistics of the federal decision process in this area.

The inadequacy of such study to date does not mean that the public's business in allocating resources is handled carelessly or inefficiently in the common sense of these terms. Inefficient management can be assessed on two quite different conceptual levels. One—the more common one—appraises performance in implementing a determined decision. It asks whether a given objective has been achieved with appropriate economy in the use of resources, with an absence of diversion or redundancy in application of assigned funds, and with an appropriate accounting for actions taken. The other concept, less commonly encountered, asks quite a different question. Should this decision be made at all? Or, at least, should it be made in this way, at this time, in this informational context? The question looks in two directions. The first considers alternative ends and alternative assignments of resources. The second considers what may be achieved in relation to what must be invested—which is what is often called cost-utility analysis. The concept requires a wealth, detail, and array of information altogether different from that called for in the narrow concept of efficiency. And the precise character of that information cannot be determined before there has been more study of the entire decision process. This involves examining at least two sorts of complex issues. One is concerned with the kinds of decisions that public administrators should make, as a reflection of the ultimate objectives of the federal government at this stage of the nation's development. The other is concerned with the process of public decision-making: its scope, timing, and sequence.

As noted previously in this book, the initial step in designing a program budget for the non-defense sector of the federal government must come to grips directly with the conceptual issue, and the way to do this is to acquire a better understanding of the logic and the process of decision-making. The existing organization structure and existing decision practices may not significantly assist, in fact may only obfuscate, such understanding. The bureaucratic structure that is now in being and in operation is largely the product of a historic response to political pressures and expedient adjustments thereto, or, in some instances, to haphazard acts of creation for the most part unresponsive to a planned analysis of the needs of efficient decision design. Considering the circumstances of its invention, there is little reason for the bureaucratic structure to reflect a logical decision-determined architecture. From this it also follows that the kinds of decisions made in the current annual budgetary exercise—their character, locale, timing, etc.—cannot be taken as reliable guides to future planning for a rationally ordered program budget. In fact, out of the existing structure and its operating habits must be expected resistance and opposition, corresponding to the familiar human disposition to protect established seats of power and procedures made honorable by the mere facts of existence and custom.

We should be careful to observe that this does not mean that in executing the recommended research the existing bureaucratic structure and the ways in which it gets its business done should be ignored or summarily rejected. We do suggest, however, that the first and most important task is to explore the fundamental issue of the objectives and functions in the federal government, the kinds of problems that arise and demand decision, the ordering of information that would effectively serve administrators confronted with these responsibilities. At a later stage, due attention should be given to existing organizations and practices, both to discover additional clues to new insights into the resource allocation process, and to anticipate operating problems of the sort dealt with later in the present chapter. We must, in short, go back to fundamentals. It should be encouraging to note that this is what was done in the first stage of the work that led to the design of the program budget in the Department of Defense.

We emphasize, then, that the desirable decision structure emerging from such study might or might not resemble the existing bureaucracy. The possibility that a new program budget, if adopted and installed, might be implemented more easily or effectively through a new management structure is a separate issue not germane to the present discussion. There may be powerful reasons for retaining all, or most, of the existing structure while installing a new program budget. There are ways of accommodating process and structure that may be well worth using for a considerable period of time. In the long run, of course, it might be reasonable to expect an adjustment of structure to process, but this would not exclude a parallel adjustment of process to structure. Operational experience has a wonderful disposition to smooth jagged organizational interfaces when they are in a continual state of mutual abrasion. Again, we can observe that this process has been at work in the Department of Defense.

The heart of the conceptual problem described above is, of course, the fact that in many areas of government activity, including some in which expenditures in recent years have aggregated billions of dollars annually, few of the objectives have been clearly defined. In view of this circumstance, the recommended research would be pioneer work, subject to all the difficulties and vicissitudes that such an undertaking must confront.

A related conceptual problem must also be dealt with. A program budget structure can be developed around one or several definitional elements. One obvious possible structural element would be end objectives and sub-components thereof. (In the military's program budget this would correspond to, say, strategic retaliatory forces further divided into aircraft and missile systems.) Another approach might be an attempt to distinguish between means and ends. This would come to grips with such questions as the classification of irrigation projects as means (to support agricultural development, for example), or as ends in themselves and therefore to be distinguished as discrete items for decision in a program budget structure. Other possibilities will need to be explored, including designs that bear no readily identifiable relation to the kind of distinctions suggested here.

In any event, it should be recognized that the initial program budget structure will need thorough testing in the early years of its use. It is certain that this design will call for amendment and modification—perhaps involving substantial change—as a result of experience in the decision process. Again, it is instructive that private business organizations which have installed information-decision systems that resemble the program budget concept have commonly discovered a need to revise their systems in the light of practice and to accord, as well, with the changing nature of their own dynamic decision processes.

OPERATING PROBLEMS OF THE PROGRAM BUDGET

When we pass from the conceptual phase to the operating phase of the program budget, we confront a new series of problems. One of these transition problems is suggested by the gap between identifying a group of activities as an appropriate cluster for a single program or program element and actually bringing together the information applicable to making a program decision about the activity cluster. It will often be the case that activities that make a logical program package are currently scattered through several government departments, bureaus, and divisions. One illustration of such a situation can be found in the international economic activities that can be discovered in a number of administrative units spread throughout the federal establishment. Other examples can be found in activities involved with the development, protection, and exploitation of natural resources; still another, in the field of educational activities. Operating techniques will have to be developed for identifying such elements and assembling them for program budget array and decision.

Doing this is no simple accomplishment. There is the initial task of discovering the relevant cells in multiple departmental budgets. This task, it may be anticipated, might be handicapped by potential bureaucratic resistance stemming from both the desire to retain power and status and the fear that duplications and inconsistencies may be revealed. The resistance arising in the public bureaucracy may be reinforced by opposition from the clients served by and benefiting from existing budgetary arrangements. It would be natural for them to fear any shifts, even of a statistical character, that might invite decisions less advantageous to their interests.

Probably a much broader range of difficulties should be anticipated as a result of the fact that things are not likely to work out neatly and promptly after the introduction of program budgeting. For a time, many component cost estimates will probably be extremely poor, in fact may have to be achieved in a somewhat arbitrary fashion. Suddenly, instead of adding the costs of personnel for jurisdictional units with well-established identities and interlocks, personnel and their costs will be allocated among a new set of categories. This immediately suggests many difficult questions. What about personnel that service several different program elements? How should these costs be treated? Or what about operations and maintenance equipment and activities that serve several program elements? Public officials with middle management responsibilities must, perforce, make many of these cost identification determinations, and it would be unreasonable to expect that they will promptly understand what is wanted in a planning decision contest and be motivated to deliver it. What this projects is a fair amount of initial confusion, error, and disappointment.

Troubles with the program element structure are also inevitable. One would like to design program elements so that they are relatively independent. In that fortunate case, officials could consider change proposals for the flood-control program element without worrying about repercussions on sewage disposal, disease control, fish and wild life, recreation, grazing lands, and other program elements. Unfortunately, life is complex, and it is impossible to devise program elements (or even broad programs) that are not, in some degree, interdependent. This means that there should and will be considerable groping at first for an improved program-element structure. As a consequence, there may also be a certain amount of initial frustration with the whole decision-making apparatus. The interdependencies are also one of the reasons that a program-budget format should be accompanied by the use of such tools as cost-utility analysis to aid program decisions. Thinking in terms of outputs can be clearer than thinking in terms of inputs (with inputs, the interdependencies can be overwhelming), but there are still important spillovers that must be traced out by special analyses.

Moreover, it is likely that the old budget structure will continue to exist side by side with the new one. Congress would in all likelihood wish to use the input categories to which it is accustomed. In addition, for some time agency officials would continue to need the old structure and the services of budgeteers familiar with it. The reason is that program-element costs, at least during the transition, would be so amorphous that, although they would serve for broad allocative decisions, they would not serve for program management or "frying the fat" out of programs. For some inputs it may not be wise to constrain the amounts, program element by program element, yet still desirable to constrain the total amount permitted. Cutting and managing such inputs may need to be done in terms of the old appropriations structure rather than in terms of the new format.

With the two structures, however, there will develop large amounts of paperwork, conflicts between program decisions and decisions about input categories, and difficulty in gearing the new system to an annual budget cycle. The nature of the paperwork is obvious, although people are likely to underestimate its extent. Conflicts between program decisions and input cuts may need explanation. As long as some decisions are made in terms of specific input categories, cutting across program elements, they can on occasion disrupt the program budget system, vitiate particular program change decisions, and cause considerable confusion.

Moreover, the possibility of such conflicts makes it desirable to gear the new system rather closely to the annual budget cycle. Other considerations also make this desirable. In principle it would be convenient to let the program budget be altered at any time and to eschew any budget ceilings or deadlines. In fact, however, there *is* an annual cycle (Congress is not about to authorize two-year budgets), and one should have cut-off dates and at least ball-park ceilings for the program budget as well as for the old style budget. Indeed, adjusting to the annual cycle and keeping it an orderly one may be the only way to preserve any energy and time for a serious look at the the future program years.

In the longer run, there are other possible difficulties that should be considered. Program budgeting that includes a mechanism for enforcing central decisions may possibly be conducive to centralization of authority. There is no inherent necessity for such a relationship. It is possible to visualize, on the one hand, a decisive and powerful department head (or Bureau of the Budget) without program budgeting, or, on the other hand, a decentralized system in which officials are motivated to make use of the information generated by a program budget. Nonetheless, looking at trade-offs and interdependencies more systematically, making decisions in the light of these trade-offs and interrelationships and enforcing these decisions may make increased centralization appear to be more rewarding or less costly than before.

If program budgeting does not contribute any impetus to centralization, many of the following costs should not be charged to the budgeting system. They should be charged instead to whatever forces bring about increased centralization, and program budgeting will simply help decisions to be better than would otherwise be the case.[1] Even if program budgeting does lead to more centralization, of course, it will often be worthwhile. As an analogy, improved techniques for high-voltage transmission will probably lead to increased centralization in the production of electric power. But most people would agree that the net effects will be good, for the disadvantages will be slight (i.e., the costs of having this decrease in competition) and the gains large.

If program budgeting might facilitate the growth of central control, however, there are some possible long-run costs that should be weighed against the benefits. Perhaps more importantly, these costs should be considered in *designing* the system, so that steps can be taken to reduce the costs and increase the benefits wherever possible. Determining the appropriate degree of central control is a difficult task. In a small agency the long-run consequences could scarcely be serious, but in a comprehensive program embracing many activities these costs could be large. There are certainly ways to use program budgeting without excessive centralization (some of which will be discussed later), but the problems and possibilities deserve careful thought.

The nature of these problems can be illustrated in terms of a hypothetical natural resources program. Assume the program packages to be (1) Agriculture, (2) Water Supply and Use, (3) Forests, (4) Outdoor Recreation Capabilities, and (5) Grazing. Because decisions about these matters need to be coordinated, a "Secretary of Resources" has the authority to make final program decisions and enforce them. Approved programs are recorded in a five-year plan. The agencies responsible for the component activities are to submit change proposals whenever a change would increase total obligational authority or transfer resources in excess of designated thresholds. Below-threshold changes are to be listed, submitted to the Office of the Secretary of Resources (OSR), and periodically incorporated in the five-year plan. A reporting system enables OSR to detect departures from the approved program. To illustrate various points, we will keep referring to this hypothetical arrangement.

How it would work out depends on many factors, one critical influence being the extent to which lower level officials continue to make significant decisions. If their authority thresholds are low, almost all decisions must be made at the top of the organization. If top management does not give relevant guidance, if lower levels devote their efforts to fighting the system, or if lower levels lose incentives, more and more decision-making authority may move upward to the OSR. Consider some of the possible effects of such a development.

One consequence could be the inadvertent suppression of alternatives, despite the fact that a properly functioning program budget should help officials to explore alternatives systematically. If the agencies responsible for the component activities—Water Supply, Agriculture, Forests, and so on—ended up with virtually no bargaining power, their dissenting and clashing views might have no impact. They might speak up, at least for a while, each urging its own position and making alternative proposals, but possibly with diminishing force and influence.

In this circumstance, the views of one group (OSR) would come to play a larger role than before. These views are important, even when analytical tools play major roles, because in many government choices judgment has to be decisive. Suppose, for example, the Secretary of Resources was an unswerving proponent of irrigation, but had relatively little regard for outdoor recreation. Cost-utility analysis could not settle this issue, because non-quantifiable considerations and uncertainties play too large a role. (The effects of outdoor recreation on personality adjustment and crime may or may not be extremely important; the development of "infant regions" by means of irrigation projects may or may not be of great value. The cost-utility analyst cannot measure these impacts.) Whatever OSR's particular convictions, centralization of authority might foreclose earnest consideration of some alternatives that vigorous inter-agency bargaining would air more seriously. In the long run, we would need both inter-agency rivalry and OSR coordination to flush out new alternatives and criticize obsolete functions.

If OSR began to control the sprawling activities in Agriculture, Water Supply, Forests, Recreation, and Grazing, in much detail, simplifying its task would become imperative. Fast screening and disposition of alternatives, and the use of rules of thumb, would be required. In other words, if OSR took on too much, the cost of fully exploring numerous alternatives would become high, and fewer options would be designed and considered. Even if OSR expanded tremendously, its incentives might not be persistently strong without *effective* debate and criticism by the individual agencies.

Without effective bargaining power, the agencies might find *their* incentives to invent and urge alternatives weakened. If they could not get even a toe in the door on new activities, could not influence decisions, could not initiate studies or pilot projects to show how good their proposals were and how bad rival schemes were, they would find it less rewarding than before to think about innovations. Fretting about these matters requires effort. The lower the rewards and the greater the pressures for compliance alone, the less energy there would be to devote to designing alternative courses of action. Would the agencies find it rewarding to analyze choices that were to be made by someone else? In such circumstances, the individual agencies might find it more rewarding just to refrain from rocking the boat.

This influence could shrink the menu of alternatives considered in studies, research, and development pertaining to natural resources projects, investments, and operations. Central control of the studies program could result in harsh screening from a particular point of view. If only one group was out "looking for business," rather than several groups, a narrower menu of studies might seem worth authorizing. There would be only one customer instead of several to consider novel ideas. Thus, if one group and one long-range plan dominated the picture, another aspect of long-range planning (the exploration of unconventional ideas) might be partially sacrificed.

Another aspect is the tendency for analyses of alternatives to become "design studies." When a cost-utility analysis is begun within an agency, participants and successvie echelons of reviewers perceive that their superiors frown upon certain alternatives. It seems useless, perhaps even risky, to put the strongest case possible for the unpopular alternatives. Gradually, the arguments against them are stressed or those alternatives are dropped from the study. The project turns into a design study—the design of one "required" system rather than an objective comparison of alternative courses of action.

These studies are still helpful as long as there are rival agencies, because the competition encourages alternative proposals. If the lower level agencies lose too much bargaining power, however, they may lose the motivation to stay in the study competition. OSR itself may become the only producer of studies. Yet those, too, may eventually become design studies. Persons assigned to prepare analyses will recognize what their superiors prefer. (If the secretary is indifferent, his subordinates are likely to have preferences.) The course of action believed to be favored may be compared with "straw men," or the unpalatable alternatives may drop out of the study entirely.

Consider, also, investment and operations in the several program packages. If authority is too centralized, the five-year plan itself may discourage the quest for alternatives. It projects the approved programs for several years ahead. If the coordinating central group is to exercise control, departures from the programs must be appraised by the group. This means that changes become more difficult than they would be if only over-all budgetary limits were being enforced. In other words, it becomes more costly or less rewarding for the organization to design numerous alternatives, consider them, and implement approved innovations.

Moreover, there is likely to be a trend toward proliferation of program elements—the compartments among which resource shifts require special permission. If the central group tries to manage the programs in detail, the responsible employees may feel their need for better "visibility" more keenly than the over-all need for flexibility. They may keep shredding out more compartments or program elements, which helps higher authorities to see what is going on but makes resource transfers more difficult.

If there is excessive program control by one group, there are still other factors that may cause resistance to change. Any group that reaches decisions and records them in an official plan quite understandably defends those decisions and resists changes. Also, Congress is likely to complain about excessive reprogramming. Despite the old saying that a wise man changes his mind, most of us believe that frequent changes suggest scatterbrained decision-makers. In any organization, dispersal of bargaining power is often required to effect extensive changes.

Other difficulties may develop if our hypothetical OSR is harried and short of staff or if the rival agencies are left with too little bargaining power. Central responsibility for programs several years ahead and a natural desire to deep the agencies from constantly reopening issues may convert what ought to be sequences of decisions into one-shot decisions. For example, choices about research on the conversion of salt water into fresh water, the advanced development of facilities, and investment in specific operational installations ought to be a sequence of decisions. But a long-term plan coupled with excessive centralization might aggregate the tendency to pick the "best" prematurely and become unnecessarily committed to that course of action.

Another long-run consequence of excessive central control of programs could be neglect of part of their impacts. This might strike with special force at one aspect of any proposal's costs and gains—uncertainty. The reasons are the same as those discussed earlier. The judgments of one group would not be as diverse as the judgments of several branches and agencies. One group would be keenly aware of and give emphasis to some contingencies; for example, to the chances of a technological breakthrough in the desalinization of water. Another group might stress some other uncertainty—for instance, the extent of population shifts, or the political feasibility of re-allocating water from irrigation to urban use— but have few doubts about technological developments. There are, in fact, uncertainties about all of these and other factors. If bargaining among the groups plays much of a role in shaping program decisions, all of these uncertainties are likely to be aired. If one group faces too few checks and balances, its convictions about the future may shape the decisions, and the full range of uncertainties is less likely to be considered.

Because of the possible neglect of uncertainties, it is often felt that program budgeting and increased centralization would give a conservative bias to the pattern of choices. In many instances program budgeting might be able to show officials rather formidable cost streams without being able to indicate, in any tangible way, the enormous gains that might be in the offing. This may seem to be a small danger, for pressures in government usually make officials feel potential benefits more keenly than costs. Nonetheless, we should recognize that the *attempt* to make decisions more rational and less responsive to bargaining pressures might introduce a conservative bias. Would the transcontinental railroad or the Panama Canal have made the grade in a regime of long-term program budgeting? In such a decision-making environment, would research and development or expenditures on education have fared as well as they have done in the past? Again there is no inherent necessity of introducing an unduly conservative bias in government choices. It would have to come from misuse rather than from proper use of these tools. But the misuse of tools should be recognized as a possibility when designing or introducing them.

In addition, as suggested earlier, the magnitude of the task of central control may make it essential to simplify decision-making. One natural way to simplify a decision is to disregard uncertainties. All of us, but especially those with complex administrative responsibilities, continually search for rules of thumb to simplify the process of choosing. It is tempting, indeed often imperative, to neglect the qualifications, the contingencies, the less probable outcomes. A slight dispersal of bargaining power, however (and this is compatible with achieving the major aims of program budgeting) may limit the tendency to shelve part of the uncertainties and simplify decisions.

A further reason why central control of programs may cause uncertainties to be neglected is that lower level groups may also become biased in favor of "safe" proposals. Consider, for example, projects that have high expected values but also a significant probability of turning out poorly. The costs of hedging against these uncertainties or of allowing for them are often hard to explain and justify. Such projects may not seem to be attractive to a cost-conscious central group. Or, if such proposals are accepted, they may involve over-runs, which spell trouble and perhaps internal conflict for the agency. As a result, an agency may veer toward "safer" proposals, with less variable outcomes, although with lower expected values.

If experience developed along these lines, few offbeat studies would survive the screening process, and bold ideas might rarely seem worth exploring. In research and development, where costs and gains are clouded with uncertainties, there would be only one customer rather than several who might sponsor a proposal. If only a few types of ideas or only well understood ideas could pass the test, explorations would be somewhat like walking down Main Street. In connection with R&D choices particularly, it may be advisable to implement program budgeting in such a way as to assure roles for a diversity of judgments.

Still another way in which program budgeting with central control might facilitate the neglect of uncertainty, although there is no inherent necessity of its doing so, is by increasing the extent of concurrent planning. Segregating the development costs, investment costs, and operating costs of a proposal ought to emphasize that these decisions can be made sequentially. Coupled with central control, a one-group view of uncertainties, and pressures for a one-shot decision, however, may encourage the planning of these activities concurrently. This seems to happen with central control within branches or agencies—now it might occur in the management of broad programs. Just what is the correct course of action is never clear. Obviously, *all* activities should not be undertaken concurrently. Just as obviously, *all* activities should not be undertaken sequentially, with everything being reviewed every thirty minutes and everything else held in abeyance until each screw is put in place in sequence. Between these extremes, the spectrum of possibilities is very wide, and we do not know what is optimal. Nonetheless, really major uncertainties should usually be cleared up before reaching interrelated decisions. Anyway, *if* we want greater awareness of uncertainties and less concurrent planning, a greater degree of decentralization may be called for. The kind of planning that is appropriate varies from one program to the next and from one situation to the next. This is clear in one's personal life. A business trip in which the objectives are crystal clear and the destinations are familiar can be planned and scheduled in great detail—with firm appointments and airline, hotel, and rental car reservations. An exploration of the Kalahari desert or Arctic lands must also be planned carefully, yet in a very different manner. In the latter case the emphasis will be on planning for contingencies, not on planning for precise appointments and reservations. These two ways of looking ahead can be thought of as "Cook's Tour planning" and "Lewis-and-Clark planning."

In some government programs there are great uncertainties, and good reason for trying to invent new courses of action. Objectives are unclear, and there is indeterminancy about human judgments. In other programs there are fewer uncertainties and less reason for hedging against them or exploring new alternatives. Objectives are relatively clear, and human judgment, although always fallible, can hardly stray far from the mark. In the former programs we need something akin to Lewis-and-Clark planning. In the latter we can use something farther along the spectrum toward Cook's Tour planning.

We should plan on the basis of projections that are as accurate as possible. For some programs an accurate projection is that population shifts and consumer demands are highly uncertain (although we will have best guesses), that technological breakthroughs may or may not occur, that certain programs may or may not have major impacts on juvenile delinquency and crime, that political developments affecting related programs are quite unpredictable, and so on. For other programs an accurate projection is that particular events and outcomes are quite likely to occur. Program budgeting and the accompanying control devices should be designed to accommodate these different situations. It should not be a procrustean bed that forces all decisions and activities to adjust to a single procedure and a single degree of central control.

Before ending this section, we would like to make sure that these issues are viewed in the proper perspective. In the discussion we have called attention to some costs or disadvantages that may be attributable, at least in part, to program budgeting. These should be kept in mind; but we must also keep in mind the shortcomings of the alternatives to program budgeting, say, the conventional one-year budget in terms of categories that are more nearly like inputs. In calling attention to the limitations and risks of program budgeting, we do not wish to obscure its potential benefits or the limitations of alternative ways of reaching budgetary choices. Similarly, it is appropriate to call attention to the unpleasant side effects of penicillin, but it would be foolish to allow this to obscure its benefits or the limitations of alternative medical treatment.

WAYS TO ALLEVIATE THE DIFFICULTIES

Thus far we have discussed the potential difficulties of program budgeting combined with central controls and the different kinds of planning that are appropriate in different situations. Let us turn now to the possible implications for the design of program budgeting systems. What might be done to avoid or reduce the difficulties and to facilitate the right kind of planning?

Accept diversity of arrangements.

First, we should be well advised to accept a diversity of program budgeting procedures and not aim for a single arrangement that applies uniformly to all governmental programs or all components of programs. A variety of arrangements would no doubt arise anyway, but this may be a virtue rather than a defect. Each arrangement should be specifically adapted to the individual situation.

Link program budgeting with the annual cycle.

In principle one might like to avoid any announced budget ceilings, or "firm" programs, or deadlines for submission of change proposals. In this way any change proposals could be considered on their merits at any time; if the prospective gains from a change exceeded the prospective costs, the change would be incorporated in the program. However, Congress is unlikely to abandon the regular annual budget cycle. In addition, such a cycle may be better than the practicable alternatives because it produces a kind of orderliness that may be necessary and it gets decisions made.

Program budgeting needs to be linked with this cycle, so that decisions in terms of program elements do not conflict with decisions in terms of the appropriations categories, and so that decisions can be, to some extent, decentralized. Programs in their entirety need to be reviewed by lower levels—not just change proposals that initiators think it judicious to offer and not just change proposals taken one at a time. Such reviews have to be executed in the light of deadlines and ceilings—not ceilings that are inviolable in some mystical sense, but ceilings and deadlines that give temporary guidance to lower levels. If program reviews are handled in this way and linked with the annual cycle, then (1) some of the work can be decentralized more effectively, and (2) cuts in terms of the appropriations categories near the end of the cycle will not have to be deep slashes.

Try to maintain future flexibility.

Although a five-year program is supposed to be flexible and provide specific mechanisms for change, it may, in some ways that are obvious and others that are subtle, make change more costly than before. Whenever commitments should be postponed, it would be better not to record tentative decisions in the official programs. This could be done by leaving an empty place here and there or by inserting a tentative level of effort but not identifying specific activities. This is bound to occur occasionally (e.g., for basic research), and we are simply emphasizing that this is a good practice, and one that should probably be adopted more frequently.

Keep "considerable" decision-making authority in the hands of lower levels.

We cannot say what "considerable" decentralization of authority means, because it should vary according to the situation. We can discuss it, however, even if the meaning is imprecise. The intention would be partly to keep top levels from being overburdened with minor decisions so that they could focus their attention on the major ones, particularly major planning decisions involving interdependencies among departments or bureaus. The intention would be partly to maintain flexibility by making it simpler to reach certain decisions, make substitutions, and implement resource shifts. But the aim would also be to maintain lower level incentives to seek alternatives, to worry about uncertainties, and to criticize competing proposals.

The design of the program budget system can influence these matters. First, and perhaps most important, the thresholds at which lower levels must get the central group's permission to make changes should be fairly high. There is no single figure that should apply to all programs, and any individual threshold should be adjusted as experience is acquired. But the magnitude of these thresholds is important, because they play a major role in determining what decisions are left to lower levels, what decisions must be turned over to the central authority, and how much influence and bargaining power the lower levels have. Relatively high thresholds would give lower levels some influence, and help maintain their incentives to keep "looking for business." To be sure, branches and agencies would have more leeway to make mistakes and to get at least a toe in the wrong door occasionally, but this would be worthwhile in the long run. Flagrant abuses could probably be deterred; the central authority could make an after-the-fact review, perhaps on a sample basis, of below-threshold changes and should have authority to punish such abuse by shifting functions from one branch to another.

Second and closely related, the conventional budget reprogramming "thresholds" and rules should be relaxed somewhat in comparison with present congressional requirements. The thresholds described above would apply to future program years, but if Congress retained the conventional budget also, reprogramming rules would apply to the current year and the fiscal year in the budget submitted to Congress. Again, although reprogramming cannot be free of central supervision, relatively high thresholds would help to maintain agency bargaining power, initiative, and incentives.

Third, where a diversity of judgments is especially desirable, as in the authorization of studies and exploratory development, the thresholds should be particularly high. Indeed, one can argue that a central program authority (like our hypothetical OSR) should give freedom to a diversity of lower level branches to allocate their budgets for studies and exploratory development. It might be worthwhile, that is, to accept some partial duplication and irrelevant research to ensure against a review process that would make these activities consistent with only one view of the future. In areas like basic research and exploratory development, the dollar amounts involved are typically relatively small. Therefore, the cost of duplication and irrelevant research would also be small.

Before we conclude this discussion of operating problems connected with the program budget, it is important to recognize at least one additional difficulty. The program budget structure recommended in this book requires forward projection of cost estimates for several years in all situations where the cost stream is an essential ingredient of a rational resource allocation decision. Perhaps a five-year projection might be taken as an acceptable general requirement for most programs, although shorter periods might be appropriate for some and longer periods for others (such as a major power, reclamation, and irrigation project; or a long-term commitment for federally financed highway development).

Public administrators and legislators have little experience in developing, evaluating, or using such extended-term cost estimates. The current practice in the case of most new, large activities is to estimate and request funding for only first-year costs, with hardly more than "blue-sky" or "pencil" projections for later time periods. As noted earlier, this has been done not only in the interest of avoiding difficult analysis of future requirements, but also to take advantage of camel's nose tactics in winning support for proposals by publicizing relatively modest entrance expenses. Compulsion to think through the total cost implications of long-term undertakings and to give full exposure to their magnitude constitutes a significant part of the argument for the program budget. Rational decision-making in assigning such a scarce resource as budget dollars demands more than a knowledge of going-in costs.

The implementation of this new requirement will have to face up to the existing staff inexperience in the development of such cost estimates in terms of realism and validity. It will also call for strategies to overcome or counter opposition from those interested parties who prefer to hide or disguise the true long-term price tags attached to their favored projects.

Extensive educational efforts and strengthening of staff capabilities for cost estimating and analysis will be required in the executive departments, the Bureau of the Budget, and, probably, the staffs of at least some congressional committees. The major gains to be derived from the use of the program budget as an effective instrument for analysis, planning, and control will depend in large part on the quality of the data presented in the budget operation.

INSTITUTIONAL PROBLEMS OF THE PROGRAM BUDGET

Finally, some comment is in order about the institutional problems that should be anticipated in the design, installation, and operation of the program budget concept. We are dealing here with an operating instrument, not an exercise in arithmetic. The immediate significance of this observation is found in the proposed use of the new tool as the central device in the government's fundamental decisions about the objects and magnitude of federal financial support. This will inevitably be viewed throughout the organizational bureaucracy as a threat to existing, familiar, and manipulatable institutional arrangements. Such a view will by no means be confined to the executive branch of the government. Allied to each executive unit, as sponsors or clients, are legislative and private interests. To many of these interests, the program budget will probably appear as a disturbing influence, if not as an outright threat. Its promise to provide better information that is better organized for better decision-making will not necessarily assure its welcome. It is unfortunately true that improved decision-making grounded in a more rational approach to the resource allocation problem will not be universally appraised as desirable progress. One of the characteristics of better decisions will be identification and possible removal of overlapping and redundant activities. Another will be exposure of ineffective or inefficient employment of resources. A third will be brighter illumination of the long-range cost implications of proposals with relatively painless initial expenses, and consequent harder screening with an accompanying higher rejection rate. And one should not overlook the threat to the existing organization structure and client relationships that many will sense as implicit in the program budget at some indeterminate time following its introduction.

In short, we should anticipate being confronted with the fact that the goals of an enterprise are not necessarily consistent with the goals of its individual component units, or with the goals of individual administrators. This is in no sense an argument for withdrawing the proposal. It does, however, urge the importance of frank assessment of future problems and imaginative design of political, organizational, and social strategies to build support for the proposal in both its acceptance and installation phases, and to implement it in such a way as to maximize its usefulness.

In the Executive Office of the President, most importantly in the Bureau of the Budget, one should be able to count on understanding and strong support. Hopefully, key committee chairmen in both the Senate and the House may see in the program budget a decision tool that will help resolve the mass of information with which they struggle annually. Outside the federal government it should be possible to recruit active supporters for the proposal: among business leaders who know from their own management experience the importance of organizing comprehensive and valid information in a planned relationship to a rational decision strategy; among economic, political, and social analysts in business, trade associations, research institutions, and universities; and generally among all informed citizens who want to see their tax dollars used more purposefully and effectively.

NOTE:

[1]If decision-making were *sufficiently* centralized, one might possibly prefer that decision-makers work with poorer rather than better information, but in most parts of "democratic" governments this degree of centralization seems a little far-fetched.

18.
Planning–Programming–Budgeting Systems and Project PRIME*
LT. CDR. STEVEN LAZARUS, USN

PPBS stands for Planning–Programming–Budgeting Systems. These words have so pervaded government in the last year that the letters used by themselves have come to suggest a magical panacea for all management ills. This is unfortunate. When a basically good idea is translated into a "buzz" word, it often suffers from distortion and mis-interpretation. If it fails to solve all problems or live up to its inflated billing, it is abruptly discarded. Usually a critic is readily available to pronounce the epitaph—I told you it wouldn't work in the first place.

The purpose of this article is to place PPBS in perspective by briefly describing its historical antecedents in DOD; outlining the process as it was implemented and refined from 1961 to 1965; and, most impor-tantly, describing the changes which are being made in it in DOD under the collective name of Project PRIME.

HISTORICAL ANTECEDENTS.

Control by Legislature.

The framers of the Constitution were aware that the British Parliament in 1688 had abrogated the historic right of the king to raise armies in time of peace according to his own good pleasure. Motivated by the conviction that the American executive should be similarly deprived of the power to raise and the sole power to regulate fleets and armies, the founding fathers expressly provided in Article 1, Section 8 of the Consti-

*Lt. Cdr. Steven Lazarus, USN, "Planning-Programming-Budgeting Systems and Project PRIME," *Defense Industry Bulletin*, 3:1 (January, 1967), 1–4. Steven Lazarus is a Lieu-tenant Commander in the U. S. Navy and Special Assistant to the Assistant Secretary of Defense (Comptroller).

tution that Congress shall have the power to "provide for the common defense," "raise and support armies," "provide and maintain a navy," and to make all laws necessary to execute these powers.

This "control by legislature" over a single War Department seemed appropriate for the small permanent military establishment contemplated in 1787. But by 1793 the incursions of the barbary pirates had forced Congress to consider the construction of a fleet and the managerial difficulties connected with this enterprise led in part to the establishment in 1798 of the Department of the Navy.

Throughout the nineteenth century Congress continued to assert its primacy in military affairs through its control of the purse. The President had no statutory authority to act on budgetary matters and, although the Secretary of the Treasury received department estimates, he was required to transmit them to Congress without revision.

The century, however, had also seen a tremendous national expansion, and with the acquisition of territory, the increase in population, and the growth of industry, had come a larger and increasingly more complex military establishment.

 . . . *Predecessors of the so-called technical and staff services of the Army became firmly established as statutory institutions in their own right and created major problems of coordination and command within the War Department itself. A similar trend toward a proliferation of specialties manifested itself in the Navy, culminating in 1842 with the establishment of the Bureaus which created the same kind of problems within that Department. . . .*[1]

This organizational form accommodated neatly to the legislative tendency to control by means of hundreds of discrete and separate appropriations. As recipients of specific appropriations, the heads of special activities achieved an almost autonomous status. The content of such appropriations was frequently established through a process of personal negotiation between the chief of a bureau and influential members of the congressional committees handling the appropriations.

Strengthening the Executive.

It was the failure of these organizational structures and management practices during wartime that prompted reform. The managerial difficulties encountered during the Spanish American War led to Secretary of War Root's recommendations of 1903 which, among other things, resulted in the creation of the Office of the Army Chief of Staff. The vast increase in expenditures during World War I made it evident that budgetary reforms were necessary and Congress responded by enacting the Budget and Accounting Act of 1921 which concentrated the responsibility for preparation and transmittal of the executive budget in the hands of the President. By strengthening the executive, the legislative branch was inevitably acquiescing to the curtailment of its own power.

Throughout the 1920's and 1930's the movement toward a unified defense establishment grew stronger and, as Charles Hitch comments, the experience of World War II finally overcame the last opposition. It was also plain that Congress could no longer exercise effective stewardship over the defense establishment by parceling out hundreds of discrete appropriations and by counseling independently with dozens of separate military officials. Massive, world-wide, total war demanded integrated and coordinated planning, finding and execution.

Although it was a major step in the right direction, the National Security Act of 1947 proved not quite equal to these tasks and was, therefore, strengthened and amended in 1949. Title IV was added to the Act creating the Office of the Assistant Secretary of Defense (Comptroller) and providing for uniform budget and fiscal procedures throughout the department. The position of comptroller was held by W. H. McNeil for ten years (1949–1959), a record for longevity at such a level. McNeil's skill and energy, coupled with his tenure, enabled him to build selectively upon the recommendations of the first and second Hoover Commissions to lay the foundation for modern financial management in DOD.

The Process from 1961 to 1965.

Relating Costs to Missions.

McNeil accomplished much to bring order out of chaos in the DOD management control process, and the reorganizations of 1953 and 1958 further strengthened the position of the Secretary of Defense. The problem, however, was already moving beyond the new systems and structure. The Defense budget was gradually rising toward its current level, new weapon systems were becoming unimaginably expensive, and the quest for a rational method of making choices and balancing forces was becoming imperative.

Congress chafed at its inability to know what it was paying for. Ohio Congressman Clarence Brown, commenting on the 1952 Appropriation Bill, said, ". . . I speak as one of those who is not at all certain just what this Bill provides or what all the items in it mean. . . ."[2] By 1959,

Congressman George Mahon, then Chairman of the House Defense Appropriations Subcommittee, was stressing the importance of looking at the Defense program and budget in terms of major military missions, and asking the Secretary of Defense "for more useful information and for a practical means of relating costs to missions. . . ."

Congress was not alone in recognizing these needs. Arthur Smithies, a noted economist, said in 1957, ". . . Neither the Congress, nor the President, nor I suspect the Secretary of Defense and the Service secretaries have the information needed to relate the financial figures in the budget to any meaningful concept of military effectiveness. . . ."[3]

In presenting the Army budget in 1960, General Maxwell Taylor described a mission-oriented budget in terms of six programs, and suggested horizontal cross-Service review. Perhaps the most articulate observer was Charles Hitch, Chief Economist of the Rand Corporation, who crystallized the problem in a book entitled, *The Economics of Defense in the Nuclear Age.*

Hitch examined the method of budget formulation, known as the "budget ceiling" approach, which entailed a process of squeezing service budget requests to make their total fit within an initial over-all limitation established by the Bureau of the Budget acting for the President. He found that "its consequences were precisely what could have been predicted:

1. Each service tended to exercise its own priorities.

  a. Favoring its own unique missions to the detriment of joint missions;

  b. Striving to lay the ground work for an increased share of the budget in future years by concentrating on alluring new weapon systems; and

  c. Protecting the over-all size of its own forces even at the cost of readiness. . . .

2. Because attention was focused on only the next fiscal year, the services had every incentive to propose large numbers of 'new starts,' the full cost dimensions of which would only become apparent in subsequent years. . . .

3. Almost complete separation between budgeting and military planning.

  a. These critically important functions were performed by two different groups of people. . . .

  b. Budget control was exercised by the Secretary of Defense, but planning remained essentially in the services. . . .

  c. Whereas the planning horizon extended four or more years into the future, the budget was projected only one year ahead. . . .

  d. Planning was done in terms of . . . outputs; budgeting . . . in terms of inputs. . . .

e. Budgeting, however crudely, faced up to fiscal realities; the planning was fiscally unrealistic, and therefore of little help to the decision-maker. . . .

f. Military requirements tended to be stated in absolute terms, without reference to their costs.[4]

New Guidance.

In 1961, President Kennedy abandoned the budget-ceiling approach as far as defense was concerned. He gave his new Secretary of Defense, Robert McNamara, two general instructions:

· Develop the military force structure necessary to support our foreign policy without regard to arbitrary budget ceilings.

· Procure and operate this force at the lowest possible cost.

Charles Hitch became McNamara's Assistant Secretary of Defense (Comptroller) and clearly stated what was required to translate this guidance into action:

We need an economically realistic future program so that long-lead decisions on program components will have a reasonable chance of turning out to be right. To develop such a program, it is essential that the decision-makers have before them the total cost implications of alternatives—not only total in the sense of cutting across appropriation categories, but also in the sense of being projected forward over a five-year period.[5]

Hitch, aided by some able systems designers, developed such a mechanism—the Five-Year Defense Program—in the phenomenal time of about six months. He also established two new organizational elements—a programming division to superintend the Five-Year Defense Program, and a systems analysis division to conduct analytic comparisons of alternative inputs to that program.

PPBS.

The mechanism was a three-phase operation: Planning–Programming–Budgeting. The first phase—planning and requirements determination—was to be a year-round operation initiated by the Joint Strategic Objectives Plan proposed by the Joint Chiefs of Staff. It was to consist of military economic studies which would compare alternative methods of accomplishing national security objectives to determine the one that contributes the most for a given cost or achieves a given objective for the least cost. Today these are commonly called cost-effectiveness studies or systems analyses.

The second phase—the programming system—integrated combinations of men, equipment and installations into program elements whose effectiveness could be measured as a whole and related to national security objectives. The B-52 bomber force with all its resources was one such element. The elements were aggregated into the major missions of the Defense Department. Each aggregation had a common set of purposes and could, for decision-making, be treated as a whole. In 1965, there were nine such aggregations or programs (Figure 1).

A mechanism which allowed for continuous update and change was provided, and data were projected for eight years in the case of military forces, and for five years in all other cases. This immense amount of data under continuous change required computerization in order to remain manageable. The availability of modern data-processing equipment made feasible what otherwise would have been an impossible task.

The budget process was not susceptible to rapid alteration and, therefore, remained structured in terms of object classes, vast accumulations of inputs such as military personnel, procurement, etc. It was necessary to translate the program into budget terms by means of a "torque conversion" or matrix which broke the program into various appropriations categories. The accounting systems of DOD were also aligned with the budget structure, and thus progress reporting related to the program had to be accomplished by means of special studies and separate reports. The programming system had filled a vital planning need but, as yet, was unable to serve the needs of field managers.

In 1965, Robert N. Anthony became Assistant Secretary of Defense

FIVE YEAR DEFENSE PROGRAM*

New	*Old*
I. Strategic Forces	Strategic Offensive Forces
II. General Purpose Forces	Continental Air & Missile Defense Forces
III. Specialized Activities (Includes MAP)	General Purpose Forces
IV. Airlift and Sealift	Airlift/Sealift Forces
V. Guard and Reserve Forces	Reserve and Guard Forces
VI. Research and Development	Research and Development
VII. Logistics	General Support
VIII. Personnel Support	Retired Pay
IX. Administration	Military Assistance

* For explanation of changes, see DOD publication, "A Primer on Project PRIME," Nov. 1966, pp. 34–35, available from the Office of Asst. Secretary of Defense (Comptroller), Room 3B857, The Pentagon, Washington, D.C.

Figure 1.

(Comptroller). It was to be Anthony's task to build upon the foundation of the programming system and create within DOD a management control system which would serve the needs of managers at all levels from the congressman to the corporal.

PROJECT PRIME.

Progress Against Plan.

In 1955, the second Hoover Commission on Organization of the Executive Branch of the Government made a series of recommendations for changes in accounting and budgeting procedures. Among these were suggestions that operating budgets be cost-based and that government accounting be kept on the accrual basis to show currently, completely and clearly all resources and liabilities, and the costs of operations. These particular recommendations were adopted and enacted in 1956 as Public Law 863.

As late as 1965, Charles Hitch had reflected that "·· . . Ideally, I suppose, the program should be costed in terms of accrued expenditure, which is closest to the concept of resources consumed. However, the accounting difficulties appeared so overwhelming that we did not attempt that approach. . . ."[6]

Finally, President Johnson asked that the pace of the Joint Financial Management Improvement Program be accelerated, and in a special memorandum asked each agency to ". . . see that the Agency's managers are given the basic tools they need—responsibility centered cost-based operating budgets and financial reports. . . ."

Operating Costs.

Anthony began by defining the problem in order to reduce it to manageable proportions. He identified two essential different types of cost—investment costs and operating costs—used in DOD management. Investment costs related to items such as ships, planes and facilities which maintained their identity during their cycle of use and were financed by means of "continuing" appropriations. These were planned for and managed on an individual item basis. They were treated consistently in both programs and budget and, thus, no significant changes were contemplated in their case.

Full attention was then focused on operating costs—the costs of the labor, materials and services required to operate the defense establishments.

The first goal was to achieve a correspondence in terms of operating costs among program, budget, accounting system, and reporting system. Such consistency would eliminate the necessity for the unrewarding process of "torque conversion," would lay the groundwork for budget submission to Congress in mission-oriented terms, and would create within the accounting system the capability for progress reporting back against the program.

In order to do this, a single entity would have to serve as the basic unit, or building block, of both program and management system. This was achieved by revising the content of the Five-Year Defense Program and defining program elements very carefully. The revised program structure is shown in Figure 1. The synchronization is demonstrated in Figure 2.

Figure 2.

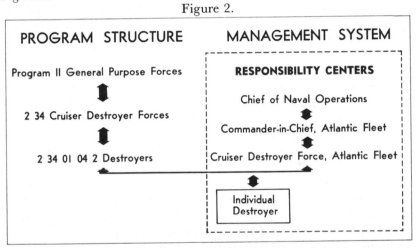

The second goal was to charge an organization with 100 per cent of the measurable expenses that it incurred, and to account thereafter in terms of expenses. Such an accounting would yield hard, actual and total cost data to the planners working on revisions to the program and, simultaneously, would display to the manager the full cost of his activity. It would, additionally, show the congressman what his operating appropriations were buying. Finally, it would give managers throughout DOD the ability to determine the real costs of specific missions, to measure actual performance against planned performance, and to relate resources consumed to work done.

While rough approximations of these relationships could have been made in the past using statistical pro-rations and special studies, what was now proposed was to derive them routinely and accurately by means of a disciplined debit and credit accounting system.

Basically, four steps were necessary to accomplish this goal:
• Revise the accounts structure.
• Charge military personnel costs to organization units.
• Purify the appropriation definitions so as to include only items of an expense nature in the operating appropriation.
• Extend the use of working capital mechanism to encompass all items of an expense nature.

The Four Changes.

A uniform account structure has been developed and will provide a common basis for the Military Departments and Defense Agencies to report expenses. It is only a skeleton and each DOD component has developed, or is developing, amplifying systems to meet its own management needs. The basic accounting structure ties directly back to the Five-Year Defense Program as shown in Figure 3.

Functional categories will serve the purposes of functional managers and aggregate to program element. Expense elements will replace object classes as the basic modules in the accounting system. There will also be subsidiary cost systems such as one for wholesale supply depots which will subdivide functional categories into sub-functional breakdowns. Such breakdowns will supplement, but not replace, accounting by expense element.

Military personnel costs will be charged to the using activity by means of a standard cost. This will have the effect of costing at the user level the largest single category of operating resources not now so charged. It is hoped that DOD will be permitted to employ a single appropriation for each DOD component for all operating costs combining the existing appropriations for military personnel and operations and maintenance. Such an amalgamation would greatly facilitate the budgeting and accounting for operating costs. But even if two separate appropriations are maintained, DOD will still combine them for internal purposes and convert for external reporting purposes at the headquarters level. The Navy is already receiving reports which reflect full costs including costs of military personnel of all units of both the Atlantic and Pacific fleets.

The third change is the purification of appropriations so that all expense items are associated with the operating appropriations and none with the procurement or construction appropriation. Primarily, this involves shifting many items of spare parts and similar consumables from

Figure 3.

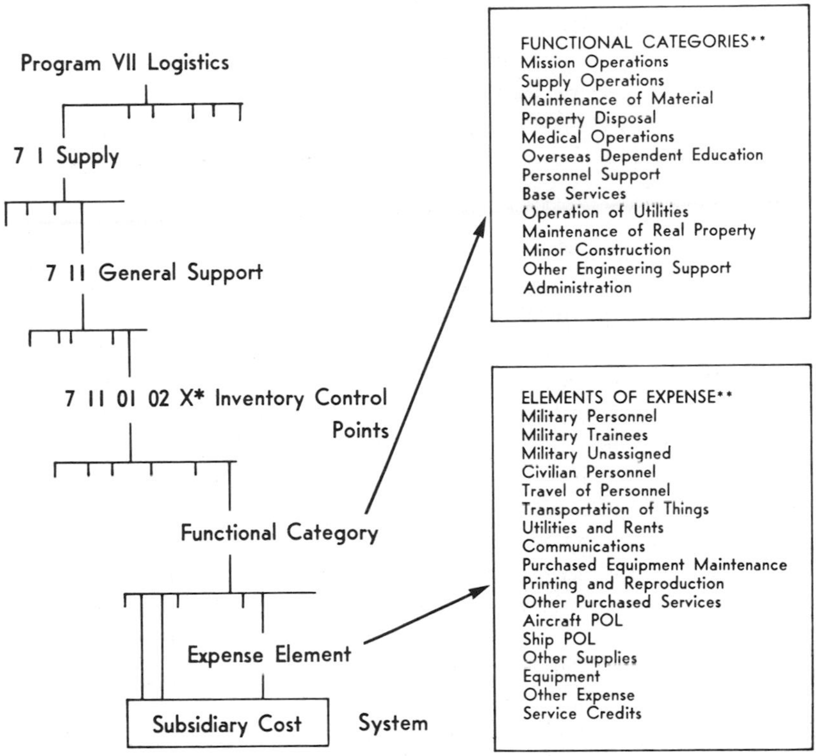

Program VII Logistics

7 I Supply

7 II General Support

7 II 01 02 X* Inventory Control Points

Functional Category

Expense Element

Subsidiary Cost   System

FUNCTIONAL CATEGORIES**
Mission Operations
Supply Operations
Maintenance of Material
Property Disposal
Medical Operations
Overseas Dependent Education
Personnel Support
Base Services
Operation of Utilities
Maintenance of Real Property
Minor Construction
Other Engineering Support
Administration

ELEMENTS OF EXPENSE**
Military Personnel
Military Trainees
Military Unassigned
Civilian Personnel
Travel of Personnel
Transportation of Things
Utilities and Rents
Communications
Purchased Equipment Maintenance
Printing and Reproduction
Other Purchased Services
Aircraft POL
Ship POL
Other Supplies
Equipment
Other Expense
Service Credits

* Indicates DOD component identified—Army, Navy, Air Force, etc.

** For definitions, see DOD Instruction 7220.20, "Expense Data Requirements," December 20, 1966.

continuing appropriations to operations. It also involves moving a few capital items from operations appropriations to continuing appropriations. Once this is fully accomplished, all expenses, and only expenses, will be included in the operating appropriation. DOD Instruction 7040.5, "Definition of Expenses and Investment Costs," dated Sept. 1, 1966, carefully spells out the criteria governing this purification. The care with which the instruction was developed is demonstrated by the fact that it consumed five months of steady effort, went through thirteen separate revisions, and was analyzed in three separate DOD-wide reviews.

The final action necessary to achieve the goal of charging 100 per cent of measurable expenses to operating activities is the extension of working capital to cover all items in the operating appropriation. Such an extension allows the association of costs with the using activity at time of use. Under the former system, purchases were often made and the appropriation charged by a central organization long before and far from the time and place of use. Centrally procured fuel or aviation spare parts are examples of this. Such material was then furnished "free" to the ultimate user. Since these expenses were not charged to him, the user had little motivation to give them the kind of management attention he gave to items which actually cost him money. Working capital solves this problem by permitting costs to be held in suspense from the time of purchase until the time of issue for consumption. At the time of issue for consumption, they are charged to the user.

Working capital is not a new concept. Many supply items are currently held in stock funds, and many services in industrial funds. Stock funds will be extended to include all consumable material, at both wholesale and retail levels, and industrial funds will be expanded to include those wholesale service activities not now under them. Finally, working capital accounts within the operating appropriation will be established for local services, such as maintenance and the motor pool. The realities of a combat environment will be recognized by charging for operating resources at the time of movement to the theater.

Effect on the Budget.

The budget process will change radically as a consequence of Project PRIME. The FY 1968 budget will be converted to expense terms prior to July 1, 1967, when the new system becomes effective. FY 1968 will see a full-scale combined program/budget submission and review in expense terms by program elements and organization units within DOD. Congress, of course, will retain the option of receiving it on this basis.

Outlook for the Future.

Project PRIME means that the manager's flexibility in deciding on what resources to use should be increased. He should be encouraged to think about, for example, the best balance between military personnel, civilian personnel and contract personnel, or the optimum degree of mechanization, in a wide variety of situations. With the financial segregations that now exist, managers have little incentive for investigating such alternatives.

It means also that there should be a tendency on the part of top management to move in the direction of control of aggregates and away from control by bits and pieces. It would be expected that, as time goes on, there will be less emphasis on individual items of expense—less detailed control of manpower and less detailed consumption rules for example—and more emphasis on expenses as a whole.

Finally, the system should motivate managers to be more concerned about the efficient use of resources. Of course, efficiency is only one criterion for judging a manager, and attention to efficiency must never be permitted to overshadow the criterion of effectiveness, which means getting the job done, and done well. But managers do need to know how efficiently their subordinates are performing their assigned missions, and the new system will help them learn this. Moreover, as performance measurement criteria change to incorporate this additional information, the motivation will be increased for managers to be concerned with the wise use of resources, thereby reducing the need for exhortation, inspection, specified constraints, and other devices that are now used as a substitute for a built-in motivation.

CONCLUSION.

When Project PRIME "goes live" on July 1, 1967, it will not function as a perfect and complete invention. The system faces many modifications and probably years of refinement. While the first programming system directly affected a few hundred people working in the Pentagon, Project PRIME will affect thousands throughout the entire Defense establishment. The extent of the job to be done in education alone is staggering.

Nevertheless, Project PRIME will achieve one fundamental goal of PPBS. It takes off from a meaningful structure for planning and makes possible realistic appraisal of the degree to which the performance has fulfilled the plan.

The environment never stands still and the defense management control process in the United States is constantly seeking to overtake a continually changing problem. Project PRIME may represent a large enough step to overcome this situation for a while and, thus gain some time for beleaguered defense managers. It will, at least, restore to the legislature visibility with respect to defense matters that some believe has been seriously eroded over 130 years, and will materially assist in the proper discharge of its constitutional responsibilities.

PPBS is no panacea. It is a good idea, a part of an evolutionary stream of ideas. It requires refinement and innovation if it is to remain useful in coping with a dynamic environment moving at an accelerating pace.

NOTES:

[1]Hitch, Charles, "H. Rowan Gaither Lectures in Systems Sciences." 1965.
[2]Kolodziej, Edward A., "The Uncommon Defense and Congress" 1945–1963.
[3]NAVEXOS P-2416, Aug. 1962.
[4]Hitch, Charles J., "Decision Making for Defense," Berkeley: 1965, pp. 24–26. For further discussion of these same points, see David Novick (ed.), "Program Budgeting: Program Analysis and the Federal Government," (Cambridge: Harvard University Press, 1965), pp. 81–119.
[5]*Ibid.*
[6]Hitch, *op. cit.*

19.

The Political Economy of Efficiency: Cost-Benefit Analysis, Systems Analysis, and Program Budgeting*

AARON WILDAVSKY

There was a day when the meaning of economic efficiency was reasonably clear.

An objective met up with a technician. Efficiency consisted in meeting the objective at the lowest cost or in obtaining the maximum amount of the objective for a specified amount of resources. Let us call this "pure efficiency." The desirability of trying to achieve certain objectives may depend on the cost of achieving them. In this case the analyst (he has graduated from being a mere technician) alters the objective to suit available resources. Let us call this "mixed efficiency." Both pure and mixed efficiency are limited in the sense that they take for granted the existing structure of the political system and work within its boundaries. Yet the economizer, he who values efficiency most dearly, may discover that the most efficient means for accomplishing his ends cannot be secured without altering the machinery for making decisions. He not only alters means and ends (resources and objectives) simultaneously but makes them dependent on changes in political relationships. While he claims no special interest in or expertise concerning the decision apparatus outside of the market place, the economizer pursues efficiency to the heart of the political system. Let us call this "total efficiency." In this vocabulary, then, concepts of efficiency may be pure or mixed, limited or total.

*Reprinted from Aaron Wildavsky, "The Political Economy of Efficiency: Cost-Benefit Analysis, Systems Analysis, and Program Budgeting," *Public Administration Review*, 26:4 (December 1966), 292–310, by permission of the author and publisher. Aaron Wildavsky is chairman of the department of political science at the University of California, Berkeley.

A major purpose of this paper is to take the newest and recently most popular modes of achieving efficiency—cost-benefit analysis, systems analysis, and program budgeting—and show how much more is involved than mere economizing. *Even at the most modest level of cost-benefit analysis, I will try to show that it becomes difficult to maintain pure notions of efficiency. At a higher level, systems analysis is based on a mixed notion of efficiency. And program budgeting at the highest levels leaves pure efficiency far behind its over-reaching grasp into the structure of the political system. Program budgeting, it turns out, is a form of systems analysis, that is, political systems analysis.*

These modes of analysis are neither good for nothing nor good for everything, and one cannot speak of them as wholly good or bad. It is much more useful to try to specify some conditions under which they would or would not be helpful for various purposes. While such a list could not be exhaustive at this stage, nor permanent at any stage (because of advances in the art), it provides a basis for thinking about what these techniques can and cannot do. Another major purpose of this paper, therefore, is to describe cost-benefit and systems analysis and program budgeting as techniques for decision-making. I shall place particular stress upon what seems to me the most characteristic feature of all three modes of analysis: the aids to calculation designed to get around the vast areas of uncertainty where quantitative analysis leaves off and judgment begins.

COST-BENEFIT ANALYSIS

. . . One can view cost-benefit analysis as anything from an infallible means of reaching the new Utopia to a waste of resources in attempting to measure the unmeasureable.[1]

The purpose of cost-benefit analysis is to secure an efficient allocation of resources produced by the governmental system in its interaction with the private economy. The nature of efficiency depends on the objectives set up for government. In the field of water resources, where most of the work on cost-benefit analysis has been done, the governmental objective is usually postulated to be an increase in national income. In a crude sense, this means that the costs to whomever may incur them should be less than the benefits to whomever may receive them. The time streams of consumption gained and foregone by a project are its benefits and costs.

The aim of cost-benefit analysis is to maximize "the present value of all benefits less that of all costs, subject to specified restraints."[2] A long view is taken in that costs are estimated not only for the immediate future but also for the life of the project. A wide view is taken in that indirect consequences for others—variously called externalities, side-effects, spillovers, and repercussion effects—are considered. Ideally, all costs and benefits are evaluated. The usual procedure is to estimate the installation costs of the project and spread them over time, thus making them into something like annual costs. To these costs are added an estimate of annual operating costs. The next step involves estimating the average value of the output by considering the likely number of units produced each year and their probable value in the market place of the future. Intangible, "secondary," benefits may then be considered. These time streams of costs and benefits are discounted so as to obtain the present value of costs and benefits. Projects whose benefits are greater than costs may then be approved, or the cost-benefit ratios may, with allowance for relative size, be used to rank projects in order of desirability.

Underlying Economic and Political Assumptions

A straightforward description of cost-benefit analysis cannot do justice to the powerful assumptions that underlie it or to the many conditions limiting its usefulness. The assumptions involve value judgments that are not always recognized and, when recognized, are not easily handled in practice. The limiting conditions arise partly out of the assumptions and partly out of severe computational difficulties in estimating costs, and especially benefits. Here I can only indicate some major problems.

Cost-benefit analysis is based on superiority in the market place,[3] under competitive conditions and full employment, as the measure of value in society. Any imperfection in the market works against the validity of the results. Unless the same degree of monopoly were found throughout the economy, for example, a governmental body that enjoys monopolistic control of prices or outputs would not necessarily make the same investment decisions as under free competition. A similar difficulty occurs where the size of a project is large in comparison to the economy, as in some developing nations. The project itself then affects the constellation of relative prices and production against which its efficiency is measured. The assumption based on the classical full employment model is also important because it gives prices special significance. Where manpower is not being utilized, projects may be justified in part as putting this unused resource to work.

The economic model on which cost-benefit analysis depends for its validity is based on a political theory. The idea is that in a free society the economy is to serve the individual's consistent preferences revealed and rationally pursued in the market place. Governments are not supposed to dictate preferences nor make decisions.

This individualist theory assumes as valid the current distribution of income. Preferences are valued in the market place where votes are based on disposable income. Governmental action to achieve efficiency, therefore, inevitably carries with it consequences for the distribution of income. Projects of different size and location and composition will transfer income in different amounts to different people. While economists might estimate the redistributive consequences of various projects, they cannot, on efficiency grounds, specify one or another as preferable. How is this serious problem to be handled?

Benefit-cost analysis is a way of trying to promote economic welfare. But whose welfare? No one knows how to deal with inter-personal comparisons of utility. It cannot be assumed that the desirability of rent supplements versus a highway or dam can be measured on a single utility scale. There is no scientific way to compare losses and gains among different people or to say that the marginal loss of a dollar to one man is somehow equal to the gain of a dollar by another. The question of whose utility function is to prevail (the analyst versus the people involved, the upstream gainers versus the downstream losers, the direct beneficiaries versus the taxpayers, the entire nation or a particular region, and so on) is of prime importance in making public policy.

The literature on welfare economics is notably unable to specify an objective welfare function.[4] Ideally, actions would benefit everyone and harm no one. As an approximation, the welfare economist views as optimal an action that leaves some people better off and none worse off. If this criterion were applied in political life, it would result in a situation like that of the Polish Diet in which anyone who was damaged could veto legislation. To provide a way out of this impasse, Hicks and Kaldor proposed approval of decisions if the total gain in welfare is such that the winners could compensate the losers. But formal machinery for compensation does not ordinarily exist and most modern economists are highly critical of the major political mechanism for attempting to compensate, namely, log-rolling in Congress on public works projects.[5] It is a very imperfect mechanism for assuring that losers in one instance become winners in another.

Another way of dealing with income distribution is to accept a criterion laid down by a political body and maximize present benefits less costs subject to this constraint. Or the cost-benefit analyst can present a series of alternatives differing according to the individuals who pay and prices charged. The analyst must not only compute the new inputs and outputs, but also the costs and benefits for each group with whom the public authorities are especially concerned. No wonder this is not often done! Prest and Turvey are uncertain whether such a procedure is actually helpful in practice.[6]

Income redistribution in its most extreme form would result in a complete leveling or equality of incomes. Clearly, this is not what is meant. A more practical meaning might be distributing income to the point where specific groups achieve a certain minimum. It is also possible that the operational meaning of income redistribution may simply be the transfer of some income from some haves to some have nots. Even in the last and most minimal sense of the term it is by no means clear that projects that are inefficient by the usual economic criteria serve to redistribute income in the desired direction. It is possible that some inefficient projects may transfer income from poorer to richer people. Before the claim that certain projects are justified by the effect of distributing income in a specified way can be accepted, an analysis to show that this is what actually happens must be at hand.

Since the distribution of income is at stake, it is not surprising that beneficiaries tend to dominate investment decisions in the political arena and steadfastly refuse to pay for what they receive from government tax revenues. They uniformly resist user charges based on benefits received. Fox and Herfindahl estimate that of a total initial investment of three billion for the Corps of Engineers in 1962, taxpayers in general would pay close to two-thirds of the costs.[7] Here, greater use of the facilities by a larger number of beneficiaries getting something for nothing inflates the estimated benefits which justify the project in the first place. There may be a political rationale for these decisions, but it has not been developed.

In addition to redistributing income, public works projects have a multitude of objectives and consequences. Projects may generate economic growth, alleviate poverty among some people, provide aesthetic enjoyment and opportunities for recreation, improve public health, reduce the risks of natural disaster, alter travel patterns, affect church attendance, change educational opportunities, and more. No single welfare criterion can encompass these diverse objectives. Has many of them should be considered? Which are susceptible of quantification? The further one pursues this analysis, the more impassable the thicket.

LIMITATIONS IN THE UTILITY OF COST-BENEFIT ANALYSIS

One possible conclusion is that at present certain types of cost-benefit analysis are not meaningful. In reviewing the literature on the calculus of costs and benefits in research and development, for example, Prest and Turvey comment on "the uncertainty and unreliability of cost estimates . . . and . . . the extraordinarily complex nature of the benefits. . . ."[8]

Another conclusion is that one should be cautious in distinguishing the degree to which projects are amenable to cost-benefit analysis.

. . . When there are many diverse types of benefits from a project and/or many different beneficiaries it is difficult to list them all and to avoid double counting. This is one reason why it is so much easier to apply cost-benefit analysis to a limited purpose development, say, than it is to the research and development aspects of some multi-purpose discovery, such as a new type of plastic material. . . . It is no good expecting those fields in which benefits are widely diffused, and in which there are manifest divergences between accounting and economic costs or benefits, to be as cultivable as others. Nor is it realistic to expect that comparisons between projects in entirely different branches of economic activity are likely to be as meaningful or fruitful as those between projects in the same branch. The technique is more useful in the public-utility area than in the social-services area of government.[9]

If the analysis is to be useful at all, calculations must be simplified.[10] The multiple ramifications of interesting activities can be taken into account only at the cost of introducing fantastic complexities. Prest and Turvey remark of one such attempt, that "This system . . . requires knowledge of all the demand and supply equations in the economy, so is scarcely capable of application by road engineers."[11] They suggest omitting consideration where (1) side effects are judged not terribly large or where (2) concern for these effects belongs to another governmental jurisdiction.[12]

If certain costs or benefits are deemed important but cannot be quantified, it is always possible to guess. The increasing use of recreation and aesthetic facilities to justify public works projects in the United States is disapproved by most economists because there can be a vast, but hidden, inflation of these benefits. For example, to attribute the same value to a recreation day on a reservoir located in a desert miles from any substitute source of water as to a day on an artificial lake in the heart of natural lake country is patently wrong. Economists would prefer to see recreation facilities listed in an appendix so that they can be taken into account in some sense, or, alternatively, that the project be presented with and without the recreation facilities, so that a judgment can be made as to whether the additional services are worth the cost.[13]

Economists distinguish between risk, where the precise outcome cannot be predicted but a probability distribution can be specified, and uncertainty, where one does not even know the parameters of the outcomes. The cost-benefit analyst must learn to live with uncertainty, for he can never know whether all relevant objectives have been included and what changes may occur in policy and in technology.

It is easy enough to cut the life of the project below its expected economic life. The interest rate can be raised. Assumptions can be made that costs will be higher and benefits lower than expected. All these methods, essentially conservative, are also highly arbitrary. They can be made somewhat more systematic, however, by sensitivity analysis in which length of life, for instance, is varied over a series of runs so that its impact on the project can be appraised.

Lessening uncertainty by hiking the interest or discount rate leads to greater difficulties, for the dominance of "higher" criteria over economic analysis is apparent in the frustrating problem of choosing the correct interest rate at which to discount the time streams of costs and benefits essential to the enterprise. Only an interest rate can establish the relationship between values at different periods of time. Yet people differ in preferences for the present versus the intermediate or long-run value. Moreover, the interest rate should also measure the opportunity cost of private capital that could be used to produce wealth elsewhere in the economy if it had not been used up in the form of tax income spent on the project under consideration. Is the appropriate rate the very low cost the government charges, the cost of a government corporation like TVA that must pay a somewhat higher rate, the going rate of interest for private firms, or an even higher rate to hedge against an uncertain future? As Otto Eckstein has observed, ". . . the choice of interest rates must remain a value judgment."[14]

If the efficiency of a project is insensitive to interest costs, then these costs can vary widely without mattering much. But Fox and Herfindahl discovered that if Corps of Engineer projects raised their interest (or discount) rate from 2⅝ to 4, 6, or 8 per cent, then 9, 64, and 80 per cent of their projects, respectively, would have had a benefit-cost ratio of less than unity.[15] This single value choice among many has such large consequences that it alone may be decisive.

THE MIXED RESULTS OF COST-BENEFIT ANALYSIS

Although cost-benefit analysis presumably results in efficiency by adding the most to national income, it is shot through with political and social value choices and surrounded by uncertainties and difficulties of computation. Whether the many non-economic assumptions and consequences actually result in basically changing the nature of a project remains moot. Clearly, we have come a long way from pure efficiency, to verge upon mixed efficiency.

Economic analysts usually agree that all relevant factors (especially non-market factors) cannot be squeezed into a single formula. They therefore suggest that the policy-maker, in being given the market costs and benefits of alternatives, is, in effect, presented with the market value he is placing on non-market factors. The contribution of the analyst is only one input into the decision, but the analyst may find this limited conception of his role unacceptable to others. Policy-makers may not want this kind of input; they may want *the* answer, or at least an answer that they can defend on the basis of the analyst's legitimized expertise.

The dependence of cost-benefit analysis on a prior political framework does not mean that it is a useless or trivial exercise. Decisions must be made. If quantifiable economic costs and benefits are not everything, neither would a decision-maker wish to ignore them entirely. The great advantage of cost-benefit analysis, when pursued with integrity, is that some implicit judgments are made explicit and subject to analysis. Yet, for many, the omission of explicit consideration of political factors is a serious deficiency.

The experience of the Soil Conservation Service in lowering certain political costs may prove illuminating. For many years the Service struggled along with eleven major watershed projects involving big dams, great headaches, and little progress. Because the watersheds were confined to a single region, it was exceedingly difficult to generate support in Congress, particularly at appropriations time. The upstream-downstream controversies generated by these projects resulted in less than universal local approval. The SCS found itself in the direct line of fire for determining priorities in use of insufficient funds.

Compare this situation with the breakthrough which occurred when SCS developed the small watershed program. Since each facility is relatively inexpensive, large numbers can be placed throughout the country, markedly increasing political support. Agreement on the local level is facilitated because much less land is flooded and side payments are easier to arrange. A judicious use of cost-benefit analysis, together with ingenious relationships with state governors, places the choice of priorities with the states and yet maintains a reasonable level of consistency by virtue of adherence to national criteria. Errors are easier to correct because the burden of calculation has been drastically reduced and experience may be more easily accumulated with a larger number of small projects.

Consider the situation in which an agency finds it desirable to achieve a geographical spread of projects in order to establish a wider base of support. Assume (with good reason) that cost-benefit criteria will not permit projects to be established in some states because the value of the land or water is too low. One can say that this is just too bad and observe the agency seeking ways around the restriction by playing up benefits, playing down costs, or attacking the whole benefit-cost concept as inapplicable. Another approach would be to recognize that federalism—meaning, realistically, the distribution of indulgences to state units—represents a political value worth promoting to some extent and that gaining nation-wide support is important. From this perspective, a compromise solution would be to except one or two projects in each state or region from meeting the full requirement of the formula, though the projects with the highest benefit-cost ratio would have to be chosen. In return for sacrificing full adherence to the formula in a few instances, one would get enhanced support for it in many others.

Everyone knows, of course, that cost-benefit analysis is not the messiah come to save water resources projects from contamination by the rival forces of ignorance and political corruption. Whenever agencies and their associated interests discover that they cannot do what they want, they may twist prevailing criteria out of shape: Two projects may be joined so that both qualify when one, standing alone, would not. Costs and benefits may be manipulated, or the categories may be so extended that almost any project qualifies. On the other hand, cost-benefit analysis has some "good" political uses that might be stressed more than they have been. The technique gives the responsible official a good reason for turning down projects, with a public-interest explanation the congressman can use with his constituents and the interest-group leader with his members.

This is not to say that cost-benefit analysis has little utility. Assuming that the method will continue to be improved, and that one accepts the market as the measure of economic value, it can certainly tell decision-makers something about what they will be giving up if they follow alternative policies. The use of two analyses, one based on regional and the other on national factors, might result in an appraisal of the economic costs of federalism.

The burden of calculation may be reduced by following cost-benefit analysis for many projects and introducing other values only for a few.

To expect, however, that the method itself (which distributes indulgences to some and deprivations to others) would not be subject to manipulation in the political process is to say that we shall be governed by formula and not by men.

Because the cost-benefit formula does not always jibe with political realities—that is, it omits political costs and benefits—we can expect it to be twisted out of shape from time to time. Yet cost-benefit analysis may still be important in getting rid of the worst projects. Avoiding the worst where one can't get the best is no small accomplishment.

SYSTEMS ANALYSIS

The good systems analyst is a "chochem," a Yiddish word meaning "wise man," with overtones of "wise guy." His forte is creativity. Although he sometimes relates means to ends and fits ends to match means, he ordinarily eschews such pat processes, preferring instead to relate elements imaginatively into new systems that create their own means and ends. He plays new objectives continuously against cost elements until a creative synthesis has been achieved. He looks down upon those who say that they take objectives as given, knowing full well that the apparent solidity of the objective will dissipate during analysis and that, in any case, most people do not know what they want because they do not know what they can get.

Since no one knows how to teach creativity, daring, and nerve, it is not surprising that no one can define what systems analysis is or how it should be practiced. E. S. Quade, who compiled the RAND Corporation lectures on systems analysis, says it "is still largely a form of art" in which it is not possible to lay down "fixed rules which need only be followed with exactness."[16] He examined systems studies to determine ideas and principles common to the good ones, but discovered that "no universally accepted set of ideas existed. It was even difficult to decide which studies should be called good."[17]

Systems analysis is derived from operations research, which came into use during World War II when some scientists discovered that they could use simple quantitative analysis to get the most out of existing military equipment. A reasonably clear objective was given, and ways to cut the cost of achieving it could be developed, using essentially statistical models. Operations research today is largely identified with specific techniques: linear programming; Monte Carlo (randomizing) methods; gaming and game theory. While there is no hard and fast division between operations research and systems analysis, a rough separation may perhaps be made. The less that is known about objectives, the more they conflict, the larger the number of elements to be considered, the more uncertain the environment, the more likely it is that the work will be called a systems analysis. In systems analysis there is more judgment and intuition and less reliance on quantitative methods than in operations research.

Systems analysis builds models that abstract from reality but represent the crucial relationships. The systems analyst first decides what questions are relevant to his inquiry, selects certain quantifiable factors, cuts down the list of factors to be dealt with by aggregation and by eliminating the (hopefully) less important ones, and then gives them quantitative relationships with one another within the system he has chosen for analysis. But crucial variables may not be quantifiable. If they can be reduced to numbers, there may be no mathematical function that can express the desired relationship. More important, there may be no single criterion for judging results among conflicting objectives. Most important the original objectives, if any, may not make sense.

It cannot be emphasized too strongly that a (if not the) distinguishing characteristic of systems analysis is that the objectives are either not known or are subject to change. Systems analysis, Quade tells us, "is associated with that class of problems where the difficulties lie in deciding what ought to be done—not simply how to do it—and honors go to people who . . . find out what the problem is"[18] Charles Hitch, the former Comptroller of the Defense Department, insists that:

> . . . *learning about objectives is one of the chief objects of this kind of analysis. We must learn to look at objectives as critically and as professionally as we look at our models and our other inputs. We may, of course, begin with tentative objectives, but we must expect to modify or replace them as we learn about the systems we are studying—and related systems. The feedback on objectives may in some cases be the most important result of our study. We have never undertaken a major system study at RAND in which we are able to define satisfactory objectives at the beginning of the study.*[19]

Systems analysts recognize many good reasons for their difficulties in defining problems or objectives. Quade reaches the core: "Objectives are not, in fact, agreed upon. The choice, while ostensibly between alternatives, is really between objectives or ends and non-analytic methods must be used for a final reconciliation of views."[20] It may be comforting to believe that objectives come to the analyst from on high and can be taken as given, but this easy assumption is all wrong. "For all sorts of good reasons that are not about to change," says Hitch, "official state-ments of national objectives (or company objectives) tend to be nonexis-tent or so vague and literary as to be non-operational."[21] Objectives are not only likely to be "thin and rarified," according to Wohlstetter, but the relevant authorities "are likely to conflict. Among others there will be national differences within an alliance and within the nation, inter-agency, interservice, and intraservice differences. . . ."[22]

Moreover, even shared objectives often conflict with one another. De-ference of atomic attack might be best served by letting an enemy know that we would respond with an all-out, indiscriminate attack on his population. Defense of our population against death and destruction might not be well served by this strategy,[23] as the Secretary of Defense recognized when he recommended a city-avoidance strategy that might give an enemy some incentive to spare our cities as well. Not only are objectives large in number and in conflict with one another, they are likely to engender serious repercussion effects. Many objectives, like mor-ale and the stability of alliances, are resistant to quantification. What is worth doing depends on whether it can be done at all, how well, and at what cost. Hence, objectives really cannot be taken as given; they must be made up by the analyst. "In fact," Wohlstetter declares, "we are al-ways in the process of choosing and modifying both means and ends."[24]

Future systems analysts are explicitly warned not to let clients deter-mine objectives. A suggestive analogy is drawn with the doctor who would not ignore a patient's "description of his symptoms, but . . . can-not allow the patient's self diagnosis to override his own professional judgment."[25] Quade argues that since systems analysis has often resulted in changing the original objectives of the policy-maker, it would be "self-defeating to accept without inquiry" his "view of what the problem is."[26]

I have stressed the point that the systems analyst is advised to insist on his own formulation of the problem because it shows so closely that we are dealing with a mixed concept of efficiency.

Adjusting objectives to resources in the present or near future is difficult enough without considering future states of affairs which hold tremendous uncertainty. Constants become variables; little can be taken for granted. The rate of technological progress, an opponent's estimate of your reaction to his latest series of moves based on his reaction to yours, whether or not atomic war will occur, what it will be like, wheth-er we shall have warning, whether the system we are working on will cost anything close to current estimates and whether it will be ready within five years of the due date—on most of these matters, there are no objective probabilities to be calculated.

An effective dealing with uncertainty must be a major goal of systems analysis. Systems analysis is characterized by the aids to calculation it uses, not to conquer, but to circumvent and mitigate some of the pervasive effects of uncertainty. Before a seemingly important factor may be omitted, for example, a sensitivity analysis may be run to determine whether its variation significantly affects the outcome. If there is no good basis for calculating the value of the factor, arbitrary values may be assigned to test for extreme possibilities. Contingency analysis is used to determine how the relative ranking of alternatives holds up under major changes in the environment, say, a new alliance between France and Russia, or alterations in the criteria for judging the alternatives, such as a requirement that a system work well against attacks from space as well as earth. Contingency analysis places a premium on versatility as the analyst seeks a system that will hold up well under various eventualities even though it might be quite as good for any single contingency as an alternative system. Adversary procedures may be used to combat uncertainty. Bending over backwards to provide advantages for low-ranking systems and handicaps for high-ranking systems is called *a fortiori* analysis. Changing crucial assumptions in order to make the leading alternatives even, so that one can judge whether the assumptions are overly optimistic or pessimistic, is called break-even analysis.[27] Since all these methods add greatly to the burden of calculation, they must be used with some discretion.

A variety of insurance schemes may also be used to deal with uncertainty. In appraising what an opponent can do, for instance, one can assume the worst, the best, and sheer inertia. In regard to the development of weapons, insurance requires not one flexible weapon but a variety of alternatives pursued with vigor. As development goes on, uncertainty is reduced. Consequently, basic strategic choice involves determining how worthwhile paying for the additional information is by developing rival weapons systems to the next stage. The greater the uncertainty of the world, the greater the desirability of having the widest selection of alternative weapons to choose from to meet unexpected threats and opportunities. Alchian and Kessel are so wedded to the principle of diversified investment that they "strongly recommend this theorem as a basic part of systems analysis."[28]

As a form of calculation, systems analysis represents a merger of quantitative methods and rules of thumb. First, the analyst attempts to solve the problem before he knows a great deal about it. Then he continuously alters his initial solution to get closer to what he intuitively feels ought to be wanted. Means and ends are continuously played off against one another. New objectives are defined, new assumptions made, new models constructed, until a creative amalgam appears that hopefully defines a second best solution, one that is better than others even if not optimal in any sense. In the famous study of the location of military bases conducted by Albert Wohlstetter and his associates at the RAND Corporation, widely acknowledged as a classic example of systems analysis, Wohlstetter writes:

The base study . . . proceeded by a method of successive approximations. It compared forces for their efficiency in carrying a payload between the bases and targets without opposition either by enemy interceptors or enemy bombers. Then, it introduced obstacles successively: first, enemy defenses; then enemy bombardment of our bombers and other elements needed to retaliate. In essence, then, the alternative systems were tested for their first-strike capability and then they were compared for their second-strike capacity. And the programmed system performed in a drastically different way, depending on the order in which the opposing side struck. In the course of analyzing counter-measures and counter-counter-measures, the enemy bombardment turned out to be a dominant problem. This was true even for a very much improved overseas operating base system. The refueling base system was very much less sensitive to strike order. It is only the fact that strike order made such a difference among systems contemplated that gave the first-strike, second-strike distinction an interest. And it was not known in advance of the analysis that few of the programmed bombers would have survived to encounter the problem of penetrating enemy defenses which had previously been taken as the main obstacle. The analysis, then, not only was affected by the objectives considered, it affected them.[29]

The advantage of a good systems study is that by running the analysis through in theory on paper certain disadvantages of learning from experience may be avoided.

If the complexity of the problems encountered proved difficult in cost-benefit analysis, the burdens of calculation are ordinarily much greater in systems analysis. Many aspects of a problem simply must be put aside. Only a few variables can be considered simultaneously. "Otherwise," Roland McKean tells us, "the models would become impossibly cumbersome, and . . . the number of calculations to consider would mount in the thousands."[30] Formulas that include everything may appear more satisfactory but those that cannot be reduced "to a single expression are likely to convey no meaning at all. . . ."[31] Summing up their experience, Hitch and McKean assert that:

. . . analyses must be piecemeal, since it is impossible for a single analysis to cover all problems of choice simultaneously in a large organization. Thus comparisons of alternative courses of action always pertain to a part of the government's (or corporation's) problem. Other parts of the over-all problem are temporarily put aside, possible decisions about some matters being ignored, specific decisions about others being taken for granted. The resulting analyses are intended to provide assistance in finding optimal, or at least good, solutions to sub-problems: in the jargon of systems and operations research, they are sub-optimizations.[32]

Although admitting that much bad work is carried on and that inordinate love of numbers and machines often get in the way of creative work,[33] practitioners of systems analysis believe in their art. "All of them point out how the use of analysis can provide some of the knowledge needed, how it may sometime serve as a substitute for experience, and, most importantly, how it can work to sharpen intuition."[34] Systems analysis can increase explicitness about the assumptions made and about exclusions from the analysis. The claim is that systems analysis can be perfected; sheer intuition or unaided judgment can never be perfect.

Yet there is also wide agreement that systems analysts "do philosophy,"[35] that they are advocates of particular policy alternatives. What Schelling calls "the pure role of expert advisor" is not available for the analyst who "must usually formulate the questions themselves for his clients."[36] Beyond that, Wohlstetter argues that systems analysts can perform the function of integrating diverse values. New systems can sometimes be found that meet diverse objectives.[37] The politician who gains his objectives by inventing policies that also satisfy others, or the leader of a coalition who searches out areas of maximum agreement, performs a kind of informal systems analysis.

All these men, however, work within the existing political structure. While cost-benefit analysis may contain within it implicit changes in existing governmental policies, it poses no direct challenge to the general decision-making machinery of the political system. Program budgeting is a form of systems analysis that attempts to break out of these confines.

PROGRAM BUDGETING

It is always important, and perhaps especially so in economics, to avoid being swept off one's feet by the fashions of the moment.[38]

So this new system will identify our national goals with precision . . .[39]

On August 25, 1965, President Johnson announced that he was asking the heads of all federal agencies to introduce "a very new and revolutionary system" of program budgeting. Staffs of experts set up in each agency would define goals using "modern methods of program analysis." Then the "most effective and the least costly" way to accomplish these goals would be found.[40]

Program budgeting has no standard definition. The general idea is that budgetary decisions should be made by focusing on output categories like governmental goals, objectives, end products or programs instead of inputs like personnel, equipment, and maintenance. As in cost-benefit analysis, to which it owes a great deal, program budgeting lays stress on estimating the total financial cost of accomplishing objectives. What is variously called cost-effectiveness or cost-utility analysis is employed in order to select "alternative approaches to the achievement of a benefit already determined to be worth achieving."[41]

Not everyone would go along with the most far-reaching implications of program budgeting, but the RAND Corporation version, presumably exported from the Defense Department, definitely does include "institutional reorganization to bring relevant administrative functions under the jurisdiction of the authority making the final program decisions." In any event, there would be "information reporting systems and shifts in the power structure to the extent necessary to secure compliance with program decisions by the agencies responsible for their execution."[42] Sometimes it appears that comprehensiveness—simultaneous and complete examination of all programs and all alternatives to programs every year—is being advocated. Actually, comprehensiveness has been dropped (though not without regret) because "it may be too costly in time, effort, uncertainty, and confusion."[43] There exists considerable ambivalence as to whether decisions are implicit in the program categories or merely provide information to improve the judgment of governmental officials.

Programs are not made in heaven. There is nothing out there that is just waiting to be found. Programs are not natural to the world; they must be imposed on it by men. No one can give instructions for making up programs. There are as many ways to conceive of programs as there are of organizing activity,[44] as the comments of the following writers eloquently testify:

It is by no means obvious . . . whether a good program structure should be based on components of specific end objectives (e.g., the accomplishment of certain land reclamation targets), on the principle of cost separation (identifying as a program

any activity the costs of which can be readily segregated), on the separation of
means and ends (Is education a means or an end in a situation such as skill-
retraining courses for workers displaced by automation?), or on some artificially
designed pattern that draws from all these and other classification criteria.[45]

Just what categories constitute the most useful programs and program elements is
far from obvious . . . If one puts all educational activities into a broad package of
educational programs, he cannot simultaneously include school lunch programs or
physical education activities in a Health Program, or include defense educational
activities (such as the military academies) in the Defense Program. . . . In short,
precisely how to achieve a rational and useful structure for a program budget is not
yet evident.[46]

In much current discussion it seems to be taken for granted that transportation is
a natural program category. But that conclusion is by no means obvious.[47] *A first*
question one might ask is whether, given their nature, health activities merit a
separate, independent status in a program budget. The question arises because these
activities often are constituents of, or inputs into, other activities whose purpose or
goal orientation is the dominating one. Outlays by the Department of Defense for
hospital care, for example, though they assist in maintaining the health of one
segment of the population, are undertaken on behalf of national defense, and the
latter is their justification.[48]

The difficulties with the program concept are illustrated in the space
program. A first glance suggests that space projects are ideally suited for
program budgeting because they appear as physical systems designed to
accomplish different missions. Actually, there is a remarkable degree of
interdependence between different missions and objectives—pride, scientific research, space exploration, military uses, etc.—so that it is impossible to apportion costs on a proper basis. Consider the problem of a
rocket developed for one mission and useful for others. To apportion
costs to each new mission is purely arbitrary. To allocate the cost to the
first mission and regard the rocket as a free good for all subsequent missions is ludicrous. The only remotely reasonable alternative—making a
separate program out of the rocket itself—does violence to the concept of
programs as end products. The difficulty is compounded because the facilities that have multiple uses like boosters and tracking networks tend to
be very expensive compared to the items that are specific to a particular
mission.[49] Simple concepts of programs evaporate upon inspection.

Political realities lie behind the failure to devise principles for defining
programs. As Melvin Anshen puts it, "The central issue is, of course,
nothing less than the definition of the ultimate objectives of the Federal

government as they are realized through operational decisions." The arrangement of the programs inevitably affects the specific actions taken to implement them. "Set in this framework," Anshen continues, "the designation of a schedule of programs may be described as building a bridge between a matter of political philosophy (what is government for?) and . . . assigning scarce resources among alternative governmental objectives."[50]

Because program budgeting is a form of systems analysis (and uses a form of cost-benefit analysis), the conditions that hinder or facilitate its use have largely been covered in the previous sections. The simpler the problem, the fewer the interdependencies, the greater the ability to measure the consequences of alternatives on a common scale, the more costs and benefits that are valued in the market place, the better the chances of making effective use of programs. Let us take transportation to illustrate some of the conditions in a specific case.

Investments in transportation are highly interdependent on one another (planes versus cars versus trains versus barges, etc.) and with decisions regarding the regional location of industry and the movements of population. In view of the powerful effects of transportation investment on regional employment, income, and competition with other modes of transport, it becomes necessary to take these factors into account. The partial equilibrium model of efficiency in the narrow sense becomes inappropriate and a general equilibrium model of the economy must be used. The combination of aggregative models at the economy-wide level and inter-region and inter-industry models that this approach requires is staggering. It is precisely the limited and partial character of cost-effectiveness analyses, taking so much for granted and eliminating many variables, that make them easy to work with for empirical purposes. Furthermore, designing a large-scale transportation system involves so close a mixture of political and economic considerations that it is not possible to disentangle them. The Interstate Highway Program, for example, involved complex bargaining among federal, state, and local governments and reconciliation of many conflicting interests. The development of certain "backward" regions, facilitating the movement of defense supplies, redistribution of income, creating countervailing power against certain monopolies, not to mention the political needs of public officials, were all involved. While cost-utility exercises might help with small segments of the problem, J. R. Meyer concludes that: "Given the complexity of the political and economic decisions involved, and the emphasis on designing a geographically consistent system, it probably would be difficult to improve on the congressional process as a means of developing such a program in an orderly and systematic way."[51]

On one condition for effective use—reorganization of the federal government to centralize authority for wide-ranging programs—proponents of program budgeting are markedly ambivalent. The problem is that responsibility for programs is now scattered throughout the whole federal establishment and decentralized to state and local authorities as well. In the field of health, for example, expenditures are distributed among at least twelve agencies and six departments outside of Health, Education, and Welfare. A far greater number of organizations are concerned with American activities abroad, with natural resources and with education. The multiple jurisdictions and overlapping responsibilities do violence to the concept of comprehensive and consistent programs. It "causes one to doubt," Marvin Frankel writes, "whether there can exist in the administrative echelons the kind of overall perspective that would seem indispensible if Federal health resources are to be rationally allocated."[52] To G. A. Steiner it is evident that "The present 'chest of drawers' type of organization cannot for long be compatible with program budgeting."[53] W. Z. Hirsch declares that "if we are to have effective program budgeting of natural resources activities, we shall have to provide for new institutional arrangements."[54] Yet the inevitable resistance to wholesale reorganization would be so great that, if it were deemed essential, it might well doom the enterprise. Hence, the hope is expressed that translation grids or crossover networks could be used to convert program budget decisions back into the usual budget categories in the usual agencies. That is what is done in Defense, but that department has the advantage of having most of the activities it is concerned with under the Secretary's jurisdiction. Some program analysts believe that this solution will not do.

Recognizing that a conversion scheme is technically feasible, Anshen is aware that there are "deeply frustrating" issues to be resolved. "The heart of the problem is the fact that the program budget in operation should not be a mere statistical game. Great strategic importance will attach to both the definition of program structure and content and the establishment of specific program objectives (including magnitude, timing, and cost.)"[55] The implications of program budgeting, however, go far beyond specific policies.

It will be useful to distinguish between policy politics (which policy will be adopted?), partisan politics (which political party will win office?), and system politics (how will decision structures be set up?).

Program budgeting is manifestly concerned with policy politics, and not much with partisan politics, although it could have important consequences for issues that divide the nation's parties. *My contention is that the thrust of program budgeting makes it an integral part of system politics.*

As presently conceived, program budgeting contains an extreme centralizing bias. Power is to be centralized in the Presidency (through the Budget Bureau) at the national level, in super-departments rather than bureaus within the executive branch, and in the federal government as a whole instead of state or local governments. Note how W. Z. Hirsch assumes the desirability of national dominance when he writes: "These methods of analysis can guide Federal officials in the responsibility of bringing local education decisions into closer harmony with national objectives."[56] G. A. Steiner observes that comprehensiveness may be affected by unrestricted federal grants-in-aid to the states because "such a plan would remove a substantial part of Federal expenditures from a program budgeting system of the Federal government."[57] Should there be reluctance on the part of state and local officials to employ the new tools, Anshen states "that the Federal government may employ familiar incentives to accelerate this progress."[58] Summing it up, Hirsch says that "It appears doubtful that a natural resources program budget would have much impact without a good deal of centralization."[59]

Within the great federal organizations designed to encompass the widest ramifications of basic objectives, there would have to be strong executives. Cutting across the sub-units of the organization, as is the case in the Department of Defense, the program budget could only be put together by the top executive. A more useful tool for increasing his power to control decisions vis-a-vis his subordinates would be hard to find.[60]

Would large-scale program budgeting benefit the Chief Executive? President Johnson's support of program budgeting could in part stem from his desire to appear frugal and also be directed at increasing his control of the executive branch by centralizing decisions in the Bureau of the Budget. In the case of foreign affairs, it is not at all clear whether it would be preferable to emphasize country teams, with the budget made by the State Department to encompass activities of the other federal agencies abroad, or to let Commerce, Agriculture, Defense, and other agencies include their foreign activities in their own budgets. Program budgeting will unleash great struggles of this kind in Washington. An especially intriguing possibility is that the Bureau of the Budget might prefer to let the various agencies compete, with the bureau coordinating (that is, controlling) these activities through a comprehensive foreign affairs program devised only at the presidential level.

Yet is it not entirely clear that presidents would welcome all the implications of program budgeting. It is well and good to talk about long-range planning; it is another thing to tie a president's hands by committing him in advance for five years of expenditures. Looking ahead is fine but not if it means that a president cannot negate the most extensive planning efforts on grounds that seem sufficient to him.[61] He may wish to trade some program budgeting for some political support.

In any event, that all decisions ought to be made by the most central person in the most centralized body capable of grabbing hold of them is difficult to justify on scientific grounds. We see what has happened. First pure efficiency was converted to mixed efficiency. Then limited efficiency became unlimited. Yet the qualifications of efficiency experts for political systems analysis are not evident.[62]

We would be in a much stronger position to predict the consequences of program budgeting if we knew (a) how far toward a genuine program budget the Defense Department has gone and (b) whether the program budget has fulfilled its promise. To the best of my knowledge, not a single study of this important experiment was undertaken (or at least published) before the decision was made to spread it around the land. On the surface, only two of the nine program categories used in the Defense Department appear to be genuine programs in the sense of pointing to end purposes or objectives. Although strategic retaliation and continental defense appear to be distinct programs, it is difficult to separate them conceptually; my guess is that they are, in fact, considered together. The third category—general purpose forces—is presumably designed to deal with (hopefully) limited war anywhere in the world. According to Arthur Smithies, "The threat is not clearly defined and neither are the requirements for meeting it. Clearly this program is of a very different character from the other two and does not lend itself as readily to analysis in terms either of its components or of its specific contribution to defense objectives."[63]

What about the program called airlift and sealift? These activities support the general purpose forces. Research and development is carried on presumably to serve other defense objectives, and the same is true for the reserve forces.

No doubt the elements that make up the programs comprise the real action focus of the budget, but these may look less elegant when spread into thousands of elements than they do in nine neat rows. When one hears that hundreds of program elements are up for decision at one time,[64] he is entitled to some skepticism about how much genuine analysis can go into all of them. Part of the argument for program budgeting was that by thinking ahead and working all year around it would be possible to consider changes as they came up and avoid the usual last minute funk. Both Hitch[65] and Novick[66] (the RAND Corporation expert on defense budgeting) report, however, that this has not worked out. The services hesitate to submit changes piecemeal, and the Secretary wants to see what he is getting into before he acts. The vaunted five-year plans are still in force but their efficacy in determining yearly decisions remains to be established.

One good operational test would be to know whether the department's systems analysts actually use the figures from the five-year plans in their work or whether they go to the services for the real stuff. Another test would be whether or not the later years of the five year projections turn out to have any future significance, or whether the battle is really over the next year that is to be scooped out as part of the budget. From a distance, it appears that the services have to work much harder to justify what they are doing. Since McNamara's office must approve changes in defense programs, and he can insist on documentation, he is in a strong position to improve thinking at the lower levels. The intensity of conflict within the Defense Department may not have changed, but it may be that the disputants are or will in the future be likely to shout at a much more sophisticated level. How much this is due to McNamara himself, to his insistence on quantitative estimates, or to the analytic advantages of a program budget cannot be determined now. It is clear that a program budget, of which he alone is master, has helped impose his will on the Defense Department.

It should also be said that there are many notable differences between decision-making in defense and domestic policy that would render suspect the transmission of procedures from one realm to the other. The greater organizational unity of Defense, the immensely large amounts of money at stake, the extraordinarily greater risks involved, the inability to share more than minimal values with opponents, the vastly different array of interests and perceptions of the proper roles of the participants, are but a few of the factors involved.

The Armed Services and Appropriations Committees in the defense area, for example, are normally most reluctant to substitute their judgment on defense for that of the President and the Secretary of the Department. They do not conceive it to be their role to make day-to-day defense policy, and they are apparently unwilling to take on the burden of decision. They therefore accept a budget presentation based on cavernous program categories even though these are so arranged that it is impossible to make a decision on the basis of them. If they were to ask for and to receive the discussion of alternative actions contained in the much smaller program elements on which McNamara bases his decisions, they would be in a position to take the Department of Defense away from its Secretary.

There is no reason whatsoever to believe that a similar restraint would be shown by committees that deal with domestic policies. It is at least possible that the peculiar Planning, Programming, and Budgeting System adopted in Defense could not be repeated elsewhere in the federal establishment.

POLITICAL RATIONALITY

Political rationality is the fundamental kind of reason, because it deals with the preservation and improvement of decision structures, and decision structures are the source of all decisions. Unless a decision structure exists, no reasoning and no decisions are possible. . . . There can be no conflict between political rationality and . . . technical, legal, social, or economic rationality, because the solution of political problems makes possible an attack on any other problem, while a serious political deficiency can prevent or undo all other problem solving. . . . Non-political decisions are reached by considering a problem in its own terms, and by evaluating proposals according to how well they solve the problem. The best available proposal should be accepted regardless of who makes it or who opposes it, and a faulty proposal should be rejected or improved no matter who makes it. Compromise is always irrational; the rational procedure is to determine which proposal is the best, and to accept it. In a political decision, on the other hand, action never is based on the merits of a proposal but always on who makes it and who opposes it. Action should be designed to avoid complete identification with any proposal and any point of view, no matter how good or how popular it might be. The best available proposal should never be accepted just because it is best; it should be deferred, objected to, discussed, until major opposition disappears. Compromise is always a rational procedure, even when the compromise is between a good and a bad proposal.[67]

We are witnessing the beginning of significant advances in the art and science of economizing. Having given up the norm of comprehensiveness, economizers are able to join quantitative analysis with aids to calculation of the kind described by Lindblom in his strategy of disjointed incrementalism.[68]

Various devices are employed to simplify calculations. Important values are omitted entirely; others are left to different authorities to whose care they have been entrusted. Here, sensitivity analysis represents an advance because it provides an empirical basis to justify neglect of some values. Means and ends are hopelessly intertwined.

The real choice is between rival policies that encapsulate somewhat different mixes of means and ends. Analysis proceeds incrementally by successive limited approximations. It is serial and remedial as successive attacks are made on problems. Rather than waiting upon experience in the real world, the analyst tries various moves in his model and runs them through to see if they work. When all else fails, the analyst may try an integrative solution reconciling a variety of values to some degree, though meeting none of them completely. He is always ready to settle for the second or third best, provided only that it is better than the going policy. Constrained by diverse limiting assumptions, weakened by deficiencies in technique, rarely able to provide unambiguous measures, the systems, cost-benefit, and program analyst is nonetheless getting better at calculating in the realm of efficiency. Alas, he is an imperialist at heart.

In the literature discussed above there appears several times the proposition that "the program budget is a neutral tool. It has no politics."[69] In truth, the program budget is suffused with policy politics, makes up a small part of President Johnson's partisan politics, and tends toward system politics. How could men account for so foolish a statement? It must be that they who make it identify program budgeting with something good and beautiful, and politics with another thing bad and ugly. McKean and Anshen speak of politics in terms of "pressure and expedient adjustments," "haphazard acts . . . unresponsive to a planned analysis of the needs of efficient decision design." From the political structure they expect only "resistance and opposition, corresponding to the familiar human disposition to protect established seats of power and procedures made honorable by the mere facts of existence and custom."[70] In other places we hear of "vested interests," "wasteful duplication," "special interest groups," and the "Parkinson syndrome."[71]

Not so long ago less sophisticated advocates of reform ignored the political realm. Now they denigrate it. And, since there must be a structure for decision, it is smuggled in as a mere adjunct of achieving efficiency. Who is to blame if the economic tail wags the political dog? It seems unfair to blame the evangelical economizer for spreading the gospel of efficiency. If economic efficiency turns out to be the one true religion, maybe it is because its prophets could so easily conquer.

It is hard to find men who take up the cause of political rationality, who plead the case for political man, and who are primarily concerned with the laws that enable the political machinery to keep working. One is driven to a philosopher like Paul Diesing to find the case for the political:

> . . . the political problem is always basic and prior to the others. . . . This means that any suggested course of action must be evaluated first by its effects on the political structure. A course of action which corrects economic or social deficiencies but increases political difficulties must be rejected, while an action which contributes to political improvement is desirable even if it is not entirely sound from an economic or social standpoint.[72]

There is hardly a political scientist who would claim half as much. The desire to invent decision structures to facilitate the achievement of economic efficiency does not suggest a full appreciation of their proper role by students of politics.

A major task of the political system is to specify goals or objectives. It is impermissible to treat goals as if they were known in advance. "Goals" may well be the product of interaction among key participants rather than some "deus ex machina" or (to use Bentley's term) some "spook" which posits values in advance of our knowledge of them. Certainly, the operational objectives of the Corps of Engineers in the Water Resources field could hardly be described in terms of developing rivers and harbors.

Once the political process becomes a focus of attention, it is evident that the principal participants may not be clear about their goals. What we call goals or objectives may, in large part, be operationally determined by the policies we can agree upon. The mixtures of values found in complex policies may have to be taken in packages, so that policies may determine goals at least as much as general objectives determine policies. In a political situation, then, the need for support assumes central importance. Not simply the economic, but the *political* costs and benefits turn out to be crucial.

A first attempt to specify what is meant by political costs may bring closer an understanding of the range of requirements for political rationality.[73] Exchange costs are incurred by a political leader when he needs the support of other people to get a policy adopted. He has to pay for this assistance by using up resources in the form of favors (patronage, log-rolling) or coercive moves (threats or acts to veto or remove from office). By supporting a policy and influencing others to do the same, a politician antagonizes some people and may suffer their retaliation. If these hostility costs mount, they may turn into re-election costs—actions that decrease his chances (or those of his friends) of being elected or re-elected to office. Election costs, in turn, may become policy costs through inability to command the necessary formal powers to accomplish the desired policy objectives.

In the manner of Neustadt, we may also talk about reputation costs, i.e. not only loss of popularity with segments of the electorate, but also loss of esteem and effectiveness with other participants in the political system and loss of ability to secure policies other than the one immediately under consideration. Those who continually urge a president to go all out—that is, use all his resources on a wide range of issues—rarely stop to consider that the price of success in one area of policy may be defeat in another. If he loses popularity with the electorate, as President Truman did, Congress may destroy almost the whole of his domestic program. If he cracks down on the steel industry, as President Kennedy did, he may find himself constrained to lean over backwards in the future to avoid unremitting hostility from the business community.

A major consequence of incurring exchange and hostility costs may be undesirable power-redistribution effects. The process of getting a policy adopted or implemented may increase the power of various individuals, organizations and social groups, which later will be used against the political leader. The power of some participants may be weakened so that the political leader is unable to enjoy their protection.

The legitimacy of the political system may be threatened by costs that involve the weakening of customary political restraints. Politicians who try to suppress opposition, or who practice election frauds, may find similar tactics being used against them. The choice of a highly controversial policy may raise the costs of civic discord. Although the people involved may not hate the political leader, the fact that they hate each other may lead to consequences contrary to his desires.

The literature of economics usually treats organizations and institutions as if they were costless entities. The standard procedure is to consider rival alternatives (in consideration of price policy or other criteria), calculate the differences in cost and achievement among them, and show that one is more or less efficient than another. This typical way of thinking is sometimes mis-specified. If the costs of pursuing a policy are strictly economic and can be calculated directly in the market place, then the procedure should work well. But if the costs include getting one or another organization to change its policies or procedures, then these costs must also be taken into account.[74] Perhaps there are legal, psychological, or other impediments that make it either impossible or difficult for the required changes to be made. Or the changes may require great effort and result in incurring a variety of other costs. In considering a range of alternatives, one is measuring not only efficiency but also the cost of change.

Studies based on efficiency criteria are much needed and increasingly useful. My quarrel is not with them as such, at all. I have been concerned that a single value, however important, could triumph over other values without explicit consideration being given these others. I would feel much better if political rationality were being pursued with the same vigor and capability as is economic efficiency. In that case I would have fewer qualms about extending efficiency studies into the decision-making apparatus.

My purpose has not been to accuse economizers of doing what comes naturally. Rather, I have sought to emphasize that economic rationality, however laudible in its own sphere, ought not to swallow up political rationality—but will do so, if political rationality continues to lack trained and adept defenders.

NOTES:

The paper, written while the author was a Research Political Scientist at the Center for Planning and Development Research, University of California, Berkeley, was originally presented at a conference on public policy sponsored by the Social Science Research Council.
Credits from the author: I am more than ordinarily indebted to the people who have improved this paper through their comments. Win Crowther, John Harsanyi, John Krutilla, Arthur Maass, Arnold Meltsner, Nelson Polsby, William Riker, and Dwight Waldo saved me from errors and contributed insights of their own. The responsibility for what is said is entirely my own.
[1]A. R. Prest and R. Turvey, "Cost-Benefit Analysis: A Survey," *The Economic Journal,* Vol. LXXV (December, 1965), 683–735. I am much indebted to this valuable and discerning survey. I have also relied upon:

Otto Eckstein, "A Survey of the Theory of Public Expenditure Criteria," in *Public Finances: Needs, Sources, and Utilization,* National Bureau of Economic Research (New York: Princeton University Press, 1961), pp. 439–504.

Irving K. Fox and Orris C. Herfindahl, "Attainment of Efficiency in Satisfying Demands for Water Resources," *American Economic Review,* May, 1964, pp. 198–206.

Charles J. Hitch, *On the Choice of Objectives in Systems Studies* (Santa Monica, Calif.: The RAND Corporation, 1960).

John V. Krutilla, "Is Public Intervention in Water Resources Development Conducive to Economic Efficiency?" *National Resources Journal,* January, 1966, pp. 60–75.

John V. Krutilla and Otto Eckstein, *Multiple Purpose River Development* (Baltimore: Johns Hopkins Press, 1958).

Roland N. McKean, *Efficiency in Government Through Systems Analysis with Emphasis on Water Resources Development,* (New York: John Wiley & Sons, Inc. 1958).

[2]Prest and Turvey, *ibid.,* p. 686.

[3]In many important areas of policy such as national defense it is not possible to value the product directly in the market place. Since benefits cannot be valued in the same way as costs, it is necessary to resort to a somewhat different type of analysis. Instead of cost-benefit analysis, therefore, the work is usually called cost-effectiveness or cost-utility analysis.

[4]A. Bergson, "A Reformulation of Certain Aspects of Welfare Economics," *Quarterly Journal of Economics,* February, 1938; N. Kaldor, "Welfare Propositions and Interpersonal Comparisons of Utility," *Economic Journal,* 1939, pp. 549–52; J. R. Hicks, "The Valuation of Social Income," *Economica,* 1940, pp. 105–24; I.M.D. Little, *A Critique of Welfare Economics,* (Oxford: Clarendon Press, 1950), W. J. Baumol, *Welfare Economics and the Theory of the State* (Cambridge, Mass.: 1952), T. Scitovsky, "A Note on Welfare Propositions in Economics," *Review of Economic Studies,* 1942, pp. 98–110; J. E. Meade, *The Theory of International Economic Policy,* Vol. II; *Trade and Welfare* (London: Oxford University Press, 1955).

[5]For a different view, see James M. Buchanan and Gordon Tullock, *The Calculus of Consent: Logical Foundations of Constitutional Democracy* (Ann Arbor: University of Michigan Press, 1962).

[6]Prest and Turvey, *op. cit.,* p. 702. For a contrary view, see Arthur Maass, "Benefit-Cost Analysis: Its Relevance to Public Investment Deci-

sions," *The Quarterly Journal of Economics,* Vol. LXXX (May, 1966), 208–226.

[7]Irving K. Fox and Orris C. Herfindahl, "Attainment of Efficiency in Satisfying Demands for Water Resources," *American Economic Review,* May, 1964, p. 200.

[8]Prest and Turvey, *Op. Cit.,* p. 727.

[9]*Ibid.,* pp. 729, 731.

[10]David Braybrooke and Charles Lindblom, *A Strategy for Decision* (New York: The Free Press, 1963).

[11]Prest and Turvey, op. cit., p. 714.

[12]*Ibid,* p. 705.

[13]See Jack L. Knetch, "Economics of Including Recreation as a Purpose of Water Resource Projects," *Journal of Farm Economics,* December, 1964, p. 1155. No one living in Berkeley, where "a view" is part of the cost of housing, could believe that aesthetic values are forever going to remain beyond the ingenuity of the quantifier.

There are also costs and benefits, such as the saving and losing of human life, that can be quantified but can only be valued in the market place in a most peculiar (or ghoulish) sense. See Burton Weisbrod, *The Economics of Public Health; Measuring the Economic Impact of Diseases* (Philadelphia: University of Pennsylvania Press, 1961), for creative attempt to place a market value on human life. Few of us would want to make decisions about public health by use of this criterion, not at least if we were the old person whose future social value contribution is less than his cost to the authorities.

[14]Otto Eckstein, *op. cit.,* p. 460.

[15]Fox and Herfindahl, *op. cit.,* p. 202.

[16]E.S. Quade, (ed.) *Analysis for Military Decisions* (Chicago: Rand McNally, 1964), p. 153.

[17]*Ibid.,* p. 149.

[18]*Ibid.,* p. 7.

[19]Charles J. Hitch, *op. cit.,* p. 19.

[20]E.S. Quade, *op. cit.,* p. 176.

[21]Charles J. Hitch, *op. cit.,* pp. 4–5.

[22]Albert Wohlstetter, "Analysis and Design of Conflict Systems," in E.S. Quade, *op. cit.,* p. 121.

[23]See Glenn H. Snyder, *Deterrence and Defense* (Princeton: Princeton University Press, 1961).

[24]Wohlstetter in Quade, *op. cit.,* p. 122.

[25]E. S. Quade, *op. cit.,* p. 157. Quade attempts to soften the blow by saying that businessmen and military officers know more about their business than any one else. But the import of the analogy is clear enough.

[26]*Ibid.,* pp. 156–57.

[27]Herman Kahn and Irwin Mann, *Techniques of Systems Analysis* (Santa Monica: The RAND Corporation, 1957), believe that: "More than any single thing, the skilled use of a fortiori and break-even analyses separate the professionals from the amateurs." They think that convincing others that you have a good solution is as important as coming up with one.

[28]Armen A. Alchian and Reuben A. Kessel, *A Proper Role of Systems Analysis* (Santa Monica: RAND Corporation, 1954), p. 9.

[29]Albert Wohlstetter in E. S. Quade, *op. cit.,* pp. 125–26.

[30]R. N. McKean, "Criteria," in E. S. Quade, *op. cit.,* p. 83.

[31]E. S. Quade, *op. cit.,* p. 310.

[32]Charles J. Hitch and Roland N. McKean, *The Economics of Defense in the Nuclear Age* (Cambridge, Mass.: Harvard University Press, 1961), p. 161.

[33]See Hitch on "Mechanitis-putting . . . machines to work as a substitute for hard thinking." Charles Hitch, "Economics and Operations Research: A Symposium, II," *Review of Economics and Statistics,* August, 1958, p. 209.

[34]E. S. Quade, *op. cit.,* p. 12.

[35]*Ibid.,* p. 5.

[36]T. C. Schelling, "Economics and Operations Research: A Symposium. V. Comment," *Review of Economics and Statistics,* August, 1958, p. 222.

[37]Albert Wohlstetter in E. S. Quade, *op. cit.,* p. 122.

[38]Prest and Turvey, *op. cit.,* p. 684.

[39]David Novick, Editor, *Program Budgeting* (Cambridge, Mass.: Harvard University Press, 1965), p. vi.

[40]*Ibid.,* pp. v–vi.

[41]Alan Dean, quoted in D. Novick, *ibid.,* p. 311.

[42]R.N. McKean and M. Anshen in D. Novick, *ibid.,* pp. 286–87. The authors say that this aspect of program budgeting is part of the general view adopted in the book as a whole.

[43]Arthur Smithies in *ibid.,* p. 45.

[44]A look at the classic work by Luther Gulick and Lyndall Urwick, *Papers on the Science of Administration* (New York: Columbia University

Press, 1937), reveals considerable similarity between their suggested bases of organization and ways of conceptualizing programs.

[45]M. Anshen in D. Novick, *op. cit.,* pp. 19–20.

[46]G. A. Steiner in *ibid.,* p. 356.

[47]A. Smithies in *ibid.,* p. 41.

[48]Marvin Frankel in *ibid.,* pp. 219–220. I have forborne citing the author who promises exciting discussion of the objectives of American education and ends up with fascinating program categories like primary, secondary, and tertiary education.

[49]See the excellent chapter by M. A. Margolis and S. M. Barro, *ibid.,* pp. 120–145.

[50]*Ibid.,* p. 18.

[51]J. R. Meyer in *ibid.,* p. 170. This paragraph is based on my interpretation of his work.

[52]M. Frankel, *ibid.,* p. 237.

[53]*Ibid.,* p. 348.

[54]*Ibid.,* p. 280.

[55]*Ibid.,* pp. 358–59.

[56]*Ibid.,* p. 206.

[57]*Ibid.,* p. 347.

[58]*Ibid.,* p. 365.

[59]*Ibid.,* p. 280.

[60]See my comments to this effect in *The Politics of the Budgetary Process* (Boston: Little, Brown, 1964), p. 140. For discussion of some political consequences of program budgeting, see pp. 135–142.

[61]See William H. Brown and Charles E. Gilbert, *Planning Municipal Investment: A Case Study of Philadelphia* (Philadelphia: University of Pennsylvania Press, 1961), for an excellent discussion of the desire of elected officials to remain free to shift their commitments.

[62]It may be said that I have failed to distinguish sufficiently between planning, programming, and budgeting. Planning is an orientation that looks ahead by extending costs and benefits or units of effectiveness a number of years into the future. Programming is a general procedure of systems analysis employing cost-effectiveness studies. In this view program budgeting is a mere mechanical translation of the results of high level systems studies into convenient storage in the budgetary format. No doubt systems studies could be done without converting the results into the form of a program budget. This approach may have a lot to be said for it and it appears that it is the one that is generally followed in

the Department of Defense in its presentations to Congress. But if the systems studies guide decisions as to the allocation of resources, and the studies are maintained according to particular program categories and are further legitimatized by being given status in the budget, it seems most unlikely that programming will be separated from budgeting. One is never sure whether too much or too little is being claimed for program budgeting. If all that program budgeting amounts to is a simple translation of previous systems studies into some convenient form of accounting, it hardly seems that this phenomenon is worth so much fuss. If the program categories in the budget system are meaningful then they must be much more than a mere translation of previously arrived at decisions. In this case, I think that it is not my task to enlighten the proponents of program budgeting, but it is their task to make themselves clear to others.

[63]A. Smithies in Novick, *op. cit.,* p. 37.

[64]See U.S. House Appropriations Committee Sub-Committee on Department of Defense Appropriations for Fiscal 1965, 88th Congress, 2nd Session, IV, p. 133. McNamara asserted that some 652 "subject issues" had been submitted to him for the fiscal 1965 budget.

[65]Charles Hitch, *Decision Making for Defense* (Berkeley: University of California Press, 1965).

[66]Novick, *op. cit.,* p. 100.

[67]Paul Diesing, *Reason in Society* (Urbana: University of Illinois Press, 1962), pp. 198, 203–4, 231–32.

[68]Braybrooke and Lindblom, *op. cit.* See Also Lindblom, *The Intelligence of Democracy* (New York: The Free Press, 1965).

[69]M. Anshen in D. Novick, *op. cit.,* p. 370.

[70]*Ibid.,* p. 289.

[71]*Ibid.,* 359.

[72]Paul Diesing, *op. cit.,* p. 228.

[73]I am indebted to John Harsanyi for suggestions about political rationality.

[74]In the field of defense policy, political factors are taken into account to the extent that the studies concentrate on the design of feasible alternatives. In the choice of overseas basing, for example, the question of feasibility in relation to treaties and friendly or unfriendly relationships with other countries is considered. Thus it seems permissible to take into account political considerations originating outside of the country, where differences of opinions and preferences among nations are to some extent accepted as legitimate, but apparently not differences internal to the American policy.

APPENDIX

EXECUTIVE OFFICE OF THE PRESIDENT
BUREAU OF THE BUDGET
WASHINGTON, D.C 20503

BULLETIN NO. 66-3   October 12, 1965

TO THE HEADS OF EXECUTIVE DEPARTMENTS AND ESTABLISHMENTS

SUBJECT: Planning–Programming–Budgeting

1. *Purpose.* The President has directed the introduction of an integrated Planning–Programming–Budgeting system in the executive branch. This Bulletin contains instructions for the establishment of such a system. It will be followed by additional instructions, including more explicit policy and procedural guidelines for use of the system in the annual Budget Preview.

2. *Application of instructions.* This Bulletin applies in all respects to the agencies listed in Section A of Exhibit 1. The agencies listed in Section B of that Exhibit are encouraged to apply the principles and procedures for the development and review of programs to the extent practical. (In this Bulletin, the word "agency" is used to designate departments and establishments; the word "bureau" is used to designate principal subordinate units.)

3. *Background and need.* A budget is a financial expression of a program plan. Both formal instructions (such as those contained in Bureau of the Budget Circular No. A-11) and training materials on budgeting have stressed that setting goals, defining objectives, and developing planned programs for achieving those objectives are important integral parts of preparing and justifying a budget submission.

Under present practices, however, program review for decision-making has frequently been concentrated within too short a period; objectives of agency programs and activities have too often not been specified with enough clarity and concreteness; accomplishments have not always been specified concretely; alternatives have been insufficiently presented for consideration by top management; in a number of cases the future year costs of present decisions have not been laid out systematically enough;

and formalized planning and systems analysis have had too little effect on budget decisions.

To help remedy these shortcomings the planning and budget system in each agency should be made to provide more effective information and analyses to assist line managers, the agency head, and the President in judging needs and in deciding on the use of resources and their allocation among competing claims. The establishment of a Planning, Programming, and Budgeting System in accordance with this Bulletin will make needed improvement possible.

While the improved system is intended for year-round use within each agency, its results will be especially brought into focus in connection with the spring Preview. It should lead to more informed and coordinated budget recommendations.

4. Basic concepts and design.

a. The new Planning–Programming–Budgeting system is based on three concepts:

(1) The existence in each agency of an *Analytic* capability which carries out continuing in-depth analyses by permanent specialized staffs of the agency's objectives and its various programs to meet these objectives.

(2) The existence of a multi-year *Planning and Programming* process which incorporates and uses an information system to present data in meaningful categories essential to the making of major decisions by agency heads and by the President.

(3) The existence of a *Budgeting* process which can take broad program decisions, translate them into more refined decisions in a budget context, and present the appropriate program and financial data for Presidential and Congressional action.

b. Essential to the system are:

(1) An output-oriented (this term is used interchangeably with mission-oriented or objectives-oriented) program structure (sometimes also

called a program format) which presents data on all of the operations and activities of the agency in categories which reflect the agency's end purposes or objectives. This is discussed in more detail in paragraph 5, below.

(2) Analyses of possible alternative objectives of the agency and of alternative programs for meeting these objectives. Many different techniques of analysis will be appropriate, but central should be the carrying out of broad systems analyses in which alternative programs will be compared with respect to both their costs and their benefits.

(3) Adherence to a time cycle within which well-considered information and recommendations will be produced at the times needed for decision-making and for the development of the President's budget and legislative program. An illustrative cycle which does this is described in paragraph 9.

(4) Acceptance by line officials (from operating levels up to the agency head), with appropriate staff support, of responsibility for the establishment and effective use of the system.

c. The products of the system will include:

(1) A comprehensive multi-year *Program and Financial Plan* systematically updated.

(2) *Analyses,* including Program Memoranda, prepared annually and used in the budget Preview, Special Studies in depth from time to time, and other information which will contribute to the annual budget process.

d. The over-all system is designed to enable each agency to:

(1) Make available to top management more concrete and specific data relevant to broad decisions;

(2) Spell out more concretely the objectives of government programs;

(3) Analyze systematically and present for agency head and Presidential review and decision possible alternative objectives and alternative programs to meet those objectives;

(4) Evaluate thoroughly and compare the benefits and costs of programs;

(5) Produce total rather than partial cost estimates of programs;

(6) Present on a multi-year basis the prospective costs and accomplishments of programs;

(7) Review objectives and conduct program analyses on a continuing, year-round basis, instead of on a crowded schedule to meet budget deadlines.

e. The entire system must operate within the framework of over-all policy guidance—from the President to the agency head, and from the agency head to his central planning, programming, and budgeting staffs and to his line managers. Fiscal policy considerations and other aspects of Presidential policy will be provided by the Bureau of the Budget in accordance with the President's program. Modifications will also have to be made from time to time to reflect changing external conditions, Congressional action, and other factors.

5. *The program structure.*

a. An early and essential step for each agency is the determination of a series of output-oriented categories which, together, cover the total work of the agency. These will serve as a basic framework for the planning, programming, and budgeting processes (including work on systems analysis, reporting, evaluation of accomplishments, and other aspects of management) and for relating these processes to each other. The following principles should guide the development of such output categories.

(1) *Program categories* are groupings of agency programs (or activities or operations) which serve the same broad objective (or mission) or which have generally similar objectives. Succinct captions or headings describing the objective should be applied to each such grouping. Ob-

viously, each program category will contain programs which are complementary or are close substitutes in relation to the objectives to be attained. For example, a broad program objective is improvement of higher education. This could be a *program category,* and as such would contain federal programs aiding undergraduate, graduate and vocational education, including construction of facilities, as well as such auxiliary federal activities as library support and relevant research programs. For purposes of illustration and to aid understanding, Exhibit 2 shows some program structures as they might be applied to two organizational units within different agencies; the same approach, of course, applies to the agency as a whole.

(2) *Program sub-categories* are sub-divisions which should be established within each program category, combining agency programs (or activities or operations) on the basis of narrower objectives contributing directly to the broad objectives for the program category as a whole. Thus, in the example given above, improvement of engineering and science and of language training could be two program sub-categories within the program category of improvement of higher education.

(3) *Program elements* are usually sub-divisions of program sub-categories and comprise the specific products (i.e., the goods and services) that contribute to the agency's objectives. Each program element is an integrated activity which combines personnel, other services, equipment and facilities. An example of a program element expressed in terms of the objectives served would be the number of teachers to be trained in using new mathematics.

b. The program structure will not necessarily reflect organization structure. It will be appropriate and desirable in many cases to have the basic program categories cut across bureau lines to facilitate comparisons and suggest possible trade-offs among elements which are close substitutes. It is also desirable to develop program formats which facilitate comparisons across agency lines (e.g., in urban transportation and in recreation).

c. Basic research activities may not be and frequently are not mission or output oriented. Whenever this is the case, such activities should be identified as a separate program category or sub-category as appropriate. However, applied research and development is usually associated with a specific program objective and should be included in the same program category as the other activities related to that objective.

d. To facilitate top level review, the number of program categories should be limited. For example, a Cabinet Department should have as many as fifteen program categories in only a rare and exceptional case.

e. Program categories and sub-categories should not be restricted by the present appropriation pattern or budget activity structure. (Eventually, however, it may be necessary and desirable for the "Program by Activity" portion of the schedules in the Budget Appendix to be brought into line with the program structure developed according to this Bulletin.)

6. *The Multi-year Program and Financial Plan.*

a. The entire process is designed to provide information essential to the making of major decisions in a compact and logical form. A principal product of the process will be a document, the Multi-Year Program and Financial Plan of the agency.

b. Thus, the process is concerned with developing for agency head review, and, after his official approval or modification, for Bureau of the Budget and Presidential review (as summarized in Program Memoranda, per paragraph 7c) a translation of concretely specified agency objectives into combinations of agency activities and operations designed to reach such objectives in each of the stated time periods.

c. The Program and Financial Plan will:

(1) Be set forth on the basis of the program structure described in paragraph 5, above.

(2) Cover a period of years, usually five, although the number will vary with the considerations pertinent to particular agencies; for example, a longer time span would be appropriate for timber production and for large multiple-purpose water resource projects. The multi-year feature is not to be compromised by the expiration of legislation at an earlier date, since extension or renewal, with possible modification, of the legislation should be reflected in the plan.

(3) Include activities under contemplated or possible new legislation as well as those presently authorized.

(4) Show the program levels which the agency head thinks will be appropriate over the entire period covered by the multi-year plan.

(5) Express objectives and planned accomplishments, wherever possible, in *quantitative* non-financial terms. For example, physical description of program elements might include the additional capacity (in terms of numbers to be accommodated) of recreational facilities to be built in national forests, the number of youths to be trained in Job Corps camps along with measures of the kinds and intensity of training, the number of hours of Spanish language broadcasts of the Voice of America, the number of children to receive pre-school training, and the number of patients in federally-supported mental hospitals. In some programs, it may not be possible to obtain or develop adequate measures in quantitative physical terms such as these but it is important to do so wherever feasible. In any case, objectives and performance should be described in as specific and concrete terms as possible.

(6) Where relevant, relate the physical description of federal programs to the entire universe to be served. For example, a poverty program plan directed at aged poor should describe not only the numbers receiving specific federal benefits but might well show what proportion of the entire aged poor population is being benefited.

(7) Associate financial data with the physical data to show the cost of carrying out the activity described. Cost data should be expressed in systems terms. That is, *all* costs—such as capital outlay, research and development, grants and subsidies, and current costs of operations (including maintenance)—which are associated with a program element should be assigned to that element. These component costs generally can be derived from existing appropriation and accounting categories. Where there are receipts, such as the collection of user charges or proceeds from sales of commodities or other assets, an estimate of receipts should also be included.

(8) Translate the costs and receipts used for analytic purposes, as described in the preceding subparagraph, into the financial terms used in federal budget preparation, presentation, and reporting.

d. The Program and Financial Plan as approved by the agency head will be submitted to the Bureau of the Budget. The Bureau of the Budget will also be kept abreast of significant revisions and updatings (see sub-paragraphs *e* and *f*, immediately below).

e. The Program and Financial Plan, as approved or modified by the agency head in conformity with guidance received from the Bureau of the Budget and the President (usually following the annual spring Preview), will form the basis for the agency's budget requests. Therefore, it should not be changed except in accordance with a procedure approved by the agency head. Appropriate arrangements should be made for participation of the Budget Bureau in significant changes.

f. Provision will be made for a thorough reappraisal and updating of the Program and Financial Plan annually. In this process, one year is added on to the plan. Other changes to the plan are to be expected from time to time and a procedure may be useful for making minor changes to the plan without requiring agency head approval.

7. *Analysis*. An analytic effort will be undertaken to examine deeply program objectives and criteria of accomplishments. Whenever applicable this effort will utilize systems analysis, operations research, and other pertinent techniques. The analysis should raise important questions, compare the benefits and costs of alternative programs and explore future needs in relationship to planned programs. The sources of data used will be many, including most importantly, the Program and Financial Plan, special studies done throughout the agency, and budget, accounting and operating data. It is important to have continuity in the work of staffs doing this work and to build expertise in them over a period of years. As expertise is developed, more and more of the agency's activities can be subjected to these analytical techniques.

a. *Special Studies* on specific topics should be carried out in response to requests by the agency top management, the Budget Bureau, or at the initiative of the analytic staff itself. Suggestions should also be made by line operating managers. The special studies may involve intensive examination of a narrow subject or broad review of a wide field. The broad program studies envisioned here will often be hampered by a dearth of information and gaps in our knowledge which can be filled only by project studies and other micro-economic studies. Nevertheless, these broad studies should be assigned top priority in the agency's analytic effort.

b. *Questions* should be posed by the analytic staffs to other elements of the agency on program objectives, measures of performance, costs and the like.

c. A broad *Program Memorandum* should be prepared annually on each of the program categories of the agency. The Program Memorandum will summarize the Program and Financial Plan approved by the agency head for that category and present a succinct evaluation and justification. It should appraise the national needs to be met for several years in the future (covering at least as many years as the Program and Financial Plan), assess the adequacy, effectiveness, and efficiency of the previously approved plan to meet those needs, and propose any necessary modifications in the previously approved plan, including new legislative proposals. Thus, the Program Memorandum should:

(1) Spell out the specific programs recommended by the agency head for the multi-year time period being considered, show how these programs meet the needs of the American people in this area, show the total costs of recommended programs, and show the specific ways in which they differ from current programs and those of the past several years.

(2) Describe program objectives and expected concrete accomplishments and costs for several years into the future.

(3) Describe program objectives insofar as possible in quantitative physical terms.

(4) Compare the effectiveness and the cost of alternative objectives, of alternative *types* of programs designed to meet the same or comparable objectives, and of different *levels* within any given program category. This comparison should identify past experience, the alternatives which are believed worthy of consideration, earlier differing recommendations, earlier cost and performance estimates, and the reasons for change in these estimates.

(5) Make explicit the assumptions and criteria which support recommended programs.

(6) Identify and analyze the main uncertainties in the assumptions and in estimated program effectiveness of costs, and show the sensitivity of recommendations to these uncertainties.

d. In sum, the analytic effort will:

(1) Help define major agency objectives and subobjectives.

(2) Analyze and review criteria by which program performance is measured and judged, and help to develop new, improved criteria.

(3) Compare alternative programs, both in terms of their effectiveness and their costs, old as well as new.

(4) Develop reliable estimates of total systems costs of alternatives over the relevant span of years.

(5) Analyze the validity of cost data.

(6) Identify and analyze program uncertainties; test the sensitivity of conclusions and recommendations against uncertain variables.

(7) Carry out systems analyses to aid in making program choices.

8. *Relation of the system to the budget process.*

a. Two products of the system will be utilized in the spring Budget Preview: the Program Memoranda (which incorporate in summarized form the relevant portions of the Program and Financial Plan) and Special Studies.

b. All annual budget requests in the fall will be based on and related to the first year of the current multi-year Program and Financial Plan, subject to such modifications as may be required by changing circumstances since the plan was last reviewed and approved by the agency head. Within this framework the detailed formulation and review of the budget will take place.

c. The introduction of the Planning, Programming, and Budgeting system will not, by itself, require any changes in the form in which budget appropriation requests are sent to Congress. Further, this Bulletin is not to be interpreted to set forth changes in the format of annual budget submissions to the Budget Bureau. Circular No. A-11 will be revised as needed to provide guidance on such budget submissions.

d. Over the next few years agency operating budgets used to allocate resources and control the day-to-day operations are to be brought into consistency with the Program and Financial Plan. Performance reports that show physical and financial accomplishments in relation to operating budgets should also be related to the basic plan.

e. The Planning, Programming and Budgeting functions are closely related and there must be close coordination in the work of the various staffs.

9. *An illustrative annual cycle.* Program review is a year-round process of re-evaluating and updating program objectives, performance, and costs. The annual cycle described below is presented for purposes of illustration and will be refined and changed over time. It is intended to identify check-points to assure that essential steps are taken and that current reviews, revisions and recommendations are given consideration at appropriate times in the budget cycle. Insofar as this schedule affects internal agency operations and does not affect Bureau of the Budget scheduling, it may be modified by each agency head to suit his needs. The illustrative annual cycle shows in outline form how the system would work after it is established and operating for an agency participating in the Preview.

January. Changes are made by the agency to the prior multi-year program plan to conform to Presidential decisions as reflected in the budget sent to the Congress.

March. By March bureaus or similar major organizational units within the agency will submit to the agency head their current appraisals of approved program objectives and multi-year plans and their proposals for (a) needed modifications, including measures to meet new needs and to take account of changing and expiring needs, and (b) extension of plans to cover an added year (e.g., 1972). The Director of the Bureau of the Budget will advise the agency head of any change in the over-all policies and objectives upon which the currently approved plan is based.

April. On the basis of instructions from the agency head following his review of bureau submissions, bureaus develop *specific* program plans.

May. Analytic staffs complete Program Memoranda. Agency head reviews program plans and approves Program Memoranda for submission to the Bureau of the Budget. He may want to assign additional studies on the basis of this review.

May–June. The budget preview is conducted by the Bureau of the Budget. The basic documents for this preview are the Program Memoranda prepared by agencies which are to be submitted to the Bureau of the Budget by May 1, and Special Studies to be submitted over a period of several months preceding this date. Presidential guidance will be obtained, where necessary, on major policy issues and on the fiscal outlook.

July–August. Appropriate changes to program plans are made on the basis of the guidance received and of congressional legislation and appropriations. Budget estimates, including those for new legislative proposals, are developed on the basis of the first year of the currently approved program plans (e.g., 1968).

September. Budget estimates and agency legislative programs are submitted to the Bureau of the Budget.

October–December. Budget Bureau reviews budget estimates, consults with agencies, and makes its recommendations to the President. Presidential decisions are transmitted to agencies, the budget is prepared for submission to Congress, and the legislative program is prepared.

January. Changes are again made by the agency to the multi-year program plan to conform to Presidential decisions as reflected in the budget sent to the Congress.

10. *Responsibility and staffing.*

    a. Personal responsibility for the Planning, Programming, and Budgeting system rests with the head of each agency. Since planning, programming, and budgeting are all essential elements of management, line managers at appropriate levels in the agency must also take responsibility for, and participate in, the system. Responsibility should be so fixed that the agency head receives the recommendations of his principal managers (e.g., bureau chiefs) on program plans as well as on the findings and recommendations of centrally prepared analytical studies. Similarly, arrangements should be made for obtaining original suggestions, and views from other echelons in a manner consistent with the assignment of responsibility and authority.

b. Specialized staff assistance is also essential in all but the smallest agencies. Such assistance will be especially useful in the preparation and review of Program and Financial Plans and in the preparation of the appropriate analytical studies. Each agency will, therefore, establish an adequate central staff or staffs for analysis, planning and programming. Some bureaus and other subordinate organizations should also have their own analytical planning and programming staffs.

c. No single form of organization is prescribed since agency circumstances differ. Planning–Programming–Budgeting activities are functionally linked but it is not essential that they be located in the same office so long as they are well coordinated. However, it is important that the head of the central analytic staff be directly responsible to the head of the agency or his deputy.

11. *Initial action under this Bulletin.* The head of each agency listed in Exhibit 1 should see that the following steps are taken by the dates indicated. It is recognized that this is a tight schedule. Nonetheless, the President's interest in the prompt establishment of the new Programming, Planning, and Budgeting system requires that each agency exert every possible effort to adhere to this schedule.

a. *Within 10 days* after issuance of this Bulletin—the agency head should designate an official to be responsible for the development of the Planning–Programming–Budgeting system for the entire agency and inform the Bureau of the Budget of his choice.

b. *By November 1, 1965*—each agency head should have tentatively decided, in cooperation with the Bureau of the Budget, the broad program categories to be used initially in the system. Bureau of the Budget staff are prepared to make suggestions on these categories.

c. *By December 31, 1965*—agency instructions, procedures, or regulations for the Planning–Programming–Budgeting system should be issued, and a copy forwarded to the Bureau of the Budget. If is is not possible to have these in polished form by this date, they should be issued at least in such form as will allow the agency to proceed without delay on the steps necessary to produce the material required by May 1, 1966, with the more complete and polished instructions or regulations issued as soon as feasible but not later than March 31, 1966.

d. *By February 1, 1966*—each agency head should have approved the basic program structure (including program categories, program sub-categories, program elements, and the non-financial units for measuring program objectives and accomplishments in quantitative terms) to be used in the program plan.

e. *By April, 1, 1966*—a comprehensive, multi-year Program and Financial Plan should be completed for consideration and review by the agency head. The Program and Financial Plan, as approved by the agency head, will be forwarded to the Bureau of the Budget.

f. *By May 1, 1966*—for the spring Preview, Program Memoranda described above will be forwarded to the Bureau of the Budget. By this date or earlier, Special Studies will also be forwarded. More specific guidance and instructions will be provided by the Bureau of the Budget.

Exhibit 1
BULLETIN NO. 66-3

A. *AGENCIES TO BE COVERED BY THE PREVIEW*

Department of Agriculture
Department of Commerce
Department of Defense—separate submission for:
  Military functions (including Civil Defense)
  Corps of Engineers, Civil functions
Department of Health, Education, and Welfare
Department of Housing and Urban Development

Department of Interior
Department of Justice
Department of Labor
Post Office Department
Department of State (excluding Agency for International Development)
Treasury Department
Agency for International Development
Atomic Energy Commission
Central Intelligence Agency
Federal Aviation Agency
General Services Administration
National Aeronautics and Space Administration
National Science Foundation
Office of Economic Opportunity
Peace Corps
United States Information Agency
Veterans Administration

B. *OTHER AGENCIES FOR WHICH A FORMAL PLANNING–PROGRAMMING–BUDGETING SYSTEM IS ENCOURAGED*

Civil Aeronautics Board
Civil Service Commission
Export-Import Bank of Washington
Federal Communications Commission
Federal Home Loan Bank Board
Federal Power Commission
Federal Trade Commission
Interstate Commerce Commission
National Capital Transportation Agency
National Labor Relations Board
Railroad Retirement Board
Securities and Exchange Commission
Selective Service System
Small Business Administration
Smithsonian Institution
Tennessee Valley Authority
United States Arms Control and Disarmament Agency

Exhibit 2
BULLETIN NO. 66-3

PROGRAM CATEGORY EXAMPLES

Coast Guard

Present Appropriation Structure

General and Special Funds:

Operating expenses
Acquisition, construction and improvements
Retired pay
Reserve training

Intragovernmental Funds:

Coast Guard Supply Fund
Coast Guard Yard Fund

Present Activity Schedule
Vessel Operations
Aviation Operation
Shore Stations and Aids Operations
Repair and Supply Facilities
Training and Recruiting Facilities
Administration and Operational Control
Other Military Personnel Expense
Supporting Programs

Proposed Program Structure

Search and Rescue
Aids to Navigation
Law Enforcement
Military Readiness
Merchant Marine Safety
Oceanography and Other Operations
Supporting Service

PROGRAM CATEGORY EXAMPLES

Forest Service

Present Appropriation Structure

Forest protection and utilization
Cooperative range improvements
Forest roads and trails
Access roads
Acquisition of lands for national forests:

Superior National Forest
Special Acts
Cache National Forest
Wasatch National Forest

Assistance to States, tree planting
Expenses, brush disposal
Roads and trails for States
Other Forest Service permanent appropriations

Proposed Program Structure

Timber Production
Outdoor Recreation
Natural Beauty
Wildlife
Water
Forage
Minerals and Mining
Research
Other

APPENDIX

EXECUTIVE OFFICE OF THE PRESIDENT
BUREAU OF THE BUDGET
WASHINGTON, D.C. 20503

SUPPLEMENT TO BULLETIN NO. 66-3   February 21, 1966

TO THE HEADS OF EXECUTIVE DEPARTMENTS AND ESTABLISHMENTS

SUBJECT: Planning—Programming—Budgeting

1. *Purpose.* Bureau of the Budget Bulletin No. 66-3 outlined the concept of an integrated Planning–Programming–Budgeting system. Pending the consolidation of all instructional materials on the Planning–Programming–Budgeting system in a circular issuance, this Supplement is being issued to provide necessary details on two of the central documents in this system, the Program and Financial Plans (PFP) and Program Memoranda (PM). Both the Financial Plans and the Program Memoranda are to be forwarded by May 1, 1966, to the Bureau of the Budget by the agencies listed in Part A of Exhibit 1 of Bulletin 66-3. These documents will form the basis for this year's Spring budget preview.

2. *Constraints.* No explicit financial guidelines or constraints are provided to agencies. Each agency head is to recommend the mix and level of programs for his agency. However, the basis of program decisions is *choice* among alternatives, and assessment of priorities. Future federal budgets, as past ones, cannot provide unlimited resources—choices will have to be made. It is important that the Program and Financial Plans and Program Memoranda be prepared with as much attention paid to reducing and modifying obsolete and low priority programs as expanding others and introducing new ones.

3. *Program and Financial Plans.*

   a. *Composition.* Each Program and Financial Plan should consist of three parts:

   Part I will tabulate program output.

   Part II will tabulate program costs and other financial data, in a format paralleling that of Part I.

   Part III will include special tabulations.

The Plan will consist only of these tables, together with such brief explanatory notes as may be necessary. All descriptive and analytic material will be included in the Program Memoranda.

(1) *Part I. Tabulation of Program Output.* The Program Output tabulation will consist of tables showing agency physical outputs. Stub headings of the tables are the program categories, sub-categories and elements of the agency's program structure. All categories, sub-categories and elements approved by the agency head should be shown. Activities requiring legislation should be so noted. The column headings should be fiscal years—FY 1965 through FY 1967, plus FY 1968 through the last fiscal year of the planning period (FY 1972 in the case of those agencies developing five-year plans).

One principal indicator of physical output or services rendered will be shown for each program element. The output measure chosen should be that which is the most important single quantitative measure of program performance. For urban highway construction, for example, output might be number of lane-miles of highways built. For an on-the-job training program, it might be number of workers trained.

Using the on-the-job training example, the program output table would look as follows, assuming that the program category was "Manpower Development Assistance," the sub-category, "Manpower Training," and the element, "On-the-job Training":

	FY							
	65	66	67	68	69	70	71	72
I. Manpower Development Assistance								
A.								
B. Manpower Training								
1.								
2. On-the-job training (No. of workers trained—000)	XX	XX	XX	XX	XX	XX	XX	XX

In the majority of cases no single measure of output is satisfactory. In the case of the urban highways, for example, some measure of traffic-handling capacity might be needed as well as a statement of lane-mileage. Similarly, in the case of Manpower Training, some measure of the number of hours of training per worker, or training costs per worker, or the intended effect of training on earning capacity might be shown. In all such cases, the agency should submit, as part of the special tabulations in Part III, additional tables showing these supplementary measures of output.

(2) *Part II. Financial Tabulations.* The first tabulation in this part should be a Program Cost tabulation which will have the same stub and column headings as the Program Output tabulation. The total federal program costs shown for each year should be based on the system cost concept described in the Bureau of the Budget Bulletin No. 66-3. It should display the total agency costs, required to achieve the comparable output shown in Part I, whether funded through appropriations, trust funds, revolving funds, or otherwise. Where the accounting system of the agency is oriented towards the present appropriation and activity structure and is unable to produce program cost data with precision, costs should be estimated as closely as possible.

The cost tabulation for on-the-job training would appear as follows:

FY	($ rounded to tenths of millions)						
65	66	67	68	69	70	71	72

I. Manpower Development Assistance
  A. . . . . . .
  B. Manpower Training
    1. . . . . . .
    2. On-the-job training . . .

XX	XX	XX	XX	XX	XX	XX	XX

Totals and sub-totals should be shown for program categories and sub-categories.

The services performed by one agency for another should be reflected in the plan of both agencies. For example, administrative support services provided overseas to another agency by the State Department on a reimbursable basis would be shown as a cost in the serviced agency's Program and Financial Plan, and as a cost and an output in the State Department's Program and Financial Plan.

Data on the New Obligational Authority and Expenditure implications of the proposed programs need not be forwarded to the Bureau of the Budget, unless specifically requested. Such data should be developed in the form which is most convenient for each agency.

(3) *Part III. Special Tabulations.* Many agencies will be asked to tabulate revenues received, and to show major capital investment plans. For some agencies, tables on federal manpower requirements and sources of financing may be required. As noted above, it will also be desirable in the case of some programs to identify measures of program output in addition to those listed in Part I. The Bureau of the Budget will work out with each agency the special tabulations to be included.

b. *Other information.* Other information may be required later. The schedule for developing this information will be worked out by the Bureau of the Budget separately with each agency. Some of the tables in this category are:

(1) Tabulations of state and local government programs (or in the case of some foreign affairs agencies, foreign programs) and in some cases activities of the private sector (including federal corporations) where these are closely related to federal government programs.

(2) Program element data sheets—one for each program element—which will provide a brief factual description of each element.

(3) A crosswalk between the costs shown in program terms in Part II, and the agency appropriation accounts and other sources of financing, together with a reconciliation of total program costs under each source of financing to new obligational authority and expenditures.

4. *Program Memoranda.* Bulletin 66-3 provided that a Program Memorandum is to be prepared annually on each of the program categories shown in the Program and Financial Plan. Certain exceptions can be made, however. Unless specifically requested, Program Memoranda need not be submitted for any residual category; e.g., "General Support" or "Other." Additionally, where no major program choices appear to be open, or where a joint analysis of several program categories appears preferable, separate Program Memoranda may not be required. In each such case, however, the decision should be taken after consultation with the Bureau of the Budget.

The Program Memorandum for a particular program category provides the analytic backup for the programs described in the Program and Financial Plan. These Memoranda should serve as basic planning documents not only by agency top management and the Bureau of the Budget but throughout the agency. Moreover, they should be regularly updated so that at any given time they provide a current statement of agency objectives and programs. They will provide the focus for the Bureau of the Budget's Spring Preview.

On the basis of Bureau of the Budget comments and of continuing internal agency review, these Memoranda should then be modified as background to FY 1968 budget proposals. The Memoranda, as modified, together with the decisions taken in the President's budget recommendations, will form the point of departure for the Memoranda to be submitted in the Spring of the following year. The Memoranda will thus be the focal points for the continuous development, refinement, and change of concepts and programs.

a. *Format and content.*

(1) Program Memoranda should be prepared in the form of Memoranda from the agency head to the Director of the Bureau of the Budget.

(2) Part I should (a) state the recommendations made, noting the relation of such recommendations to those of the prior year; (b) summarize the Memorandum, including the alternatives analyzed, in not more than two pages; and (c) include a copy of the PFP for the program category.

(3) Part II should present the factual and analytic basis for the program proposals. It should be a hard, quantitative analytic document, not an essay, and not merely a budget justification. It should (a) specify national needs in the area covered by the memorandum; (b) define the agency's objectives with respect to those needs in precise and concrete terms; (c) analyze the probable effectiveness and the long-term costs of the programs proposed to attain those objectives; (d) outline and compare alternative programs for meeting the same objectives; and (e) make clear and precise the priorities within program sub-categories and categories and state the relative emphasis among broad program categories. In the course of this presentation the assumptions and the criteria used must be made explicit. Where relevant factors have not yet been ade-

quately analyzed, they must be identified, and an indication given of the nature of the data needed or the studies still to be performed.

Where special studies or other analyses of particular pertinence have been completed, they may be made appendices to the Program Memoranda.

b. *Length.* There is no fixed requirement as to length, but thorough coverage of an important program category, including tables, will ordinarily take from 20 to 50 pages, single spaced.

c. *Method.*

(1) In general, there are more important questions deserving analysis than there is analytic capacity available to do the work. The Program Memoranda should focus on the central questions. In some cases these have been identified in the program issues posed by the Bureau of the Budget. Choices on which subjects should be given highest priority should be decided after consultation with Bureau of the Budget staff.

(2) The Memoranda should be as specific and as quantitative as possible. Broad, general statements of national needs, such as the "development of a safe and efficient civil aviation system" or the "elimination of poverty," though adequate for some purposes, cannot form a basis for analysis. The adequacy of specific programs cannot be assessed unless their goals are stated precisely—quantitatively wherever possible—and the time span for their accomplishment is specified. Correspondingly, specific goals should not be adopted until the costs of achieving them have been assessed.

(3) In many cases program analysis can be greatly assisted by a development of a formal program model. Such a model would show, usually on the basis of statistical data, the relationship of outputs the program inputs. All such models are simplified versions of the phenomena being described, but they help clarify the effectiveness of existing programs, and of possible new programs.

(4) The Memoranda must carefully identify assumptions. Some assumptions will be about facts; for example, the level of economic activity or the rate of family formation. Others will be assumptions about values; for example, the specific level of health to which our Indian

population should be brought. Some indication should be given of the degree to which alternative assumptions affect conclusions.

(5) It will often be desirable to analyze explicitly the effect on program choice of making alternative assumptions.

(6) It is often useful to discuss program uncertainties about future programs. In general, the further into the future a program is projected, the greater the uncertainty about needs and objectives—but also the greater the range of options. For this reason it may be useful to outline a strategy in which certain actions are taken now which both keep open future options and help provide the data or analysis needed to eventually choose between them. The reduction of uncertainty by data gathering, by research or simply by the passage of time may then make possible wiser choices than could now be made, and those choices will still be open because the decisions made now were designed to keep them open.

(7) Where estimates of effectiveness or cost are uncertain, it is sometimes illuminating to do a "breakeven analysis," that is, an analysis which compares the uncertain program with one on which there are adequate data. For example, an unproven mail sorting machine of known costs might be compared with existing mail sorting methods by calculating the performance which would make the new machine just competitive with the old methods. Conversely, if the mail sorting ability of the new machine were specified, one could calculate how much the Post Office could pay for it and be as well off as with existing methods.

(8) Quantification should not be attempted where it is inappropriate or meaningless. In many cases, the effectiveness of programs is difficult to quantify; for some activities, it is impossible. Even in these cases, however, cost can be estimated, and a more precise knowledge of program costs can provide a partial basis for the over-all judgments which are made in any event. As in the case of the Program and Financial Plan, all costs shown should by systems costs; i.e., all costs incurred in the production of a given output or service.

d. *Legislative implications.* New programs proposed in the Program Memoranda will often require authorizing legislation. The Program Memoranda should, where possible, outline the essential features of the required legislation including timing.

5. *Handling of documents.* The Program and Financial Plans and Program Memoranda will be submitted to the Bureau of the Budget in 25 copies. These documents will be handled in accordance with Bureau of the Budget Circular No. A-10, "Responsibilities with Respect to the Budget."

6. *Inquiries.* Questions on format and substance that arise during the course of preparing agency Program and Financial Plans and Program Memoranda should be brought to the attention of Bureau of the Budget examining staff for assistance and advice.

CHARLES L. SCHULTZE
Director

EXECUTIVE OFFICE OF THE PRESIDENT
BUREAU OF THE BUDGET
WASHINGTON, D.C. 20503

BULLETIN NO. 68-2   July 18, 1967

TO THE HEADS OF EXECUTIVE DEPARTMENTS AND ESTABLISHMENTS

SUBJECT: Planning–Programming–Budgeting (PPB)

1. *Purpose.* This Bulletin contains current guidelines for the continued development of integrated Planning–Programming–Budgeting (PPB) systems within agencies of the executive branch. It is not intended to change the instructions for the preparation of the 1969 budget previously communicated by letter to the agencies listed in section 1 of the Attachment, and it is consistent with the current revision of Bureau of the Budget Circular No. A-11. This Bulletin replaces Bulletin No. 66-3 and the supplement thereto.

2. *Application of instructions.* The Bulletin applies in all respects to the agencies listed in section 1 of the Attachment. It is applicable not later than January 1, 1968, to the agencies listed in section 2. Agencies listed in section 3 should prepare to develop and integrate their planning and programming with budgeting as fully as practicable, but specific time limits are not prescribed herein. Bureau staff will be available for consultation on the nature, extent, and timing of the application of these instructions to the agencies listed in section 3.

3. *Principal objective of PPB.* The principal objective of PPB is to improve the basis for major program decisions, both in the operating agencies and in the Executive Office of the President. To do this, it is necessary to have clear statements of what the decisions are and why they were made. Program objectives are to be identified and alternative methods of meeting those objectives are to be subjected to systematic comparison. Data are to be organized on the basis of major programs, and are to reflect future as well as current implications of decisions. As in the case of budgeting generally, PPB applies not only to current programs, but to proposals for new legislation. The budget is the financial expression of the underlying program plan. The budget review will therefore be conducted *primarily in program terms* for each agency to which this Bulle-

tin applies. It is essential that the Program Memoranda, Program and Financial Plan, and Special Studies provide adequate bases for these decisions. The budget, however, is submitted and must be justified to the Congress in terms of individual appropriations. The program decisions must, therefore, be translated into appropriation requests, and the relationship of these requests to the program decisions must be clearly set forth.

4. *Elements of the system.* The PPB system is built upon three types of documents:

   a. *Program Memoranda* (PM) which succinctly present the agency head's major program recommendations to the President within a framework of agency objectives, identify the alternatives considered, and support the decisions taken on the basis of their contribution to the achievement of these objectives;

   b. A comprehensive multi-year *Program and Financial Plan* (PFP) which is periodically updated and presents in tabular form a complete and authoritative summary of agency programs (initially those recommended by the agency head and, subsequently, those adopted by the President) in terms of their outputs and costs; and

   c. *Special Studies* (SS) which provide the analytic groundwork for decisions reported in the Program Memoranda.

The Program Memoranda and the PFP are organized around a program structure.

5. *Program structure.* The program structure groups the activities of an agency into a set of program categories that facilitates analytic comparisons of the costs and effectiveness of alternative programs. Individual program categories establish the scope of the related Program Memorandum. The program categories should, therefore, be chosen so far as possible to permit a self-contained analysis of programs with common outputs or with common objectives.

   a. The program categories used in each agency should provide a suitable framework for considering and resolving the major questions of mission and scale of operations which are the proper subject of decision at the highest level within the agency and within the Executive Office of the President. These program categories will not necessarily be consistent with appropriation categories or with organizational structures.

b. Normally, an agency will have between five and ten major program categories. Most program categories will contain one or more subordinate levels, called sub-categories and program elements. Some of the sub-categories and program elements will complement others within the same main category. Some may be competitive with others.

c. Each agency is responsible for proposing its own program structure and for reviewing it regularly and proposing its amendment where appropriate. The Bureau of the Budget should be consulted with respect to program structure and its approval obtained for changes therein.

d. The Bureau of the Budget will provide leadership in seeking to fit agency program structures into a government-wide structure. As progress is made in this effort, agencies may be asked to adjust their structures to permit achieving a comprehensive and compatible structural pattern across agency lines.

6. *The Program Memoranda.* Each agency should prepare a Program Memorandum (PM) for each program category.

The Program Memoranda should outline the broad program strategy upon which the agencies' plans and programs are to be built for the future years and provide background for the development of annual budget and legislative programs. They define long-range goals and objectives and anticipated program accomplishments.

a. With respect to the *annual* budget and legislative processes the Program Memoranda serve two major purposes:

(1) They contain the major program recommendations of each agency for the upcoming budget, and define authoritatively the strategy underlying those program recommendations. As such they convey the tentative program recommendations of the agency head, and also provide internal guidance for the preparation of the agency's detailed budget submission. For this purpose, the Program Memoranda must record all of the major program decisions within each category.

(2) In addition to showing *what* choices have been made, the Program Memoranda should make clear *why* particular choices have been made, by identifying agency objectives in a measurable way, and comparing alternative programs in terms of their costs and their achievement of the objectives. In short, the Program Memoranda should provide an *explicit* statement of program strategy, with the basis for major program decisions explicitly stated. The documents should be concise enough to be used directly by agency heads and by the Director of the Bureau of the Budget.

b. The basic PM should stand on its own and in no case should it be longer than twenty pages. It should be prefaced by a two- or three-page summary.

c. The treatment of decisions in the Program Memoranda may vary. Wherever there are major policy issues relating to a program, the Program Memorandum should, at least, identify the issues in terms of the alternative courses of action among which choices must be made and the recommended course of action. Wherever possible, it should summarize the analytic basis for the choice. Where Special Studies carry the detailed analysis and have been made available, a Program Memorandum need only summarize the findings, making reference to the study reports without repeating their contents. Supporting analyses may also be contained in separate appendices to the basic PM.

d. The limits imposed by the availability of analytic staff resources or other circumstances may in some cases make it impossible to provide full treatment of alternatives and their analysis in each Program Memorandum. Such instances will diminish as the PPB system is developed. Nevertheless, since the Program Memoranda are to constitute the principal basis for major program decisions in the budget review process, it is essential that such decisions in each program category be recorded in the PM and that the reason for the decisions be stated. Minor decisions will, of course, be reflected in the PFP and all decisions will be reflected in the appropriation requests. This selectivity will not only produce desirable brevity in the Program Memorandum, but will also permit the focusing of the limited number of studies that can be done on the issues where they can have the greatest effect.

e. When a program is an experimental one or a demonstration, the PM should clearly identify this fact. If it is necessary to proceed for more than one year on an experimental or demonstration basis, the PM should indicate why a decision to start a full-scale program is being postponed, what is being done to reach a conclusion on expansion or termination, and the date when a decision is expected.

f. The PM should deal explicitly with the legislative implications of the alternatives presented in it.

7. *Multi-year Program and Financial Plan.* The PFP presents in tabular form, and for a period of several years, pertinent data relating to the outputs, cost, and financing of agency programs. These data are to be presented in a set of tables that reflect the decisions on agency programs contained in the Program Memoranda as well as minor program decisions not set forth there. The PFP should show the future implications of current decisions. The output and costs are to be shown for each program element, grouped in terms of the program structure by category and sub-category, and for each year of the planning period covered by the PFP—the fiscal year just past, the current year, and the budget year, plus at least four future years.

a. *Presentation of future year data.* The years beyond the budget year are included primarily to show the future implications of current (past and present) decisions. This projection, therefore, is not designed to predict comprehensively future budget totals for agencies or for major programs.

(1) This approach permits, on the output side, a showing of the expected results of development or demonstration projects and the fruition of multi-year investment projects; and, on the cost side, a reflection of future requirements that are the results of program decisions for the budget year. For current decision-making purposes, this will make a more effective presentation where program levels are prescribed by law, where a program involves investments and future operating costs spread over several years, where program levels are determined by factors outside government control (such as increases in population), or where a program is undertaken as an experiment or demonstration to provide a basis for future program decisions.

In the latter case, the PFP should identify, by a footnote, the year in which the next decision will be required on the program. Thus, if the current decision does not provide for full-scale operation of a program, costs and outputs should not be projected beyond the next decision point. (For major program decisions, the expected cost and output of the full-scale program, the evidence being accumulated to warrant expansion or termination, as well as the timing of the next decision point should, of course, be discussed in the PM.)

(2) Where an existing program is expected to continue throughout the planning period, but no decision has been made as to its future level, it should be shown at its current levels unless (a) mandatory or built-in changes are required under existing law, by uncontrollable workload, or by demographic or other factors, or (b) explicit justification for some other pattern is provided in the Program Memorandum (or if the decision is a minor one, reflected succinctly in a footnote to the PFP).

(3) The PFP therefore is to show the implications of current decisions and will not necessarily reflect accurate estimates of agency budget totals for the years beyond the budget year, because it omits new programs not yet recommended and fails to reflect program level changes, including the termination of some existing programs, decisions which are not part of the current budget cycle. The fact that the PFP is designed to show the future implications of current decisions is *not* meant to imply that in Program Memoranda or Special Studies, or for their own internal use, agencies should not develop and evaluate alternative individual program policies, costs, and outputs for a five-year period. They are encouraged to do so. The PFP, itself, however, is meant to be a record of the present and future budgetary and output consequences of the current year's decisions. In brief, the long-run program strategy outlined and analyzed in the Program Memoranda need not—and in many cases should not—be confined to decisions taken in the coming budget. The data shown in the PFP, however, should.

b. *Outputs.* Table I of the PFP will display outputs—that is, a quantitative measure of end products or services produced by a program element. Where it is meaningful to do so, outputs should be aggregated by sub-category and category of the program structure.

(1) Outputs by program element in Table I are to reflect the best measure of what is produced by that element. Outputs will not necessarily measure the achievement of a program objective, nor the benefits of the program. Such measures are vital to the PPB process—they should be identified as soon as practicable, and should be given full considera-

tion in the Program Memoranda and Special Studies. Wherever meaningful measures of achievement and effectiveness are available for a program, the PFP should display them either on a separate line in Table I,
properly identified, or by means of a supplementary table. In certain
cases, such as research programs, where meaningful measures of output
cannot be defined, the best available quantitative non-financial descriptions of the program should be used (e.g., the number of projects initiated, continued, and completed, number of research workers engaged, or
the number of researchers trained).

(2) In some cases—a recreation program, for example—costs in the
PFP may best be related to the capacity of proposed recreation facilities,
and this might serve as the best output measure. Attainment of the objective of the program, however, may best be shown by a measure of the
use of the facilities—which is an important factor for decision-making on
the program. Both of these measures, therefore, are relevant and appropriate for presentation.

(3) In the case of an on-the-job training effort, the simplest measure
of output in relation to cost might be the number of workers trained, or
the student weeks of training supplied. The number of workers trained
might also have added significance since it may reflect the diminution
of dependence on public assistance. But the ultimate purpose of the program presumably is to improve the earning capacity of the worker
trained. The best measure of the success of the effort, therefore, might be
the increase in income that results from the training. It is possible that a
program which showed "low output"—in terms of the numbers of workers trained—might be more effective on this criterion because it was better taught, or focused on skills in shorter supply, than a program that
showed a higher "output."

(4) In short, where objectives are complex, as they often are for
government programs, it may be impossible to find a single, conceptually clear output measure that will satisfy all the needs of decision-making
on a program. Basically, the PFP should show measures of what is produced as a result of a program effort, supplemented where appropriate
by one or two other measures of achievement and effectiveness, with
the relationship of these measures and the pertinent costs explained in
the PM's and Special Studies.

c. *Costs.* Parallel to the display of output in Table I, Table II of the PFP presents a tabular statement of financial requirements in terms of program costs to be incurred for program activities. In addition to the display of program costs for each program element, the NOA requirements for the budget year for each program category should be set forth. Differences between budget year NOA and program cost that are greater than 10 per cent of the larger item should be explained in a footnote. The definitions of "program cost" and "NOA" are those established by Circular No. A-11 for the program and financing schedules in the budget appendix. (Agencies desiring to use any other financial concept in lieu of program costs should consult the Bureau of the Budget.)

(1) The financial data presented in the PFP for each program element should reflect total program costs inclusive of the program-oriented research and development, investment, and operating costs required to produce the ouptut shown in Table I. Where there exists a significant difference between the total program costs and the costs funded by the particular federal agency, both the cost to the given agency and the total net cost to other agencies, other units of government, the private sector, or other sources, should be identified and shown in three separate lines—one for the given agency, one for other federal agencies, and the third for all other sources.

(2) For programs financed with earmarked receipts or with their own generated receipts, such as loan programs, government corporation activities, and revolving funds, Table II of the PFP should show the total level of resources committed or applied, as well as cost to the government and obligational authority. In difficult or unusual cases, the agency should consult with the Bureau of the Budget on this display.

(3) It should be noted that costs in the PFP are defined in a more limited sense than the costs which may—and usually should—be utilized in the Program Memoranda or in Special Studies. For decision-making purposes, the analysis of a problem should include the consideration of economic opportunity costs, marginal costs, and systems costs.

(4) For the year immediately past, the presentation is to be based upon cost data that are adequately supported in the agency accounting system. Where the maintenance of specific accounts for program classifications is not justified as an efficient and practical approach, cost

data for the past year may be developed through cost allocation or analysis techniques: in such cases there should be a technical note appended to the PFP to indicate the techniques used. Cost distribution practices should be so developed as to provide a suitable basis for program decisions and to provide to the managers concerned reliable information that will permit them to evaluate results actually obtained in relation to the resource allocation decisions made under PPB.

d. *Reconciliation of program costs to appropriations.* The PFP will include as Table III a reconciliation—a "cross-walk"—of the NOA shown for the budget year in the PFP, with NOA estimates by appropriation and fund account. However, this table need not necessarily go to the level of program element; and translation can be done at the level of program category or sub-category, whichever is appropriate. Similarly, for this purpose, appropriations of funds which are grouped into a single "building block" under Circular No. A-11 (for example, certain relatively inactive accounts) may also be so grouped for the purposes of this tabulation. The purpose is to provide a reconciliation between program costs and the budget submission, sufficient to insure that the budget submission is consistent with the intent of the program decisions. The PFP constitutes a link between the marginal systems costs in the PM that are pertinent to decision-making, and the financing needed to carry out programs.

8. *Special Studies.* Special Studies are a vital element of PPB. By providing the analytic basis for decisions on program issues in the PM, they determine the quality of the PPB system's contribution to the decision-making process. Special Studies will, in general, formulate and review program objectives in terms useful for making program comparisons; they will review in terms of costs and benefits the effectiveness of prior efforts, compare alternative mixes of programs, balance increments in costs against increments in effectiveness at various program levels with attention to diminishing returns and limitations of physical resources, and assess the incidence of benefits and costs as well as their totals. Normally, a Special Study will not be co-extensive with a program category. Most will deal with specific phases of a program; some studies will cut across program category lines. In every case a Special Study will contain specific recommendations for future action. There is no fixed length or format for Special Studies.

A Special Study should normally be made whenever a proposal for major new legislation is involved. Such a study should spell out the purposes, costs, and expected accomplishments under the legislation, and the alternatives considered for accomplishment of the purpose.

9. *Timing for production of documents.* PPB is a continuous process. The analytic work cannot produce once-and-for-all answers. Successive analyses should assist in producing successively better government decisions and in responding to new initiatives and changing circumstances. The decisions to which PPB contributes are basically incorporated in two annual processes—the annual executive budget of the government and the annual legislative program of the President. Consequently, it is necessary that the preparation and presentation of PPB documents fit the schedules for these two processes. Similarly, the documentation under this instruction should be coordinated with and be consistent with the submissions made under Circular No. A-11 on the budget and Circular No. A-19 on legislation. In fact, the PM and the PFP are integral parts of each covered agency's budget submissions.

The timing for the major documents is as follows:

a. *Program Memoranda.* Program Memoranda will be drafted each year for each program category. The Bureau of the Budget will identify well in advance certain issues it may wish to have especially considered. The Bureau of the Budget will also generally indicate a staggered schedule of dates for the submission of draft Program Memoranda, usually over the period from February 15 through July 15. The draft Program Memoranda should contain or be accompanied by tables showing for the planning period the output and cost data covering at least the major issues dealt with in the PM for the given program category.

Wherever possible, the Bureau will respond to the draft PM with comments on recommendations and supporting rationale. Revisions should then be made in the PM to reflect the agency head's consideration of the Bureau's comments and to reflect any further developments in the agency analysis. The PM should then be submitted in final form by September 30.

b. *Program and Financial Plan.* The Program and Financial Plan is to be prepared annually and transmitted to the Bureau by September 30. It should be consistent with the Program Memoranda and the rest of the budget submission which is due at the same time.

The PFP should be revised as necessary for use within the agency to reflect major changes in the program plans taking place, but submission of any such revised PFP to the Bureau of the Budget is not required as a routine matter. The PFP should be revised for consistency with the President's budget in January. Where congressional action on the agency budget is completed appreciably ahead of September 30, a further revision would be appropriate to reflect such action.

    c. *Special Studies.* Agencies should maintain a continuing program of Special Studies. These may extend over more than one year of the budget cycle and need not follow a uniform time pattern.

    (1) A list of Special Studies contemplated by the agency should be submitted to the Bureau of the Budget not later than January 15, covering the new calendar year. The Bureau may make additional suggestions with reference to proposed studies, giving particular emphasis to studies which may be needed for the forthcoming budget cycle each year, and the dates by which such studies should be submitted. Special studies requested by the Bureau, and such others as the agency head believes appropriate for submission, should be forwarded to the Bureau as soon as they have been reviewed by the agency head. The Bureau of the Budget will give substantive and technical comment as promptly as feasible.

    (2) Draft Program Memoranda and Special Studies should be submitted to the Bureau of the Budget in six copies, or such other number as may be requested by Bureau representatives. Each final PM and PFP should be submitted in the same number as is specified in Circular No. A-11 for annual budget submissions, or in such other number as Bureau of the Budget representatives may specify.

10. *Illustrative annual cycle.* In summary, a typical annual cycle is as follows:

September: Agency submits PM's in final form, PFP's, the annual budget, and the annual legislative program to the Bureau of the Budget.

October–   Bureau reviews and recommends to the President; Presi-
December: dential decisions made and communicated to the agency.

January: Executive budget is presented to the Congress; major elements in the legislative program are indicated in the State of the Union message, the budget message, the economic report, or in other communications to Congress.

January: Agency reviews special study program and submits proposed list for the calendar year to the Bureau.

January: Agency updates the PFP to conform to the executive budget.

February: Bureau indicates to agency its request for Special Studies and for issues to be covered in Program Memoranda during the upcoming budget cycle.

February–   Agency brings Special Studies to completion and prepares
July: drafts of Program Memoranda.

April–   Budget Bureau responds on Special Studies and draft Pro-
August: gram Memoranda.

July–   Agency head makes final decisions on his program recom-
September: mendations; agency revises draft Program Memoranda; agency updates PFP, adding one year and making it conform to agency head recommendations.

Year around: Special Studies are begun, carried on and completed, as appropriate.

11. *Responsibility, staffing and training.* Responsibility for the development and use of Planning-Programming-Budgeting systems rests with the head of each agency. Since planning, programming and budgeting are all essential elements of management, it is necessary that line managers at appropriate levels participate in the system. Management responsibility should be so fixed that the agency head receives the recommendations of his principal managers on all major program issues. It may be desirable to provide principal managers with small analytic staffs to insure their meaningful participation in Special Studies and other analytic work. Similar arrangements for obtaining the views of other echelons may be made, consistent with the agency's assignment of responsibility.

a. Whether or not analytic staffs are provided the principal managers, each agency should establish a specialized analytic staff reporting directly to the agency head or to his deputy. The principal duties of this staff will be to coordinate the analytic and planning work done in the subordinate bureaus or other organizations of the agency; to initiate and conduct Special Studies; where appropriate, to provide first drafts of Program Memoranda; and to supervise or monitor research for program analysis.

b. Each agency should take such action as is needed to provide, within the management system of the agency, for an automatic provision of pertinent data on the results of the resource allocation decisions made under PPB. Agency information systems should be designed to provide timely data on outputs and costs in budget execution—suited to the needs of the managers concerned with agency programs—so that programs may be effectively carried out according to plans and related operating budgets, and to provide information useful for planning and programming in the next cycle of operations.

c. To make PPB a fully effective system, a general understanding of the methods and purposes of PPB must be created throughout the agencies. Agencies are, therefore, encouraged both to make maximum use of the various training and educational programs offered through the Civil Service Commission, and also to establish their own internal orientation and training courses.

CHARLES L. SCHULTZE
Director

Attachment

Section 1
  Department of Agriculture
  Department of Commerce
  Department of Defense—separate submission for:
    Military functions (including Civil Defense)
    Corps of Engineers, Civil functions
  Department of Health, Education, and Welfare
  Department of Housing and Urban Development
  Department of the Interior
  Department of Justice

Department of Labor
Post Office Department
Department of State (excluding Agency for International
  Development)
Department of Transportation
Department of the Treasury
Agency for International Development
Atomic Energy Commission
Central Intelligence Agency
General Services Administration
National Aeronautics and Space Administration
National Science Foundation
Office of Economic Opportunity
Peace Corps
United States Information Agency
Veterans Administration

Section 2
Civil Service Commission
Federal Communications Commission
Federal Power Commission
Federal Trade Commission
Interstate Commerce Commission
Securities and Exchange Commission
Small Business Administration
Tennessee Valley Authority

Section 3
Export-Import Bank of Washington
Federal Home Loan Bank Board
Federal Mediation and Conciliation Service
National Labor Relations Board
Railroad Retirement Board
Selective Service System